My Heart Toward Home

My Heart Toward Home

LETTERS OF A FAMILY

DURING THE CIVIL WAR

Eliza Woolsey Howland

Georgeanna Woolsey Bacon

Edited by Daniel John Hoisington

Edinborough Press

Printed in Canada.
Type set in Adobe Caslon.
Research Associate: Daniel Aaron Hoisington

Photographs, except as noted, used by permission of the Bellamy-Ferriday
House & Garden, a property of the Antiquarian and Landmarks Society.
For more information, contact the Bellamy-Ferriday House & Garden,
P. O. Box 181, Bethlehem CT 06751.

Publisher's Cataloguing–in–Publication Data
Georgeanna Woolsey Bacon and Eliza Woolsey Howland
My Heart Toward Home: Letters of a Family during the Civil War
Edited with an introduction by Daniel John Hoisington.
p.   cm.
ISBN 1-889020-07-9
1. United States–History–Civil War, 1861-1865–Personal narratives;
2. United States–History–Civil War, 1861-1865–Hospitals.
3. United States–History–Civil War, 1861-1865–Women.
I. Bacon, Georgeanna II. Howland, Eliza III. Hoisington, Daniel John.
IV. Title.

E464.B13 2001
Library of Congress Card Number 00-108076

Edinborough Press
P.O. Box 13790
Roseville Minnesota 55113
1-888-251-6336
www.edinborough.com

Contents

The Woolsey Family of New York

I peer into the darkness,
And the crowding fancies come:
The night wind, blowing northward
Carries all my heart toward home.

For I 'listed in this army
Not exactly to my mind;
But my country called for helpers
And I couldn't stay behind.

—*Mary Woolsey Howland*

To the dear memory of the
loving mother
whose lofty faith, unfailing charity
and great courage
were the inspiration of all that was best
in her children
this fragment of the war-story
is dedicated.

— from the original edition

Jane Eliza Newton Woolsey
"Moremamma"
1801–1872

Abby Howland Woolsey
1828–1893

A. H. W.

Jane Stuart Woolsey
1830–1891

J. S. W.

Mary Elizabeth Watts Woolsey Howland
1832–1864
with Abby Roberta Howland

M. W. H.

Eliza Newton Woolsey Howland
1835–1917

E. W. H.

Georgeanna Muirson Woolsey Bacon
"Georgy"
1833–1906

G. M. W.

Harriet Roosevelt Woolsey Hodge
"Hatty"
1837–1878

H. R. W.

Caroline Carson Woolsey Mitchell
"Carry"
1838–1914

C. C. W.

Charles William Woolsey
"Charley"
1840–1907

C. W. W.

Robert Howland
1820–1887
Mary's Husband

R. S. H.

Joseph Howland
1834–1886
Eliza's Husband

J. H.

Francis Bacon
1831-1912

F. B.

8 Brevoort Place
10th St
Friday Aug 2nd

My dear Girls.

With this I suppose
you will receive some packages of
papers. 12 Independents which Charlie
put up for the Columbia, or any
other hospital. & some packets for
the Chaplain of the 16th, tho' directed to you. By the
way is there such a person, and what
is his name. If you will tell me,
I can direct papers from time to
time immediately to him. Please say
whether it is best to send anything
thus by mail to the camp, or whether
the additional postage, from Washington down & the trouble
of transmitting to the camp are
against it. I have sent some
time ago a couple of packages to
Joe's address in camp — for distribution to the men — just a few
illustrated papers. Were these received
and is it worthwhile to send any

Abby Woolsey to Georgeanna Woolsey and Eliza Howland, August 1861
Woolsey Collection, Ferriday Archives

Introduction

The Inner Personal History of the War

IN A NOTE pasted into family scrapbooks, Eliza Howland wrote, "The chief family event of 1898 was the printing for private distribution of the *Letters of a Family.*" With her sister, Georgeanna Bacon, Howland sat down with their carefully organized letters to tell the story of the Woolsey family during the Civil War. Spurred by the recent deaths of sisters Jane and Abby, they hoped to record "the inner personal history of the war." It is a remarkable story.

The Woolseys represent the best of antebellum New York society. Charles Woolsey—son of a New York merchant—and Jane Newton married in 1830. Ten years later, Charles died in a ship explosion as he returned on a late night voyage to his family. He left his widow with seven daughters, and one son, Charles, who arrived a month after his father's death. The widow and her family moved from their Boston home, returning to live in New York City, where they were supported by inheritances and wealthy relatives. They settled at 17 Rutgers Place, moving to a new home at 8 Brevoort Place in 1850.

The children were well educated and cultured. The girls attended private academies, including the Rutgers Female Institute. Charles graduated from University College (later New York University) in 1861. They were avid readers, and knew French, Italian, and German. Following formal education, they filled their days with improvements to the mind and spirit through a host of fashionable pursuits—attending the opera and ballet, summering in Lenox, Massachusetts, and touring Europe. They also grew up with a warm sense of humor—as the reader will learn.

While they enjoyed the comfortable life of upper class New York, their mother raised them with a sense of moral and social responsibility.

They were active church members at Market Street Church (Dutch Reformed), where the older daughters taught Sunday School and called on the sick. They took church history and Bible classes at Union Theological Seminary, taught by a cousin, Henry Boyton Smith. Abby served as assistant manager at the House of Industry—a training program for poor women. Charles was president of his college's YMCA.

This moral sensibility translated into politics. The family held strong views and clearly saw disunion and slavery as the sins of the age. As the sisters wrote, "When the members of the Woolsey family gave up toys, they took up politics. Brought up by a mother who hated slavery, although her ancestors for generations had been Virginia slave-holders, they walked with her in the straight path of abolitionism." They listened to lectures by noted abolitionists such as Wendell Phillips and Dr. George Cheever, and Abby attended special prayer services on the day of John Brown's execution.[1]

When the Confederacy fired on Fort Sumter, the two oldest sisters, Abby and Jane, were in their thirties. It is likely that without the war, they would have passed the years in relative leisure and quiet. Mary and Eliza married their cousins—Robert and Joseph Howland. Mary settled into the domestic life as the wife of a church rector and mother of three children. In 1859, Eliza and her husband purchased a comfortable Hudson River estate, Tioronda, where he took up the life of gentleman farmer. A friend's words about Jane are an apt description of the family as a whole. Sarah Chauncey Woolsey wrote that when the war began, life "...found her, safe, seated in the golden haze of youth and ease, living luxurious days." Yet, when the war came, they answered the call to service.[2]

Among the several hundred accounts written by Civil War nurses, this book stands out because it gives the fullest description of the earliest organizational efforts. Georgeanna volunteered for a program guided by Dr. Elizabeth Blackwell—the rare attempt at professional instruction under the supervision of the country's first woman doctor. After a month's training, she traveled to Washington, D.C. with her sister, Eliza, and served under Dorothea Dix, Superintendent of Army Nurses. Of those first days, she wrote:

No one knows, who did not watch the thing from the beginning, how much opposition, how much ill-will, how much unfeeling want of thought, these women nurses endured. Hardly a surgeon whom I can think of, received or treated them with even common courtesy. Government had decided that women should be employed, and the army surgeons—unable, therefore, to close the hospitals against them—determined to make their lives so unbearable that they should be forced in self-defence to leave. It seemed a matter of cool calculation, just how much ill-mannered opposition would be requisite to break up the system.

Some of the bravest women I have ever known were among this first company of army nurses. They saw at once the position of affairs, the attitude assumed by the surgeons and the wall against which they were expected to break and scatter; and they set themselves to undermine the whole thing. None of them were 'strong-minded.'

I have known surgeons who purposely and ingeniously arranged these inconveniences with the avowed intention of driving away all women from their hospitals. These annoyances could not have been endured by the nurses but for the knowledge that they were pioneers, who were, if possible, to gain standing ground for others,—who must create the position they wished to occupy.[3]

Even in the midst of events, they saw their story as more than a personal odyssey, but one that embraced the whole vocation of women as nurses.[4]

Georgeanna served as a nurse from the beginning to the end of the war. In the first years, Jane volunteered in New York City hospitals, then worked full-time as a nurse from late 1862 until mid-1865. She held an important administrative position as Superintendent of Nurses at the Fairfax Seminary Hospital in Alexandria, Virginia. Eliza's career was shorter, linked closely to her husband's military career. Hatty, Carry, and Charley served short stints as nurses. Their mother rushed to Gettysburg in the aftermath of battle and nursed the wounded for three weeks.[5]

Within this one family, we glimpse the breadth of the Northern war experience. Their activities were so far-flung that Mother Woolsey remarked, "We think of adding 'Army Gen'l Directory' to our door-plate, so many people of all sorts come to us for information, and for aid in various enterprises." Abby became an important organizer of sewing circles and other supply efforts, working with Louisa Schuyler and the Women's Central Association of Relief. Mary wrote patriotic poems, which were printed at family expense and distributed in the camps. The Woolseys devoted the spring of 1864 to preparations for the great New York Metropolitan Fair. [6]

It is not simply the story of women in the war. Charles enlisted in the home militia, worked with the Sanitary Commission, and eventually secured a post in the Army of the Potomac. He was present when Lee surrendered to Grant at Appomattox. Joseph Howland volunteered and headed south with the Sixteenth New York Volunteers. Quickly rising the rank of Colonel, he saw action in the Peninsula campaign. After ill health forced his resignation, Howland remained an active recruiter for the army. Dr. Francis Bacon, Georgeanna's confidante, held several key positions, including medical commander of the Department of the Gulf. Henry Hopkins, who served alongside Jane at the Fairfax Seminary Hospital, wrote reports about the spiritual state of the army.

The story is compelling because they witnessed not just the great events of the war, but the small illuminations as well. Although the family was primarily associated with the United States Sanitary Commission, Eliza, Georgy, and Charles assisted Vincent Colyer with the work of the Army Committee of the YMCA—a precursor to the U. S. Christian Commission. Mother and Abby saw the devastating results of the New York Draft Riots of July 1863, lamenting the fate of their friends' homes and possessions. They toured Richmond shortly after Appomattox—Georgy left newspaper clippings about the horrors of Andersonville prison on Robert E. Lee's doorstep. They cheered the heroics of George Custer as he reined in his runaway horse during the Grand Review in May 1865. In one touching scene, we catch a glimpse of President Lincoln. A letter noted, "Georgy met him by chance one morning in the White House garden, and found him greatly changed since last summer. He was walking slowly, eating an apple, dragging

"Tad" along by the hand and gazing straight before him, afar off,
—older, grayer, yellower, more stooping and harassed-looking...."[7]

This book is also a social history as we glimpse the life of New York's
upper class. In the midst of war, they attended rehearsals of the New
York Philharmonic and lectures and parties. Mary Howland wrote of
one Christmas season:

> Night before last was devoted to a brilliant little party for the chil-
> dren Hatty and Carry,—a very handsome and successful affair. I
> did not go, my wardrobe presenting only the alternative of bogy
> or bride, either black silk or a too dressy white silk, but Robert
> and I feasted on some of the remains last night, on our round-
> about way home from Mr. Everett's lecture at the Academy of
> Music.

During the summer season, the family retreated to Lenox, Massachusetts—where they hobnobbed with social luminaries Fanny Kemble
and Mrs. Ellery Sedgwick—and to Brattleboro, Vermont—where they
visited the hospitals. Even at the front, Eliza and Georgy were accompanied by their servant, Stanislas Moritz.

Three decades after the war, Georgeanna and Eliza looked back at
those years as they edited the family letters. The book's narrative voice
is complex, since it represents two historic perspectives: first, the original letters and journals; second, the connecting narrative written thirty
years after the events. In one sense, they provided their own footnotes.
For example, they explained cryptic references to an "Agnew" with a
description of the flannel shirts that they wore on the hospital transports.

There are some differences between the original manuscripts and the
edited versions. The sisters left out much of the social history—the
daily mechanics of life—as unimportant for the historic record. The
perspective of thirty years tempered many harsh judgments. In her
journal on June 13, 1862, Georgeanna condemned the military medical
service, writing, "The governments' boats have been unprovisioned &
unmedicated & unstored in all ways. And if the Commission had not
been here the men would have starved." Rumors, so important at the

time, are often excluded from the published letters. For example, on March 9, 1862, Georgeanna wrote, "It is rumored that Mr. Lincoln will be requested by the Radical party to resign—that he will appeal to the army for support." Thirty years later, this gossip held no resonance.[8]

Sadly, for the family and the historian, these letters are only a partial representation of a much larger correspondence. The sisters wrote,

> These few happen to have been saved from a much larger number, which, coming almost daily at times from the brother (Charles), at the Headquarters of the Army of the Potomac, and the sisters in Hospital service, were carefully filed by the eldest sister, Abby, in orderly succession, and, when the home was broken up, were stored in the Morrell warehouse in New York. There, later, with all our Mother's household possessions, they were destroyed by fire, to the deep and lasting regret of all who knew the writers and the times they had passed through.[9]

As a result, the book has an uneven quality, weighted heavily toward the early war years when Georgeanna and Eliza kept their daily journals. The sisters never formally published *Letters of a Family during the War for the Union* but printed several hundred copies and distributed them to friends and family.

It is a book about service. In 1895, Georgeanna addressed the graduating class of the Connecticut Training School for Nurses, saying, "It was in 1860, on the breaking out of our Civil War, that American women woke up to a knowledge of their responsibilities and opportunities." The two sisters wrote this book, hoping to pass on this knowledge to a new generation of Woolseys. In the introduction to the *Letters*, they told their nieces and nephews that, "As you read, you will see that this was a family of earnest Americans, having no other thought at that time, than to give themselves and their possessions freely—as thousands of other families did—to the service of the men in the field."[10]

It is also a story about family. They saw their individual work as pieces of a whole. For example, the sisters, describing the Sanitary Commission, noted, "With its work, we, *as a family*, were associated from its beginning." That is how others remembered them. Their friend,

Henry Hopkins, recalled an evening at Brevoort Place, writing, "The house was all aglow with light and warmth; there was an atmosphere of earnest faith, courage, and good cheer, that filled me with a new sense of the sacredness of the cause of our country." Samuel Chapman Armstrong, founder of the Hampton Institute, aptly called them "the splendid Woolsey family of New York." This is their story.[11]

✖

In preparing the text for publication, we corrected obvious spelling and typographical errors. We let stand nineteenth-century spellings (such as "to-day") and inconsistencies in capitalization, hyphenation, and commas. There is one major deletion. The sisters asked Charles to contribute a recollection about his wartime service. His submission is different in narrative style and added little to the text. At several points, the sisters inserted footnotes with genealogical information, directed to their young nieces and nephews. We have deleted these references.

Special thanks are due to Barbara Bradbury Pape, Site Administrator, and Arleen Mitchell, Project Archivist, Bellamy-Ferriday House and Gardens, Bethlehem, Connecticut.

Endnotes

1. This text was first published as Georgeanna Woolsey Bacon and Eliza Woolsey Howland, *Letters of a Family during the War for the Union, 1861-1865* (New Haven: Tuttle, Morehouse and Taylor, 1899), 79-82. For additional biographical information, see Anne Austin, *The Woolsey Sisters of New York: A Family's Involvement in the Civil War and a New Profession* (Philadelphia: American Philosophical Society, 1971).

2. Woolsey Collection, Ferriday Archives, Bellamy-Ferriday House and Garden.

3. *My Heart Toward Home*, 79-80.

4. See Jeanie Attie, *Patriotic Toil: Northern Women and the American Civil War* (Ithaca, NY: Cornell University Press, 1999) and Judith Ann Giesberg, *Civil War Sisterhood: The U. S. Sanitary Commission and Women's Politics in Transition* (Boston: Northeastern University Press, 2000).

5. Elizabeth D. Leonard's *Yankee Women: Gender Battles in the Civil War* (NY: W. W. Norton, 1994) is a fine introduction to Civil War nursing. Kirstie Ross gives a careful analysis of the hospital transport service in her dissertation, "'Women are needed here': Northern Protestant Women as Nurses during the Civil War" (Ph.D. dissertation, Columbia University, 1993). See Katherine Wormeley, *The Other Side of War* (Boston: Ticknor and Co., 1889) for another view of the hospital transport work. A recent popular study is Nancy Garrison, *With Courage and Delicacy: Civil War on the Peninsula* (Mason City, Iowa: Savas Publishing Company, 1999).

6. *My Heart Toward Home*, 354; See Jeanie Attie, *Patriotic Toil: Northern Women and the American Civil War* (Ithaca, NY: Cornell University Press, 1999) and Judith Ann Giesberg, *Civil War Sisterhood: The U. S. Sanitary Commission and Women's Politics in Transition* (Boston: Northeastern University Press, 2000). Also see Barbara Gordon, *Bazaars and Fair Ladies: The History of the American Fundraising Fair* (Knoxville: University of Tennessee Press, 1998); Daniel John Hoisington, "Who Will Come to the Fair?" *The Citizens' Companion* 7 (June 2000): 12-19.

7. *My Heart Toward Home*, 304; Cephas Brainerd, *Christian Work in the Army, prior to the Organization of the United States Christian Commission* (NY: John Medole, 1866), 18-19.

8. For an excellent review of the forms of Civil War narratives, see Jane E. Schultz, "Women at the Front: Gender and Genre in Literature of the American Civil War" (Ph.D. dissertation, University of Michigan, 1988).

9. *Letters of a Family during the War for the Union*, 1861-1865, i.

10. Georgeanna Woolsey Bacon, "Sketch on the Foundation of the Connecticut Training School for Nurses," Woolsey Collection, Ferriday Archives, Bellamy-Ferriday House and Garden; *Letters of a Family during the War for the Union*, 1861-1865, i.

11. Francis Greenwood Peabody, *Education for Life* (Garden City: Doubleday, 1918), 103.

My Heart Toward Home

LETTERS OF A FAMILY

DURING THE CIVIL WAR

Procession of the Republican Wide-Awakes.
Harper's Weekly, October 13, 1860

CHAPTER ONE

The Steady March to the Inevitable

W HEN the members of the Woolsey family gave up toys they took
up politics. Brought up by a mother who hated slavery, although
her ancestors for generations had been Virginia slave-holders, they
walked with her in the straight path of abolitionism and would none of
the Democratic party.

As long ago as 1856, when the Fremont campaigners, with misguided
zeal and loud enthusiasm, proposed to sing the "Pathfinder" into the
White House, night after night this family, with the many young men
who flocked to their standard, sang, doors and windows being all open,
hour after hour, the patriotic doggerel of the campaign song book; and
many a song went hot from No. 8 Brevoort Place, the New York home,
to the campaign printing office, and was shouted at political meetings
for the furtherance of a result which a merciful Providence averted.

We all cut our political teeth on the *New York Tribune,* and were
in the right frame of mind to keep step with the steady march to the
inevitable through the Kansas perplexities, the John Brown raid and
the election of Mr. Lincoln, to the firing of the first gun by the rebels
upon the national flag at Fort Sumter.

In the spring of 1859, Abby not having been very well during the
winter, Mother planned a little trip to the South for her benefit, making
up a party with Robert, Mary, and little Mary.

They spent several days in Charleston, and vexed their righteous
souls with the sights and sounds of an auction of slaves.

Abby writes to her cousin, Harriet Gilman:

CHARLESTON, S. C., FEBRUARY 6, 1859
Slave auctions are of daily occurrence, and one of these we attended,

seeing what perhaps no lady-resident of Charleston has seen. But for that sad insight we might have thought things had a pretty fair aspect, generally. Certainly nothing forced itself unpleasantly on our attention, only every black face in the street reminded us of the system. I enclose you the list of some we saw sold. It is the list of only "one lot" put in by one trader. I could not get a full catalogue of sale; it seemed very long, and the men who held them were marking off the names and the prices which they brought. One man, a great stout thorough African, ran up to $780, but that was "cheap." The sale was in Chalmers street—a red flag indicating the spot—hardly a stone's throw from the hotel. The slave yard was probably the largest in Charleston, a great empty square, with high walls on three sides and a platform where the auctioneer stood and around which the bidders were grouped. On the fourth side was a five or six-story brick building, dirty, ragged-looking, like our rear tenements, where the poor crowd were lodged.

The gentlemen of our party, Mr. Robert Howland, and Mr. Charles Wolcott of Fishkill (who is here with his wife on a hasty tour), went in among the bidders. We ladies stood at the gate and looked in. Whole families of all ages were standing back against the walls, being questioned by purchasers and waiting their turn. A poor old woman, her head bowed, was sold with her son. They told us families are never separated except on account of bad behavior when they wish to get rid of some bad fellow—that this is so much the custom that the opposite course would not be tolerated. But mortgages, sheriffs' sales, sudden death of the owner, etc., must often, as we can imagine, infringe on this custom.

Among the saddened lookers on, all colored women except ourselves, was a middle-aged black woman, with a child in her arms. Mother had much talk with her. "Ah! Misses," she said, "they leave me some of the little ones. They sell my boys away, but I expect that, and all I wish is that they may get a good Master and Misses. There! Misses, that's one of my boys on the stand now! I don't mind that, but it's hard to have the old man (her husband) *drifted away*. But what can I do? My heart's broke, and that's all." He had been sold some time ago, and was gone she didn't know where. We turned home sickened and indignant. The bidders were gentlemanly-looking people, just such as we met every day at the hotel table. The trader had come down with this very gang in the cars with the

Wolcotts the day before, and was so drunk then he could hardly stand. Isn't Dr. Cheever justified?

MARCH 18, 1859.

Though this is March, the Japonicas are just passing out of blossom and the roses are in their first fresh glory—yellow and white Banksia, the Lamarque, and all those choice fresh varieties. I'll just run down in the garden here and pick you a rosebud. There it is—my voucher for the floral stories.

While we were at the Pulaski in Savannah, the great sale of Pierce Butler's slaves took place, and there all the gentlemen interested were congregated. You would never suppose the young meek pale little man, Pierce Butler, to be either a slave owner or Mrs. Kemble's husband. He is the indignant vestryman, I am told, who walked out of Rev. Dudley Tyng's Church when that sermon was preached. I am glad to hear that Mrs. Kemble has never drawn a dollar of her alimony, $3,000 a year, but allows it to accumulate for the children. She has the honest pride of maintaining herself, under the circumstances. Of course, you have read the *Tribune's* account; the girls sent it to us, and we have kept it well concealed, I assure you, for there are fire-eaters in the house, who would not hesitate to insult us. But now it is copied into the *New York Herald*—the only northern daily sold here—and has gone all through the city. There is a shrewd Philadelphian here, with his wife, Mr. Ashmead. He knew the agent at that sale. He attended the sale; took notes of course, as every northerner had to do, and now and then made a modest bid—to appear interested as a buyer. He says: "All I can say of Doe-stick's account is it does not go one bit beyond the reality—hardly comes up to it, indeed." He heard all the remarks quoted about Daphney's baby; says the story of Dorcas' and Jeffrey's love is true; and it was to himself and one other that the negro driver's remarks about the efficacy of pistols were made. He thought Mr. Ashmead was one of the same sort! The latter was a Buchanan man; he goes home an Abolitionist, and says: "Now I can believe that everything in Uncle Tom's Cabin might really happen."

As properly part of the history of the war, the following *New York*

Tribune's account of this sale is valuable. It was found among Abby's papers, dated March 9th, 1859:

A Great Slave Auction.
400 Men, Women, and Children sold.

The largest sale of human chattels that has been made in Star-Spangled America for several years took place on Wednesday and Thursday of last week at the Race Course, near the City of Savannah, Georgia. The lot consisted of four hundred and thirty-six men, women, children and infants, being that half of the negro stock remaining on the old Major Butler plantations which fell to one of the two heirs to that estate—Mr. Pierce M. Butler, still living and resident in the city of Philadelphia, in the free state of Pennsylvania. They were, in fact, sold to pay Mr. Pierce M. Butler's debts.

The sale had been advertised largely for many weeks, and as the negroes were known to be a choice lot and very desirable property, the attendance of buyers was large. Little parties were made up from the various hotels every day to visit the Race Course, distant some three miles from the city, to look over the chattels, discuss their points, and make memoranda for guidance on the day of sale. The buyers were generally of a rough breed, slangy, profane and bearish, being, for the most part, from the back river and swamp plantations where the elegancies of polite life are not, perhaps, developed to their fullest extent.

The negroes were brought to Savannah in small lots, as many at a time as could be conveniently taken care of, the last of them reaching the city the Friday before the sale. They were consigned to the care of Mr. J. Bryan, auctioneer and negro broker, who was to feed and keep them in condition until disposed of. Immediately on their arrival they were taken to the Race Course and there quartered in the sheds erected for the accommodation of the horses and carriages of gentlemen attending the races. Into these sheds they were huddled pell-mell, without any more attention to their comfort than was necessary to prevent their becoming ill and unsalable.

The chattels were huddled together on the floor, there being no sign of bench or table. They eat and slept on the bare boards, their food being rice and beans, with occasionally a bit of bacon and corn bread. Their huge bundles were scattered over the floor, and thereon the slaves sat or reclined, when not restlessly moving about or gathered into sorrowful groups discussing the chances of their future fate. On the faces of all was an expression of heavy grief.

The negroes were examined with as little consideration as if they had been brutes; the buyers pulling their mouths open to see their teeth, pinching their limbs to find how muscular they were, walking them up and down to detect any signs of lameness, making them stoop and bend in different ways that they might be certain there was no concealed rupture or wound.

The following curiously sad scene is the type of a score of others that were there enacted:

'Elisha,' chattel No. 5 in the catalogue, had taken a fancy to a benevolent-looking middle-aged gentleman who was inspecting the stock, and thus used his powers of persuasion to induce the benevolent man to purchase him, with his wife, boy, and girl. "Look at me, Mas'r; am prime rice planter; sho' you won't find a better man den me; no better on de whole plantation; not a bit old yet; do mo' work den ever; do carpenter work, too, little; better buy me, Mas'r; I'se be good sarvant, Mas'r. Molly, too, my wife, Sa, fus rate rice hand; mos as good as me. Stan' out yer, Molly, and let the gen'lem'n see."

Molly advances, with her hands crossed on her bosom, and makes a quick, short curtsy and stands mute, looking appealingly in the benevolent man's face. But Elisha talks all the faster. "Show Mas'r yer arm, Molly—good arm cat, Mas'r—she do a heap of work mo' with dat arm yet. Let good Mas'r see yer teeth, Molly—see dat, Mas'r, teeth all reg'lar, all good—she'm young gal yet. Come out yer Israel; walk aroun' an' let the gen'lm'n see how spry you be"—

Then, pointing to the three-year-old girl who stood with her chubby hand to her mouth, holding on to her Mother's dress and uncertain what to make of the strange scene,—"Little Vardy's on'y a chile yet; make prime gal by and by. Better buy us, Mas'r; we'm fus' rate bargain"—and so on. But the benevolent gentleman found where he could drive a closer bargain, and so bought somebody else.

In the intervals of more active labor the discussion of the re-opening of the slave-trade was commenced, and the opinion seemed to generally prevail that the reestablishment of the said trade is a consummation devoutly to be wished, and one red-faced Major, or General, or Corporal, clenched his remarks with the emphatic assertion that "We'll have all the niggers in Africa over here in three years—we won't leave enough for seed."

One huge brute of a man, who had not taken an active part in the discussion save to assent with approving nod to any unusually barbarous proposition, at last broke his silence by saying in an oracular way, "You may say what you like about managing niggers; I'm a driver myself, and I've had some experience, and I ought to know. You can manage ordinary niggers by lickin' 'em and given' 'em a taste of the hot iron once in a while when they're extra ugly; but if a nigger really sets himself up against me I can't never have any patience with him. I just get my pistol and shoot him right down; and that's the best way."

The family of Primus, plantation carpenter, consisting of Daphney his wife, with her young babe, and Dido a girl of three years old, were reached in due course of time. Daphney had a large shawl, which she kept carefully wrapped around her infant and herself. This unusual proceeding attracted much attention, and provoked many remarks, such as these:

"What do you keep your nigger covered up fer? Pull off her blanket!"

"What's the fault of the gal? Ain't she sound? Pull off her rags and let us see her!"

"Who's going to bid on that nigger, if you keep her covered up? Let's see her face!"

At last the auctioneer obtained a hearing long enough to explain that there was no attempt to practice any deception in the case—the parties were not to be wronged in any way; he had no desire to palm off on them an inferior article, but the truth of the matter was that Daphney had been confined only fifteen days ago, and he thought that on that account she was entitled to the slight indulgence of a blanket, to keep from herself and child the chill air and the driving rain.

Since her confinement, Daphney had travelled from the plantations to Savannah, where she had been kept in a shed for six days. On the sixth or seventh day after her sickness she had left her bed, taken a railroad journey across the country to the shambles, was there exposed for six days to the questionings and insults of the negro speculators, and then on the fifteenth day after her confinement was put up on the block with her husband and her other child, and, with her new-born baby in her arms, was sold to the highest bidder.

It was very considerate in Daphney to be sick before the sale, for her wailing ailing babe was worth to Mr. Butler all of a hundred dollars. The family sold for $625 apiece, or $2,500 for the four.

There were some thirty babies in the lot; they are esteemed worth to the master a hundred dollars the day they are born and to increase in value at the rate of a hundred dollars a year till they are sixteen or seventeen years old, at which age they bring the best prices.

Jeffrey, chattel No. 319, being human in his affections, had dared to cherish a love for Dorcas, chattel No. 278; and Dorcas, not having the fear of her master before her eyes, had given her heart to Jeffrey.

Jeffrey was sold. He finds out his new master; and, hat in hand, the big tears standing in his eyes and his voice trembling with emotion, he stands before that master and tells his simple story:

"I loves Dorcas, young Mas'r; I loves her well an' true; she says she loves me, and I know she does; de good Lord knows I love her better than I loves any one in de wide world—never can love another woman half so well. Please buy Dorcas, Mas'r. We'll be good servants to you long as we live. We're be married right soon, young Mas'r, and de chillun will be healthy and strong, Mas'r, and dey'll be good sarvants, too. Please buy Dorcas, young Mas'r. We loves each other a heap—do, really, true, Mas'r."

At last comes the trying moment, and Dorcas steps up on the stand.

But now a most unexpected feature in the drama is for the first time unmasked; Dorcas is not to be sold alone, but with a family of four others. Full of dismay Jeffrey looks to his master who shakes his head, for, although he might be induced to buy Dorcas alone, he has no use for the rest of the family. Jeffrey reads his doom in his master's look, and turns away, the tears streaming down his honest face.

And tomorrow Jeffrey and Dorcas are to say their tearful farewell, and go their separate ways in life to meet no more as mortal beings.

That night, not a steamer left that southern port, not a train of cars sped away from that cruel city, that did not bear each its own sad burden of those unhappy ones.

Abby's account from Charleston goes on:

On Sunday Mother and I went to the African Baptist Church, and had a most interesting service, remaining to their communion. The new members, nine of them, were seated in the front pews; the young women, in white dresses, shawls, and white ribbons on their straw bonnets. We had a seat of honor just behind them. The pastor, a slender, meek man in spectacles—a black man you know—"Dr. Cox," gave them the right hand of fellowship, with many touching words of counsel and passages of scripture. He and we, too, were equally moved, as to one (free) woman he said, "If the Son shall make you free, ye shall be free indeed," and to another, "Stand fast, therefore, in the liberty wherewith God shall make you free." He is free himself, I hear, but the Methodist minister is a slave. He is well taken care of—given his whole time, and is considered in an enviable position.

The church was crowded—bandannas of every shade, and style of tie—and no small sprinkling of the gayest bonnets. The minister was a quiet, excellent speaker; "two broders" who assisted were roaring ones, and the "broder officers" who officiated were such real darkies, and the singing was so like stories I have read, that altogether I had more a sense of sight-seeing than of worshipping, I am afraid. The service was very solemn, however, and we were deeply interested. There must have been three or four hundred communicants, for it was not close communion. The bread and wine were carried to every one, and up in the galleries too, and the eight baskets were emptied and the eight goblets were all emptied and filled three times. We shook hands with "Dr. Cox," who seemed gratified that we had remained, and as for us, we would not have missed it for a great deal.

Abby's heart was full of the thought of the slave market when, six months later, John Brown put his belief into action and attempted to bring about the forcible liberation of the slaves, acting as he thought and said "by the authority of God Almighty." Death by hanging was his reward. He left the jail at Charlestown and met his fate "with a radiant countenance and the step of a conqueror." At the hour appointed for the execution, December 2d, 1859, thousands of Northern hearts were with him, and in Dr. Cheever's church, New York, prayers were offered.

A. H. W. to E. W. H.

8 BREVOORT PLACE, DECEMBER 5, 1859.

My dear Eliza:

I went round to Dr. Cheever's lecture room for half an hour. I found it crowded with men and women—as many of one as the other—hard-featured men, rugged faces, thoughtful faces, some few Chadband faces; plain, quiet women; none that looked like gay, idle, trifling people. I entered just as some one suggested five minutes of silent prayer, which I have no doubt every soul of us made the most of, and then Dr. Cheever, who had the chair, gave out that hymn, "Oh, glorious hour! Oh, blest abode! I shall be near and like my God," etc. Mr. Brace made a fervent prayer for John Brown. Then a Methodist brother made a few remarks—said "it did him good to cry Amen. It proved you to be on the right side and that you were not afraid to make it known, and it didn't need a polished education to help you do that much for truth." Then they sang, "Am I a Soldier of the Cross?" everybody singing with a will, and, indeed, throughout the meeting there was much feeling—some sobs and many hearty Amens.

The public feverish excitement constantly increased and carried our family along in its stream.

Abby writes:

8 BREVOORT PLACE, DECEMBER 17, 1859.

Dear Eliza:

Georgy has gone to Professor Smith's class on church history and Jane has been out for a little air and exercise, to see if her head would feel better. She is in a highly nervous state, and says she feels as if she had brain fever, the over-excitement being the result of last night's meeting at the Cooper Institute, with speeches from Dr. Cheever and Wendell Phillips. She and Georgy went with Charley, and they say that the moment Dr. Cheever opened his mouth, Pandemonium broke loose. There seemed to be a thousand mad devils charging up and down the aisles with awful noises, and one of the rowdies near them plucked Charley and tried to draw him into a quarrel. This frightened Jane, but though Charley grew very white with rage he stood firm, and then Mr. Rowse joined them, and, as they couldn't get out, by degrees they worked their way to the platform, over the backs of the seats, and were high and dry and safe, and heard Phillips through. He was not so ornate in style as they expected, but a charming speaker.

All this had such an exciting effect on Jane that in her sleep last night she walked about; went into the little room next to ours and locked herself in; barricaded the door with baskets and chairs, throwing one of the latter over and breaking it. She had previously closed the doors between our room and Mother's, so that Mother only heard the sounds indistinctly. Jane lay down on the little bed, without covering, and toward morning the cold waked her, to her great bewilderment.

In the summer of 1860 Robert and Mary, with little Mary and Bertha, went to Europe, taking with them Hatty and Carry, and on November 20th, 1860, Mary's fourth little girl, baby Una, was born in Rome at the Casa Zuccara, via Quattro Fontane. She was christened Una Felice, in water brought from the Aqua Felice fountain. Mother's note refers to it all, and several of the following letters give peaceful little touches of home life before the storm broke:

SATURDAY MORNING, DECEMBER, 1860.

My dear Eliza,

Your very modest little, "may I Mother?" leads me to an immediate reply. Yes, my dear child, come and welcome, just as often as you possibly can and never feel it necessary to ask if you may *come home,* for this you know is only another home. I am happy to enclose you a foreign letter bringing still further pleasant news. How much we have all to be thankful for that the travellers have so much enjoyment and so little interruption to it. Dear Mary finds, I dare say, comfort enough in the little new baby to compensate in a great measure for all the suffering consequent upon its arrival.

What do you think of Felice added to Una? Our opinions will be useless now, however, as before the last letters reach, the baptism will have *been done.* Did you see the paragraph stating that the continual assassinations in the streets of Rome render it unsafe to strangers and to residents after dark! This is very comforting to anxious families who have friends there! Hatty and Carry are certainly having a gay time at Naples. Just think of Vesuvius, a hurried dinner, rush to the Crocelli to meet a party of naval officers, a fourteen-oared boat excursion, dancing, and other festivities on board the Admiral's ship-of-war, supper, etc., etc., all on one day! And after that the return civility of an egg nogg party! I am very glad they are under the care of a clergyman and his wife!

J. S. W. to a Friend in Paris.

NEW YORK, DECEMBER 5, 1860.

We came down to Centre Harbor on the 6th of November (the great day) and there the Republican majorities came rolling in for Abraham Lincoln. Our host in that place was of a practical turn, and, having no artillery and having some rocks to blast in the garden, laid his trains and waited for the news; and when the stage coach came in from Meredith village he "stood by to fire," and all the rocks went off at once and made a pretty good noise. Georgy and I stopped in New Haven for a visit and had some delicious breezy, rushing, sparkling little sails in the bay and in the sound. We took to the salt water with a keen relish after nearly five months of mountains. Miss Rose Terry was in New Haven. She has just published a little volume of poems, and is writing New England stories for the magazines. Think of our national bird being in danger of splitting at last, like that odious fowl, the Austrian Eagle—a step toward realizing the vision of a "Bell-everett" orator in the late campaign, whose speech I read, and who saw the illustrious biped with "one foot upon the Atlantic shore, one on the golden strand, and one upon the islands of the main!" Not that I care for secession; let them go! We are told we "mustn't buy too many new dresses this winter," but *still* I say no matter—no compromises. Millions for defence, not one cent for tribute. I can live on a straw a day. "So can *I*," Georgy puts in here, "if one end of it is in a sherry cobbler." But what a sight we must be to other peoples. Just as morning breaks over Italy with sunshine and singing, this evil cloud comes up in our heaven. Must there be a sort of systole and diastole in civilization, and must one nation go down in the balance as another goes up, till the great day that makes all things true? You read all this stuff in the papers: how the North "hurls back with scorn the giant strides of that Upas Tree, the slave power!" and how the South will no longer be "dragged at the chariot wheels of that mushroom, the Northwest!" The money men look blue and the dry-goodsy men look black. Charles Rockwell has just gone to Georgia, rather against the advice of some of his friends, for the R's are stout Republicans and given to being on their own side. Now and then an incident "comes home" that doesn't get into the papers. Here is one that came under my own knowledge. A young lady, being rather delicate, decided three or four weeks ago to go to her friends in Georgia for the winter. For some reason they could not send for her, or even meet her at Savannah, so she set out alone. During the little voyage there was some talk in the cabin about John Brown. "But we must allow he was a *brave* man," she said;—nothing more. The steamer arrived in the night, and she with some others waited on board till morning. Soon after daybreak, while she was making ready to go ashore, three gentlemen presented themselves to her; "understood she had expressed abolition sentiments, regretted the necessity," etc.—the usual stuff—"if she would consult her safety she would leave immediately by the Northern train; her luggage *had already been transferred;* they would see her safely to the station." She denied the charges, told who her relatives were (staunch Democrats), etc., in vain. They, with great politeness, put her into a carriage, escorted her to the station, presented her with a through ticket and sent her home, where she arrived safely, a blazing Abolitionist.

Thanksgiving day is lately past, and the burden of the sermons was peace, peace and concession. Mr. Beecher preached a tremendous Rights-of-Man and Laws-of-God sermon, and I was told that once when a fine apostrophe to freedom came in, and there were movements to hush signs of enthusiasm, he paused a moment, and said in his peculiar manner: "Oh, it isn't Sunday!" and all the great audience broke into long applause. And why not? In the Church's early days they used to applaud and shout "Pious Chrysostom!" "Worthy the Priesthood!" And in the meantime: Garibaldi! The word is a monument and a triumphal song. I should like to have one of the turnips from that island farm of Caprera. Now, when the "deeds are so few and the men so many" it is surely a great thing to find a noble deed to do, and to do it! What a scene that was, the meeting and the crowning at Speranzano; for *that* was the real crowning, when Garibaldi said to Victor, "King of Italy!" We fairly cried—don't laugh—over that scene. And now he is like Coleridge's Knight:—

> "In kingly court,
> Who having won all guerdons in the sport
> Glides out of view, and whither none can find."

While I am writing they are screaming "President Buchanan's message" in the streets. I capture an extra and try to make "head and tail" of it for you, without success. Our family friends are snugly settled in Rome, and "as quiet as in North Conway." Baby Bertha begins to speak, and her first articulate word is "Viva!"

G. M. W. to the Sisters in Europe.

PHILADELPHIA, DECEMBER, 1860.

Dear Girls:

Mother and Abby have just come down from Fishkill, Mother declaring that she feels like a different person in consequence of her visit. We are none of us making a time over Christmas presents this year. Abby has had a little bureau just to fit shirts made for Mr. Prentiss, who was in high delight while they lived abroad because he had *a drawer* to keep his things in. No calls will be received at No. 8 this New Year and indeed I don't think there will be many made, people are so depressed about the times.

The papers today report from Washington that "alarming news has been received from Charleston. Apprehensions of immediate collision with the Federal government are entertained. Influential Northern men are doing their utmost to avert the calamity. The intention of the people of North Carolina is to seize the forts and arsenals and to prevent the government from collecting the revenues. Despatches have been received stating that the forts would be taken in less than twenty-four hours. The Cabinet is in council. It has not transpired what course the government will pursue. A naval fleet will probably be despatched to Charleston. The amendment of the Constitution to settle the controversy between North and South forever, by a division of the country from ocean to ocean on the parallel of the Missouri line, is the great subject of discussion." Notwithstanding all this trouble, and the secession ordinance which was published on Saturday, "the stocks of the North have gone up steadily for some days both before and after the fulmination of the ordinance. Never was the strength of the business condition of the northern and central states more decisively proved than now." I hope you are interested in all this; politics are the only things talked of among all classes of men and women here in this country, now, and foreign affairs relating to the "state of Europe" are comparatively of no importance. In fact, all interest given to Italy centres in the "Casa Zuccara" and especially on our 'Donna and child. We only wish the Southerners could see how prosperous and happy we look, on the outside at least! "O, yes, Doctor," one of them said the other day to Dr. Hodge, "it's a beautiful city this of yours, but in a little while the grass will be growing in the streets." Lenox's reports from down town are that it is suggested that the governors of the states should have the troops of the different states in readiness for any emergency, since the South is busy making its preparations, and thus far we have been doing nothing. I took the news word for word from the paper this morning, from the Washington correspondent, and you must take it for what it is worth. People think it worse than anything thus far, though Mr. Seward predicts that in sixty days the troubles will have past away. Only think how jolly! There's an ordinance in Charleston forbidding the sale of Boston crackers and including farina.

Several pleasant surprises came to lessen the depression of this Christmas. Mr. Martin, a young gentleman returning from Rome, brought to Mother a promised ring—"a Mosaic of a carrier pigeon, which lifted up and displayed a shining curl of the new little baby's hair," and Abby writes: "Uncle Edward [Our dear Uncle and guardian, Edward John Woolsey, of Astoria, L. I.] gave me some of Father's early water-colors, interesting to us—the work of a boy of fourteen,—and when Mother and I drove in after spending the day with him what do you think we found besides?—a box with a scarlet camel's hair shawl for Mother with Cousin William Aspinwall's best wishes." (This shawl is now Alice's.)

On December 20th, 1860, South Carolina "in convention assembled" had declared the union subsisting between that state and other states to be "hereby repealed." Other southern states were rapidly following the insane example.

All sorts of efforts, private and public, were made to compromise and patch up, and family friends and relatives on both sides made last attempts to join hands. Abby writes Eliza, "What do you think? I wrote Minthorn Woolsey a long letter the other day asking for information as to the position he holds on secession."

When we were all children and spending, as usual, our summer with Grandfather Woolsey at Casina there arrived one day a new and charming cousin, Benjamin Minthorn Woolsey, from Alabama. He belonged to the Melancthan Taylor branch of the family, and none of us had ever seen him before. A warm friendship began and was continued until the mutterings of secession were heard. Abby, unwilling to give him up, argued and entreated in vain. The letter from which the following extracts are taken was probably her last to him and will give an idea of her clear and forcible thinking and writing. Many families decided at this point to meet again only as enemies.

My dear Cousin,

I hasten to answer your letter, for, as events march, mail facilities may soon be interrupted between North and South. When the great separation is a recognized fact postal treaties, along with others, may be arranged. Meantime, it is one of the curious features of your anomalous position that you are making use of a "foreign government" to carry your mails for you, on the score of economy. Congress may cut off the Southern service and occasion some inconvenience and delay, but I am told it will save the government about $26,000 weekly, that being the weekly excess of postal expenditure over revenue in the six seceding states.

I thank you very sincerely for your letter. It was very kind in you to write so promptly and fully and in so sedate a tone. But what a sober, disheartening letter it was! We have been slow to believe that the conservative men of the cotton states have been swept into this revolution. I could not believe it now but for your assurance as regards yourself and your state. "Not a hundred Union men" as we understand it, in Alabama! We had supposed there were *many* hundreds who would stand by the Union, unconditionally if need be, and uphold the Constitution, not according to any party construction, but as our fathers framed it, as the Supreme Court expounds it, and as it will be Mr. Lincoln's wisest policy to administer it. Not a hundred Union men in your state! Truly not, if Mr. Yancey speaks for you and Alabama when he avows himself as "utterly, unalterably opposed to any and all plans of reconstructing a Union with the Black Republican states of the North. No new guarantees, no amendments of the Constitution, no repeal of obnoxious laws can offer any the least inducement to reconstruct our relations." Then compromisers in Congress, in convention, everywhere, may as well cease their useless efforts. Not a hundred Union men in Alabama! Who then burned Mr. Yancey himself in effigy? Have those delegates who refused to sign the secession ordinance yet done so? and what constituencies do they represent? Why was it refused to refer the action of convention to the people?

Whatever the Border states may have suffered, and, as in the case of the John Brown raid, have swiftly and terribly avenged, you of the Gulf states can hardly think that your wrongs have been so intolerable as to make revolution necessary. True, you describe us as standing with a loaded pistol at your breast, but the heaviest charge we have ever put in is non-extension of slavery in the territories. If slavery cannot stand that; if, surrounded by a cordon of free states, like a girdled tree it dies, then it cannot have that inherent force of truth and justice—that divine vitality which has been claimed for it. This is as favorable a time as we could have to meet the issue and settle it peacefully, I trust, forever. And here comes up the subject of compromises, the Crittenden measures particularly. How does it happen that the Southern demands have increased so enormously since last year? *Then* the Senate declared by a vote of 43 to 5 that it was not necessary to pass a law to protect slavery in the territories. *Now,* you "secede" because you cannot get what Fitzpatrick, Clay, Benjamin, Iverson, and others declared you did not need. *Then* you asked the Democratic convention at Charleston to put a slavery code into the party platform, and you split your party about it. *Now* you come to the opponents who fairly outvoted you and your platform and ask them to put the same protective clause,—where?—*into the Constitution!* We can never eat our principles in that way, though all fifteen of the states secede. The right of eminent domain, by which South Carolina claims Fort Sumter, inapplicable as it is, is a respectable demand compared with what has been practiced further south—the right of seizure. If you attack Sumter you may precipitate a collision. Meantime, never was a people calmer than ours here, in the face of great events. We have scarcely lifted a finger, while the South has been arming in such hot haste and hurrying out of the Union, in the hope of accomplishing it all under Floyd's guilty protectorate. We all hope much from the new administration. We think well of a man who for so long has managed to hold his tongue. We shall try to help him and hold up his hands, not as our partisan candidate but as the President of the Nation. If we become two confederacies we shall not shrink from this race with *your* Republic, which in the heart of christian America and in the middle of the Nineteenth Century lays down slavery as its corner stone, and finds its allies in Spain, Dahomey, and Mohammedan Turkey.

A. H. W. to E.

8 BREVOORT PLACE, FEBRUARY 1, 1861.

My dear Eliza:

As Charley was away at Astoria Georgy sent round for young Herdman, and she and I went with him to hear Wendell Phillips' lecture. I never saw him before, and found it a perfect treat. A more finished and eloquent sketch I never heard, enlivened by telling anecdotes, and that quiet, shrewd wit which distinguishes the speaker. He made the lecture an indirect argument of course for the negro race; twice in the course of it mentioned John Brown's name, which was received with a storm of applause, and once, in speaking of the courage of the blacks, he said: "Ask the fifty-two thousand of LeClerc's soldiers who died in battle. Go stoop with your ear on their graves! Go question the dust of Rochambeau and of the eight thousand who escaped with him under the English Jack! and if the answer is not loud enough, come home!" and (dropping his voice) *"come by the way of quaking Virginia!"* There was a great crowd, but we went early and had excellent seats, and were perfectly charmed.

On Friday Rose Terry (who is at the Danas) and Dr. Bacon are to dine here. Rose wrote the "Samson Agonistes" it seems,—the fragment about John Brown in the *Tribune* which we all liked.

J. S. W. to Cousin Margaret Hodge.

FEBRUARY 7, 1861.

Night before last a Virginia gentleman said to us: "Don't be too san-guine. Union does not mean in Virginia what it means in New York. There it means only delay—it means Crittenden's compromise; it means secession, not today but tomorrow." The same gentleman said: "Floyd was no gentleman. No Virginia gentleman would ask him to dinner" (the climax of earthly honors I suppose) and that "he was intoxicated at the Richmond dinner and not responsible for his speech." This Virginian said he would "stake his existence," or something of the sort, on the honor of the South in paying, to the last cent, everything it owes the North. As an offset to this, Mr. Lockwood last night repeated to us the contents of three letters he had read yesterday, sent to acquaintances of his in answer to requests for payment. One said: "I shall pay, of course, every farthing I owe you, in cash, but not till I pay it in the currency *of the Southern Confed-eracy.*" Another sent a note to the effect: "I promise to pay, etc., five min-utes after demand, to any Northern Abolitionist the same coin in which we paid John Brown, endorsed by thousands of true Southern hearts." The third said: "I cannot return the goods, as you demand, for they are already sold, and the money invested in muskets to shoot you—Yankees!" Georgy was at a party last night at Amy Talbot's, where nothing but politics was talked. Uncle Edward has just popped in, for a minute, and says: "All I am afraid of now is that Virginia and the other Border states *will stay in;* and we shall have the curse of their slavery on our shoulders without the bless-ings of a complete union."

Dr. Roosevelt dined with us on Saturday, and I said: "What do you go for, Doctor?" "I go for gun-powder!" he answered. Mrs. Eliza Reed hears from her brother-in-law, a clergyman in Beaufort, S. C., that she "ought to be very thankful that her property is safely invested at the South" (partly in his own hands) and that he is "sorry he is *not able to forward her the interest now due,*" the fact being that she has not had a cent of her income this winter.

One more anecdote and then my gossip is over. Mrs. Dulany overheard two negresses talking on a corner in Baltimore. "Wait till the fourth of March," said one of them, "and then won't I slap my missus' face!"

Abraham Lincoln was inaugurated President of the United States on the fourth of March, 1861. In closing his inaugural address he said to the Southern seceders: "In your hands my dissatisfied fellow country-men, and not in mine, is the momentous issue of Civil War. You can have no conflict without being yourselves the aggressors. You have no oath registered in Heaven to destroy the government, while I shall have the most solemn one to preserve, protect, and defend it."

The Seventh Regiment, New York Volunteers, Cortland Street
April 19th, 1861
Frank Leslie's Illustrated Newspaper

CHAPTER TWO

A Most Extraordinary Mixture of Feeling

THE REBEL BATTERIES in the neighborhood of Charleston had been built and armed in the last three months of the imbecile administration of Mr. Buchanan and his traitorous Cabinet, and on April 12th, 1861, they opened fire upon Major Anderson, Fort Sumter, and the national flag, and easily forced a capitulation from troops left by the government without food or ammunition.

A. H. W. to E. W. H.

APRIL 14, 1861.

What awful times we have fallen upon! The sound last night of the newsboys crying till after midnight with hoarse voice, "Bombardment of Fort Sumter," was appalling. Cousin William Aspinwall was seen at a late hour going into the Brevoort House—no doubt to give what little comfort he could to Mrs. Anderson. This storm, which has been raging a day or two at the South, and has just reached us, has scattered the fleet sent to reinforce and provision Fort Sumter, and the vessels can neither rendezvous nor co-operate with Major Anderson who is there without food, without help, and without instructions. Is Providence against us too?

April 15th, 1861, President Lincoln issued the first call to arms, summoning the militia of the several states to the aggregate number of 75,000 men to serve for three months, and ordering the oath of fidelity to the United States to be administered to every officer and man.

At once the Governors of all the Northern states called out their militia, and preparations for war began in earnest, with a great burst of patriotic self-devotion on the part of men, women, and children. Regiments almost immediately began to arrive in New York en route for

Washington. Mother and all her family enlisted promptly for the war, and the home, 8 Brevoort Place, New York, became a sort of headquarters for all the family friends. The little strong mahogany table which our uncle Commodore Newton had had made for Charley, on his flagship, the "Pensacola," and which Charley and the younger sisters had used at their play in the old Rutgers Place nursery, was brought down and established in the parlor. A bandage-roller was screwed to it, and for months bandage-rolling was the family fancy-work, and other festivities really ceased.

A. H. W. to E.

APRIL 19, 1861.

My Dear Eliza:

Your's and Joe's note and the box of birthday flowers for Charley came yesterday morning, and the latter we have all had the benefit of. Charley did not want to give any away, so we used them for the dinner-table and parlor, and looked and smelled "lovely" last night when we entertained eight young men callers. Charley did not have any of his friends to dinner or supper. On Wednesday he said he should keep his birthday on Thursday, and on Thursday he said he had kept it the day before. I think he preferred not having any special celebration this year. Meantime, the candy pyramid stands untouched, consolidating gradually into a huge sugary drop. The city is like a foreign one now; the flag floats from every public building and nearly every shop displays some patriotic emblem. Jane amused herself in shopping yesterday, by saying to everyone: "You have no flag out yet! Are you getting one ready?" etc. Shopkeepers said in every instance: "No—well—we mean to have one; we are having one prepared," etc. She met Mr. Charles Johnson, of Norwich, who had been down to see the Massachusetts contingent off—a splendid set of men—hardy farmers, sailors from Marblehead, some in military hats, some in fatigue caps, some few in slouched felts—all with the army overcoat. C. J. had a talk with some of them in their New England vernacular, which he described as very funny, "thought there might be some fightin', but by golly! there's one thing we want to do—a lot of us—just pitch into an equal number of South Carolinas." C. J. says a few gentlemen in Norwich came in to the "Norwich Bank" to his father and authorized him to offer Governor Buckingham $137,000 as a private subscription. This is beside the $100,000 offered by the other bank the "Thames."

Yesterday Mother and I went round to see Mary Carey, who was out, but seeing policemen about the door of the Brevoort House, colors flying, and a general look of expectancy on the faces of people in opposite windows, we hung round and finally asked what was going on? "Why nothing ma'am, only Major Anderson has just arriv'." Sure enough, he had driven up rapidly, reported himself at General Scott's headquarters, and then driven round to the hotel. In five minutes the crowd on foot had got wind of it and came surging up Eighth street with the Jefferson Guard, or something of that sort—a mounted regiment—who wished to give the Major a marching salute. Band playing, colors flying, men's voices cheering lustily, and everywhere hats tossed up and handkerchiefs waving—it was an enthusiastic and delightful tribute! We clung to an iron railing inside an adjoining courtyard and, safe from the crush of the crowd, waved our welcome with the rest and saw Major Anderson come out, bow with military precision several times and then retire. He looked small, slender, old, wrinkled, and grey, and was subdued and solemn in manner. Charley Johnson was on hand, of course—he is up to everything—and later in the day pressed his way in with some ladies, shook hands impressively and prayed, "God bless you, Sir!" "I trust He will!" said Major Anderson, and expressed himself honored by the interest felt in him. Our Charley went round in the evening, found Mr. Aspinwall in close conversation with the Major in the parlor, but not liking to intrude, looked his fill at him through the crack of the door.

Yesterday was "one of the days" in 10th street—a steady stream of people all day. While Mother and I went out for a few calls and had our little adventure, as above described, Jane took a short constitutional. C. Johnson, whom she met, gave her a flag, and as she walked up Broadway a large omnibus, with six horses, passed, gaily decked with flags and filled with gentlemen—some delegation—going to wait on Major Anderson as they supposed. Jane said she could not help giving her flag a little twirl—not daring to look to the right or left—and instantly the whole load of men broke out into vociferous cheers. They tell us that quantities of Union cockades were worn in the streets yesterday, and I should not be surprised if they should become universally popular. Just at dusk Will

Winthrop came in to say good bye. To our immense surprise, he said he and Theodore joined the Seventh Regiment a week ago—he as a private in the ranks and Theodore in the artillery in charge of a howitzer—and they were all to leave this afternoon for Washington. It seemed to bring war nearer home to us. Mother was quite concerned, but I cannot but feel that the Seventh Regiment is only wanted there for the moral influence. It will act as guard of honor to the Capitol and come home in a fortnight. However, the demand for troops in Washington is very urgent. They are telegraphing here for all the regular officers. Even Colonel Ripley, the Dennys' cousin, who arrived on government business yesterday on his way to Springfield, was overtaken by a telegram as he took his seat in the New Haven train and ordered back by night train to Washington. Other men received similar despatches, and the idea is that Washington may be attacked at once now that Virginia has gone out, and the fear is that if done this week it may be taken. Troops are hurrying on. The Rhode Island contingent passed down at nine this morning, the Seventh goes at three—that will be a grand scene! We shall be somewhere on Broadway to see them pass. Georgy has been busy all the morning cutting up beef sandwiches and tying them up in white papers as rations. Each man tonight must take his supply with him for twenty-four hours, and Theodore Winthrop, who was in last night, suggested that we should put up "something for him and Billy in a newspaper." The Seventh is likely to have more than it needs in that way; it is being greatly pampered; but it all helps to swell the ardor of those who stay behind I suppose. The more troops who can be sent off to Washington the less chance for fighting. The immensity of our preparations may over-awe the South. Last night we had rather jolly times, joking and telling war anecdotes, and worked ourselves up into a very merry cheerful spirit. It is well that we can sometimes seize on the comic points of the affair or we should be overwhelmed by the dreadful probabilities.

J. S. W. to Cousin Margaret Hodge.

APRIL, 1861.

My dear Cousin Margaret:

I fancy that you may like to know how we have gone through the dreadful turmoil and excitement of the last few days, and so I send you an incoherent line tonight, though my wits are scarcely under command of my fingers.

The three great local incidents this week have been the arrival of Major Anderson, the leaving of the Seventh Regiment, and the great mass-meeting today in Union Square, or rather whose centre was Union Square, for the huge sea of men overflowed the quadrangle of streets where the speakers' stands were, and surged down Broadway, up Broadway, through Fourteenth street and along Fourth avenue far beyond the Everett House. We were in a balcony at the corner of Union Square and Broadway and saw the concourse, though we could not distinguish the words of any speaker. We could only tell when the "points" were made by the thousands of hats lifted and swung in the air and by the roar of the cheering. Every house fronting the square, and up and down the side streets, was decorated with flags and festoons, and the Sumter flag, on its splintered staff, hung over the stand where the gentlemen of the Sumter command were. The Puritan Church had a great banner afloat on its tower. Trinity set the example to the churches yesterday, when a magnificent flag was raised on its tall spire with a salvo of artillery. The sight was a grand one today, and in some of its features peculiar. As the tide rolled up under our balcony we could see scarcely a man who was not earnest-looking, grave, and resolved, and all seemed of the best classes, from well-dressed gentlemen down to hardworking, hard-fisted dray men and hodcarriers, but no lower. There was not a single intoxicated man as far as we could see, or a single one trying to make any disturbance or dissent. You will see by the reports of the meeting who were the officers, speakers, etc., and judge how all colors of opinion were represented and were unanimous. New York, at any rate, is all on one side now—all ready to forget lesser differences, like the household into which grief has entered. Almost every individual, man, woman and child, carried the sacred colors in some shape or other, and the ladies at the windows had knots of ribbon, tri-colored bouquets, and flags without number. There was not a policemen to be seen from our outlook, though no doubt there were some about the square, but the crowd kept itself in order and perfect good nature, and whenever the flag appeared at the head of any procession or deputation it fell back instantly and respectfully to let it pass through. The resolutions, Committee for Patriotic Fund, etc., you will see in the papers.

I have given the first place to the meeting because it was the most recent, but yesterday was a more exciting and saddening day than this. Beside Meredith Howland, Captain Schuyler Hamilton, Howland Robbins and other friends and acquaintances in the "Seventh," our two cousins Theodore and William Winthrop went. All these are privates except Merry, who is on the staff—Paymaster. The Winthrops came in their accoutrements at one o'clock to get their twenty-four hours' rations (sandwiches which Georgy had been making all the morning), and we filled their cases and liquor flasks, with great satisfaction that we were able to do even such a little thing for them. We gave them a hearty "feed," helped them stow their things with some economy of space, buckled their knapsack straps for them, and sent them off with as cheerful faces as we could command. They were in excellent spirits, on the surface at any rate, and promised to come back again in glory in a little while. We in our turn promised to go down to them if they needed us. Poor fellows! It was heart-sickening to think of any such necessity. Then we went down to a balcony near Prince street, in Broadway, and saw them off. The whole street was densely crowded, as today, and the shops and houses decorated—only there were three miles of flags and people. After long waiting we began to see in the distance the glimmer of the bayonets. Then the immense throng divided and pressed back upon the sidewalks, and the regiment came,—first the Captain of Police with one aid, then the Artillery corps, then company after company, in solid march, with fixed faces, many of them so familiar, so pleasant, and now almost sacred. The greeting of the people was a thing to see! The cheers were almost like a cannonade. People were leaning forward, shouting, waving handkerchiefs, crying, praying aloud, and one block took up the voice from the other and continued the long, long cry of sympathy and blessing through the entire route. Some friends of the soldiers who marched all the way with them to the Jersey cars, said the voice never ceased, never diminished, till they reached the end of that first triumphal stage of their journey. It was a triumph though a farewell. At Ball and Black's Major Anderson was in the balcony with Cousin John's and Cousin William Aspinwall's families, and each company halted and cheered him as it passed. Except for this, they looked neither right nor left, but marched as if at that moment they were marching into the thick of battle. They were not long in passing, and the crowd closed in upon them like a parted sea. We watched the bayonets as far and long as we could see them, and the last we saw was a late warm beam of sunshine touching the colors as they disappeared.

Great anxiety is felt tonight about their arrival in Washington and what they may meet there. Many gentlemen here think the forces in the District quite inadequate and blame anybody and everybody for not hurrying on more troops. A gentleman was here late this afternoon looking for Cousin William Aspinwall. They were hunting him up everywhere where there was any chance of his being found, to make instant arrangements for steam vessels to take reinforcements tomorrow. Several regiments are ready, only waiting orders and means of transit. Uncle Edward came to the meeting today—very grave indeed—and I don't doubt very efficient and open-handed, as usual, in anything that needed his help. He has ordered a great flag for the "barrack." Joe has set one flying from his house-top. He (J. H.) has joined a cavalry company in Fishkill who are drilling for a Home Guard or a "reserve." Charley has joined a similar company (foot) in town. He is uneasy and wants to "do something." Uncle Edward says: "Stay at home, my boy, till you're wanted, and if the worst comes to the worst I'll shoulder a musket myself!"

Major Anderson was the hero of Cousin Anna's party last night. Only Charley represented us; we didn't feel "up to it." C. said it was a very handsome party, as usual with their entertainments, and that a portrait of Major Anderson was hung in the picture gallery, wreathed with laurel, and all the "Baltic's" flags decorated the hall and supper room. Thirty of the expected guests had marched at four o'clock with the Seventh. Major Anderson is very grave, almost sad, in expression and manner, as a man may well be who has been through such scenes and looks with a wise eye into such a future; but if anything could cheer a man's soul it would be such enthusiasm and almost love as are lavished on him here. He says "they had not had a biscuit to divide among them for nearly two days, and were almost suffocated." They say he talks very little about it all; only gives facts in a few modest words. He is "overwhelmed" with the sight of the enthusiasm and unanimity of the North; "the South has no idea of it at all." He says that he "felt very much aggrieved at being attacked at such disadvantage;" that "for four weeks he only received *one* message from government, and was almost broken down with suspense, anxiety, and ignorance of what was required of him." He went to all the stands today at the mass-meeting, and was received with a fury of enthusiasm everywhere. Yesterday he was obliged to leave the balcony at Ball and Black's, the excitement and applause were so overpowering; and he goes about with tears in his eyes all the time.

Mrs. Gardiner Howland is very anxious and sad about Merry in the Seventh. She says she is "no Spartan mother." Mary G. G. has sent to Kate Howland withdrawing her invitations for her bridesmaids' dinner on Tuesday. She is not in spirits to give it. [Kate Howland was married April 2, 1861, to Richard Morris Hunt.] Two regiments start tonight instead of tomorrow to go by rail to Philadelphia and thence by steamboats, outside. There are the gravest fears that they may be too late. . . . I have been writing while the others have gone to the Philharmonic concert. They have come back and had a splendid scene at the close—singing of the Star-Spangled Banner, solo, and chorus by the Lierderkranz and the whole huge audience, standing, to the hundred stringed and wind instruments of the orchestra, while a great silken banner was slowly unrolled from the ceiling to the floor. Then followed rounds of vociferous applause, and three times three for everything good, especially for Major Anderson, and the Seventh.

The Massachusetts contingent passed through on Thursday, and then we got the news of the cowardly assault in Baltimore. [The Sixth Massachusetts, crossing Baltimore to the Washington depot, were set upon by a furious mob of roughs and pelted with stones and brickbats. Two soldiers were killed and eight wounded, and the troops forming in solid square with fixed bayonets at last forced their way through the crowds.] The poor fellows tasted war very soon. Tonight the city is full of drum-beating, noise and shouting and they are crying horrible extras, full of malicious falsehoods *(we hope)*. G. G., we hear, is going from home to his Mother's and back again, all the evening, contradicting them. There should be authentic news by this time of the progress of the Seventh, but people will not believe these horrible rumors, and refuse to believe anything.

There is the most extraordinary mixture of feeling with everyone—so much resistless enthusiasm and yet so much sadness or the very cause that brings it out. It seems certainly like a miracle, this fresh and universal inspiration of patriotism surmounting the sorrow, like a fire kindled by God's own hand from his own altar—and this alone ought to inspire us with hope of the future.

The following letter from our special cousin, Sarah Chauncey Woolsey, to G. M. W. describes the making of the Connecticut flags and their presentation, and the farewell to the Second Connecticut Volunteers on the New Haven Green. Dr. Bacon (now "Uncle Frank") marched with them as Assistant Surgeon:

Our beautiful flags are nearly done and are to be presented to the Second Regiment before they leave. The regimental banner is worked with the arms of the state, which are far more beautiful than those of any other state, with a heavy wreath of palm worked in gold-colored silk around the shield and mounted on a staff headed with a battle-axe and spear plated with gold. Won't it be beautiful? The other flag is the Union flag and just as handsome in its way. F. B. was here last night with stripes on his trousers, but wisely withholding the full splendors of his "miling-tary" attire until we become gradually accustomed to it. He looked very handsome and is as coolly delighted at the chance of a little fighting as anyone I have seen. We are both highly entertained just now by the pertinacity with which our friends here persist in engaging us to each other. I was telling him last night of a lady who called the other day and would not listen to any denials on my part, asseverating that Miss —— assured her that she knew it to be a fact; whereon Frank, putting himself in an attitude, informed me that "being on the eve of battle and about risking his life in his country's defence, he *could not* feel that it was his duty to engage the affections of any young and lovely female and withdraw her from the bosom of her own family," whereon I begged him not to apologize, and explained that "being on the point of joining the Nightingale Regiment and putting myself in the way of catching a fever, I could not feel justified in allowing my naturally susceptible feelings to run away with me," etc. I don't know why I tell you all this stuff—only it makes you laugh a little. . . .

Later.—Dora and I went up at four o'clock to see our flags given to the Second Regiment, on their way to the "Cahawba," which waited to carry them off, no one knows where, under sealed orders,—but probably to Washington or Fortress Monroe. The colors were presented on the Green at the foot of the liberty pole, where the Home Guard formed a hollow square enclosing all the ladies who had worked on or were interested in the flags, and when the regiment marched up they took their places inside the square, which widened and kept off the crowd outside. Two pretty girls held the flags, assisted by two gentlemen. Mr. Foster made a short and spirited address to the regiment, and their Colonel replied in a few brave words, and then Dr. Leonard Bacon read the twentieth Psalm, "in the name of our God we will set up our banners," etc., and made a beautiful prayer, and amid the shouts and cheers of the crowd, the frantic waving of handkerchiefs and flags and the quiet weeping of some who were sending off their dearest ones to all the chances of war, the glittering waving splendors were lifted aloft and the regiment swept on—carrying in its ranks Frank, who found time in the midst of the confusion to ride his horse round to the place where here we stood, and hold my hand tenderly for two or three minutes while he whispered some good-bye words, especially his "farewells to Miss Georgy," greatly to the satisfaction of some old ladies near, who, fondly fancying that I am engaged to him, probably wondered at my comparative composure. Yes! the good-byes are hard enough even if it is for the country, and I have had a heartache all day at the thought that I shall see the dear fellow no more for so long a time, and of how much we shall all miss him. He looked tired, with these last days of hurry. We stood two hours nearly, on the Green. We heard all about the doings in Norwich from Captain Chester and Lieutenant Coit of the "Buckingham Rifles." They are both pleasant young fellows, and we made their acquaintance while sewing green stripes on the trousers of the company and brass buttons on their coats—the very garments which were made on Sunday by the Norwich ladies. It was funny work, as the men all had to be sent to bed before we could be put in possession of their apparel, and the officers being in the same quandary all were comfortably tucked up in their quarters and their trousers under way when sixteen Norwich gentlemen called to see them, and had to be received by them "lying in state!"

About this time the national flag was printed in colors on note paper, and on slips for use in books and wherever it could be displayed on anything, and this next letter of Jane's bears it, as a matter of course, on the first page.

J. S. W. to the Sisters Abroad.

Seventh Regiment safe and jolly. No fighting yet,—April 29th, 1861.

Eliza has been making a flag for their church. It was her part to cut out and sew on the stars. She sent for a large number of very small testaments, for knapsacks, for the Fishkill Regiment, and we have found some sheets of flags on paper, like stamps, to paste in them, each with an appropriate verse—"Fight the good fight;" "Endure hardness as a good soldier of Jesus Christ," etc.

On Thursday evening Charley had a few friends to supper—a substitute for the birthday party—and we decorated the table with flags, bunting, red, white and blue mottoes, etc. They seemed to have a gay time and sang many songs to a squealing accompaniment from Pico. It is by no means unlikely that a Home Guard will be needed with all the militia ordered away and seditious people biding their time in town. Mansfield Davies is with his regiment at Fort Schuyler, drilling. They go south next week. George Betts goes today as Lieutenant-Colonel Second Zouaves. The great barracks in the park are nearly finished—meant as a mere shelter for troops in transit and there is a camp in the Battery—officers' marquee and a whole fleet of tents. We hear from Norwich that last Sunday was spent by Dr. Bond's congregation in making red flannel shirts for the regiment who were to leave next day. Mr. Davies asks us for bandages, etc., for their surgeon, which we shall supply with great readiness. Mother has made a great deal of beautiful lint. There is an organization of medical men to train nurses for the camp; lectures are to be given and bands of ten ladies are to walk some wards in the hospitals, as a preparation. Georgy has been to some of the lectures with Mrs. Trotter, and would like to go as a nurse, but would no doubt be rejected, as none but "able-bodied and experienced" women are to be taken. While I write a company goes down Broadway with the eternal Reveille. We had a grand patriotic sermon last Sunday from Dr. Prentiss, and now we have only patriotic prayers and psalms, with the petition for the President borrowed bodily from the Prayer Book.

This morning I got, to my surprise and pleasure, an official document containing a letter from Will Winthrop of the Seventh, written, no doubt, in acknowledgment of the little kindnesses we were able to show him on leaving. I quote, as it's far too bulky to send:

"Washington, April 26. Dear Cousin: Here we are in "marble halls" the adored of everybody, the heroes of the hour. Members of Congress frank our letters; hotel men fetch the sparkling wines; citizens cheer us with tears and rapture. Wherever we appear vivas greet us—now the triple cheer, now the *"bully for you!"* This P. M. we paraded in the Capitol grounds, and forming in a grand square took the oath of allegiance, all together, repeating it sentence by sentence after the magistrate. Green grass was soft under foot, trees in spring attire exhaled fragrance, the marble halls gleamed on every side. Every man was clean and beautiful of moustache, pipe-clayed as to belts of snowy whiteness, well-dinnered internally. Brass plates and bayonets glistened in the sun. The band played the national hymns and the Valence polka. Abe and wife walked happy and beaming along the line. All was brilliant and imposing. Night before the last we were staggering along the line of railroad from Annapolis, wearied to exhaustion, stiff with cold and swamp damps, almost starved, with nothing but a little salt pork or jerked beef in our haversacks and no water in our canteens, feet sore with tramping—wretched beyond expression; yet all the time forced to build bridges destroyed by the enemy, and relay railroad track, torn up (rails and sleepers); also to push along before us heavy platform-cars carrying our howitzers; also to scout in the van and watch on all sides for the enemy who might be ambushed anywhere. This we had done during the day, now under a hot sun, now rained on by heavy showers; but at night in the dark and fog and cold it was cruelly severe, and to all of us the most terribly wearisome experience of our lives. Whenever we halted to hunt missing rails and lay track, our men who were not thus employed would sink down and instantly fall asleep, and often could not be roused without violent shaking. Many a time during the night did I thank (1) the cherub that sits up aloft for having put me in the way of roughing it in Minnesota; (2) the blessed women whose brandy helped to give heart to many a miserable beside myself. On the day before this forced march we were in clover in Annapolis doing parade drill on the Academy ground, sniffing the sea breeze and the fruit blossoms, swelping down oysters on the demishell. On the day before this, we were packed in the transport, either stifled in the steerage in odors of uncleanness and water drips, or broiling on the deck, each man with a square foot or two to move in, and all subsisting on the hardest of tack. The day before, we woke at dawn in Philadelphia and foraged for provisions around the railroad station, bearing off loaves on our bayonets, entertained by Quakers with eggs and cakes, lingering all day at the station, utterly in doubt about the future—ending with a hot fatiguing walk across the city to take the transport. The day before, the triumphal march down Broadway! Such are the vicissitudes of a week, the most eventful and strange in the lives of all of us—a week of cheers, tears, doubt, peril, starvation, exhaustion, great dinners, woe, exultation, passion. And the sweetest thing of all has been the brotherhood and fraternization. We share in common, give, relieve and love each other. . . . We were disappointed that we could not have a chance at Baltimore; also that we had no brush with the enemy in Maryland. We only saw them scampering over the distant hills. They could tear up the track, but were too craven to meet us. There were but few troops here in Washington; everybody was in doubt and dread, and when we marched up toward the White House with colors flying, full band playing and perfect lines, the people rushed out in tears and shouting welcome. Our importance is, of course, over-estimated, but *moi* I feel that I never before was so useful a member of the Republic.

We are quartered in the stunning Representatives Hall and march down three times a day to our browsings at the hotel. This is luxury, but pretty soon we go into camp on Georgetown heights. Regiments arrive all the while and the city is awake and brilliant—guards and watchings everywhere. Washington is not in immediate danger, but all are ready to resist an attack at any moment."

All very graphic and interesting. Now we shall be eager to know how *you* take all this stupendous news, and whether it affects in any way your plans. Perhaps you will think best to spend the summer abroad—Isle of Wight, or something. For many reasons we should be quite satisfied to have you. Perhaps on the other hand you will be for rushing home;—natural but after all, useless. One thing, look out for Jeff. Davis' privateers, and don't come in any ship that hasn't arms of some sort on board. This sounds ridiculous, so did the siege of the Capitol, ten days ago; so did the prophecy that New York would be nothing but a barrack full of marching regiments.

Uncle E. has a turn of gout. Abby is going out to spend the day there. Some day soon Mr. Aspinwall is going to drive Major Anderson out, for Aunt E.'s gratification. I shall keep my letter open for tomorrow's news. Nothing immediate is expected, but a collision *must* come soon. We shall send every day's papers and you must look out for them.

Tuesday.—The news this morning is the final departure of Virginia and the call for more troops by the President. We can send as many as are wanted and more.

On April 25th, 1861, the first steps were taken by fifty or sixty New York women towards organizing systematic work for the sick and wounded.

From this "Woman's Central Association of Relief," together with Boards of Physicians and Surgeons proposing to furnish hospital supplies in aid of the army, came the first suggestion to the Department of War at Washington that a "mixed commission of civilians, medical men and military officers" be appointed, charged with the duty of organizing and directing the benevolence of the people towards the army.

As the result of this petition the great United States Sanitary Commission, was, on the 13th of June, 1861, duly appointed by Simon Cameron Secretary of War, with the signature and approval of President Lincoln.

While retaining its independence, the Woman's Central Association became at its own instance an auxiliary branch of the commission, and other branches sprang up all over the northern states.

The headquarters of the commission were in Washington, where also was stationed Mr. Frederick Law Olmsted, its life and soul. With its work we, as a family, were associated from the beginning.

Eliza and Joe were just taking possession of their beautiful new home, "Tioronda," at Fishkill, and all the little details of E.'s home letters have a pathos of their own in view of the speedy closing of the house and the sudden change from peaceful loveliness to the grimness of civil war. Meantime, E. was busy, as all of us began to be, in work for the disabled soldiers.

E. W. H. to A. H. W.

Dear Abby:

I was just going to write you a note this P. M. when the Kents came in for a long call and stayed on for an early tea. We sat in the *library* where the books are now all arranged and the cushion we ordered at Soloman and Hart's in its place in the bay-window. To be sure there is no carpet down, and we have no tables or chairs, but it already has a very habitable look, and we feel quite at home in presence of our old book-friends. They make a very good show, though there are still a number of empty upper shelves which will fill up by degrees. James Kent had been in town for a couple of days and had a good deal to say about military matters. While Joe was in town I did a good deal of cutting out and have three dozen army pillow-cases and six double-gowns under way. Tomorrow I shall attack the drawers and night-shirts, for which I borrowed a good simple pattern of Mrs. Kent. I smile when I think of the sang-froid with which you and I discussed the cut of drawers and shirts with that pleasant young doctor the other day. I see that Georgy is excluded from the corps of nurses by being under thirty.

A. H. W. to E.

Friday.

Dear Eliza:

We got off our first trunk of Hospital supplies for Colonel Mansfield Davies' Regiment yesterday and feel today as if we were quite at leisure. You have no idea of the number of last things there were to do, or the different directions we had to go in, to do them. Mr. Davies came in at breakfast yesterday, in his regimentals, quite opportunely, to tell us what to do with the trunk. It went down to his headquarters at 564 Broadway and thence by steamer to Fort Schuyler for the sick soldiers there. Charley and Ned drove out there yesterday afternoon from Astoria to see the drill, and saw the box safely landed within the walls. It was the old black ark which you and G. had in Beyrout, Syria, marked with a capital H, which now answers for *Hospital*. There were in it as follows—for you may be curious to know:—

42 shirts,
12 drawers,
6 calico gowns,
24 pairs woolen socks,
24 pairs slippers,
24 pocket handkerchiefs,
18 pillow sacks,
36 pillow-cases,
18 damask napkins,
36 towels,
24 sponges,
4 boxes of lint,

beside old linen, oiled silk, tape, thread, pins, scissors, wax, books (Hedley Vicars and the like), ribbon, cloth, etc., and fifty bandages.

This morning Mother has been putting up a tin box of stores for Mr. Davies—sardines, potted meats, arrow root, chocolate, guava and the like, with a *box* of cologne, a jar of prunes and a morocco case with knife, fork and spoon, fine steel and double plated, "just out" for army use. Lots more. The box, a square cracker box, holds as much in its way as the trunk. I am glad you are in the library at last. You will grow accustomed to it and find it pleasanter even than the dining-room.

J. S. W. to a Friend in Paris.

8 BREVOORT PLACE, FRIDAY, MAY 10, 1861.

I am sure you will like to hear what we are all about in these times of terrible excitement, though it seems almost impertinent to write just now. Everything is either too big or too little to put in a letter. Then one can't help remembering sometimes that you are that august being, a "Tribune's Own," and as unapproachable on your professional pinnacle as the ornament of the Calendar whom Georgy *will* persist in calling Saint Simeon Stalactites. But the dampest damper to enthusiastic correspondents on this side is the reflection that what they write as radiant truth today may be "unaccountably turned into a lie" by the time it crosses the "big water".

So it will be best perhaps not to try to give you any of my own "views" except indeed, such views of war as one may get out of a parlor window. Not, in passing, that I haven't any! We all have views now, men, women and little boys,

> "Children with drums
> Strapped round them by the fond paternal ass
> Peripatetics with a blade of grass
> *Betwixt their thumbs,*"—

from the modestly patriotic citizen who wears a postage stamp on his hat to the woman who walks in Broadway in that fearful object of contemplation, a "Union bonnet," composed of alternate layers of red, white and blue, with streaming ribbons "of the first." We all have our views of the war question and our plans of the coming campaign. An acquaintance the other day took her little child on some charitable errand through a dingy alley into a dirty, noisy, squalid tenement house. "Mamma," said he, "isn't this South Carolina?"

Inside the parlor windows the atmosphere has been very fluffy, since Sumter, with lint-making and the tearing of endless lengths of flannel and cotton bandages and cutting out of innumerable garments. How long it is since Sumter! I suppose it is because so much intense emotion has been crowded into the last two or three weeks, that the "time before Sumter" seems to belong to some dim antiquity. It seems as if we never were alive till now; never had a country till now. How could we ever have laughed at Fourth-of-Julys? Outside the parlor windows the city is gay and brilliant with excited crowds, the incessant movement and music of marching regiments and all the thousands of flags, big and little, which suddenly came fluttering out of every window and door and leaped from every church tower, house-top, staff and ship-mast. It seemed as if everyone had in mind to try and make some amends to it for those late grievous and bitter insults. You have heard how the enthusiasm has been deepening and widening from that time.

A friend asked an Ohio man the other day how the West was taking it. "The West?" he said, "the West is all one great Eagle-scream!" A New England man told us that at Concord the bells were rung and the President's call read aloud on the village common. On the day but one after that reading, the Concord Regiment was marching into Fanueil Hall.

Somebody in Washington asked a Massachusetts soldier: "How many more men of your state are coming?" "All of us," was the answer. One of the wounded Lowell men crawled into a machine shop in Baltimore. An "anti-Gorilla" [That was the newspaper's way of spelling "Guerilla."] citizen, seeing how young he was, asked, "What brought you here fighting, so far away from your home, my poor boy?" "It was the stars and stripes," the dying voice said. Hundreds of such stories are told. Everybody knows one. You read many of them in the papers. In our own little circle of friends one mother has sent away an idolized son; another, two; another, four. One boy, just getting over diphtheria, jumps out of bed and buckles his knapsack on. One throws up his passage to Europe and takes up his "enfield." One sweet young wife is packing a regulation valise for her husband today, and doesn't let him see her cry. Another young wife is looking fearfully for news from Harper's Ferry, where her husband is ordered. He told me a month ago, *before Sumter,* that no Northman could be found to fight against the South. One or two of our soldier friends are surgeons or officers, but most of them are in the ranks, and think no work too hard or too mean, so it is for The Flag. Captain Schuyler Hamilton was an aid of General Scott's in Mexico, and saw service there, but he shouldered his musket and marched as a private with the Seventh. They wanted an officer when he got down there, and took him out of the ranks, but it was all the same to him; and so on, indefinitely.

The color is all taken out of the "Italian Question." Garibaldi indeed! "Deliverer of Italy!" Every mother's son of us is a "Deliverer." We women regretfully "sit at home at ease" and only appease ourselves by doing the little we can with sewing machines and patent bandage-rollers. Georgy, Miss Sarah Woolsey and half a dozen other friends earnestly wish to join the Nurse Corps, but are under the required age. The rules are stringent, no doubt wisely so, and society just now presents the unprecedented spectacle of many women trying to make it believed that they are over thirty!

The Vermont boys passed through this morning, with the "strength of the hills" in their marching and the green sprigs in their button-holes. The other day I saw some companies they told me were from Maine. They looked like it—sun-browned swingers of great axes, horn-handed "breakers of the glebe," used to wintering in the woods and getting frost-bitten and having their feet chopped off and conveying huge fleets of logs down spring-tide rivers in the snow and in the floods.—The sound of the drum is never out of our ears.

Never fancy that we are fearful or gloomy. We think we feel thoroughly that war is dreadful, especially war with the excitement off and the chill on, but there are so many worse things than gun-shot wounds! And among the worst is a hateful and hollow peace with such a crew as the "Montgomery mutineers." There was a dark time just after the Baltimore murders, when communication with Washington was cut off and the people in power seemed to be doing nothing to reestablish it. It cleared up, however, in a few days, and now we don't feel that the "social fabric"—I believe that is what it is called—is "falling to pieces" at all, but that it is getting gloriously mended. So, "Republicanism will wash"—*is* washed already in the water and the fire of this fresh baptism, "clothed in white Samite, mystic, wonderful," and has a new name, which is *Patriotism.*

From the first moment of the firing on Fort Sumter J. H. had felt that "solemn and compelling impulse" that forced men, almost in spite of themselves, into the service of the government. Making his decision quietly, seriously, he gave up the new home and all that it meant, and early in May, 1861, joined the Sixteenth New York Volunteers—a fine regiment from the northern counties of the state, then forming at Albany under the command of Colonel Thomas A. Davies,—into which he was mustered as Lieutenant and Adjutant.

E. W. H. to Mother.

MAY 11, 1861.

Dear Mother:

Joe had a note from his Colonel last night requesting him to report himself at headquarters, 678 Broadway, on Wednesday of this week. This may be merely to take the oath, receive his commission, etc., but he will arrange matters to stay if required. He is now under orders and not his own master. It is generally known now that he is going, and hearty blessings and congratulations pour in upon him. He wrote to Uncle Edward and his sisters last night, and was busy till a very late hour settling business matters and explaining things to me. He goes off with rather a sad heart, but he feels that he is *doing right,* and I can give him nothing but encouragement. Our friends here have been most kind in their sympathy and in offers of service to me; and, as for me, if I can have all or any of you here I shall be very courageous. Don't forget our big house in making your summer plans. I would rejoice in having you with me.

Uncle Edward to J. H.

MAY 13, 1861.

My dear Joe:

My eyes are so weak that I must use your Cousin Emily's pen to express the surprise caused by the announcement in your letter that your sense of duty had obliged you to accept the adjutancy of a regiment.

Had the question been propounded to me, I should have replied that I did not think you possessed the physical endurance needed for such a post, nor the requisite knowledge of military law and tactics; also that you could be ten times more usefully employed in aiding the cause than by a *personal* devotion to the duties of an officer of the army. If there had been a deficiency of able men anxious to serve, then the duty might have been imperative to stand forward and offer personal services. There are, however, five men offering to each man required. All this I state, because you wish my candid opinion, though I am fully aware that now, having taken the step under your own sense of duty, it is perhaps well that you had not an opportunity of consulting me previous to your decision.

May God's presence accompany you; and if during your absence I can be of any use to Eliza let her come to me as freely as to a father.

Your Cousin Emily joins with me in all love and desires to do anything in her power for you or Eliza.

Yours with sincere affection,

E. J. Woolsey.

From Mother.

MAY 15, 1861.

My dear Eliza:

Thank you and Joe for your letters received this morning. I was hoping to see you here today, and on reading these letters telling of Joe's sudden departure, and thinking of you as all alone at your house, I at once concluded to go up, Charley and I, by the three o'clock train. I was all packed up to start when your telegram was brought in. I felt relieved to get it, because I was going off in a little uncertainty as to whether we might not possibly pass you on the road, on your way to us. I hope you will come, and Joe too, if he can. He must now I suppose *obey orders*—a somewhat new position for him! Should the regiment be ordered to Washington, perhaps you might feel like going on there for a while, at least, But remember, my dear child, your home is with us still, for as long as you choose."Indeed, I think you had better come to us altogether—at any rate we must manage to keep an eye over you, and all of us must look on the bright side and hope for the best. How comforting to fall back at such times to that invisible arm which is ever ready for our support and which, I trust, is leading in all this movement Charley waits for the letter, and I will only add my tender love to you both. Many thanks to Joe for his letters. *Your loving Mother.*

Among many kind notes from friends at this time was the following from Mrs. Professor Smith:

My dear Mrs. Howland:

I thank you very much for the beautiful flowers, which are a great delight to us all, and I thank you especially for thinking of our pleasure when your heart must have been so full. I could hardly be reconciled at first to Mr. Howland's going, but now I am glad that such a man should go. Surely the cause is worthy of the best and noblest, and he will have the same Protector there as at home, and the constant loving prayers of many hearts will be like a shield of defence.

A. H. W. to E.

FRIDAY, MAY 17, 1861.

My dear Eliza:

Your nice long letter of yesterday from Albany came this morning at breakfast. I say your "nice" letter in the sense of its being long and circumstantial. That anything concerning Joe's going off is nice, I shall never be brought to say. It seems as if you both had been snatched up and swept away from us by some sudden and awful fate. No time for thought about it and no use for regrets! I hardly think he himself realized all he was pledging himself to—the bothering duties, I mean, of an Adjutant's office, a great deal of work and no glory; a sort of upper servant to an exacting Colonel; though some people tell us that the Adjutant's post is a highly military one, requiring fine military education—a knowledge, at least, of theories and laws, etc. I am glad that Colonel Davies impresses you pleasantly.

Do find out from Joe's Dr. Crandall what style of garments he thinks best for hospital wear, as we are constantly cutting them out, and may as well make them with reference to his wants. Should the night-shirts be of unbleached or canton flannel, and drawers ditto? Should the shirts be long or short? and are extra flannel shirts necessary for hospital wear? I am going to the Cooper Union today to try and get some simple pattern for calico gowns. They advertise to supply paper patterns of garments to ladies, and their published circular, a copy of which I have seen, is far more particular and satisfactory in its directions than the one we have had.

I went to Astoria day before yesterday and came back yesterday noon. Aunt E. and I spent all the time in Casina library. The women dusted the books and I checked them off on the catalogue to see if they were all right and to leave them in good order for G. G. Howland, who moves up next week. I saw the transport go up to Riders' Island with George Betts' Zouaves—the Hawkins' Zouaves as they are called. We can see the barracks built for them from Casina. I thought if Robert were at home he would be flying about in his sailboat, visiting these points, and could make many a call on Joe if he were to be at Fort Schuyler. I found on coming home from Astoria that Georgy had fairly begun at the hospital—the City Hospital on Broadway—but as she has requested me not to "discuss her" with anybody I had better leave her to tell her own story. She and Mrs. Trotter go down daily at twelve o'clock, and yesterday, Mother tells me, they went before breakfast beside, at 6 A. M. Two such visits a day, when a singing lesson and a German lesson come in between, are rather too much, *I* think, but this insane war is making men and women insane,—Mr. —— of Alexandria, for instance. Mother had a letter from him this morning written in the true Southern style—so highfalutin—with abuse and melancholy, martial ardor and piety, beautifully commingled. Mother wrote the other day to find out something about them, and this letter was to say that her's had been received and forwarded to his wife and daughters at Lexington, Virginia, where he had removed them "to be out of the reach of the licensed outrages of our Northern outcasts, who make up the Northern army!"

Today we are going to try and decide on our wedding presents for Jenny Woolsey. Just think of Susan Johnson, too! and now Sarah Winthrop tells us of *her* engagement to Mr. Weston, a friend of her brother Will's. It reminds me of the days of Noe when there was marrying and giving in marriage and the flood came and drowned them all. Love to Joe. What is his title now? We cannot call him plain Mister!

As part of their excellent work, the Woman's Central Relief Association organized a nursing staff for the army, selecting one hundred women and sending them to the various hospitals in New York city for such drill as could be secured in a few weeks, through the kindness of the attending staff. The Sanitary Commission undertook to secure recognition for these women from the War Department with the pay of privates; and they were sent on to the army hospitals on requisition from Miss Dix and others, as needed.

I (G.) still have my blue ticket, or pass, signed by (Mrs.) Christine Kean Griffin, Secretary of the Ladies' Committee, and Dr. Elisha Harris, of the Hospital Committee, on which I, "No. 24," was admitted to the old New York Hospital for a month's seasoning in painful sights and sounds. The old New York Hospital property comprised a square on Broadway bounded by Worth street on the north and Duane on the south.

Later in the war it happened that the Sanitary Commission wanted contributions to the "Spirit of the Fair," published during the great Fair held for the Commission, and I gave them my experiences in getting ready to be a nurse three years before. They may interest you and I quote from them. You will be amazed to know that your aunt was considered by some of the committee as too young and too pretty! to be sent to the front. That was thirty-seven years ago though!—

It was hard work getting myself acceptable and accepted. What with people at home, saying "Goodness me! a nurse!" "All nonsense!" "Such a fly-away!" and what with the requisites insisted upon by the grave committees, I came near losing my opportunity.

First, one must be just so old, and no older; have eyes and a nose and mouth expressing just such traits, and no others; must be willing to scrub floors, if necessary, etc., etc. Finally, however, by dint of taking the flowers out of my bonnet and the flounce off my dress; by toning down, or toning up, according to the emergency, I succeeded in getting myself looked upon with mitigated disapprobation, and was at last sat upon by the committee and passed over to the Examining Board. The Board was good to me. It had to decide upon my physical qualifications; and so, having asked me who my grandfather was, and whether I had had the measles, it blandly put my name down, leaving a blank, inadvertently, where the age should have been, and I was launched, with about twenty other neophytes, into a career of philanthropy more or less confused.

Then began serious business. Armed with a blue ticket, I presented myself with the others at the door of a hospital and was admitted for instruction. 'Follow me,' said our guide, and we followed in processing. 'this will be your ward; you will remain here under so and so, and learn what you can; and this, yours: and this, *yours.'* That was *mine!* I shall never forget the hopeless state of my mind at this exact point. To be left standing in the middle of a long ward, full of beds, full of sick men—it was appalling! I seized another nurse, and refused to be abandoned. So they took pity, and we two remained, to use our eyes and time to the advantage of the Army of the Potomac which was-to-be. We took off our bonnets and went to work. Such a month as we had of it, walking round from room to room, learning what we could—really learning something in the end, till finally, what with writing down everything we saw, and making elaborate sketches of all kinds of bandages and the ways of applying them, and what with bandaging everybody we met, for practice, we at last made our 'reverses' without a wrinkle; and at the end of the month were competent to any very small emergency, or very simple fracture.

In looking over my little note book of those first days at the New York Hospital I find it full of extracts from the lectures of Dr. Markoe and Dr. Buck at the bed-side of the patients, and with sketches of four-tailed, six-tailed and many-tailed bandages. I remember it gave me a little shock that first day in the ward to hear the young "house" say peremptorily: "Nurse, basin!" I presented the basin promptly, and as promptly tumbled over in a faint at seeing a probe used for the first time. I came out from this ignominy to find that my associate-nurse was dashing my face with water from a tumbler in which she dipped her fingers before offering it to me to drink from.

Before the summons from the army, though, came sickness among our soldiers passing through the great cities. Measles and typhoid fever began almost immediately. New wards in hospitals had to be opened, and the beds were filled faster than we could make them. Such nice fellows, too, from the country villages as were brought in.

My first patient of the war was a Duryea's Zouave, not a country boy though, but one of those poor desolate creatures, so many of whom the army has sheltered, giving them the first *home* they have ever known. My Zouave was dying when he enlisted; he had no friends, no place to live in, no place to die in, so he told me, and came into the army for the sake of finding one. "I felt the sickness coming on, and I knew if I was a soldier they would put me into a hospital, and then I could die there."

Poor soul! he was young and refined, in look and manner, and so comforted by little attentions, so appreciative of them;—and never to have had anything of the kind given him through all his lonely life!

Now, in these few last days of it there was a satisfaction in doing everything for him, in being as good to him as possible, in bringing him all that a gentleman's son might have had. So, with his poor tired head on my arm, I fed him with jellies and ices, and in little ways tried to comfort him. We owed him all the blessing we could bring into these last few moments of a dreary life.

My Zouave died, and they buried him in his fine new clothes—the best he had ever had—and put him to sleep in his own bed; now, at last, *his own,* that no one would dispute with him; no one grudge him possession of forever.

What our common soldiers understood the war to mean is shown in this extract from a letter of one of them, taken ill on the march through New York from Connecticut and nursed by me in the New

York Hospital. The rough draft in my hospital note book is sandwiched between directions for a "figure of 8" bandage and a receipt for boiling farina. The letter was to his old mother in Ireland:

"We are having a war here in America. The Southern states want to have a flag of their own and as many slaves as they can buy or steal. The North wants to keep the old flag and the country as Washington left it, and not to have slavery go any further; so they have gone to war about it, and I have enlisted and hope to fight for right and the country."

This gives the cause of the war in a very few words.

What the spirit was which these Northern men and women had to meet when they "enlisted for the war" is shown for instance in the proceedings of the "open session of the Confederate Congress," May, 1861, where the "assistance of The Most High" was impiously asked with the following blatherskite: "To protect us from those who threaten our homes with fire and sword; our domestic circles with ruthless lust; our fathers' graves with the invader's feet, and our altars with infidel desecration."

As soon as J. H. was mustered in, G. began to urge that she and E. should go as army nurses. Mother writes: "Georgy is more earnest than ever about being a nurse for the soldiers. *I shall never consent* to this arrangement unless some of her own family go with her."

G. herself writes to E.

May 15, 1861.

I supposed you would go to Albany; I am sure I should, and I hope you will take into serious consideration the small plan I suggested to you about being a nurse—at any rate about fitting yourself as far as you can for looking after the sick, if you go, as I suppose you will want to, to Washington in the fall with Joe. I invite you to join me. Mrs. Trotter and I were yesterday examined by the Medical Committee, Drs. Delafield, Wood and Harris, and with ten other women admitted to the course of instruction at the New York Hospital. We are to learn how to make beds for the wounded, cook food properly for the sick, wash and dress wounds, and other things as they come along in the proper care of the wards—fresh air, etc. Not that we have any idea of really going south now, no one will

till the fall, and two or three companies of ten each who are fitting themselves at Bellevue Hospital will at any rate go first. Then if there is really
a necessity for more nurses we shall send substitutes agreeing to pay their
expenses,—unless the opposition in the family has come to an end, in
which case, having tested our strength and endurance a little in this training, we shall be very glad to carry out our plan and go. We three might
very usefully employ ourselves in Washington if we went no further south,
and I shall not be satisfied at all to stay at home while Joe is down there.
So, my dear, be keeping the little plan in view in making your arrangements, and don't say a word to anybody about our being at the Hospital;
I don't want to have to fight my way all through the course, and be bad-
gered by the connection generally, besides giving a strict account of myself
at home. We all mean to be very brave about Joe, and I am sure you will
be;—it's a way you have; especially as you and I, and perhaps Mrs. Trotter,
will be near him in Washington at one of the hotels or hospitals.

A. H. W. to the Sisters Abroad.

[Robert and his family and Hatty and Carry were still in Europe, but
hurrying their return on account of the breaking out of the war.]

NEW YORK, MAY 21, 1861.

Dear Girls:

We hope soon to have more particulars about your interview with Mrs.
Browning, what *she* said, and "said he" and "said they."

I hardly know what to tell you about home. I have been trying to think
what questions about public affairs you are longing to have answered, the
whys and wherefores of things, but am afraid I might hit on the very wrong
ones. We cannot see into details ourselves; we live only on newspaper
rumors, and the only peace of mind we get is by mentally consenting to
leave everything in the hands of Scott, satisfied of his patriotism, wisdom
and skill. The best statesmanship of the country is at work for its good;
many knowing heads are contriving and planning; many brave hearts and
steady hands are executing the will of government; the monied men, who
have so much to save or lose, feel that their only hope of extrication is in
the vindication of our laws and constitution; the military men know the
true weakness of the South and predict its ultimate ruin; and above all and
over all, as Mr. Prentiss preached to us on Sunday, "this continent belongs

to Christ. He has a greater stake in it than any of us, who are here only for our little day, can have. If it should be destroyed, where on earth has God such another country so suited to His great providential designs? Be sure He will see to it that America is delivered out of all her troubles in His own time."

We hear the bugle-call now constantly floating down the streets. It is used as a rallying sound in the field—as in Europe—by the French and the German volunteers, and by some of our own regiments, I think. Going down Broadway you pass a great many "headquarters" or recruiting offices, and the crossed bayonets at the door or the sentry marching up and down have a very foreign look. You should see Charley in his Home Guard martial array. It is a sight to strike awe into feeble sisters—a grey tight-fitting coat, with red cuffs and collar edged with white cord, and a red and grey cap trimmed with white braid.

From Eliza and Joe at Albany we hear as follows: Joe was summoned there to report for duty, as the regiment is quartered in barracks, along with others, four thousand troops in all. The regiment and officers were sworn into United States service last Wednesday, drawn up in a long line, and the sound of their cheers rolling down the field like thunder. Two men refused to swear from some cause or other, and a third, who had hesitated but finally stepped into the ranks, was cheered by his comrades till the tears ran down his cheeks.

They say they are "able to lick their heft in wild cats" and are pronounced the finest regiment so far accepted—all six feet or more high and experienced riflemen. Joe is well, so far, and busy, and does not for a moment regret the step he has taken. The duties of adjutant are honorable and responsible ones, and purely military.

A. H. W. to the Sisters still Abroad.

JUNE, 1861.

We are gradually growing accustomed to things that a few weeks ago would have appalled us, or which we should have received as horrid jokes—such, for instance, as Georgy's training at the hospital. She comes home fagged-looking but determined to "stick it out." Did you know, Carry, that Miss Bessie and Miss Mattie Parsons are walking the hospitals in Boston? Some of the ladies there fainted every day for a week, when

Dr. Bigelow made them very mad by telling them "they had tried it long enough; they were unfit for it and must go home." It will not surprise us if by and by Georgy starts for the wars. *Nothing* astonishes us nowadays; we are *blasées* in revolutions and topsy-turvyings; or, as Joe elegantly expresses it: "How many exciting things we have had this winter! First, parlor skates, and now, civil war!"

I am reminded to say that the best thing that Theodore Winthrop has ever done, after volunteering for this war, is to write an account of the eventful journey of the Seventh Regiment in "THE ATLANTIC" for June. You will get it in England—Sampson and Low no doubt receive it. It is very bright—just sentimental enough—and has its value given it in the fact that his feelings went along with it in the writing and our feelings go with it in the reading. He describes the fraternization of the New York Seventh with the Massachusetts Eighth, and says they began to think that there was *nothing* the Eighth couldn't do. All trades and professions were represented. The man that helped to build the locomotive, you know, stepped out of the ranks to repair it, at Annapolis; others sailed the good ship Constitution; others laid rails; others mended leaky canteens, as tinsmiths; and Theodore says he believes if the order had been given, "poets to the front!" or "sculptors! charge bayonets!" a baker's dozen would have stepped from each company in answer to the summons.

Don't let me forget to give you Charley's message which is to countermand the purchase of his carriage blanket and to beg you to buy his gloves a trifle larger than the size he mentioned, as his hands have spread, as well as his appetite, since he began to drill.

Mr. Dayton, the new French minister, will have arrived in Paris before you leave, and perhaps Mr. Charles Francis Adams may be in London in time for you to see him. I hope Robert will see and consult one or both of them as to the state of things at home and the safety of taking passage in an American steamer. You can do nothing, of course, but take the best advice and then do what seems best to yourselves. The summer is going to be a broken one at any rate. We have given up our rooms in Conway. We cannot leave Eliza *entirely alone,* as she will be at Fishkill. Joe has gone "for the war" if he lives and it lasts, and Eliza reverts to our love and protection. The summer will be harassed by skirmishes in Virginia—possibly a great battle may be fought if General Scott thinks we are ready. He is bothered more than anything by the haste of ignorant, injudicious men who think they are great military geniuses, and want to push the matter on. June is a great month for battles in the world's history—*we* may add another to the catalogue—but it looks more as if the hard work, especially that in the far South and in the gulf, would be postponed till fall. A rebellion that has been thirty years in maturing isn't going to be put down in a day.

We went on Sunday night to a grand meeting of the Bible Society where reports were read of the distribution of Testaments and Bibles to the volunteer troops. Twenty-three thousand have been given away, and many interesting anecdotes were told and most stirring addresses made by Professor Hitchcock and Dr. Tyng. They began in a very sober Sunday-night spirit, but before we got through there was the most rampant patriotism—stinging sarcasms about Jeff Davis; kissing of flags which draped the platform; storms of applause, and a great time generally. . . . You would not judge by the streets that we were at war. The shops are thronged by gay women making cheap purchases. Indeed, it seems difficult to pay *more* than two and sixpence a yard for a new dress—double width at that.

E. fancying at first that she ought to stay behind to care for "the stuff" when J. went to the war, sent cheerful bulletins to him of home matters:

E. W. H. to J. H. at Albany.

FISHKILL, MAY 21, 1861.

Everything goes on nicely. I have made the rounds this morning and the report is all satisfactory. Thomson has bought a very nice bay mare to take Dick's place for $130, and a third pig, as there was too much food for the others. The men are all at work, the potatoes in and the corn will be finished tonight. Then the sodding and grading will be resumed. Mechie has bought dahlia poles and is now finishing the flower beds outside the greenhouse, which looks finely. A superb box of flowers came up this morning. . . . Everyone expresses the greatest interest in you and your movements. Moritz says the country wasn't as "lonesome" all winter as it was the first few days of your absence. . . . I don't doubt James will go with you, but I wouldn't let him decide hastily. Thompson would go with you himself in a minute but for his family. . . . I have had a very busy morning and haven't had a chance to miss you.

SUNDAY (BETWEEN CHURCHES), MAY 26.

I am going over to the Dutch Church at the Corners more, I confess, to hear the news from Washington than for the sermon's sake. The rumor by telegraph this morning was that Washington was on fire. I am restless and anxious. There *must* be important movements on one side or the other before long, now that we have advanced beyond the Potomac.

In yesterday's papers the great camp preparing on Staten Island is described—10,000 acres on the southeast slope of the island, with room for the tents and evolutions of an army of 60,000 men. Is it likely that you will be ordered there?

Mr. Masters told me this morning to tell you you were not forgotten in the village, for the boys have organized a company and are drilling under the name of the "Howland Guard." Mother thinks it should be called *Mrs. Howland's Guard.* . . .

May 27. This morning I deposited Mother with the papers at the old chestnut tree seat and helped Thomson and Mechie get a good line for the turf on the carriage road. It is not right yet, but shall be made so. Thomson says: "We'll na gie it up, ma'am till you say it's right." The sodding round the door and kitchen end is a great improvement and gives quite a finished look. We all took a turn in the wagon after dinner, stopping for me to get some cut-out work from the Women's Army Association, which is fairly under way now, with Mrs. David Davis as President, Mrs. James Kent Secretary and Miss Rankin Treasurer. Five or six dozen shirts were given out today. . . . I have a note this morning from L. H. H. asking me to make them a visit at Newport and saying Mr. H. would come on for me and bring me back. It is very kind, but I shall stand by my post here this summer. . . .

Mr. Masters told us an anecdote of old R—— who was in a tavern bar-room the other day with a party of rough fellows discussing the war, when one of them declared that "any man who would refuse to go *now that Mr. Howland had gone* ought to be drummed out of the community."

A. H. W. to E.

JUNE 1, 1861.

Dear Eliza:

We had a funny communication from Theodore Winthrop this morning written at Fortress Monroe, where he is acting as Military Secretary to Major General Butler, in the very middle of the middle of things—"Headquarters Department of Virginia." He tells about the negroes who are flocking to them, and begs that on the sly we will manage a patriotic job for them—get some sort of kepi, turban or headgear, which shall make them more respectable to look at and more formidable to the enemy. Of course, General Butler is to know nothing of it *officially* but since the poor ragged fellows must be clothed they will be glad to have a sort of coarse uniform for them—shirt, trousers and cap—if the ladies will do it privately, and forward to Fortress Monroe.

Last night and night before G. and I each made three havelocks, and Georgy is going to take them down to the Battery Encampment and distribute the six to the six men who fled the hospital. *They*, at least, must be supplied, as they had had inflamed eyes already from wearing the hot caps. If the Fishkill ladies want work say there is a demand for 3,000 havelocks, 3,000 grey flannel shirts and 3,000 grey or red drawers, and more will be needed. *Those* are needed today.

Yesterday Charley went about a good deal trying to find a room as a depot for receiving and distributing books and magazines for the troops. He had seen one or two notices on the subject in the papers, but last night's *Post* showed us that some gentlemen of the Evangelical Alliance are already in the field.

E. W. H. to J. H. at Albany.

8 BREVOORT PLACE, JUNE 13, 1861.

We are waiting for our travellers who are due now at any moment by the "Adriatic." Abby and I came down this morning from Fishkill leaving a lovely summer morning behind us, but bringing some of it in the shape of flowers, strawberries and vegetables. Mother has everything in nice order for the girls, cribs for the babies, little novelties and conveniences for the girls, plenty of lovely flowers, etc., etc. It will be a tight squeeze to accommodate them all, but it will be done, with Mother's usual faculty,

and there would have been a place for you, too, if you could have come. . . .
How wretched the Southern news is; such bungling and such frightful
and unnecessary loss of life. That battle of Bethel must injure us very
much and give strength to the rebels. I suppose you have seen the death
of poor Theodore Winthrop—one of its victims. It has shocked us all and
brought the matter very close.

Major Winthrop was shot in the fight at Great Bethel, June 10th,
1861. From the *Yale College Obituary Record* this extract is taken:

While gallantly leading a charge on the battery he fell mortally wounded
and died in a few minutes. His body was buried near the spot where he
fell. It was subsequently disinterred, and after obsequies in New York City
was brought to New Haven, where, on the 28th of June, 1861, with unusual
demonstrations of respect from military, civic and academic bodies, and
from the people-at-large, it was laid to rest in the burial-place of his
father.

All the students and faculty marched in procession to the grave.

As the coffin was brought through New York it was taken to the Seventh Regiment Armory. There Mother and G. saw it resting on a gun
carriage, when they went for a last farewell. They had, so short a time
before, helped to pack and buckle on his knapsack!

E. W. H. to J. H. (still in Albany.)

NEW YORK, JUNE 14, 1861.

At 10 P. M. the expected telegram arrived saying the "Adriatic" would be
at her wharf by 11, and Charley and Mr. S. left at once in carriages to bring
the girls up. The travellers all look remarkably well and by no means as
seedy and seasick as they ought to by rights. Molly has a sore throat, but
is bright and very smart in spite of it, and the other children are lovely as
possible. Bertha is the *stranger* after all, for Una is like most other sweet
babies round and plump and laughing—but Bertha is a little darling,
unlike May and unlike Elsie, unlike all other children—not belonging to
anyone, in likeness or manner. She is a mere baby herself; just running

about and beginning to talk, saying, *"I will"* and *"I won't"* in the sweetest and most winning way.

Robert has been out to the country with Charley, and the rest of us have had a grand "opening" of foreign traps. Aren't you glad Harper's Ferry has been evacuated without bloodshed?

The middle of June, 1861, J. H.'s regiment, the Sixteenth New York, suddenly received orders to be ready to march, and after some little further delay it left Albany for Washington and the front. The family were now fairly in the war.

Rev. G. L. Prentiss to J. H.

NEW YORK, JUNE 19, 1861.

Abby has just told my wife that you are ordered South. Is it so? If I were not strong in faith about you, I don't know what I should say. But the path of duty is the path of safety and of honor, and if you were my own brother (you seem to me more like a younger brother than anything else) I could not lift a finger against your going—assuming always that your health and strength hold out. God bless you and have you ever, dearest friend, in His holy keeping.

Most affectionately yours,
GEORGE L. PRENTISS.

G. M. W. to E.

WEDNESDAY.

My dear Eliza:

You must feel that I am ready and glad to go anywhere and at any time with you and dear Joe. You will probably go with him to Washington, at any rate. You and I could be companions for each other at the hotel as long as the regiment camps near the city, and, judging from the way the other regiments have been disposed of, that is likely to be the arrangement for them for some time. We should be able to see them every day and perhaps go even farther south. Since Joe has taken the sick under his care we *perhaps* shall be able to be a part of the regiment, as other women have been, and may keep together in this way, doing what we can.

You know we three have travelled over rough roads together before, and have now only to take up our little bundles and commence our march again. We shall like it and we will do it if possible. Two of our bands of nurses have been sent on from the Hospital already, and with a letter of introduction from our association (which is accepted by government) *I* shall probably be able to go where I please, as far south as hospitals have been established; and so we may be able perhaps to keep up with the Sixteenth. If you can, don't you think you had better come down and be introduced to Dr. Elizabeth Blackwell and others, and go for a few days to one of the hospitals opened to us, so that you may be able to give references from our association, if necessary? It may save you some delay and be useful to you in other ways. I am ready, or shall be at the shortest notice, to do as you say. I cannot tell you how we all feel about this. We shall try and not feel at all, only our hearts are with you and Joe always.

E., who had by this time definitely abandoned the idea of trying to stay behind, alone, writes to G. from Tioronda, June 20:

We will go together, as you say, and will keep as near Joe as possible, though where it may be is entirely uncertain. They will march like others, with sealed orders. I go to Albany on Friday to see them in camp again before they leave. Will you go too? Joe has ordered a mess-chest and camp-table, and wants a *cookery-book*. I think I have seen one for army use advertised. Will you get me a simple one of any kind, civil or military, and send or bring it up? Simple directions for soups, gruels, stews, etc., are all he wants. His advice to me is to close up my affairs here and go to Mother for a while, till he can reach Washington and spy out the land. He wants us to be all ready to move but not to move hastily, and he says we must take Moritz with us as body-servant wherever we go. If any of you are near Tiffany's the next few days you might hurry the flags up.

E. W. H. to J. H.

TIORONDA, JUNE 23, 1861.

. . . I write chiefly to remind you of the stand of colors which Tiffany is making and promises for Wednesday. You may want to have them presented to the regiment the day they pass through New York, and, if so, will have to arrange the affair with the Colonel. *I* do not wish to appear in the matter, but you can present them in my name, or, if you like, perhaps Charley will be willing to, but *don't* have any fuss or parade about it, and don't let the men tramp through the city *à la* McChesney till they are exhausted. The colors will remain at Tiffany's till the Colonel sends for them or notifies me.

Mary and Robert and the children are still here and all well. Mary broke the news of my going to the servants, who were very sorry for me and for themselves. In the course of next week I shall wind up my affairs—pay my debts, etc., and go to Mother's. I shall go down on Wednesday when the regiment passes through New York, at all events, for the day and night, unless I hear to the contrary from you.

The Sixteenth left Albany for the seat of war via New York, June 25th, and, reaching the city early in the morning of the 26th, marched to Washington Square. Here at 3.30 before embarking for the South the regiment was presented with a stand of colors, state and national, made by Tiffany and Co.,—Eliza's gift.

Mr. Robert S. Hone made the presentation in E.'s name, and Colonel Davies responded for the regiment,—also saying "already my command is deeply indebted to Mrs. Howland and her family for many articles which they needed while in Albany."

Colonel Davies then delivered the state flag to the color-sergeant, who bore it to the line. Waving the national flag before the regiment, he asked each company if they would defend it. A prolonged "yes" rang from one end of the line to the other, followed by deafening cheers and waving of caps. That promise was faithfully kept.

At Gaines' Mill the color-bearers were three times shot down, and all except one of the color-guard were either killed or wounded. The regimental banner was in every march and every battle in which the regiment participated. At Crampton Gap Corporal Charles H. Conant was instantly killed by a minie ball through the head while holding one of the flags, and Corporal Robert Watson, of the color-guard, was shot through the leg in this action. These flags are now deposited with other battle-flags in the Capitol at Albany.

That same afternoon of the 26th the regiment left by transports for Elizabethport and from there by rail to Washington, via Baltimore.

Before entering the last place ammunition was issued, in remembrance of the brutal attack of the mob there on the Massachusetts Sixth and other national troops. The Sixteenth New York was the first regiment to march through that city without some form of attack.

J. H. to E. W. H.

WASHINGTON, JUNE 30, 1861.

Our journey on was a hard one. We reached Harrisburg late Friday P. M., and Baltimore at sunrise Saturday. Our passage through Baltimore was unmolested, but was one of the most impressive scenes imaginable. We marched through about 8 o'clock without music and with colors furled, in perfect silence, marching in quick time, only pausing once to rest. The streets were full of people, but we did not get one word of welcome or a single smile except from two little girls in an upper window and half a dozen old darkies standing in doorways. At the head of the column of eight hundred stern-faced men walked the Colonel with his sword sheathed and a hickory stick in his hand. Once a rough fellow in the crowd (a city official) asked tauntingly, "Where's your music?" and Colonel Davies, gritting his teeth, replied, *"In our cartridge boxes!"* We were all fully armed and supplied with ammunition, and had received full instructions how to act in case of an attack. Tramp, tramp, tramp, went the Sixteenth through Baltimore in the early morning, and the crowd looked cold and bitter at us, and we looked stern and ready at them. All the road from Harrisburg to Washington is guarded by strong bodies of federal troops, *and they are needed.*

We got here safely at noon yesterday, and, after a couple of hours' delay under the shade of the trees of the Capitol grounds, we marched out to "Camp Woolsey," for so this camp is named in your honor! There are 100,000 soldiers in Washington.

I hope to see you very soon. I don't know what you will do with yourself here, but, if you want to come, your coming will make me very happy. God bless you!

G. M. W. to E.:

NEW YORK, SUNDAY.

My dear Eliza:

In anticipation of a possible march on Tuesday I have got myself ready and hold myself under orders for any moment. As for some sort of a hospital costume, if we chance to need one, I have *two* grey cottonish cross-grained skirts, and a Zouave jacket giving free motion to the arms—so the skirts can be, one of them, always in the wash; and a white Zouave will take the place of the waist when that is in the tub. Four white aprons with waists and large pockets; two stick-out and washable petticoats to take the place of a hoop, and a nice long flannel dressing-gown, which one may put on in a hurry and fly out in, if the city is bombarded or "anything else." Then for quiet and civil costume, I have only one dress made of black grenadine, like Mary's, and a black Neapolitan straw with green ribbon will make it all very nice. I shall make up a trunk of towels and old scraps of linen and cotton, soap, cologne, oil-silk, sponges, etc., and have it stored away in the hotel in Washington for use, if necessary. Any towels or old sheets you may have to dispose of we shall probably find useful if we are able to do anything for the sick. I have also under consideration a small camp cooking affair, about two feet square, with lamp and all complete, which I shall probably get—cheap and very useful in an emergency—could cook up little things for ourselves at any rate. If we find that we shall be allowed to march with the regiment, or rather *ride,* we could easily have grey flannel skirts and shirts made in Washington. So I don't see that we may not be very comfortable and useful, and consequently happy, even in following the war.

A. H. W. to J. H.

NEW YORK, JULY 3, 1861.

My dear Joe:

It was a satisfaction to us, at least, to receive your telegram of yesterday morning about half-past four in the afternoon. I was sorry that Eliza could not have seen it before she and Georgy left, at 3 P. M. But she was in good spirits, having received your letter with the account of your strange, safe march "through Baltimore," "that *luke*-loyal, flagless city," as somebody from the Garibaldi Guard, writing to the *Post,* calls it. By the way, I think your camp and the Babel-camp of the Garibaldians must be near each other, from the accounts. I am glad yours is on that high open ground—a hitherto undefended part of Washington, too, I think. "Camp Woolsey," has a strange sound to us, there never having been any military association with the name in our family. *Naval* officers you know we have had, and there is a little village of five houses down at Pensacola named after the Commodore—"Woolsey."

I send by this mail some maps for Georgy and Eliza. Carry, Jane and I are living very quietly and miss you all sadly. Mother and Hatty intend to spend the Fourth at Astoria.

Every morning I wake up to bright sunshine and familiar sounds and sights, and think for a second that perhaps all this pageant and preparation of war has been a horrid dream! A busy reality to you I dare say, hardly giving you time to read this or even to remember.
Yours affectionately,
A. H. W.

We—Charley, E. and G.—left New York, July 2nd, to join the army and J. H. in Washington, stopping on our way over night with Cousin Margaret Hodge in Philadelphia.

G. M. W. to Cousin Margaret Hodge.

WASHINGTON, JULY 8, 1861.

My dear Cousin Margaret:

I should have begun by dating my letter Ebbitt House, we having been established here since Saturday, spending the first three days of our visit, or probation, at the "National," in the fifth story, a prey to several inconveniences, but refreshingly near processions. Joe sent his man down to meet us, and came himself after evening drill. He looks brown and well; is dashing round on horse-back all day from camp to the War Department, and back again to camp, where he must spend seven hours a day drilling. Then all the cracks are filled up with our society out there. We go out every day in time for evening drill, and stay till it is time to shut up for the night, having a nice time in the door of Joe's tent "in the cool of the day," and this sort of thing we fondly thought was going to last an indefinite length of time, till yesterday, when Joe surprised us by the news that they were ordered into Virginia, and would leave on Tuesday or Wednesday. The Colonel has been made an acting Brigadier-General, and he and Joe were eight hours in the saddle yesterday, flying round selecting three regiments to form the Brigade with the Sixteenth. Joe has been in today on the same business, being entrusted to decide upon them and take whichever he thought best; and has chosen the Eighteenth, Twenty-first and Thirty-first—all from New York. So on Wednesday I suppose they will move over the bridge, and then we shall deliver our letters of introduction and plunge into occupation of some kind.

Washington is the stillest place for a city I have ever been in; nobody knows anything, or has anything to say. Everything is guess work. A few doleful little boys call the evening papers round the doors of the hotel, but in a tone that fixes a gloom upon you. I hate the *"Eve-en-ing Star"* already, and our only news comes via New York. *The Tribune, Times* and *Herald* have a great deal of information about what goes on here, and it generally proves true. . . . One longs now and then for a real living and lying "Extra" boy, with his mouth full of fearful statements, all disproved by his paper which you imprudently buy. We went, of course, to the opening of Congress and also to hear President Lincoln's message, read on the fifth.

Charley has been about visiting the camps at Alexandria, Georgetown and Arlington, but for all this a pass is necessary, which can only be procured through General Mansfield on introduction by some one known to him. If Lenox knows anyone at home who knows the General it would save him half a day to get his letter before coming on. Charley got his through Colonel Davies who is a relative of the General's. I hope Lenox will come on, but it is too bad that he will not see Joe. . . .

Here comes a regiment down *this* street. About 15,000 men have gone over into Virginia since we came on. Joe goes up in rank with his Colonel as his aid—is now Captain and Assistant Adjutant General—and the Brigade will be in McDowell's Division. . . . The regiment has marched past—the Massachusetts Eleventh just from Harrisburg, all in beautiful order, gray uniforms and large clean havelocks. New England doesn't do anything by halves.

And here goes another company, guarding thirteen well-filled baggage wagons and followed by its regiment. We have only to flourish our handkerchiefs and the dear fellows will kiss their hands, twirl their hats and manifest affection for the entire woman population of the North. They are the Fourth Maine, and are going over into Virginia. I must put up my letter and watch them marching along. Our love to the Doctor and the boys.

C. W. W. to G. M. W.

NEW YORK, JULY 9, 4.30 P. M.

It is not quite one day since I left the "Ebbitt House," dear G., and here I am writing to you from the table in my room with Pico by my faithful side—no! the other way. I arrived at the house an hour ago for all the base lies that the railroad guide tells, and am waiting in a serene perspiration the arrival of my trunk by express from the station. Journey on long and fearfully dusty. Passed, just out of Washington, a long train full of ambulances and took a walk in Baltimore. Everyone sat on his doorstep and every *group* without exception was talking *about* the war.

The Ebbitt House in Washington was a rambling, untidy place on F street, which became a sort of Army Headquarters, filled with officers and men connected with the service. We (G. and E.) were given a large parlor on the second floor, where cot beds were set up for us, and we began a sort of half army-life, with bundles of hospital supplies stacked in all the corners and extemporized arrangements for comfort. We were close by Willards and in the midst of all that was going on, and just opposite the headquarters of the Sanitary Commission.

Charley, having seen us established, hurried home. Rather later Uncle Edward Woolsey, Robert Howland and some gentlemen friends came on for a brief view of what was going on, and took us to Mr. Lincoln's reception at the White House, where we are glad to think his great hand grasped ours for a moment. Mr. Seward, who was receiving too, was rather gruff and gave us welcome with the remark that "the fewer women there were there the better."

As soon as possible we called on Miss Dorothea Dix, who had, by a general order, been recognized in the following words:

Be it known to all whom it may concern that the free services of Miss D. L. Dix are accepted by the War Department, and that she will give at all times all necessary aid in organizing military hospitals and by supplying nurses; and she is authorized to receive and disburse supplies from individuals or associations, etc., etc.

Given under the seal of the War Department, April 23, 1861. (Signed.) SIMON CAMERON, *Secretary.*

G. M. W. writes:

Miss Dix received us kindly and gave us a good deal of information about the hospital, and this morning we went out to the Georgetown Hospital to see for ourselves. We were delighted with all the arrangements. Everything was clean and comfortable. We shall go again and take papers and magazines.

H. R. W. to G. and E.

NEW YORK, MONDAY, JULY 15, 1861.

My dear Girls:

I might as well give you the benefit of a scrawl just to thank you for the big yellow envelope in Georgy's hand-writing lying on the library table by me. It has just come and I think you are two of the luckiest fellows living to be where you are, down in the very thick of it all, with war secrets going on in the next tent and telegraph-wires twitching with important dispatches just outside of your door. "Who *wouldn't* be a nuss" under such circumstances? or would you prefer staying at home to arrange flowers, entertain P. in the evenings, devise a trimming for the dress Gonden is making for you, and go off into the country to fold your hands and do nothing?

I tell you, Georgy, you are a happy creature and ought to be thankful. Jane and Abby have been in Astoria all the week. It was a triumph of ours to make Abby loosen her hold of those abominable old women of the widow's society. She won't get back to them for some time either. . . . Mother and I went up to Northampton, Mass., one evening last week to look up summer quarters. We went via New Haven by the 11 o'clock boat. Charley saw us on board and we got to bed about twelve. Quite a good night for a boat. Mother says she slept well, and was prime for a walk over to the depot before breakfast the next morning. She is certainly made of more enduring material than the rest of us, and, after getting through our business, wanted to come back in the express train at 5.30 that evening. Mr. Frank Bond and Mr. Thomas Denny spent the other evening here. F. B. is going on to Washington very soon, and is to be with General Tyler, something or other to him, and charged me when I wrote to let you know he was coming, and renewed his invitation to you to accompany them into Virginia as chief surgeon!

Mary has cut Bertha's hair square across her forehead, which makes her look more sinful and unregenerate than ever. Polly has had her's cut, and is more comfortable. Did Robert mention the box of old wine for General Scott, from Uncle E.? Think how glorious a part to take—propping up the government with rare old wine from one's own cellar.

Our regiment, the Sixteenth New York, was about two weeks stationed at "Camp Woolsey," near the Capitol, and then crossed the Potomac and pitched its tents on Cameron Run, a little west of Alexandria, in the fields which were once the property of our great-great-Aunt Ricketts, whose plantation was famous for its flour, ground by the mill on the Run. This Aunt Ricketts, a sweet faced woman, whose likeness was among those taken by Saint Memin about 1805, brought up your dear grandmother (left an orphan in 1814) whose letter of July 19th speaks of those days:—

Mother to G. and E.

8 BREVOORT PLACE, FRIDAY, JULY 19, 1861.

My dear Girls:

A loving morning kiss to you both, and three hearty cheers for the success of the grand forward movement thus far. I have just been devouring the *"Times"*—that part of it, at least, and that only, which tells of the war movements—everything else is passed over with a very slighting glance. We feel the intensest interest now in every tramp of the soldiery as they advance southward, and wait with great impatience from night till morning, and from morning till night again, for our papers. Georgy, how deeply interesting was your letter to us, written in the doorway of the tent at Alexandria!—not the first tent letter we have had from you, but how different the circumstances of this last from any other! and how

strange to me that poor old Alexandria, where all of my eleven brothers
and sisters were born, and where my father and mother and relatives lie
buried, should be the scene of such warfare—the camping ground of my
children under such circumstances! You must have been very near the
graves of your grandparents, and that of my dear venerated great-aunt,
Mary Ricketts, who was a loving mother to me after the death of my own,
and in whose house Abby was born. Cameron, too, was one of the places
and homes of my childhood. It was the country-seat of this same good
aunt, and on the grounds, some distance from the dwelling-house, stands
a dilapidated building, in its day a fine "mansion" for that part of the country, which was the original home of the family, and where my mother was
married to a then "affluent merchant" of Alexandria.

"Cameron Run" was the scene of all our childish sports, where we used
to fish and sail and bathe and have all sorts of good times; it was then
a wide deep stream, and formed the boundary line along the bottom of
the garden at Cameron, and was lined on either side by magnolia trees;
and when the old family coach, with its grey horses, was called up to the
door on Sunday mornings to take us into town for church, we each had
our magnolia in hand, showing where our morning walk had been, and
our side of the old church was known by its perfume. All this is as fresh
in my memory as though *fifty years* had been but as many days! I perfectly
remember every spot about the old place;—but everything had changed
almost entirely when I was last there, though I look back to it still as it was
in my childhood. More than ever do I now regret my not having kept a
diary of my early life, which might have been interesting to my children.

I feel very much as you do, my dear Eliza, that "somehow or other I
cannot write letters now," and, indeed, I cannot sit down very long at anything. My mind is in a state of unsettledness, if I may coin a word—a
sort of anxious suspense, all the while, and I feel better when on the jump,
going about. I have been making up a lot of currant jelly, some of which
I will send on to the hospitals. I am going out by and by to get a work
basket for little May—her birthday present. She is to keep her birthday
and little Bertha's together, tomorrow, by having a tea-party on the lawn.
I shall fill the basket with goodies for them. . . . What an imposing sight
it must have been when the troops all set forward together, and then the
arrival at Fairfax! and then at Centreville! the rebels flying before them

and leaving all their goods behind! I hope this may be the case all along, that they will throughout have a bloodless victory! . . . We look any instant for your letters. I say constantly to myself, "What will be the next news?" I dread to hear from Manassas, but hope the enemy will continue to retreat, until the whole land is clear of rebels. I cannot help thinking it will be an easy victory, and without bloodshed. May God bless and keep you, my dear children, and graciously prepare us for whatever may be his will. Give my love and blessing to Joe when you write.
Most tenderly and lovingly yours,
MOTHER.

Our letters from Camp Cameron were among those lost in the Morrell fire, but late in the war, when the Sanitary Commission wanted items for its paper, G. sent the following sketch of the camp:

It was a pretty spot, our camp in a valley in Virginia—the hillside, covered with white tents, sloping to a green meadow and a clear bright little river. The meadow was part of my great-great-aunt's farm years ago, and in the magnolia-bordered stream my grandfather's children had fished and paddled. Now, we, two generations afterwards, had come back and pitched our tents in the old wheat fields, and made ready for war, and there were no magnolia blossoms any more.

On the hills all about us the army was gathering, white tents springing up like mushrooms in the night. With their coming, came sickness, and sickness brought men of the next brigade into a poor little shanty close behind our headquarters. There we found them, one day, wretched and neglected, and 'most improperly' at once adopted them as our own. We asked no one's permission, but went to work; had the house cleaned from top to bottom, shelves put up and sacks filled with straw; then we prescribed the diet and fed them just as we pleased. All this was a shocking breach of propriety, and I have no doubt the surgeon of the regiment was somewhere behind a fence, white with rage. Never mind, our men were delighted, and one dear little blue eyed boy, who had blown his lungs through his fife, was never tired of saying and looking his thanks. Finally we persuaded the General to break up the little den, and order all the sick sent to general hospitals, and our breaches of etiquette came to an end.

Our regiment had only been camped a few days on Cameron Run when the advance, against the enemy at Manassas was ordered, and we two (G. and E.) watched the brigade break camp and march down the peaceful country road, carrying Joe away from us. We stood alone, and looked after them as long as they were in sight, and then made our way back to Washington.

After skirmishing at Fairfax Court House and Centreville, in which the regiment was engaged more or less, the battle of Bull Run was fought, July 21st, the regiment taking position on the extreme left at Blackburn's Ford.

Here Colonel Davies, owing to the unfortunate condition of Colonel Miles, was left virtually in command of the reserve division.

J. H. writes from Camp near Centreville.

JULY 19, 1861.

We had hardly got here yesterday when we heard heavy cannonading in the S. W. It proved to be the firing at Bull's Run, where our troops were repulsed. A complete blunder—the old story of a masked battery and an insufficient infantry force sent against it. We expected a renewal of the fight last night. We slept on our arms, and were prepared for action at any hour. Nothing occurred, however. Our scouts bring in word that the enemy are receiving large reinforcements, and we on our side are also getting them. Everything points to a great battle.

July 20th. We march at 6 P. M., and there will be a great battle within twenty four hours unless the rebels retreat. Our brigade takes the advance on the left wing. We can see the enemy from a high hill near here concentrating their troops. Our pickets were firing all night, and we slept on our arms. I am well, though I feel the want of sleep and the constant anxiety. We are all in good heart, officers and men.

ON THE BATTLE FIELD NEAR BULL RUN,

SUNDAY, 21, 12.45 P. M.

Our brigade is making a demonstration in the face of the enemy and a fight is going on on the right of the line five or six miles off. The enemy's batteries do not return our fire. We see immense masses of troops moving, and the supposition is that the enemy is trying to outflank us on the left. We started (from Centreville) at half-past two this morning.

The following little note, hardly legible now, written in pencil on a scrap of soiled and crumpled paper, made its way to us at Washington and told the rest of the story:

EVENING. HALF-PAST SEVEN.

A complete rout. The Sixteenth safe. We are making a final stand. J. H.

Mother to G. and E.

MONDAY, JULY 22, 1861.

My dear Girls:

We have had an exciting night and morning. Just as we were going to bed last night we heard the distant sound of an "Extra;" it was very late; everybody in bed. We had been out to the meeting of the Evangelical Alliance at Dr. McAuley's Church. We were all undressed, but waited with anxiety till the sound approached nearer and nearer; but made up our minds not to rush down and buy one, as it might be a hoax—till at last a tremendous howl of three boys through 10th street gave us the news of a "great battle at Bull's Run." "Rebels defeated! Batteries all taken!" We thanked God for this much, and went to our beds to try and sleep patiently till morning. We have now had the newspaper accounts as far as they go, but long for further and later. Your two letters of Saturday, Georgy, we have also this morning; many thanks for both; rejoiced to hear good news from Joe so direct, and that you are both well and *busy*. It is better so. I feel this morning as if I could fly right off to Washington, and can scarcely resist the impulse to start at once. Would you like to see me?

The girls are packing a box for your distribution at the hospitals,—Jane rolling a fresh lot of bandages. Poor Kate, our house-maid, looks quite distressed to-day, thinking her brother may have been foremost in the ranks, as the paper stated "the First Massachusetts led in the advance, and had suffered much." . . . Dr. Tyng made an inspiriting address last night to a densely crowded audience. He said he was greatly surprised to see such an assemblage when he had supposed the city deserted, and thought such an audience was a sufficient appeal without a word from him, as showing the deep interest manifested in this "righteous" cause—"I say *righteous,* for I firmly believe if there ever was a righteous, holy war, direct from the hand of God, this is one." ... There were some very interesting letters read from the different chaplains, and some from the men themselves of different regiments. Dr. Hoge has resigned, and left his charge to Dr. Spring, on account of his attachment to the South! and his desire to be there at this time. *I* say joy go with him, but some of the people are unwilling to receive his resignation. . . . I have no news for you; we see no one, and are supposed to be out of town. It is perfectly cool and comfortable here, and we are at present better satisfied to be here. By and by we may run off for a while. God bless you both, my dear children! I wish I were close at your side.

Your loving Mother.

A. H. W. to G. and E.

JULY 22, 1861,

My dear Girls:

Since Mother's letter was sent this morning we have had some heavy hours. At noon we got the first extra with the despatch announcing the defeat and retreat of our troops—defeat, because retreat, or *vice versa,* whichever it was. It is a total rout of our grand army of the Union. All guns gone, etc.; but the saddest is the vast number of wounded and half dead. I have no doubt your hands are full, at some one of the hospitals. Hour after hour today went on and we heard nothing from you; had nothing but the horrible extras and our consciousness of your anxiety and suspense. We packed the trunk for you very busily and tried not to think too hard. At five P. M. your despatch came, dear E., and such a load was removed from our hearts. Joe not only was safe, but you had seen him. Thank Heaven! We could hardly make out from the confused papers what his position had been in the fight. . . .

Mary and Robert drove in at six to hear what we had heard, and met Ned at the Ferry, carrying out your despatch. Robert brought his valise in case Mother wanted him to escort her to Washington, but the immediate anxiety she felt for you having been relieved, she feels it is safest to wait till she gets a letter from you. So many troops will probably encumber the roads on the way to Washington to-morrow, and there is so much chance of a riot in Baltimore, as Robert suggests—that it is more prudent to wait. She wants to go for her *own* satisfaction as well as yours you know, so you must not think it desirable for you to oppose it. If she could only have been with you these two horrible days she would have been so glad. She is anxious to do something for the army and thinks she ought to go on and be matron in the Alexandria Hospital. We laugh, and remind her of her fortitude when Dr. Buck tried to vaccinate her! . . . And now for the boxes. Mrs. Willard Parker is ready to make the largest grants. Has packed one box today, and is anxious to have it go to you that she may know what disposition is made of the things. Let us know when you receive them—one French black trunk, one wooden packing box. Mrs. Parker has a huge box packed, but I shall advise *that* one going to the Sanitary Commission. Your box has six dozen sheets in it from her, and the trunk is filled with our shirts, slippers, etc.

In haste and with all love,

A. H. W.

P. S. Also one box of currant jelly. All will be directed to the Ebbitt House, except Mrs. Parker's box.

Thread and needles are invaluable in camp. We hear that after every march bits of uniforms fly all over the camp, and that one man patched his black shoulder with a sky-blue scrap begged from a brother volunteer. You know the men haven't always a sixpence to spare for the sutler every time a button is needed, and our two hundred thread cases will go very little way in a regiment. . . . Everybody is knitting yarn socks for the men—all the young girls and all the old women. Everybody means to make one pair each before winter. Cousin Margaret Hodge has set all her old ladies at work at the Asylum. We have set up four tonight for ourselves, and Kate and Mary the cook are to have their turn too. . . . But the deed of Mrs. Lowell of Boston, sister-in-law of the poet, puts all others to insignificance. She being a lady of means and leisure, took the Government contract for woolen shirts in Massachusetts and is having them cut and made under her own eyes by poor women at good prices, and the sum that would have gone into some wretched contractor's pocket has already blessed hundreds of needy women.

Mother to E. and G.

TUESDAY MORNING, JULY 23, 1861,

God be praised for that telegram! What a day was yesterday to us; and what a day must it have been to you, my dear Eliza! The terrible news, the conflicting reports, the almost unendurable suspense we were in, the distance from you at such a time! Altogether it was a time to be remembered!

We are thankful indeed, unspeakably so, to hear this morning by your nice letter, Georgy, of Joe's quiet sleep upon the sofa at your side! How mercifully are we dealt with! when we think of the families in our land who are this day in sorrow as the result of this terrible battle. . . . There is a tremendous sensation throughout the city in consequence of this news—crowds are rushing continually to the news offices, and all we have seen are wearing looks of sadness and disappointment, following as this does so immediately upon the accounts of the easy manner in which Fairfax, Centreville and Bull's Run were captured, and the flying of the enemy before our soldiers.

G. M. W. writes:

WASHINGTON, JULY 22, 1861.

My dear Cousin Margaret:

This is the third attempt I have made to finish a letter to you. Joe is safe and quietly sleeping on the sofa by us. You know all about this total defeat—our army is entirely broken up, all the army stores, three of the batteries, ammunition, baggage, everything, in the hands of the enemy—Centreville retaken by them, Fairfax C. H. retaken, and our troops scattered in and about Washington. Everything was in *our* hands and success seemed certain at Bull Run, when from some cause or other a panic was created, our men fell back, the rebels seized the moment for a bold rush and we were entirely routed. Joe says there never was a more complete defeat. All last night the soldiers were arriving in all sorts of conveyances, and on horses cut from ambulances and baggage wagons. An officer from Bull Run told us he saw four soldiers on one horse; and so they came flying back to Washington in all directions. Colonel Miles' division, in which Joe's regiment was, was held as a reserve at Blackburn's Ford on the left and only came into active duty when the rout began—they had a sharp engagement with 5000 in a "gully"—lost only two men from the Brigade and none from the 16th and retired in order, first to Centerville, where orders met them to fall back on Fairfax C. H. Here they slept half an hour last night, when they were again ordered to retreat to Washington, which order they have followed as far as Alexandria, and expect now to be stationed there some little time. The dead and wounded were left in the hands of the enemy, and one of the officers told me it would be unnecessary to ask for the sick, for the rebels were killing them: he knew it had been done in some cases, and undoubtedly would be in all. Colonel Davies and two of the officers came up from their camp at Alexandria with Joe, and all four of them were wretched-looking men, dirty, hungry and utterly tired out. Joe had not had his high boots off since he left Alexandria on the 16th. The day that McDowell's division marched south, Eliza and I were out at the camp to see them pass, and our own regiment march. Eleven thousand fine looking fellows filed past us as we stood at the cross-roads,—and disappeared down the quiet country lane. What a horrid coming back it has been! "We shall not see this place very soon again," they said as they packed up their things at Alexandria, and marched off, singing as they went. And in spite of all this, and in full knowledge of the great outnumbering of our men on the other side, General Scott sat quietly in St. John's Church that battle-Sunday through a tremendously heavy sermon, shook hands with me at the church door, and told us all that "we should have good news in the morning and that we were sure to beat the enemy." Colonel Davies has seen him this morning too, and he is quite cheerful and composed. The Zouaves, one Massachusetts regiment, and the 68th and 71st New York have been the greatest sufferers—very few of the Zouaves are left. The fighting was all from behind masked batteries on the enemy's side. Lieutenant Bradford told me that he had to ride down the lines and give the order to retreat. Our men were all lying on their faces, and the air filled with shot and shell and not a rebel's head to be seen. When Colonel Davies was asked what lost the day, he said "green leaves and fine officering on the enemy's side." In open field, they all say they should have beaten the rebels entirely. . . . Now he and Joe are off on business in a hard rain, and go to Alexandria at two, where the regiment is established in the old camp—at Cameron Run. Yesterday and last night were hard to bear; but what with General Scott's assurances,

General Ripley's, Mr. Dixon's and Judge Davies' comforting little visits, we got along, jumping up every few moments through the night whenever a horse dashed by the house or an ambulance rumbled along. Now we shall be as much as possible at the camp in Alexandria,—for how long I can't say. . . . We have had an encounter with Miss Dix—that is rather the way to express it. Splendid as her career has been, she would succeed better with more graciousness of manner. However, we brought her to terms, and shall get along better.

Eliza adds, also to Cousin Margaret:

The sick and wounded are doing well. Georgy and I have been to all the hospitals and find them very well supplied, for boxes of garments and stores of all kinds have poured in ever since the battle. It has been the one cheering thing of the times. . . . We hear from the surgeons we have met here that very many of the wounded who were left behind had their wounds carefully dressed before the rout began, and they are constantly being brought into the city in ambulances, having reached the camps on the other side by slow stages.

In this same battle of Bull Run the 2d Connecticut was in the thick of the fight, and its surgeon, Dr. Bacon, found himself separated from the troops and in the midst of a group of southern wounded, for whom he cared under the impression that we were victorious and he within our own lines. He ordered them to surrender their arms, threw most of these into a pond near by, and saved a pistol and two dangerous knives as trophies. They are those that afterwards hung on the banisters of his house in New Haven. One of the knives was more than a foot long and home-made from a horse shoer's file, with rough home-made scabbard; the other, an ugly dirk, was made in England and engraved *there* "Arkansas toothpick." The revolver belonged to the wounded commanding officer, Lieutenant-Colonel Gardner, leading a Georgia regiment. He insisted upon giving his watch to Dr. B. as a return for the good care received.—(It was afterwards returned to him.)—When the arms were in the horse pond and the rebels cared for, the Doctor made the startling discovery that he was alone—our army in retreat, and he virtually a prisoner to the rebels. He left hastily, before the truth dawned upon Colonel Gardner's mind!

R. S. H. to G.

ASTORIA, JULY 23.

We are trying to look things in the face,—like the great apostle, cast down but not disheartened.

Of course the first thought of us civilians is to take care of the wounded. I send enclosed a cheque from Cousin Edward and one from myself. If you find you cannot use these amounts satisfactorily at Washington let us know and we will send materials as they may be wanted. Telegraph to Howland and Aspinwall (to G. G. for me) if anything is wanted immediately. . . . If you want *anything* specifically in the way of hospital stores, wines, currant jellies, &c., telegraph first and write more fully afterwards.

H. R. W. to E.

NEW YORK, JULY 23,

Abby is in the front parlor reading the papers. It is quite useless to say anything about going into the country just now. If we are away from the daily papers, or if they are delayed an hour the girls get into a perfect fever; besides, Abby, you know, has decided never to go to the country again! Because she took a sea bath at Mary's and felt weak after it, she thinks the country doesn't agree with her! . . . Aunt Emily is going up to Lenox the last of next week, I believe. I hope so, for Uncle E. needs change; he looks miserably, has a constant cough, and seems quite run down; though when Aunt E. says, "You don't feel very bright today, do you, dear?" he is quite indignant and makes a feeble attempt to sing "the Cock and the Hen," or to whistle "Dixie."

Nurses visit New York City Hospital in training for service in the Army.
Frank Leslie's Illustrated Newspaper

CHAPTER THREE

A Company of Army Nurses

T HE REGIMENTS called out for three months were now about disbanding, though a large number of the men at once reenlisted for
the war.

A. H. W. to E.

JULY 27, 10 A. M.

My dear Eliza:

I have just been up to the corner to see a sorry sight, the return of
the 68th Regiment—oh, so shabby, so worn and weary—all sorts of hats
and shirts and some with hardly any clothes at all, staggering along under
their knapsacks which they should never have been allowed to carry up
Broadway. The surging mass of men and women locking arms and walking with the soldiers, was wonderful. It was a wild, tumultuous, promiscuous rush—not a march. Yesterday afternoon the 8th came through. I could
see from the balcony how brown they looked and sturdy, and trimmer
than the 68th. The girls and Mother saw them from Brady's window. The
cheers and applause they got down town, I suppose. There was not much
of it up here—there was too much crying. Even policemen were in tears.
What a dreadful collapse the "Grand Army" of the Potomac suffered. I
don't think the North needed such a lesson! Perhaps they did—perhaps
the people have felt as if they could march down to Richmond whenever
they chose. . . . Scott sent an inefficient general (known as a perfect wind-
bag among brother officers) without commissariat, without organization,
without proper regimental officers, against what he knew to be a fortified
camp of a hundred thousand men. The one great blunder was that the
battle was fought at all. All other minor blunders—and how many there
were! are included in this. . . .

Jefferson Davis is free now to do what he pleases—flushed with success. Everyone says this battle has been as good to him as an increase of a hundred thousand fighting men. . . . He will perhaps attack Washington itself. The papers speak of the danger of this—and we all feel that the city is in greater peril than it was in those April days. Under such circumstances we do not quite relish your idea of going to Alexandria. You would be cut off at once, in that town, from communication or escape. One thought that checked Mother's desire to go immediately to Washington last Monday was the idea that on reaching there she might find that women and children had been ordered to leave—for fear of an attack from Beauregard. That order may come yet. My dear sisters, I do not want to write anything depressing, but you must make up your minds after this disaster for a *long war*, an impoverished country, many reverses. So far, you have had but one thought—that of immediate success. General Scott's plan of closing in on the rebels in Virginia and crushing them as in his fingers, is blown to the winds. We are to have a protracted and somewhat equal struggle, but the North is in earnest; its fault has been *over*-eagerness. Men there always have been enough of,—let them have proper officers; and as to money, Congress ought to be ashamed to haggle about direct taxation but pass the bill at once and provide ways and means. . . . I am very glad the boxes had all arrived safely. Next day you would get Aunt Emily's two barrels, and Uncle Edward's $250 in money. Buy whatever you see is needed or the surgeons and nurses want. Don't wait for red tape. If it is mattresses, cots, pillows, spirit lamps, food, sheeting, flannel, etc. to wrap wounded men in, or what not. You can have plenty of money, and it could not be better spent than in fitting up a hospital even if that is government work. Carry wanted me to send you some money for her, but I told her I would wait and see whether you could buy the things you needed in Washington, or whether it had better be spent here. Please let me know. We shall have enough more things to fill a barrel early next week. Shall we put in the bandage roller, or are the hospital surgeons provided? I am sorry that Mrs. Leavitt did not send you a list of the contents of *her* boxes. . . .

Don't save up things if you see them needed. It is easy to buy more slippers and mosquito net here, and it does not cost us any time or a stitch of effort to send more clothing. The Society has plenty on hand. Mrs. Parker jumped up with pleasure when we sent round the other day to see if she could let us have a few things for the trunk, and granted enough, as you saw, to fill two boxes and over. She was delighted at the idea of their being distributed where she could hear about it, and I must manage to put some scraps of your accounts together and tell her what you say. There is a fresh lot of handkerchiefs under way. Maria Gilman hemmed them on her machine.

Mother to E.

BREVOORT PLACE, LATE IN JULY.

My dear Eliza:

If the regiments are all to be stationary for some time you and G. might run on for a *visit*. I have given up my plan of going to you for the present unless you should need me. We are now talking again of Lenox for the summer—Abby and Jane are both wilting daily in the hot city, and I feel troubled at their being here, though we are unwilling to move off further away from you girls. We don't know at what time the Southern army may make an attack. I have no idea that they will wait patiently till fall, though our side might, and the daily expectation of another battle keeps us here. It is intensely hot, noisy, dusty and distracting. The streets seem filled with a perfect rabble all the while. . . . Mary and the children are looking perfectly well. Baby Una grows fat and lovely by the hour—she is a splendid child. Bertha is a witch, but fascinating in her badness. Little May is very much interested in hemming a handkerchief for some poor soldier, which I basted for her, and am to send on to you when finished! She feels as if she had the whole army on her hands! in this important piece of work. . . . It is pleasant to know of your seeing so many friends. I think you are right to stay in Washington instead of Alexandria—the latter place must be intolerable,—but don't wear yourselves out.

Social formalities were entirely abandoned in Washington in war time. The Ebbitt House public parlors were on a level with F street and the windows were always open. Any friends in passing would catch a glimpse of us and happen in for comradeship, giving bits of news, and offering kindly services. One group of four Philadelphia officers were especially friendly and helpful. The lack of conventionality now and then, though, had its drawbacks, as G's note shows—addressed to—"Mrs. Howland—Parlor" and sent down from the bedroom one evening to E., who, not fortunate in escaping, was captured by the enemy:—

"Find out incidentally before Dr. E. goes, where Mr. Channing is to preach. Mind, I don't want to accept an invitation to go with *him*. I saw him, when I was shutting the blinds up here, pass the windows of the parlor, and stop and look in, and go on, and stop, and turn back and come in—! and then I banged the blinds with glee, and am just popping into bed. Shall expect you up about midnight."

A. H. W. to E.

10TH STREET, JULY 31.

My dear Eliza:

We were quite touched by a note and a message from your farmer Thomson, and I write at once that no time may be lost in carrying out the generous wishes of the people on the place. As soon as they received the particulars of the battle of Bull Run, Thomson took up a subscription among them, for the wounded soldiers, and raised *twenty dollars.* He took it to Mrs. Wolcott, asking her to put it into the Society's fund for buying hospital clothing. But she suggested that a more satisfactory way would be to send it to you, to be spent on the spot, in any way you thought best. . . . Thomson preferred this himself, and hopes to hear from you that the twenty dollars are well laid out.

E. to J. H. in camp.

WASHINGTON, AUGUST—.

Hurrah for you, to be offered the Colonelcy of the regiment! I am glad, however, that you have no wish to take it. I shrink from any such responsibility for you.

Dr. Bacon came in last evening and we had a nice pleasant chat. His regiment, the 2nd Connecticut, goes home today to be mustered out. We saw them march down yesterday to give up their arms and were struck with their fine manly appearance and precision in marching. Dr. Bacon is anxious to come back to the army and hopes that one regiment at least may be formed of the three just returning, in which he may serve. He has left one of his patients at the new Columbian College Hospital and commended him to our care. We shall see him this afternoon and take him jelly, slippers, etc. The slippers are from a large boxful which Lenox Hodge has sent us, our commission. They are scarce at the hospitals and in great demand. Cousin M. Hodge writes of her happiness at hearing of your safety and welfare. Columbian College Hospital is just opened and only half organized, but already crowded. It *will* be nice, but now they have few comforts or conveniences, scarcely any sheets, no water, etc. One of G's nurse friends is there working like a slave, as are the other five women nurses. We spent the morning there helping them, reading to the men, writing letters for them, etc.

G. writing in 1864 of the annoyances of those first days, said:

No one knows, who did not watch the thing from the beginning, how much opposition, how much ill-will, how much unfeeling want of thought, these women nurses endured. Hardly a surgeon whom I can think of, received or treated them with even common courtesy. Government had decided that women should be employed, and the army surgeons—unable, therefore, to close the hospitals against them—determined to make their lives so unbearable that they should be forced in self-defence to leave. It seemed a matter of cool calculation, just how much ill-mannered opposition would be requisite to break up the system.

Some of the bravest women I have ever known were among this first company of army nurses. They saw at once the position of affairs, the attitude assumed by the surgeons and the wall against which they were expected to break and scatter; and they set themselves to undermine the whole thing.

None of them were 'strong-minded.' Some of them were women of the truest refinement and culture; and day after day they quietly and patiently worked, doing, by order of the surgeon, things which not one of those gentlemen would have dared to ask of a woman whose male relative stood able and ready to defend her and report him. I have seen small white hands scrubbing floors, washing windows, and performing all menial offices. I have known women, delicately cared for at home, half fed in hospitals, hard worked day and night, and given, when sleep must be had, a wretched closet just large enough for a camp bed to stand in. I have known surgeons who purposely and ingeniously arranged these inconveniences with the avowed intention of driving away all women from their hospitals.

These annoyances could not have been endured by the nurses but for the knowledge that they were pioneers, who were, if possible, to gain standing ground for others,—who must create the position they wished to occupy. This, and the infinite satisfaction of seeing from day to day sick and dying men comforted in their weary and dark hours, comforted as they never would have been but for these brave women, was enough to carry them through all and even more than they endured.

At last, the wall against which they were to break, began to totter; the surgeons were most unwilling to see it fall, but the knowledge that the faithful, gentle care of the women-nurses had saved the lives of many of their patients, and that a small rate of mortality, or remarkable recoveries in their hospitals, reflected credit immediately upon *themselves*, decided them to give way, here and there, and to make only a show of resistance. They could not do without the women-nurses; they knew it, and the women knew that they knew it, and so there came to be a tacit understanding about it.

When the war began, among the many subjects on which our minds presented an entire blank was that sublime, unfathomed mystery—'Professional Etiquette.' Out of the army, in practice which calls itself 'civil,' the etiquette of the profession is a cold spectre, whose presence is felt everywhere, if not seen; but in the Medical Department of the Army, it was an absolute Bogie, which stood continually in one's path, which showed its narrow, ugly face in camps and in hospitals, in offices and in wards; which put its cold paw on private benevolence, whenever benevolence was fool enough to permit it; which kept shirts from ragged men, and broth from hungry ones; an evil Regular Army Bogie, which in full knowledge of empty kitchens and exhausted 'funds,' quietly asserted that it had need of nothing, and politely bowed Philanthropy out into the cold.

All this I was profoundly ignorant of for the first few months of the war, and so innocently began my rounds with my little jelly pots and socks knit at home for the boys—when, suddenly, I met the Bogie;—and what a queer thing he was! It was a hot summer morning, not a breath of air coming in at the open windows—the hospital full of sick men, and the nurses all busy, so I sat by a soldier and fanned him through the long tedious hours. Poor man, he was dying, and so grateful to me, so afraid I should tire myself. I could have fanned him all day for the pleasure it was to help him, but the Bogie came in, and gave me a look of icy inquiry. My hand ought to have been paralysed at once, but somehow or other, it kept moving on with the fan in it, while I stupidly returned the Bogie's stare.

Finding that I still lived, he quietly made his plan, left the room without saying a word, and in ten minutes afterward developed his tactics. He was a small Bogie—knowing what he wanted to do, but not quite brave enough to do it alone; so he got Miss Dix, who was on hand, to help him, and together, they brought all the weight of professional indignation to bear upon me. I 'must leave immediately.' 'Who was I, that I should bring myself and my presumptuous fan, without direct commission from the surgeon-general,' into the hospital? 'Not only must I leave at once, but I must *never return.*'

This was rather a blow, it must be confessed. The moment for action had arrived—I rapidly reviewed my position, notified myself that I was the Benevolent Public, and decided that the sick soldiers were, in some sort, the property of the B. P. Then I divulged *my* tactics. I informed the Bogies (how well that rhymes with Fogies) that I had ordered my carriage to return at such a hour, that the sun was hot, that I had no intention whatever of walking out in it, and that, in short, I had decided to remain. What there was in these simple facts, very quietly announced, to exorcise the demon, I am unable to say, but the gratifying result was that half an hour afterward Professional Etiquette made a most salutary repast off its own remarks; that I spent the remainder of the day where I was; that both the Bogies, singly, called the next morning to say—'Please, sir, it wasn't *me,* sir,—'twas the other boy, sir;' and from that time the wards were all before me."

J. S. W. to G. and E.
Dear Girls:

Your full, interesting letters have come in and given great relief. G's of today is certainly altogether more cheerful in tone than Eliza's of Tuesday,

and very naturally. We are beginning to "look up" a little, too. Your rebuff
by Miss Dix has been the subject of great indignation, but we all devoutly
hope you will not mind it in the least. . . . Whatever you do, go in and
win. Outflank the Dix by any and every means in your power, remembering that prison visitors and hospital visitors and people who really desire
to do good, have taken no notice of obstacles except to vanquish them,
and as soon as one avenue was closed have turned with perfect persistence
to another. We shall be very much disappointed if you do not establish
some sort of relations with the hospitals, at least enough to give you free
access, and to make a reliable channel for such things as we can send.
You ought certainly to get those boxes today if not sooner. . . . All your
details are very interesting. Pray, send any that you collect, and *make Joe
write out* or *dictate* to one of you a connected story of what he saw and
did from the time of the advance up to the Monday morning when he
came in. It will be invaluable, and ought to be done while it is fresh. Your
"memoires pour servir" may immortalize you yet. . . . We have seen only a
few people the last day or two, Mr. Denny, F. Bond, and Col. Perkins. All
cheerful, hopeful and undaunted, say we can have ten men to every one
lost now; that there is settled determination to use every resource to the
uttermost. Uncle E. says, setting his teeth, "to the last drop of my blood!"
Abby desponds. Thinks Scott to blame, that his tide of fortune is turning,
or that he is childish, or, at best, that he let the cabinet have its way this
time for the sake of saying, "I told you so." We begin to grin now when
Abby begins to croak, but there is certainly something in what she says.
Don't keep drumming about our going away. We should have been crazy if
we had been in suspense in some small country place the last week or two.
When things subside, and look *nearly* settled for the present, we will take
our own time and go. . . . Frank Goddard is in the rebel army at Sewall's
Point. "Hopes it will make no difference in our pleasant relations." Hm!!!
perhaps it won't.

Why don't you come home? Now's your chance, if at all. The rebel
army before Washington will melt away like a cloud and come down
again suddenly in Kentucky, Missouri, Jeff knows where, where we are
weak and unexpecting, and leave us sitting like fools behind our laborious
entrenchments that nobody means to take. . . . How can you doubt Fremont? There has been no *positive* charge against him from any respectable

source, only malevolent *rumors,* filling the air, coming no doubt from the Blairs and other malignant personal enemies who hate him, because they are slaveholders and he is just now the apostle of liberation. I announce my adhesion still and my painful anxiety that he should retrieve himself in Missouri against all the heavy odds of fortune. . . . It is pitiful to see how great and general a defection from him has grown out of absolutely nothing (so far) of any authority. . . . Take some measures to make Frank Bacon let his beard grow; tell him to go to Jericho with his "Victor Emmanuel." He is in the late fashion, by the bye; so much the worse. Why should a man who can look like a knight of the table of the blameless King voluntarily look like a Lynn shoemaker?

> "Yet, oh fair maid, thy mirth refrain,
> *Thy hand is on a lion's mane.*"

Quote me to him; who's afraid? . . . Goodbye. I hope the highly accommodating Providence which directs, or rather acquiesces in all G.'s movements, will afford you both every facility for whatever you want to do. . . .

Having established our own position and made it clear that we had no intention of being bluffed off, we were accepted by the surgeons and Miss Dix at our own valuation (purposely made high!) and from that moment our path was as a shining light. All hospitals were open to us, and our relations with Miss Dix became most cordial and friendly, as the following notes, among many received from her (nearly all undated), show.

My dear Miss Woolsey:

I am thankful you are going to the hospital. Express to the good nurses my kind regards and purpose of seeing them so soon as I am able. Thanks for the lovely flowers, with cordial regards to Mrs. H. I have very little strength; excuse brevity and abruptness. I must have some consultation with you so soon as I am *better,* concerning the position of the nurses. I fear they are over-tasked.

Very cordially yours,

D. L. Dix.

My dear Miss Woolsey:

Will you give a little attention to the hospitals at Alexandria through next week for me if convenient? Any requisition on my stores will always be promptly met.

I still feel that all the nurses who are really conscientious are very heavily tasked.

Yours most cordially,

D. L. Dix.

Receiving the nurses, and seeing that they were safely started on their way to various hospitals, and reporting to the New York committees on their services therein were among our occupations in the first year of the war.

Dr. Elizabeth Blackwell to G. M. W.

New York, July 30th.

My dear Miss Woolsey:

I was extremely glad to receive your excellent letter yesterday. Had I known that you were residing in Washington, I should have requested you some time before to collect information for our society. We had become extremely anxious about these women; we could not learn who had safely arrived, where they were, what they were doing, nor how they fared in any respect; and a check of considerable amount, sent to one of them, was unacknowledged. As we had pledged ourselves to protect these women, pay their expenses, their wages, etc., you may imagine that we felt extremely uneasy about them. . . .

I will ask you now, to find out for us where Miss E. H. and Mrs. M. S. are placed. They were sent from New York by the night train, July 25th, direct to Miss Dix, and should have reached Washington last Friday morning.

Will you also visit the Georgetown Hospital and report on two nurses whom we sent on last Saturday. We should like some unprejudiced account of the management of this Hospital. . . .

I will see that any nurse going to Alexandria in future is furnished with a certificate signed by some proper authority here. We feel much obliged to you for all the trouble you have taken in this matter. . . .

As the government payment commences August 5th, from that time our society hands the nurses over to the government.

I remain very truly yours,

E. BLACKWELL.

The nurses were required to take the oath of allegiance to the government, and to secure passes, in all of which G. helped them, also securing government ambulances to carry them to their destination:—

"Dr. Asch begs to inform Miss Woolsey that he has seen the officer in charge of the passes into Virginia. It will be impossible to procure them this evening as the office closes at 3 P. M., and in addition it will be necessary for the nurses to present themselves at General Porter's office for the purpose of making affirmation as to their loyalty,—when, on presenting the accompanying note, Dr. Asch trusts that there will be no delay in the accomplishment of their object."

SURG.-GENERAL'S OFFICE, AUGUST 27, 1861.

Dr. Wood has requested Dr. Spencer to attend to the wishes of Miss Woolsey (in regard to the ambulances).

He very much regrets he is prevented from attending personally.

Government hospitals were multiplying in Washington, Georgetown, and Alexandria. As regiments were ordered forward extemporized camp hospitals were broken up, and patients were sent back to these large general ones in the rear.

By this time J. H. had ordered his horses and carriage sent on from Fishkill for our use and we were constantly driving about, seeing where the need was in camps and hospitals and supplying wants. In order to make our way to the many outlying hospitals about Washington and also to visit Joe's camp over the river, it was necessary for us to be provided with passes—not always an easy thing to procure. General Scott, however, came to the rescue and gave the following comprehensive one which was "good daily" during the rest of our stay in Washington:—

HEADQUARTERS OF THE ARMY,
WASHINGTON, AUGUST 19, 1861.

Mrs. Joseph Howland (wife of the Adjutant of the New York 16th Regt.), sister Miss G. M. Woolsey, and man-servant (Stanislas Moritz) will be permitted to pass the Bridges to Alexandria (and return) and are commended to the courtesy of the troops.

Good daily.

WINFIELD SCOTT
By command:
H. VAN RENSSELAER,
Col. and Aid de Camp.

Armed with this we constantly dashed over the Long-Bridge, the carriage filled with all sorts of supplies from the abundant and unfailing stores committed to us by the family and friends and societies at home. Warm woolen socks were always one item. Abby and many others never ceased knitting them during the war. Wherever we found a camp-hospital in need, there we thankfully left comforts from home, or arranged that the Sanitary Commission, whose general office was directly opposite to the Ebbitt House, should supply the want.

The Commission on its side was always glad to have our report and responded promptly to all our suggestions.

A few letters among very many will be enough to show the feeling on all sides.

SANITARY COMMISSION, WASHINGTON, D. C.
TREASURY BUILDING, AUGUST 17TH, 1861.

Miss Woolsey:

In absence of Mr. Olmsted I answer your note in regard to supplies for the 25th N. Y. We will give immediate attention to this Regiment, and will gladly furnish them any supplies we have on hand for their comfort. There are now no beds or cases to fill with straw in the store-room of the Commission (but very few have ever been sent in). Mr. Olmsted, however, has sent for two hundred to be forwarded from New York as soon as possible, and when these arrive a supply shall be furnished to the 25th.

It has been the endeavor of the Secretary to send notice of the existence and objects of the Commission to the surgeon of each regiment: it may not have reached some, but the visits of the inspectors, now in progress, will ensure this notice to all.

Mr. Olmsted wishes to make the Regimental Hospital *comfortable,* but not to induce the regimental surgeons to retain patients who ought to be sent to the General Hospital.

I am glad to be able to add, that there is a reasonable prospect that a new General Hospital will be immediately established in or near Alexandria for the sick of the regiments in that vicinity. Pardon haste,
With sincere regards,
Your obedient servant,
F. N. KNAPP, *for*
     Fred'k Law Olmsted.

Rev. Edward Walker to G. M. W.

HDQRS. 4TH REG. C. V., CAMP INGALLS.

Dear Miss Woolsey:

Your kind note is just received. A week ago our hospital was in wretched condition, but, thanks to the Sanitary Commission! we are at present provided with nearly everything we want. If anything is needed, it is a few more sheets, as we have some fever patients who require frequent change of bed-clothes. The surgeon suggests that more pillows are needed and that a little Indian meal for gruel would be very acceptable.

There are 51 in the regimental hospital today—2 dangerously ill, and 30 on the sick list in the camp. . . . Should we find ourselves really in need of further aid from the Sanitary Commission I will let you know promptly, either by a note or by calling on you when I come in town.
Yours gratefully,
EDWARD ASHLEY WALKER.
Chaplain 4th C. V.

CAMP TRENTON, 1861.

Miss Woolsey, Ebbitt House:

I have the honor to acknowledge your favor of the 2nd inst., and would beg leave to say in reply, that the stores will be most acceptable, and in order that you may have no further trouble in the matter, an order signed

by our Surgeon, Dr. Grant, will be presented you by our regimental wag-
oner, who will take charge of the goods for us.

With many thanks for your interest in behalf of the regiment, I have
the honor to remain
Your obedient servant,
Saml. L. Buck,
Major 2nd Regt. N. J. V.

G. W. M. to Frederick Law Olmsted.

Washington, 1861.

My dear Mr. Olmsted:

Can the Sanitary Commission do anything to prevent a repetition of
the inhuman treatment the sick received last week, on their way from
Jamestown to Alexandria? 150 men were packed in one canal boat between
decks, stowed so closely together that they were literally unable to turn
over: without mattresses, without food, without decent attention from the
time they left till their arrival.

Among them were three or four men with the worst kind of measles
put in with all the rest: one of them died on the boat, and another on the
way from the boat to the hospital, and it will be wonderful if the disease
has not communicated itself to others among the 150. There was of course
no ventilation, and the men say that they suffered greatly from bad air. A
medical officer came down with the boat and is perhaps not responsible
for the state of things on board; some one must be, however, and it may
save further suffering if the affair could be made public. We heard this
story through a friend who was in Alexandria when the boat arrived and
has known all the facts of the case.

"Boston rockers" were an untold comfort to the men able to sit up.
The first of the many sent to us were from Daniel Gilman's father and
placed as follows:—

ALEXANDRIA HOSPITAL, AUGUST 14, 1861.

My dear Miss Woolsey:

The eight chairs are very thankfully received and shall be disposed of precisely as you proposed.

Yours in haste,

Nurse in charge.

Miss L. L. Schuyler to G. M. W.

25 COOPER UNION, N. Y., AUGUST 7TH, 1861.

My dear Miss Woolsey:

Dr. Blackwell, at our last board meeting, read a very interesting letter from you, giving details about the hospitals. We should be very much obliged if you would be willing to write us a few incidents in regard *to hospital supplies.* Any little personal anecdote relative to the pleasure caused by the receipt of these delicacies and stores, any message from a wounded soldier, would go farther to interest our country contributors, than any figure-statements of what has been, and is to be, done.

The response made to our appeals is grand, and it is a privilege to know and feel the noble spirit that animates the women of the loyal states. We have contributions not only from our own states, but from Connecticut, New Jersey, Massachusetts and Michigan. Within the last fortnight our receipts have amounted to over 7000 different articles of clothing and 860 of edibles. . . .

Our letters from the Sanitary Commission say that the hospitals near Washington are now well supplied.

A. H. W. to G. and E.

AUGUST, 1861.

Dear Girls:

Did you give the company captains my little books by Ordronneaux? If not, please do so. They have much useful advice, and as each captain ought to be the father of his company, and look after its welfare in every respect, some such little manual might be useful to them.

In regard to your enquiry about sending the *Tribune* and *Independent* to the hospitals regularly from the publication office, I would say that I have already so ordered 10 copies of the *Independent* sent every week for

the coming three months, beginning with this week's issue. It is prepaid
and will be delivered free by Adams Express at the hospital. Charlie has
gone down this morning to order the *Semiweekly World* or *Tribune* sent in
the same way. . . . You will receive 12 *Independents* which he has put up for
the Columbia or any other hospital, and some packages for the Chaplain
of the 16th. . . .

The young men of the New York Christian Association who have been
in Washington and Alexandria making the rounds of the hospitals, writing letters for the men and ministering generally, send word that they have
never known a single chaplain of any regiment present himself to enquire
for his sick or wounded, that there is no *resident* chaplain, and no one at
hand to read or pray for a dying man, or to conduct the funeral services
of the dead in the city hospitals This must be especially the case with the
Alexandria hospital—for in that town hardly any clergymen are left. . . . It
would be encouraging to know that somebody was detailed in each hospital for special chaplain's duty. Cannot some arrangement be made? . . .

You must tell us something more about the men of the 16th. . . . How
do they cook their food and how is it distributed? Is the camp kept
drained and clean? What do the men sleep on? Have they chances for
bathing, washing clothes, etc.? . . . Two-thirds of the New York regiments
as examined by the Sanitary Commission are crowded too many in a
tent—regardless of ventilation—and liable next month to some terrible
pestilence. The only sign, so far, that I can see of God's mercy and the
justice of our cause, is the absence as yet of any serious epidemic. . . . But
as carelessness, bad habits, hot weather, etc., only sow *seeds* of sickness to
ripen in autumn, we may yet have that plague too, overtake us.

Abby's informant was right. Up to this time there were no special
chaplains in the Washington and Alexandria hospitals. G. and E. felt
the need and wrote of it to Abby, who answers as follows:

A. H. W.

AUGUST, '61.

I think that the best you can do is to make your own private arrangement for missionary work two days a week, say, in the Columbia College
and two in the Alexandria hospital. I mention these because I suppose

they are the two you would be likely to have best access to, and where your suggestions would be best received. You would have to do it with the consent of, or knowledge of, the head physician, superintendent, or whatever Cerberus it is who guards the portals. . . . You need not wait to find out what anybody else is doing. You have a grand scheme on hand for making the hospitals military posts and so entitled to chaplains, but I hardly think you will succeed. . .

Shall I not apply to Professor Smith for information about a graduate of Union Theological Seminary who would be glad of such an appointment and who has qualifications for such special missionary work?—some one who could be set to work at once, under the "young men's" auspices or your private patronage, and afterward get a government commission if such are granted. . . .

How strange some of the statements in Russell's last letter are! That there was no hand to hand fighting at Bull Run. No batteries charged and taken by the Federalists. No masked batteries at all on the side of the rebels, etc., and then that horrid, insulting, false editorial from the *London Times* in yesterday's *Tribune!* I am sure *that* is aiding and abetting our enemies if anything is, and Russell as the representative of such a paper ought not to be allowed within our lines again. . . .

Do you two ever refresh yourselves by a drive out into the country—for pleasure purely,—with your thoughts so busy always?

E. following up the Hospital Chaplain plan, wrote to General Van Rensselaer, of General Scott's staff and received the following note:

HEADQUARTERS OF THE ARMY,
WASHINGTON, AUGUST, 1861.

My dear Mrs. Howland:

If you will send me the names of the persons you want appointed to act as Chaplains for the Hospitals, I will get the Lieutenant-General to give them (not a regular commission) but an authority to visit and have free access to the Hospital at all times.

This will invest with full authority, but no rank or emolument.

Yours very truly,

H. VAN RENSSELAER.

G. also wrote a private letter to President Lincoln asking that Hospital Chaplains should be appointed and handed it in herself at the back door of the White House; and, acting upon Abby's idea, E. wrote Prof. H. B. Smith of the Union Theological Seminary, asking him to suggest the right person, and soon received the following answer:

. . . I hope I have found the right man. Young Hopkins, son of President Mark Hopkins of Williams College, has just been in, and will think of it. If he can and will accept, he is as near being just the man as need be. He is not ordained, but I suppose can be, if necessary. Will you write me, if it is so? He is a Christian gentleman, every way, and a very able man intellectually. If you think well of him, and he agrees, when shall he come? Please write soon.

I have the most entire confidence in Mr. Hopkins' discretion and courtesy. He does not seek mere position, he only wants to do good.

Yours truly,

H. B. Smith.

Mr. Henry Hopkins took the position, to our great and lasting pleasure, and the friendship so begun has remained one of the best things the war brought to us.

When he sent up his letter of introduction from Professor Smith to G. and E. in Washington, he expected to be descended upon in the Ebbitt House parlor by two elderly women all ready to superintend him. A year later he wrote to G. in acknowledging her photograph, "It is the very identical countenance which demolished so delightfully my ideal Miss Woolsey with iron grey curls, black silk dress and spectacle-case."

Mr. Hopkins did most admirable work in the voluntary unofficial position he consented to occupy at first. Later, wishing a more formal connection with the army service, he secured proper official recognition in the General Hospital, and still later he accepted an appointment in the field as regimental Chaplain.

C. C. W. to G. and E.

AUGUST, '61.

Dear Girls:

I have wrenched this opportunity from Abby to take my turn in writing you. It is as good as a fight to attempt to do anything useful in this family. Each one considers it her peculiar province, and if I manage to tuck in a handkerchief or two in the next box of hospital supplies I shall consider myself successful beyond expectation—speaking of which, T. D. brought in a splendid lot last night that we had commissioned him to get the night before. . . . Abby says, "would you like three or four hundred brown duck havelocks for any of the brigade?" They can be bought ready-made. If so, find out from the quartermaster of the *DeKalb* regiment which pattern he thinks best, and let us know. In this connection I would advise that you *answer* all questions that we ask, and don't suppose that they are put in to fill up. Mother and Charley are still in Astoria; they drove out in C's little wagon Tuesday evening. I think mother repented before she got to the corner. I arranged her toes under the iron bar of the dash-board so that she could have that at least to hold on by, in case the horse went off the slow walk which Charley promised to keep to. . . . We have been holding a family conclave down in Mother's room in which it has been decided,—that is, after bullying the girls into consent,—that Charley and I go up to Lenox on Monday, and engage rooms for the following Friday *somewhere* if not in Lenox then in Lebanon. But go we must—the girls will slave themselves to death if we stay in town, and nothing short of heroic decision on our part will induce them to leave.

S. C. W. to E. W. H.

NEW HAVEN, AUGUST, '61.

The Second Connecticut Regiment returned on Monday and Willy and I rushed out to see them pass, poor, way-worn, tired fellows, as they were; and in their ranks we saw Dr. Bacon prance by, much to our surprise as well as pleasure. His family are all spending the summer in the country, and as the last duties of his place would detain him here for a few days, we offered him the shelter of our roof till they should be over, and so have had him to ourselves all the week—too tired and unwell to be as entertaining as usual, but still invaluable as a guide-book and interpreter to all the recent war movements.

I am hoping that a large blue pill which he swallowed publicly last night may make him even more graphic and interesting. . . . He gave me a charming description of his calls on you and Georgy and what you said and did, and what you meant to say and do. Oh, girls, don't I envy you, being so in the thick of everything!

. . . The reports from Lenox—(where Jenny and Harry Yardley, newly married, were settled)—are charming; the little house is just like a bower, transformed into such by all simple means and expedients. I am really getting appalled by the smartness of the girls. Dora and Lilly put carpets down themselves the other day in three rooms and did it as well as a professional. The last addition to the ornaments of the rooms was the pretty picture which Carry and Hatty brought from Rome for Jenny. Carry and Charley walked in upon them on Monday evening to their delight and surprise, having come up in search of rooms for the family—found at once quite near the Parsonage, and occupied by them to-day.

J. S. W. to a friend in Paris.

BREVOORT PLACE, AUGUST 8TH 1861.

Your response to my patriotic fervors gave me a sort of chill. We did not seem *en rapport*. . . . *We* are heartily ready to record our faith that the war is worth what it may cost, although the end may be only—*only!* the preservation of the Government, and not, just now, the liberation of the slaves. Perhaps you hold, with Mr. Phillips and Abby (I believe they comprise the entire party) that the war is not justifiable if it "means only stars and stripes." We think, or to resume the perpendicular pronoun, I think that is enough for it to mean or seem to mean at present. "The mills of the Gods grind slow," you know, or, if you will let me requote to you your own quotation, "you cannot hurry God." Don't you and Mr. Phillips want to hurry Him a little? I would rather, for my part, think with Mrs. Stowe, that the question of the existence of free society covers that other question, and that this war is Eternally Righteous even if it "means only the stars and stripes." . . . We are all getting bravely over the two or three dreadful days of a fortnight ago, and coming to think that our retreat under the circumstances was not such a bad thing after all. . . . Monday after Bull Run was a frightful day in Washington. Georgy says a thick gloom oppressed them which the knowledge of the safety of those nearest them could not lighten in the least, and that a sad procession of the wounded was passing through the streets all day under the heavy rain. . . . Many of the men are but slightly wounded, and all are perfectly patient, cheerful and only eager for another chance." "Tell her about the wound in my hand preventing me from writing," one man said, for whom Georgy was writing home. "And the wound in your leg?" G. asked. "No, never mind about that." "And I shall say you fought bravely?" "Oh, no matter about that; she'd be *sure* of *that."* They have known two or three cases of Southern barbarity to our wounded. But the poor wretches expected the same thing at our hands. Dr. Bacon, an intimate friend who has just come home with his regiment, Connecticut and, says in the battle on Sunday he came upon a piece of shade in which four or five wounded Georgians were lying, and what was very painful to him, every man believed that he had come to kill them, lying there disabled. One young fellow called out, "Don't hurt me, I'm hurt enough already," and the rest made a feeble show of defending themselves. Of course he dressed their wounds, and did what he could for them with more than usual care and gentleness, and I can bear witness how careful and gentle that must have been, but it was hard to tell which emotion was uppermost with them, gratitude or astonishment. Mr. Maclise, of the 71st, which has come home, says he found a wounded man under a tree, a Carolinian, he thinks, who begged for his life in the same way. "Bless your soul," Maclise said, "I wouldn't hurt you for the world; don't you want some water?" The poor fellow eagerly took the water from his enemy's canteen. "If I only had a cup I could give you some brandy," Mr. M. added. "Oh, just look in my knapsack and you'll find a cup." So Maclise opened the knap-sack, took out a beautiful silver cup, mixed the draught, and made his patient as comfortable as he knew how, bringing home the silver cup, at the Carolinian's most urgent entreaty, as a souvenir of that sad day. He will try and return it one of these days. But what a blackness of darkness, of falsehood and misrepresentation lies behind all this. These perfectly intelligent men devoutly believed that we would kill them, unarmed, sick and helpless! . . . The "prevailing" Prince comes and goes, and nobody seems to care much about it. We have learned something, or it is that we have too many troubles of our own to care for the pleasures of princes. He overstayed his time at Mount Vernon the other day, and there was a splendid story that he had been captured, but he spoiled the bulletins and the joke by coming back to a soiree at two o'clock at night. . . . We are going, as much for duty as pleasure, to Lenox, tomorrow or Saturday, for a few weeks, to refresh ourselves for the winter. As long as McClellan keeps quiet we shall stay. He resigned one day last week. Col. Davies dined with us yesterday and told us so, from his uncle, General Mansfield, who had seen the letter. The administration attempted some interference in his reforms, and he sent in his resignation. It was immediately hushed up, refused, of course, and he was allowed to have his way.

E. W. H. to J. H.

 EBBITT HOUSE, WASHINGTON, AUGUST 10, 1861.

Dear Joe:

We had a very successful journey in from camp yesterday, for who should be on the boat but the Prince (called by the public "Captain Paris,") McDowell, and *McClellan* himself, whom Mrs. Franklin introduced to us, and who helped us all into the carriage when we reached Washington. He and General Franklin are old and dear friends. He is singularly young and boyish-looking for so important a position, but at the same time has a look and manner that inspire respect. The Prince is exactly like the picture of his uncle. We hoped they would all discuss secrets of state, but the topic was persistently the range of different kinds of cannon. . . . G. goes to Alexandria this morning to look up a hospital Mr. Vernon told her of and take them some comforts. . . . There is no news except the sad story of Lyon's death in Missouri, and the mutiny here in the 79th, which was put down summarily by the display of six cannon, three companies of cavalry and a good many infantry, which came down upon them yesterday after noon. The ringleaders, about 26, were put under arrest last night and in irons, and the rest marched off into the darkness somewhere. The trouble was that they did not like their new Colonel, and would not serve under *Sickles* as Brigadier. In the latter we sympathize with them.

Letters from home report all well in Lenox . . . I send one from Mary. We shan't think of going North at present.

M. W. H. to G. and E. in Washington.

ASTORIA, AUGUST 12TH.

Dear Girls:

If mother and the remaining three kept to the programme, they all left for Lenox on Saturday and are at last settled in their summer quarters, much to my relief. So long as they would not come to us, I think it was highly necessary for them to go somewhere, as the city grew hotter and *smellier* and more unbearable every day.

Knowing what New York is at this season, and inferring what Washington must be, I am sure you will consider my proposition reasonable when I beg that you will come on and freshen up a little here at Astoria "by the side of a river so clear." . . . When you come Robert will sail you up to Riker's Island, in order to make you feel more at home, where the Anderson Zouaves are encamped. We went up there the other day with some illustrated papers sent by Jane to the men, and were enthusiastically received by a company of bathers, who swam round the boat for whatever we had to offer, and whom we left seated on the rocks reading *Frank Leslie*, with not so much as a button or an epaulette on by way of dress.

A. H. W. to E.

LENOX, MASS., AUGUST 25, 1861.

My Dear Eliza:

I don't believe you realize how interesting your letters always are. . . . Five nurses consigned to Georgy!—just think of it! I was going to ask you in my very next letter more particularly about the New York nurses—who they were obliged to report to on arriving in Washington, Surgeon-General Finley or Miss Dix, when lo and behold! I learn that they report to Georgy. . . . I see by the morning *Tribune* that the Sanitary Commission are said to have furnished light reading, as well as a quantity of little tables to stand on the beds with rests for the arms, etc., etc. I have thought of having some of those plain book racks made for weak or armless men. It grieves me to the bottom of my heart to think of how many men are ruined for life by surgeons who with savage glee hurry to chop off arms and legs *ad libitum*. Many a brave New England land forester or craftsman will have to earn a sorry livelihood by stumping about at a toll-gate, or peddling candies, one-armed, at railroad stations, who might by a slower and more skillful process have been saved such humiliation. [Dear Abby's gloom, and her low opinion of army of officers generally, kept the family in cheerful mood on many a doleful day.]

. . . I copied out Trench's sonnet on prayer for your young Lieut. Ferris. You know Mary has it in Trench's own handwriting given her by him with his autograph; and I also copied out a few of our least familiar hymns' thinking you could slip them among the newspapers now and then. I sent a package of *Boston* papers to Dr. Sheldon, at Alexandria, yesterday, and will do it again.

A. H. W. to G.

LENOX, AUGUST, 1861.

My dear Georgy:

You need not speak so coolly of our staying here three months. Three weeks will give us enough, I guess. It is actually *tiresome* not to have any-thing to do, after being so busy in New York. We only take one paper too now—the *Tribune*, and that does not come in till four o'clock, so that our mornings are very blank. There is a newsboy here however—think of that! who sells the New York and Boston papers every day on the hotel steps, after the arrival of the stage. And there is a brick store and a telegraph office, connecting with the telegraph in Springfield. Messages come over the wires in the short space of three days, I am told! . . . Is there not some news-stand or book-store on Pennsylvania Avenue where Moritz can buy you the illustrated papers for the hospitals? I hope so, as we cannot send anything now except perhaps a stray Boston paper which everybody here has finished. I sent word to Edward Gilman, who has been in New York, when he goes home to Maine to mail you every now and then a Bangor paper for some sick Maine volunteers. . . . When we go back, we will con-stitute *ourselves* into a society, and do things more systematically and thor-oughly.

Our letters must be few and stupid. Your last to us was Eliza's, written last Monday in camp. What scenes you must have gone through there, in the arrest and examination of those women spies! What strange romance history will be, by and bye, to May and Bertha. Gay ladies and courtly gentlemen, and ragged rebel volunteers, and city brokers, and wily politicians, all assigned their respective cells side by side, perhaps, in

Fort Lafayette. You wonder what "horse-cakes" are, which the old woman declared her packets of letters to be, when found between her shoulders. They are gingerbread of the "round heart" consistency, cut in the flat, rude shape of a prancing horse with very prominent ears and very stubbed legs, sold in various small shops in Alexandria, along with candy balls, penny whistles and fly-specked ballads. "Horse-cakes" are an Alexandria institution. You should buy a few for lunch some day in the bakery. . . . We live in the newspapers and in your letters. It is impossible to think of anything else. I have tried on successive afternoons to get interested in Motley's Netherlands, and give it up as a bad job. One reads a sentence over and over without getting the sense of it. And then, I remembered, that I *couldn't* remember a name, or fact, or date in the three volumes of Motley's other work; so what's the use of reading anything? "Fort Sumter" is ancient history enough for me. To-day we have quite a budget of news—the details of Butler's expedition to Fort Hatteras, which of course had to be successful. They went against the weakest point of the coast, with an overwhelming force. Little as it is, it serves for a subject of brag for us, and the newspapers glory over it as a splendid naval victory in the style of true *Southern* reports. We have the text of Fremont's proclamation. It is all very well in itself, but I don't see the object of setting slaves free in Missouri, and setting soldiers to catch them in Virginia;—shooting rebels out west and letting them off with "a mild dose of oath of allegiance" in Washington. . . . It is my growing conviction that nothing would be worse for the country than to be let off easy in this war. We should learn to think lightly of Divine guidance and Divine judgments. Providence means to humble and punish us' thoroughly before full success is granted, and it is best so.

M. W. H. to G.

ASTORIA, MONDAY, SEPTEMBER 2ND.

Dear Georgy:

Your interesting letter was highly appreciated by little May, as well as by her parents, who thought it very kind of you to elaborate so nice a little story out of the materials. May's artistic efforts were revived by it and all her inspirations lately breathe of camp life and army movements. I enclose the last one, "Recollections of what I saw on Riker's Island when passing in the boat," which is really not bad for a fancy sketch. You would have been amused to hear her reading the newspapers aloud to little Bertha the other day. I was writing at the time and took down verbatim one sentence. "We are sorry to state that General Brigade, a contraband of war, was taken prisoner last night at Fort Schuyler: he was on his way to visit the navy-yard at Bulls Run and was brought home dead and very severely wounded."

The children and nurses have just driven off with a carriage full of little pails and spades to spend the afternoon digging in the sand at Bowery Bay. You know the bliss, especially if the tide admits of rolling up their pantalettes and wading in. We are having lovely weather, which I wish you were sharing. Indeed, I am greatly disappointed that you will not come on while things are comparatively quiet and stay awhile with us. Robert and I have had some delicious sails in the boat, for which I have taken a great liking, and we are having a quiet but delightful summer. Today the Astoria flags are out in great numbers for our naval capture; a little victory which is refreshing after so many defeats. Abby and Cousin William are very blue up in Lenox and write desponding notes in the *Toots* style. The Micawber mood will probably follow, in which Abby will be "inscribing her name with a rusty nail" on the walls of some southern dungeon. Indeed I begin to think she must be in the confidence of the rebel leaders, from the entire assurance with which she looks for an attack by sea upon some northern port, while the land army meantime marches triumphantly to Washington.

We are looking for Sarah Woolsey this week to make a little visit, and were in hopes that Rose Terry, who was with her, would come too.

I sent your two letters to Mother, who will enjoy them as much as May did. When you write again tell us more about Joe,—how he is looking after the summer's campaign, how he really is, etc. It seems strange to think that autumn is already here and the dreaded hot weather for the troops nearly over, I suppose. If we can get anything for you in New York while the girls are away, or do any of the things for which you have depended upon them, be sure to let me know. . . . I wonder if a season will ever come when for once we can all spend it together without the need of ink and paper. Some large, generally satisfactory Utopian farm-house, where, as in Pomfret days, one vehicle and one horse (alas, poor beast!)

and Mother to drive, would be ample accommodation and style for all. Give our love and a God-speed to Joe when you see him next, and insist upon his taking good care of himself when out of your sight.

Affectionately yours,

MARY.

M. W. H. to A.

ASTORIA, SEPTEMBER, '61.

Dear Abby:

Sarah and I have been all the morning arranging flowers. . . . Our roses are most luxuriant this year, and just now we have outside the front door two large orange trees from the greenhouse which are one mass of blossom and perfume the whole place. We have been quite on the *qui vive* yesterday and today at the expected arrival of the Great Eastern at Port Morris which is that cluster of buildings, you may remember, next to Casina dock, on the opposite side of the river. The vessel comes consigned to Howland & Aspinwall. The English agents sent them word at the last minute that she would come in by the Sound, so we have been constantly on the look-out. It would be very pleasant to have her lying in sight of the windows for some days. On Saturday we had a fine view of the imperial yacht which passed up the river with royalty on board, and looked beautifully with its gold prow and the gold line running round the sides. Sarah particularly enjoys the river, bathes every day in a highly ornamental costume brought for the purpose, and floats round on the surface like a cork. We have had some charming sails too, and indeed divide our time about equally between the water and the carriage, with occasional short digressions among the rose bushes. Tell Carry that Mr. Stagg spent Saturday evening with us, and brought up the package of hand-kerchiefs which he promised her. They are a dozen of large, fine, colored-bordered ones, very much in the style of those I brought Ned from Paris, and such as I should not at all object to crib for private use. He must have intended them in case of a cold-in-the-head of the War Dept., they are on such a grand scale. However, I thanked him on behalf of the national nose, and will take charge of them for Carry.

S. C. W. writes during her visit to Astoria at this time:

The children are my delight all day, especially Bertha, whose little flower of a face tempts me to continual kisses. Dear little puss, she grows sweeter every day. Una, too, develops continually powers and talents undreamed of. She has learned to say 'R-r-ra,' which means Hurrah! and she says it with great enthusiasm whenever a steamer passes full of troops and we all rush out to the bank to wave our handkerchiefs to them,—the children held up by Ann and Maria, and solemnly gesturing with their little hands, and May waving one flag and the gardener's boy another. The group is so very patriotic that we are generally saluted by cheers from the boats.

The home letters, full of sweet air and peaceful views, were delightful to get in the dust and confusion of Washington, which, however, with all its discomforts, nothing would have induced us to leave. Among the letters of introduction which made our way simple and pleasant were those from Cousin Wm. Aspinwall to Senator Dixon and General Ripley ("a fine, blunt old gentleman") of Connecticut, and to Generals Hamilton and Van Rensselaer, on the staff of the Commanding General Scott. Also to Generals Wool, Dix and McDowell, Admiral Wilkes and family, and the household of Mr. Hodge, a cousin of our good Dr. Hodge of Philadelphia. We imagined that our unctuous way to the good graces of the Commanding General was made by the gift from J. H. of a number of very fine hams. These, cast upon the water, came home to us later in an invitation to dinner, which seemed rather to have the nature of a military summons, delivered as it was by a Colonel on the staff. We accepted with the mixed feeling which one must have who receives the "Queen's Command" to an interview.

The hams appear in the following note:

HEADQUARTERS OF THE ARMY, WASHINGTON.

Dear Mrs. Howland:

The Lieutenant General desires me to send his thanks for the hams sent to him by Mr. Howland. He considers them very fine indeed, to which opinion I beg leave to add my own.

Yours very truly,

H. VAN RENSSELAER.

E. to J. H. in camp.

EBBITT HOUSE, SEPTEMBER 5.

I hope you are not entirely without starch this damp, sticky day, and that you have kept "Manassas" [A "contraband of war" freed by the 16th N. Y.] busy all the morning bringing wood for the fire. Since my note we have had the confirmation of Jeff. Davis' death, reported yesterday. If he is really gone, I suppose we mustn't abuse him, but the fate is much too good for him.

We won't go down to camp again till we hear from you, as you ask, but meantime I am anxious to know what your plans and prospects are, and what the order to be "ready for instant action" meant.

We had a charming dinner with General Scott yesterday, and shall value the remembrance of it all our lives. We are the only ladies except Mrs. Thomas Davies whom he has entertained at his table during the war. We ought to feel highly honored, and we do. There were only the three aides present, and it was all very social and pleasant, but they didn't tell any state secrets. The General looked very well indeed, but showed his feebleness when he attempted to leave his chair. He spoke in high praise of the hams, which we suppose to be the humble cause of the politeness to us, and toasted the "absent Adjutant" in a bumper of sherry.

G. takes exceptions to the word "charming" in connection with that dinner, and perfectly recalls it as a fearful joy, where none of the aides dared speak unless spoken to, and she and E. hardly then. J. S. W., however, writing from Lenox and rising to the occasion, said: "Georgy's letter received last night with its gorgeous item of your dinner at General Scott's was very interesting. You are lucky to be so honored above all other women, and will consequently be able to brag to your posterity to the third and fourth generation of them that hate you."

Mother to G. and E.

LENOX, SEPTEMBER.

My dear Girls:

Abby, as usual, is writing away vigorously, and I am very sure her letters to you are better far than mine would be, therefore I always give place to her; but do not think me *indifferent* to you or to any little circumstance whatever connected with you in the most remote way, for I assure you every word relating to Washington has a deeper interest than I can express to you, and in all my reading of news I turn with indifference from other parts of the country and items of other regiments, to seek eagerly for some word of those immediately about Alexandria and Washington, and we look with more desire than ever for your letters. The "expected attack" dwells upon our minds and hearts, and our sympathies and fears are all alive. When will the *end* come? In God's own time, and we must only wait in patience and faith, looking to God for strength to help us in this time of need. . . . Ask counsel of some of your *wise* friends in Washington as to the prudence of your remaining for the present there. Do you not think in case of an attack upon the city you would be better elsewhere? I scarcely know where either, south of Philadelphia. Had you not better take the chance, before communication is cut off, of coming north? I should fear your being in Baltimore more than staying in Washington. I hope you will call on Mrs. McClellan and her mother, if the latter is with her. I knew them both, you recollect, in North Conway, and I would like you to make their acquaintance. You might consult with your familiar, General Scott, as to the propriety and safety of your being in Washington in case of an attack. What a nice thing for you to have dined so socially with the General. It will come in as a pleasing little incident in that history which I hope you are writing for coming generations.

A. H. W. to Harriet Gilman.

LENOX, SEPTEMBER 12, 1861.

To-day has been very beautiful. Such floating clouds and corresponding shadows, such liquid blue on the distant hills and such gold green on the nearer meadows! We saw it to advantage at sunset, from Mrs. Sedgwick's house. Only Miss Catherine was at home, and we saw her in her own little parlor, hung with photographs and engravings and one or two old choice portraits. But the picture from the window was best of all. . . . We had a charming drive one day with the Warners (of the "Wide, Wide World") to Tyringham, the Shaker settlement below Lee, which name reminds me of the story we heard of the loyalty of *that* little village. It had already sent its full proportion to the army. But that dreadful night when the news of disaster at Bull Run came, the baker told the Warners "Nobody couldn't eat nothin' and nobody couldn't sleep none." That very midnight *sixty* men of Lee started in the cars for New York and enlisted for the war. . . . I had a chance of seeing Mrs. Kemble to-day as she drove by, silks and lace and birds of paradise, several I should think by the size. She is the great woman of the place here. Her daughter, Mrs. Wistar, was with her—strikingly like her, and yet young, fair, simple and beautiful. She came back yesterday from New York with Julia Butler the sister. They had been down to see their father in Fort Lafayette.

In consequence of complaints made of the treatment of the political prisoners, Dr. Bellows, the President of the Sanitary Commission, inspected Fort Lafayette and reported to the Secretary of State October 31, 1861—"Every man has his own cot, plenty of blankets and abundance of food. They were in better condition in all respects than our own men in the field. They have many acres for play-ground. They complained of nothing though I gave them abundant opportunity."

S. C. W., writing from Lenox, says;

I was highly diverted by a story Mrs. Kane told Jenny Yardley of Mrs. Kemble. She was playing whist the other night with Mrs. Ellery Sedgwick as a partner, and became really furious because Mrs. Sedgwick played so badly. Finally, just as her rage had reached its height, Mrs. Sedgwick remarked, "I do not know what is the matter with me! somehow I can't play well, or talk straight, or do anything right this evening, and it is strange, for I certainly do know how to play whist." Whereupon the majestic Fanny exploded: "Well, I am glad to hear that. It is a comfort to know that one has for a partner an inattentive genius and not a *born fool!*"

Mrs. Kemble was most friendly with the various members of the family, though unexpected at times, as for instance when she remarked to Harry Yardley, while Lilly Woolsey was his guest, "Mr. Yardley, you have a very handsome young woman at your house; I do not refer to Mrs. Yardley." However, the people in Lenox seemed used to these little bursts. They never resented them and only made a good story of it all, which they enjoyed.

The Mansion Hospital, Alexandria, Virginia
Photographic History of the Civil War

CHAPTER FOUR

What I Can Do

E. W. H. to J. H.

September 11th, 1861.

Where do you think I am writing? In the Patent Office, where we heard the other day that a large number of sick men had been brought from the 19th Indiana regiment. We found them in a dirty and forlorn condition and have come to do what we can. The whole regiment, nearly, is down with sickness from great exposure when they first arrived, they say. The assistant-surgeon of the regiment and the matron are here all the time, and a number of Washington women come in to help every day.

From G's letter to the Sanitary Commission Fair's paper this account of the hospital is taken:—

One of the first extemporized hospitals of the war was in the top story of the Patent Office, where the 19th Indiana regiment was brought, nearly every man of them. The great, unfinished lumber room was set aside for their use, and rough tables—I can't call them beds—were knocked together from pieces of the scaffolding. These beds were so high that it was impossible to reach them, and we had to make them up with brooms, sweeping off the mattresses, and jerking the sheets as smooth as we could. About six men could be accommodated on one table. These ran the whole length of the long room, while on the stacks of marble slabs, which were some day to be the floor, we spread mattresses, and put the sickest men. As the number increased, camp-beds were set up between the glass cases in the outer room, and we alternated—typhoid fever, cog-wheels and patent churns—typhoid fever, balloons and mouse-traps (how *many* ways of catching mice there are!)—typhoid fever, locomotives, water-wheels, clocks,—and a general nightmare of machinery.

Here, for weeks, went on a sort of hospital picnic. We scrambled through with what we had to do. The floors were covered with lime dust, shavings, nails, and carpenters' scraps. We had the rubbish taken up with shovels, and stacked in barrels at one end of the ward. The men were crowded in upon us, the whole regiment soaked with a malignant, malarial fever, from exposure, night after night, to drenching rains, without tents. There was so much of this murderous, blundering want of prevision and provision, in the first few months of the war—and is *now,* for that matter.

Gradually, out of the confusion came some system and order. Climbing up to the top of the Patent Office with each loaf of bread was found not to be an amusing occupation, and an arrangement of pulleys was made out of one of the windows, and any time through the day, barrels of water, baskets of vegetables and great pieces of army beef, might be seen crawling slowly up the marble face of the building.

Here for weeks, we worked among these men, cooking for them, feeding them, washing them, sliding them along on their tables, while we climbed up on something and made up their beds with brooms, putting the same powders down their throats with the same spoon, all up and down what seemed half a mile of uneven floor;—coaxing back to life some of the most unpromising,—watching the youngest and best die.

I remember rushing about from apothecary to apothecary, in the lower part of the city, one Sunday afternoon, to get, in a great hurry, mustard, to help bring life into a poor Irishman, who called me Betty in his delirium, and, to our surprise, got well, went home, and at once married the Betty we had saved him for.

By-and-by the regiment got through with the fever, improvements came into the long ward, cots took the place of the tables, and matting covered the little hills of the floor. The hospital for the 19th Indiana became the "U. S. General Hospital at the Patent Office," and the "volunteers for emergencies" took up their saucepans and retired.

A. H. W.

LENOX, SEPTEMBER 15, 1861.
Charley talks of going down to-morrow to be inspected and mustered

into State service with the regiment—the Home-Guard. He thinks his fine for non-attendance will about equal his railroad fare down and up. He is to stay over night and will see Mary at Astoria.

C. C. W.

SEPTEMBER 18.

Charley left on Monday to be with his regiment, which has been drafted into the U. S. Service the first step towards Washington. The members singly can resign at any time, and Charley will do this when called upon to leave the city.

The family took this consoling view of Charley's duty to his country, and saw him leave Lenox without anxiety. Charley's private views developed later, when, after valuable service with the Sanitary Commission at the front, he entered the 164th N. Y. regiment and was immediately assigned as aide de camp to very active duty at Army Headquarters.

Rev. Henry Hopkins to E. W. H.

CITY HOTEL HOSPITAL, ALEXANDRIA, OCTOBER 1861.
My dear Mrs. Howland:

I want to tell you how I am coming on here in my new field, for at Washington I received the impression, which it will take a long time to wear away, that you and Miss Woolsey are cordially interested in all that concerns me in this work.

Dr. Sheldon is entirely propitious thus far. . . . Those who are religious women among the nurses hail my coming with real joy. The very first one whom I encountered was such a woman, and as I sat down in her cheerful ward before the bright fire on the hearth, talking with the men, a poor emaciated creature who was sitting wrapped in blankets, with his feet upon a pillow, asked me—"Are you a physician?" "No," I told him, "I am a clergyman." He stretched out his lean hand to me, and said—"Oh, sir, I am so glad to see you. I have been very sick, so that they gave me up, and now I am getting well, and I am not a Christian, and I *must* be." Could the most trembling faith ask more than this?

I have just come from attending the funeral of a soldier of the 27th N. Y.

regiment, who died last evening of typhoid fever. It was severely simple in all its accompaniments, only a little gathering in the hospital dining room, and a simple exercise; while a corporal's guard were the only ones to attend the body to the grave, to hear the last sad words spoken. But in the very simplicity of it, and in the peculiar circumstances of those concerned, and especially from being the first time that I had ever officiated on such an occasion, it was to me very impressive. Had I not been here it is unlikely that he would have received a Christian burial.

. . . Dr. Sheldon called me *Mr. Woolsey* this morning, and as long as that association of ideas continues I am sure of most excellent treatment.

E. W. H. to J. H.

OCTOBER I, '61.

Very little to tell you about except a few calls, including one from Mrs. General Franklin to ask us to take tea with her to-night. Lieutenant Lusk of the 78th, whom we used to know as "Willy" Lusk, also came. He seems to have grown up into a very fine young fellow, handsome and gentle-manly, and with the same sweet expression he had as a child. He was studying medicine in Europe when the war broke out, but came home at once and enlisted as Lieutenant in the 78th, where he is now Acting Captain—so many of the regiment were either killed or taken prisoners at Bull Run. Dr. E. also came again and Captain Gibson and Col. Mont-gomery of Philadelphia, so we had quite a levee.

October 2. G. and I are just going up to Columbian College to cover and arrange a nice box of books Hatty Gilman has sent on at our sugges-tion to form the nucleus of a hospital library—an excellent selection of books, histories, biographies, etc.; half worn, but the covering and label-ing we mean to put them through will make them highly respectable and attractive.

We took tea last night with Mrs. Franklin and met five or six other people, among them Major and Mrs. Webb—he on General Barry's staff. Dr. Bacon has brought G. some splendid bunches of roses this week, the finest I ever saw. He expects to be ordered off with his new regiment, the 7th Connecticut, within a few days, probably to join the Coast Expedi-tion, but this is a secret.

We have been with Captain Gibson all through the Corcoran Art

Building, now used as a government warehouse and filled with clothing and camp equipage of every kind, one item being twenty thousand tents. From the roof, to which we mounted, we had a fine view over the city and environs, the river, the opposite heights and an army balloon.

E. W. H. to J. H.

OCTOBER 6.

After dinner yesterday we drove out to the camp of the Rhode Island 2nd to see the friend of our infancy and of hay-loft and cow-stall memory—Col. Frank Wheaton, son of Dr. Wheaton of Pomfret, Connecticut, to whose farm-house Mother took us all to board, the summer after Father's death. It is about twenty years (!) since we all played together. You know it was for him that Mary got that ugly scar across her nose, in her anxiety to reach him through a glass window, and they two at the age of about seven were married in state and went to housekeeping in the cow-stall on apples and flagroot. He says he remembers it all most distinctly and still claims Mary as "his wife by right" though he has had one, and is engaged to a second.

He was very much pleased to find that he had met you too, for he was mustering-in officer at Albany when you were there, and swore in, part of the 16th. He and the others were "delighted with Adjutant Howland, who used to come to their office nearly every day and *always had his muster rolls right.*"

I was sorry to hear that the mare "Lady Jane" was so sick and I send George Carr out to camp to see if he can do anything for her. As he has known her from early youth he may understand her insides better than others do. You may be surprised at my being able to get a pass for George, but not more than I was! A mere statement of the case dissolved all the adamantine walls round the Provost Marshal, and is only another proof of our being "noble-hearted women of *luck.*"

A. H. W. writes:

How funny it is that you should have met the Wheatons again. It is one of the queer ways in which people turn up. I wonder if they remember the little school which Mother held for us every day in the porch of their father's house in Pomfret, and the yellow hymn book, and the tunes of

"Our Father in Heaven,
We hallow Thy name," and
"God is in Heaven, would He hear
If I should tell a lie?"

—and then how at times we used to see who could eat the most ears of corn! And the skeleton in his father's office, what a corner of horrors that was!

E. to J. H.

WASHINGTON, OCTOBER 7.

After dinner to-day we said good-bye to Dr. Bacon, now Surgeon of the 7th Connecticut, and he left in the night we suppose, with the regiment, to join the second great land and naval expedition for the southern coast.

October 9, '61. As I told you, Dr. Bacon left either Monday night or early yesterday for Annapolis with the 7th Connecticut. They seem to have been the first ones dispatched, for yesterday others went, and, as I write, a long train of baggage and men equipped for a journey is passing down the street. We think of sending Moritz on to Annapolis this afternoon with a basket of sea-stores for the Doctor, and he can bring us back accounts of the number of vessels, etc. Moritz is anxious to know before leaving if the troops—including the 7th Connecticut! are Union ones!

October 14. Moritz got back from Annapolis all right. Found Dr. Bacon and delivered the basket. There was no prospect of their going before next week. All the 15,000 had not yet arrived and only one transport was ready. The railroad was blocked all the way by immense trains of stores, ammunition, etc., and Moritz was from half-past two till eleven o'clock getting there.

F. B. to G. M. W.

CAMP WALTON. ANNAPOLIS, OCTOBER 18TH, 1861.

Pardon a wretched notelet, written on camp stationery with the very dregs of the day's ration of nervous energy. Everybody is both tired and busy to-night with this embarkation business.

You will readily believe they are sober enough, these long, undulating files of honest brown faces, as they pour down upon the wharves, but there are good, rousing cheers, too, as the tenders swing out into the stream and go scuttling away to the great motionless ships in the roads.

I notice with surprise, and with some apprehension as well, that the 6th and 7th Connecticut, green as I have thought them, are farther advanced in the military art than any other troops I have seen here. This is not brag, you will please consider, it is very reluctant conviction. But still, as for me, turning more sadly than ever before from the loyal North, I feel an exultation in helping to strike, as we are hoping, the heaviest blow at the great crime that it has yet felt.

Your basket is such a miracle of packing that I have hesitated to thoroughly ransack it, fearing that the attempt to restore its contents to their normal condition might reduce me to a state of hopeless idiocy, like a Chinese puzzle, or a book on political economy.

Moritz delicately hinted at French rolls as being the only things that could not defy the ravages of time, and so, one terribly stormy evening, being the second after the arrival of the basket, Chaplain Wayland, my brother the Captain and I, having our rival teapots all in a row, each singing over her own spirit-lamp, I removed the stratum of rolls and disposed of them to the immense satisfaction of the tea-party. This gave me a glimpse of the blue and gold Tennyson lying lapped among the balmy bolognas. Ever since, I have been longing for the golden moment to come when I could sit, or, more properly, lie down to my own individual, personal, particular, blue and gold Tennyson. This may probably be when every soul in the regiment except myself is helplessly, hopelessly seasick, and nobody can "come a botherin' me."

F. B. to G. M. W.

HAMPTON ROADS, OCTOBER 27TH.

We still loiter here in a seeming imbecile way, waiting now for weather and now for nobody knows what. Meanwhile patience and strength are ebbing in twelve thousand men. The condition of some of the regiments on shipboard is said to be very bad. Ours is fortunate in its ship, and they say is in better order than any other. A villain of a division-commissary, supplied fifteen days' rations of pork and no beef, for the entire expedition!

Finding this out just as we were leaving Annapolis, I felt that we could never stand it, and we have behaved so cantankerously about it, that we have secured beef enough, fresh and salt, to greatly mitigate the Sahara of pork, for this regiment. God help the others! Oh to have a Division-commissary's head in a lemon squeezer!

J. H. got a week's furlough about the middle of October and we all went North together. Just before leaving Washington E. writes:

We did a few errands, went to see the Indiana boys at the Patent Office again, and to the Columbian College Hospital, and also to call on Will Winthrop, now Lieutenant of the Berdan Sharp Shooters. He entertained us in his tent, a nice neat one, full of contrivances—painted table, book shelves and a *wash-stand*. Captain Hastings of his company received us too; and when we left, Will begged us to walk down the color-line with them as "it would increase their importance to be seen with two *rather* good-looking women. And if one of the field officers would *only* come by and ask who we were!"

On Sunday (the 13th) we went to St. John's Church and shook hands with General Scott and asked him in fun for leave of absence. He "thought we couldn't be spared!"

E. and J. H. went at once to their own home at Fishkill.

Mother to E. W. H. at Fishkill.

NEW YORK, THURSDAY, OCTOBER 17TH.

My dear Eliza:

I must write a line to you this afternoon, not only to congratulate you and dear Joe upon being together again in your own pleasant home hut to tell you how charmed I am at the prospect of seeing you here. We began to pack up immediately on the receipt of our last letter from Washington and came down from Lenox as soon as possible, reaching home yesterday in time for a six o'clock dinner. I wrote to old William we were coming and he had everything very nice and clean. . . . Mary received our letter last night, telling her we should be in town, so that this morning the first thing, Georgy—who had gone right out to Mary—and Carry rushed in upon us, and right glad were we to see Georgy again, and to find her looking so well; not entirely grey-headed and wrinkled with age from the cares and anxieties of her Washington campaign, as we expected! but really looking better and certainly fatter, than when she left home. It is delightful to hear her account of things, and it will be very charming when you are here with us too, to join in the pow-wows. We are all eager listeners to Washington doings, and I cannot bear to be out of the room a minute while Georgy is talking

Do give my kind remembrance to Thomson and his wife; I have a great respect for him. I hope you will come to us as soon as you can. We shall be all ready for you, except the "nick-nacks," and I don't mean to take any of them out. I found William had opened Joe's likeness, and set it out, as a delicate little attention to the family! Hatty waits to take my note.
Ever affectionately yours,
MOTHER.

E. writes:

On reaching home we found everything in the nicest order, gas lighted, bright fires, plenty of flowers, a delicious supper, and Thomson and his whole family, and Mechie (the gardener) with his arms full of pears and grapes, waiting to welcome us. They were all glad to have us back, and seemed unable to do enough for us. Mrs. Thomson and the gardener's niece helped Moritz, and we lived like princes for the few days on the products of the place without lifting our hands.

Joe went back to the army at the end of his week's furlough, G. and E. staying in New York a fortnight longer with Mother. On returning to Washington they found that General Scott had just resigned from the head of the army, November 1, '61, and General McClellan had been appointed commander-in-chief. They began work again at once. E. writes home the next day:—

We have been up to Columbian College Hospital and have helped Miss Dix cover a lot of books; were most affectionately welcomed by her on the field of our old conflict. Joe is in a new camp near Leesburg Pike and very comfortable. We took a lot of things to the Alexandria Hospital and to Slocum's brigade, including a number of bright prints Mother and Hatty sent on.

E. to J. H.

EBBITT HOUSE, WASHINGTON, NOVEMBER 11.

It is very late, but I scribble a line before going to bed to say we got over safely from camp, stopping on the way for Mr. Hopkins, who is going to Poolesville with us to-morrow. We got in at six o'clock and since then we have been in a blaze of glory, for there has been a splendid torchlight procession in honor of McClellan, with rockets and blue lights and all sorts of fine things. Of course we followed it with Chaplain Hopkins, bringing up at Mrs. Hodge's in H street, next door to McClellan's own house, where the procession halted and called out Seward and Lincoln and Cameron and McClellan himself, and there were several little speeches, the best of which was General Blenker's, who said: "Citizens and soldiers, when I shtand on de battle field with your thousands volunteers I will fight de enemy better as I shpeak your noble language." Then on tip-toe he patted McClellan on the back and I think kissed him! Seward's speech was highly vague and promiscuous.

We came home at midnight, just now, with our patriotic noses smutty from the torches.

At 9 this morning we start for Poolesville and have the prospect of a fine day.

The battle of Ball's Bluff near Poolesville had taken place while we were on "leave of absence" at home, and on our return to Washington, Major Potter, U. S. paymaster, and his wife, starting on an expedition to pay the troops up the Potomac, invited Chaplain Hopkins and ourselves to join the party, which we did with great delight, though it involved a three days' journey in our own carriage—a formidable thing at that time. It gave us an opportunity of visiting the scene of the desperate fight at the Bluff and the encampments at Poolesville and Darnestown and of taking supplies to these distant hospitals.

From E's Journal.

. . . The officers told us the whole story of the battle and described terrible scenes to us of cold, suffering and death by drowning which we hope to forget. . . .

While standing on the dreadful bank where our poor wounded were dragged up (and from which we plainly saw the rebel pickets across the river gathering in a little group), we understood fully and bitterly the wicked incompetency of whoever is responsible for this blunder. . . .

Bright and early next morning we left for Darnestown on the return drive. There Captain Best, of Battery F, 4th Regular Artillery, was our host, and a most kind and attentive one, he and the other officers turning out of their tents for us and treating us like queens. Frank Crosby turned up there as Senior 1st Lieutenant, a position, Captain Best told us quietly, *he* worked fourteen years for in the regular service. Our tent was the *salon* and round our little fire that evening gathered Captain Best, General Hamilton of Wisconsin, Major Crane, Lieutenant Hazzard of Battery A, R. I. Artillery, Colonel Stiles of the 9th N. Y., Captain Perkins, Lieutenants Muhlenberg and Crosby, Dr. Wier of the Battery and others. They all came laden with refreshments from the sutler's, and all seemed to enjoy the fun. . . . Next day we called at Fort Muggins, lunched with the General, dined with Lieutenant Hazzard of Battery A, and left for Washington. We were stopped on the way for lack of countersign and marched to Tenallytown between files of soldiers! but managed to establish our innocence, and finally reached the Ebbitt house at 8 P. M.

At Darnestown we received the first official confirmation of the success of the great expedition and the capture of Port Royal. Captain Rodgers of the navy was selected by the Commodore as the first man to go on shore and run up the Stars and Stripes; and Dr. Bacon, who was one of the party, was sent inland with General T. W. Sherman's proclamation, issued on his own responsibility, to the citizens of South Carolina, exhorting them to "pause and reflect upon the tenor and consequences of their acts," etc. So deserted was the whole neighborhood of all but slaves that they had to go twelve miles to find a white man to hand the proclamation to, and *he* took it with oaths and under protest."

A. H. W. to G. and E.

8 BREVOORT PLACE, THURSDAY.

The details of the landing of the fleet at Port Royal fill all minds and mouths. I hope Georgy will have, from "our own correspondent" with the expedition, a full account of the landing of the 7th Connecticut, which seems to have been the first on shore. The sight of those vessels rounding to and sailing past, with sails spread, and the bands playing, and the men crying, instead of cheering, for joy! must all have been wonderful. The poor blacks coming down to the shore, with their little bundles in their hands, is the most touching of all. Every one asks me what I think *now* of the state of the country, and I say the results of the expedition are good, as *far as they go*. We must have something more than a Hatteras fizzle this time. Flags are shown from all the private houses to-day. Our's is out again, and I dare say Broadway will be quite a sight.

F. B. to G.

TYBEE ISLAND.

The 7th was the first regiment ashore in South Carolina. It made the first reconnaissance in force; a detachment of five companies occupied Braddock's Point and its batteries, and was the first to reconnoitre Daufuskie and neighboring islands. The greater part of the regiment now holds this position, with a fragmentary German one. If you have ever wondered how I could be accessory to Sherman's proclamation in any way, let me suggest in the faintest possible whisper that I improved the occasion to issue on my own account a considerable number of small proclamations "to the loyal people of South Carolina of various shades of black and yellow scattered over the country from Beaufort to Port Royal Ferry."

C. C. W. to E.

NOVEMBER 18TH

Dear Eliza:

Your most delightful letter has just been read aloud amid the cheers of the assembled family. What a splendid time you are having with your brigadiers and serenades. How I should like to sacrifice myself and join you in a few of your "noble" sprees, and become acquainted with some of your suffering generals. We, meantime, have been devoting *ourselves,* giving all our time and energy to the work of soothing and captivating a poor nervous soldier, Major Anderson. I suppose you heard that we started on our Christian enterprise the day after you left again for the same work. When we reached Tarrytown, the scene of our labors, we were received, as such heroines should be, with a great deal of state, and as we found a dinner-party of some twenty awaiting us we rushed up stairs to dress in our red silk and our mauve. . . . The whole regiment of us encamped in the house for the night and we had a jolly time.

On Wednesday, General Anderson, wife and son arrived. Mrs. A. is a great invalid and did not appear for the first two days, and when at last she was announced I looked to see a pale shadow glide in, and was astonished by the sight of a little, fat, plumpy woman with big bare arms and a good deal of jet jewelry; quite a talkative, frisky person. The General is lovely, quiet and gentlemanly and devoted to young ladies—a very important requisite in a hero. His health is very much shattered but his loyalty is unshaken. We were speaking of a lady who was engaged to a Southerner. "Break it off," he said, "break it at once, he is a lunatic; I would as lief go into an insane asylum and argue with a man who calls himself Christ, as reason with a secessionist." Mrs. Anderson said she never saw such a change as being up in Tarrytown made in her husband. In town he was worn out by callers and indifferent people who came to see the hero and ask him why he did not do this and that and the other at Sumter; and propound their own theories as to how he should have acted . . . We told General Anderson you were in Washington doing what you could, etc., and he said "God bless them, it is a good work they are doing." . . . We were sorry to come home on Tuesday, but had to, as I had invited the ———s and Mr. ——— to dinner. When we got home about an hour before dinner not a soul was here, Mother and Abby gone to Sing Sing for the day, Jane dodging a procession on Broadway, and one dish of chops ordered for dinner. We sent William out for jelly-cake, beef, etc., and with a spread of linen and glass, which fortunately was not in the closet of which Mother had the key, we set out quite a nice little table. . . . Cousin Mary Greene, Gardiner, and little Gardy arrived yesterday; the two last are still here. Gardy cuts into every conversation, asking innumerable and unanswerable questions: is now reading Ferdinand Second as pastime! aged ten.

Lenox Hodge (Hugh's father) was ready to give us all the help in his power, and we depended upon him often to fill our commissions for the hospitals. He writes from Philadelphia, November '61.

Dear Georgy: I hope that you will duly receive the six air-beds, which agreeably to your request I have ordered. The cost was eleven dollars apiece and one dollar for express. I send also 100 pairs of slippers and 100 palm-leaf fans.

J. S. W. to G. and E.

NEW YORK, NOVEMBER, 1861.

Dear Girls:

I went to the provisional Hospital here to see if the volunteers wanted anything. Mrs. Darragh took me all over, and said she wanted woolen shirts and socks very *much.* So I sent the requisition to the society and she will get all she wants there. . . . Mrs. D. also suggests slates for the men to scribble on, cypher on, do puzzles, etc.; thought they would be very nice, in which I agree. Perhaps the idea may be useful to you. . . . Do you remember Peck, the man all twisted with rheumatism? He is getting well, and is a great gourmand. They let him have anything he wants. While we were there he remarked sentimentally, "I say, send we some more of that *roast pig,* won't you." I shall adopt the New York volunteers to the mild extent of taking them some papers occasionally. . . . Mrs. Bennett, poor old soul, called yesterday to tell of the death of her son with typhoid dysentery in the camp, and, what with her grief and childish elation at having news to tell and being an object of sympathy, was most pathetically comic,— "dead and gone! dear, dead and gone! and this is his picter that he sent home to his mar," was her greeting to everyone that came down stairs; "and I hope you'll all be ready in time, my dears. It's bad enough to be *left by the cars,* but worse not to be ready when you come to die." Her great desire seemed to be to see and thank a drummer boy, who in the last few days of her son's life walked a mile and a half every day to get him a canteen of spring water. He was consumed with thirst and could not drink the river water. . . . Do the surgeons know that you can have money at your disposal for delicacies, as well as clothes, etc.? Let them know it, if you have not, and *spend, spend* indefinitely. I say to myself often, "fifty or sixty thousand dollars would give quite a lift, why do I cumber the ground?" So if you don't want to see me dead and the ducats in my coffin directed to the Sanitary Commission, say what I can do or send.

A. H. W. to G. and E.

NOVEMBER.

Bessie Wolcott's wedding came off very brilliantly. Carry went out to Astoria the day before Mother and Hatty drove out together. Mary is said to have looked very handsome in white silk trimmed with black lace and white silk ruches. Hatty wore her crimson silk with white valencienne spencer or waist, and mother was very resplendent in velvet and feathers, stone cameos and black lace shawl. . . Charley drove out and back with his pony as rapidly as possible, as they had to drill for evacuation day, Charley's first appearance in a procession. We all stood on the curbstone and we winked, and he winked, and Captain Ben Butler and others twinkled and winked, not daring to do more, so precise and martial was their array. . . . Have you received a large brown bale that you didn't know what to make of? It is black curled hair. Eliza said *whole pillows* were much needed—underscoring the words. I don't know what she means, unless that mere empty tickings to be filled with straw don't answer. I have thought that the best way was to send you the hair, as it can be packed far closer than any number of ready-made pillows would be. The tickings are all made and will be along in Washington soon.

J. S. W. to J. H. in camp.

NOVEMBER 25.

We have been evacuating the British with great zest to-day; good weather, clean streets, and many praises for the 22nd Charley's regiment, among other battalions—praises, that is, with the exception of some vile youths of the street, near Stuart's, who shouted "hurrah for the never go 'ways!" . . . We had a very interesting meeting of the Bible Society last night, second meeting of the army branch, many excellent speeches; Dr. Roswell Hitchcock, of course, who *apropos* of the slavery question, said, "Patience; we need not be hurrying matters—*that* cause, like the soul of old John Brown, is 'marching on,' and the chorus is 'Glory, Hallelujah!'"

The allusion was charged with electricity, and the audience responded appropriately. A gentleman, I forget his name, had been to visit the Hatteras rebel prisoners and described the scene; a sad, sorry six hundred as you could well find. He made them an address on repentance (of the gospel sort), and begged them to sing, to "start something"—"Pray, sing my brothers; it will do your hearts good." So some one began "All hail the power of Jesus' name." Then followed "Jesus, lover of my soul," and last "There is rest for the weary." He said they sang well, and it was a strange and even touching sight. He said they were comfortably cared for, and he saw a lot of underclothes sent them in a wrapper marked, "from a father and mother whose son (a Union soldier) is in prison in Richmond." . . .

How are you going to spend your Thanksgiving, and what are you going specially to give thanks for? The question will rather be what to leave out, than what to put in the *action de grace.* Did you read Governor Andrews' proclamation? if you didn't, do! It is like a blast out of one of the old trumpets that blew about the walls of the strong city till they tumbled down. Have you read the Confederate President's message, in which he has contrived to out-Herod Herod? . . .

Tell the girls to get F. L. Olmsted's "Cotton Kingdom" if they want anything to read. He labors a little with his conscientiously faithful statistics, but when he breaks into his story his style runs smooth and clear, and there are few prettier pieces of travel-telling than his ride through the pine forests with the filly "Jane," for instance.

The Governors of all the loyal states issued in these dark days their annual proclamation of a day of Thanksgiving. Governor Andrews' of Massachusetts was dated November 21, '61,—the anniversary of the day on which the Pilgrims of Massachusetts on board the Mayflower united themselves in a solemn compact of government:

'Sing aloud unto God our Strength.'

The proclamation proposes to "give thanks for the privilege of living unselfishly, and dying nobly in a great and righteous cause."

These state proclamations came, heartening and sustaining a people sorely in need.

E's Journal.

NOVEMBER 28, THANKSGIVING.

We have kept the day with J. in camp. He commissioned us to ask Mrs. Franklin to meet the General, unbeknown to him. So we sent the carriage for her by half-past eight, and started a little after nine, hoping to reach camp in time for service with the regiment. The roads were very bad, however, and we were too late. We stopped at the Brigade Hospital on the way, to leave oysters, jelly, oranges, etc., keeping some for the regimental "sick in quarters." Our camp looked very neat and comfortable, tents all raised three or four feet on logs and clay, and nearly every one with a fireplace or stove. J. had arranged everything nicely for us, and his little fire and General Slocum's were running races. General Franklin soon arrived, and we all sat round the firesides till dinner time. The dining-room was the Sibley tent, charmingly ornamented with evergreens, and the dinner was a great victory in its way; for out of the little tent-kitchen appeared successively, oyster soup, roast turkey, cranberry sauce, canvas-back ducks, vegetables, and a genuine and delicious plum pudding that would do justice to any New England housekeeper. Cake, pies and ice cream were also among the good things. The whole day was delightful, ending with a visit to General Franklin's camp and the return to town with outriders.

E. to J. H.

EBBITT HOUSE, DECEMBER 1, '61.

We saw yesterday a nice dodge for enlarging your tent and making the back one more private. It is pitching the two tents three or four feet apart and spreading the fly over the intermediate vestibule. Chaplain Edward Walker of the 4th Connecticut, whom we went to see yesterday, had his two tents arranged so, and the effect was very pretty. In the front one he had the regimental library (a very nice one) and the back one was his own, and between them was the little vestibule floored like the others and boarded at the sides to keep out the cold, and in it he had his stove and washing apparatus, and from its ceiling hung a pretty wire basket filled with moss and wild flowers! a charming little bit of New England country life in the midst of civil war. He is a nice fellow, one of Dr. Leonard Bacon's Congregational boys and just the one for an army Chaplain—so cheerful and strong, and honest and kind-hearted. . . . He went with us through the camp and to the hospital, where we left them some supplies, including a lot of hair pillows which we had made from Abby's material.

G. lately drove Chaplain Wrage's wife out to her husband's camp, carrying socks, pillows, comforters, farina, etc. to the hospital. The camp was very German and dirty; no New England faculty shown in keeping *it* warm and clean, and the little German bowers looked dreary in the freezing weather. The Colonel, who addresses us as "my ladies" in a polite note, is under arrest for stealing; the Lieutenant-Colonel and Quartermaster are fools, and the men suffer in consequence.

Mother to G. and E.

THURSDAY EVENING, DECEMBER 5.

My dear Girls:

This will be a little Sunday greeting to you, probably, as I write it merely to give you my love, and your address to Mr. Charles Johnson of Norwich. He is now here spending the evening, and, as usual, very entertaining. He leaves to-morrow for Washington. He goes to secure, if possible, a paymaster's postion in one of the Connecticut regiments, and has Governor Buckingham, Mr. Foster and others interested for him. Jane has told him that perhaps you can "pull the wires" for him in some quarters! I fear we are beginning to feel proud of you, as we hear your praises sounded in various quarters, and read paragraphs in the papers of your doings. At the wedding last night, Mrs. Colby told me all she had heard from your French widow nurse, who, it seems, has told her all about your visits to the hospital, etc., and what a "sunbeam" Georgy is, and how much comfort you have both been to her, and to all the other nurses. . . . The largest box yet, stands all nailed up and marked, ready for the express, in the front hall, and when Mr. Johnson said he was going on and would take anything for us, we told him we had a small parcel which he probably saw as he came in; the poor man looked aghast at the idea! . . . How very pleasant Mr. Hopkins is, but I think he must have been quizzing you in his very flattering remark about me. I do not like this in him. You poor, dear, little girls! I wish I could place a tray before you every day or two with something relishing. A large dish has come up to-night of jumbles, which I should like to empty on your table. . . . Charley has just come in from drill, with his new military overcoat, which is quite becoming. . . . Many kisses and lots of love.

A. H. W. to G. and E.

DECEMBER 6TH.

If Mr. Craney thought the bundle of hair was a feather-bed, he will certainly think that the stocking box, when it arrives, is the bedstead following on. . . . Let me describe its contents. In the first place, E's cheque bought seven dozen and a half pairs of socks. . . . We have added as many more dozen as our own purchase, and friends sent in nearly two dozen knitted ones, so that the whole number is sixteen dozen. The pair of Mackinaw blankets looked like very heavy and handsome ones, from one of Robert's parishioners. We added two pairs more of less expensive ones, and in the folds of one are a couple of little framed pictures, out of a lot Charley brought down to be sent, but I thought two were enough to run the risk of breakage. . . . Of woolen gloves there are five dozen—Jane's purchase, etc., etc. . . . Lastly, after the box was all nailed up, came Dorus with a dozen of "country-knit socks" from the store in Friendsville, near where Annie Woolsey lives. We had the middle plank of the box taken off and stuffed them in. . . . It is unpardonable that Wrage's men, or any men, should be badly off for socks. The dishonest quartermasters are a curse to our army and our cause. . . . Mother thinks the best part of all this is to be able to put the pillows *yourselves* under the sick men's heads. What a scene your room must be with its boxes and bags! . . . We are amused to think that you admire the President's message. . . . What do you think of his muddle about the slavery question? about Government taking slaves at so much a lump for taxes? expatriating a man from the soil he was born on and loves, because he is loyal to the government and of dark complexion.

C. C. W. to G. and E.

DECEMBER 1ST.

L. came in a few evenings ago. He was at Conway last summer, and able to contradict an absurd story that was going the rounds,—that Charley and Joe having joined the army, Mother had given up housekeeping and gone into the hospitals, and all the daughters were children of the regiment!

Dr. Carmalt called too. He is very quiet, but good-looking, and ready to laugh at poor jokes, which is much in his favor. . . . I never told you what a nice dressing-gown the one you left for Abby was; and though she was immensely disgusted at your having given it, she wears it every night and looks comfortable and warm, which is what she did not look, with her flannel petticoat over her shoulders.

Abby would not spend a penny that could be helped, on herself, during the war. She casually mentioned one day with modest pride that she had spent only $300 for herself this year. Jane looked at her with surprise and remarked, "I can't imagine where you've put it!"

F. B. to G. M. W.

TYBEE ISLAND, DECEMBER 24, '61.

You speak of our hospital as a matter of course; and we are, by and by, to have one, as yet uncommenced; but we owe the medical department no thanks for this when we get it. Dr. Cooper, Medical Director of the expedition, a sensible man, urged the necessity of a hospital; Surgeon-General Finley thought otherwise—"in this mild southern climate tents would do very well for men to have fevers in." It would suit my views of the fitness of things to have Surgeon-General Finley exposed in scanty apparel to a three days' Texas norther, by way of enlarging his views of southern climates. . . .

I was just laying the foundations of a log hospital for our men at Port Royal when we were ordered here, and, as I have no compunction about committing any crime short of high treason for a hospital, I had effected a neat little larceny of a lot of windows and sawn lumber which were to work in so sweetly. It was a sad reverse to abandon it!

One great trouble has been to keep our sick men, with their lowered vitality, warm in tents. There is a popular prejudice against cannon balls which I assure you is wholly unfounded. My experience is that there are few pleasanter things to have in the family than hot shot. It would raise the cockles of your heart some of these wretchedly cold nights, to walk between the two long rows of men in my large hospital-tent just after they have been put to bed, each with his cup of hot tea and his warm thirty-two pound shot at his feet, and to see and feel the radiant stack of cherry-red balls in the middle of the floor. This is troublesome and laborious to manage, however, and we greatly need some little sheet-iron stoves. I sent for some a good while since, which should be here shortly. Your inquiry about medicines is a sagacious one, and shows that you have not neglected your hospital-walking opportunities. My dear unsophisticated friend, permit me to indoctrinate you in a dainty device whereof the mind of undepartmental man hath not conceived. Know that there is one supply-table of medicines for hospital use and another for field use. Some very important, almost essential, medicines are not furnished for field service; when your patient needs them he is to go to the hospital. Very good—where is the hospital for us? Now, before we left Washington, with a perfectly clear notion of what was likely to befall us in the way of fevers, and out of the way of hospitals, I made a special requisition for some things not in the field supply table, such as serpentaria, and some of the salts of iron, and went in person to urge it through the purveyor's office. No use.

Ask any sensible, steady-going old doctor how he would feel with a lively fever *clientele* upon his hands, and no serpentaria or its equivalent.

I declare, it seemed to me like a special providence that in my pretty extensive "perusings" about these parts, I picked up, here and there, from rebel batteries and deserted houses, both serpentaria and many other needed medicines which have turned to the best account. . . .

If you should hear some day that some rebel Major-General had been rescued from impending death by hemorrhage by the application of *Liq. Ferri Persulphat* in the hands of the surgeon of the 7th C. V., you may lay it all to that little bottle which was not the least wonderful content of that wonderful basket sent to Annapolis. The Tennyson and Barber inspired me with emotions too various and complicated here to describe; the bologna cheered and invigorated; the Castile soothed and tranquilized my soul; but at the sight of the Liquor Ferri Persulphatis!—what shall I say, except to repeat the words of our own Royston—"a halloo of smothered shouts ran through every vein!" and whenever since, I have started upon any expedition giving promise of bullets, I have popped the bottle into my pocket, hoping to use it upon some damaged rebel.

Our tents, flimsy speculator's ware at best, are now in a most deplorable state. I am distressed to think of the possibility of a long rainy season overtaking us with no other shelter. . . .

This island upon which we are now encamped, though a lonely wilderness enough and several days farther from home than that which we have left, is on the whole more interesting, as it seems to offer "a right smart chance" of a fight. At any time we can, and often we do, get ourselves shelled from Pulaski by walking upon a certain stretch of the beach. This afternoon a rifled shell came squealing along in its odd way and plumped into the ground without exploding, a few yards from where my brother and I stood. The rascals seem to have defective fuses, and as yet they have hurt no one. By creeping along under bushes we get within Sharps' rifle range of the great grim fort, and look right into its embrasures. Don't mention that fact just now. . . . Every day, about the time Pulaski begins her afternoon shelling, "Old Tatnal" ["Old Tatnal" originated the expression, "Blood is thicker than water," when as flag officer of the U. S. squadron in '57, he came to the assistance of the English commander in Chinese waters. In 1861 he turned traitor to his flag.] runs down his fleet and gnashes his teeth at us from a safe distance, but doesn't come within range of our new battery or the gunboats. We hear cannon practice at Savannah occasionally, and from one quarter or another great guns growl every few hours. On the whole, a lively place. . . .

Our jolly German neighbors have begun upon their Christmas eve with such rolling choruses right behind my tent, that I must step out to see. . . .—I find that they have a row of Christmas trees through their camp, all a-twinkle with candles, and hung with "hard-tack" curiously cut into confectionery shapes, and with slices of salt pork and beef. Sedate, heavy-bearded Teutons are sedulously making these arrangements, retiring a few paces to observe through severely studious spectacles the effect of each new pendant.

We have all the foliage orthodox for Christmas here, including holly and mistletoe with berries of scarlet and white wax. The jungly unscarred forest of this island is superb. . . . The purple grey depths of the wood all flicker with scarlet grosbeaks like flames of fire, and quaint grey and brown northern birds flit in and out with the knowing air of travelled birds, and plan the nests they will build next summer, in spite of bombs and bayonets, in New England elms and alders. . . .

I owe something to Captain Howland for keeping up my spirits, for, sometimes when I think how utterly these wretched Carolinians throw their best and their all into their bad cause as if they believed in and loved it, and then see, with a sort of dismay, how few, comparatively, of our first-rate men have come personally to the fight with self-sacrifice and out of pure love of the cause, I think of Captain Howland and take comfort of him at least.

The Trent affair, to which the next letters refer, was the capture by Captain (afterwards Admiral) Wilkes, of Messrs. Mason and Slidell, rebel emissaries, making their way to England via Havana, on board an English vessel, the Trent, with their secretaries and families. They were afterwards surrendered by the U. S. Government without an apology to England.

A. H. W. to G. and E.

December.

My dear Girls:

The news of Mason and Slidell's release has arrived since you wrote. It was generally known here about 11 A. M. Saturday. I am quite satisfied with the release and with the grounds of it. In making the claim, England runs counter to all her preceding history in the matter of maritime laws. In holding the men, we should contradict our own previous course. Is it not far better to put England in the wrong, by yielding to her claim and so negatively securing her assent to what America has so long contended for—the rights of neutrals? As the *Washington Intelligencer* said, Mason and Slidell are for a day, Maritime Law is for all nations and all time. For my part, I think our position more assured, more dignified, more honorable to us since the surrender than ever before. Of course it will not satisfy *England.* Their peremptory demand, and Lord Lyons' laconic acceptance, are in contrast with Mr. Seward's wordy, sauve, argumentative letters. They have got in part what they asked—possession of the men; they have not got what they asked—an apology for the "insult to their flag" and the violation of rights of asylum. The *Manchester Guardian* even says plainly that "whether Mason and Slidell are returned or not, war preparation on the part of England must go on, the day being not far distant when the Southern Confederacy must be recognized, and England must be prepared to support her policy." Mr. Seward, too, you know, says very plainly that recognition of the South would instantly be the signal of war between ourselves and all the recognizing powers.

J. S. W. to G. and E.

DECEMBER '61.

Dear Girls:

"We are in the midst of stirring times," as the newspapers say—or rather, stirring times are in our midst, as well as all around us. I am prepared to be astonished at nothing, and to regard all events with stoicism bordering on a fiendish glee. New York was sizzling on Monday and Tuesday; shops, omnibuses and everything, full of "don't give 'em up" and "come on, Britain." Wm. Bond was here on Monday evening and said he never saw such a state of things down town. In their office they had drawn up a subscription paper among themselves for *one privateer, with two rifled guns; to sail from New London.*—"But I thought privateering was a sort of barbarism, Mr. Bond?"—"Oh, no. It is a *relic* of a *bygone* age; that is all."—Mr. B. brought invitations to the breakfast at the Astor House to Gov. Buckingham and the officers of the 11th Connecticut. Mother, Abby and Charley went yesterday and had a very nice time. . . . The young line officers munched and crunched and giggled and clapped with the keenest enjoyment. The remarks about England were the same in tone that most sensible people make—*"prove* us wrong and we will apologize like gentlemen; if otherwise then otherwise." . . . For my part, as to war with England; I do not see it where I stand. Infinite are the resources of diplomacy, and Mr. Seward and Mr. Lincoln are cool hands.—What a horribly satisfactory thing the burning of Charleston is—retribution from within;—Sumter avenged without our responsibility. There is something quite dramatic in the denouement. "As the captain of the Illinois came by, the whole sky was one red glare, with the outlines of Fort Sumter black against it." . . . A note from Sarah Woolsey says she will be here to-night. I shall take her round to some of the fairs and things of which there is no end. The Union Bazaar is the biggest. Stewart gives a shawl—$1,500—to be raffled for; Dr. Hughes a bronze statue, ditto; Miss King a doll bride with trousseau, trunks, French maid, etc., all complete, ditto; and so on.

They took in $3,000 the first night. We have just sent off a lot of old party dresses to the Tracys for doll finery, everything we could find; you may miss something familiar when you come back. . . . I observe that when *you* write two sheets you speak of it as a letter. When *I do* it becomes a note. "We had a lot of little things already collected for F. B. and shall send them on as a little Christmas box without waiting to hear. I am going to put "Spare Hours," by author of Rab, in the box, and the jolliest tin canister of bonbons "as ever you see." . . . Anna Rockwell read us a lot of interesting letters from Charles. He is "heading home" now; he belongs to the 7th; the 7th may have to turn out yet to garrison the forts. If there is war with England Robert says he shall enlist. . . .

Mother to G. and E.

MONDAY, DECEMBER 24, 1861.

My dear Girls:

Col. D. is a godsend! I was in despair at the thought of not getting some little Christmas box off so as to reach you to-morrow, when lo! he appeared, like an angel of mercy and offered to take anything we might have to send. So of course we gathered together our duds, which we had set aside as an impossibility as Christmas gifts, to take their chance in reaching you for New Year, and have just sent off the bonnet box filled with love and best wishes in all the chinks, mixed in with the sugar-plums and covering over everything, to make all acceptable to our noble-hearted girls, who are "extending their benevolence to all within their reach." . . . I have sent Joe a cake, which you must dress with its wreath and flag, for him to take down to camp. . . . We are going to give little May a Christmas tree and have a beauty now standing in the middle parlor ready to be decorated. It is a very large one, and will take the whole of a box of one hundred colored candles which I have been arranging in little colored tin candlesticks with sharp points which fasten on to the branches. We have also a number of small colored lanterns and a great variety of beautiful and cunning toys. This is to be my Christmas gift to the children

E's Journal:

Christmas Day we spent with J. again in camp, going round by Alexandria to pick up Chaplain Hopkins and take him with us. We had taken some goodies and little traps with us for the men in the hospitals in Alexandria and were glad to find the nice arrangements that had already been made by Madame M. She had got Col. Davies to detail some of the 16th men to bring her Christmas greens, and had dressed all the wards with festoons and garlands, little flags, mottoes, etc., besides are ranging for a grand Christmas dinner for her "boys."

The Mansion House Hospital too was resplendent with bright tissue papers and evergreens and Dr. Sheldon showed us with great pride his kitchen and store-room arrangements, which are excellent in every respect. Fifty roast turkeys were preparing for the Christmas feast, sixteen large loaf-cakes iced to perfection and decorated with the most approved filigree work, pies without number, cream puffs, cranberry sauce, puddings of all sorts, etc., etc.—altogether the most Christmas-like scene we have looked upon, and all arranged with the greatest order and cleanliness.

Among the little things we took out were Mother's and Jane's socks, which we gave to men likely to go back soon to their regiments. The only boy without mittens got Mrs. Smith's.

After our own camp dinner, at which the Colonel and the Doctor joined us, we sat round the last and best chimney yet built, and talked about old times five or six months ago, which now seem like so many years. J. says his Christmas Eve was dreary enough in his tent, and they all agreed that our coming was the only thing that prevented their Christmas Day from being so too.

A. H. W. to G. and E.

DECEMBER 26.

Dear Girls:

We had a great day yesterday. *Of course,* Mother and the girls and Charley broke through the rule we had prescribed for ourselves, not to give Christmas presents, and launched upon Jane and me wholly unprepared, a flood of pretty and useful things. . . . We dined at Mary's, and there Mother was made happy by a superb dish of moss, growing and trailing over, and set in a carved walnut table or stand which Mary brought from Germany. . . . Our children's "Christmas tree" went off very successfully. Little May came over early and did the honors as nicely as could be to the arriving guests, introducing them all to each other and providing amusement. There were the three little Howlands and their mamma, the Prentisses and theirs, Mally and Willy Smith and theirs, little Kernochan, little Parker boy, and Mary and Helen Skinner with the Rhinelander children. The tree was in the back parlor with the doors closed and windows darkened, and the effect was very pretty when the candles and the lanterns were all ready and the doors were thrown open, and the tree blazed out in its own light. Each child had half a dozen little things and was delighted, choosing, when left to him or herself, the most hideous Chinese toys only intended as decorations. Then there were ice cream and jelly, which the older people helped eat, and Mr. Prentiss came in, and the children gradually went away—and we subsided into quiet.

And so, the first year of the war closed with at least a happy time for the children.

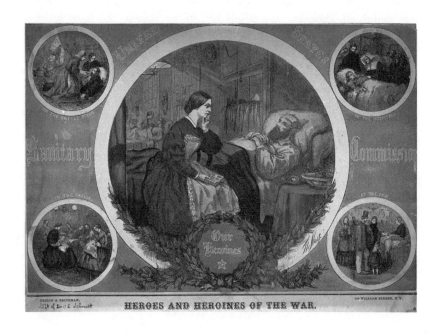

"Heroes and Heroines of the War" by Thomas Nast
Harper's Weekly, April 9, 1864

CHAPTER FIVE

From Camp

E's Journal.

JANUARY 1862.

Sunday evening James Gillette came up to our room to tell us his story. He is one of the two hundred and forty Union soldiers just released from Richmond prisons in exchange for an equal number of rebel prisoners from Fort Warren. He was with the 71st N. Y., a three months' regiment, and his time was out before the battle in which he was taken prisoner. These five months of prison life have turned him from a dapper little fellow into a sad-looking, care-worn, sick man. He and his fellows were in Prison No. 2, a tobacco factory, dirty and uncomfortable beyond description—170 men in a room 40 feet by 60. They immediately organized themselves, however, into a little military community under strict discipline.

A detail of men was made every day to police the place, and all *unnecessary* uncleanliness was punished by the court they instituted for the trial of offenders. They had plenty of water but no soap or towels. Their rations were about eleven ounces of bread daily and one ration of beef or pork, and the water in which this was boiled was served at night as soup—"Confederate swill" they called it. They had no clothing given or sent them except what came to the Massachusetts and Rhode Island men, and an occasional little bundle handed in secretly by some sympathizing citizen. . . . The principal suffering was from the ignorance and brutality of the prison guards, who treated them roughly and often shot at them. Several were killed in that way; and yet these same sentinels would let the prisoners stand guard in their places, and go off and get them whiskey; and when they themselves were drunk, our men would pass them and take an airing in the city. The sick suffered and still suffer for want of decent care and medicine. One building is given up to cases of gangrene—a sufficient commentary on the condition of things. As a rule the prisoners kept up their spirits well and used all sorts of means for entertaining themselves; a debating club, a court, menagerie exhibitions, carving in beef-bones, etc. I have a little ring cut from part of their rations. Some men, though, have grown simple, almost idiotic, from the confinement; some have gone insane; and some of good standing at home will now wrangle pitifully over a bit of cracker or meat. About one hundred of our men, he says, have already died in Richmond of sickness, besides those dying from their wounds.

Among these released Richmond prisoners were twenty-one men of the 27th N. Y., a regiment brigaded with our 16th.

E's Journal, January 11, '62, says:

Joe told us of the pretty reception they had given the returned Richmond prisoners of the 27th. It was a shockingly muddy day or the whole brigade would have marched down to meet them. As it was, the General and Staff and the 27th marched as far as the Brigade Hospital, where they met the poor fellows trudging up the hill, each with his little bundle. They gave them a grand greeting with band-playing and hand-shaking and then the procession was formed: first the band, then the prisoners at the head of the column, then the rest of the regiment, and the General and Staff bringing up the rear. As they marched through the different camps there was a perfect ovation, friends and strangers alike smothering them with hugs, cheering them, slapping them on the back and "old-fellowing" them. The regimental bands were *all* out in force and the camp of the 27th was dressed festively for the occasion, the procession entering it by an archway over which hung the words "Welcome, Comrades! Your wounds bleed afresh in our hearts." They were all more or less wounded but are now in pretty good condition and all are to have a furlough of thirty days.

J. S. W. to J. H.

SATURDAY EVENING, JANUARY, '62.

I received yesterday from Mr. Stephen Williams thirty dollars, on the part of Mr. Alexander Van Rensselaer, "for a soldiers' library." Stephen, good old soul, said, "Oh! I've got this commission; now won't you help me? *I* don't know about libraries; you can consult Howland," etc., etc. . . . It will buy about forty plain books for a hospital or regiment. Would the 16th or any regiment in the brigade like one? . . .

Lizzie Greene sent a box of flannel shirts to a Connecticut regiment lately, and put a dozen cigars and a paper of tobacco in a pocket in each—"true Christian philanthropy," William Bond says;—"send them something they ought not to have." . . . We have been trying to persuade Mother to go down to Washington with Hatty and Charley, and take a look at things, but she is not to be prevailed on, I am afraid. Charley's lame hand will prevent him from going for a while, but I think he and H. will go on while Carry is in Boston. Carry goes on Wednesday to Mrs. Huntington Wolcott's and afterwards to Miss Parsons', (lately engaged to a tall Captain Stackpole in a Massachusetts regiment now at Annapolis, expecting to go up the York river with Burnside's expedition). Abby saw Mrs. George Betts to-day, who says her husband (in Hawkins' Zouaves) expects to join the same expedition immediately. Transports are to take them at once from Hatteras to the rendezvous at Fortress Monroe. They have suffered severely at Hatteras; the mortality in George Betts' regiment has been very great. . . .

Malvina Williams says she hears G. and E. are known in Washington as the "Angels!" . . .

Mr. Prentiss came in just now for a little call, cheery and bright, asking for your photograph to put in a book he had given him for Christmas. So you can send him one. It's a good book to be in, Mr. Prentiss' good book. . . .

William Wheeler, who has been very ill with camp fever, writes home that he has received great kindness from Miss *Jane Woolsey,* meaning G., and "was delighted with her." I *begged* his friends not to mention it; it was but little I could do! But tell Georgy. . . .

Would you like three or four dozen more gloves for your men, lonely and cold sentinels, for instance? Spake the wurred. Mr. Gibson sends a lot of London papers all deep-edged with black for the Prince Consort (rest his soul) and their own sins (bad luck to them) I should hope. The "whirligig of time will no doubt bring in its revenges."

I had a vision of you to-day, as might be a year ago, sitting on the box seat of a sleigh, with a fur cap with ears, and, shall I say it, a roseate nose, visible when you turned around, skirrying over the crusty roads with the blue bloomy hills lifting, and the white fields rolling away, with the wonderful sparkling rime on everything and the heavy snow breaking down the fir-branches. The vision passed, as Cobb would say, and I tried to make another out of your present circumstances and didn't succeed at all, which proves that your normal state is not war-like.

Young people at home could not be kept on the nervous strain all the time, and an occasional festivity served as a breathing place, though the regular occupation of the family followed hard upon it.

M. W. H. to G. and E.

JANUARY.

Dear Girls:

I have only been waiting for the New Year to come fairly in and shut the door, before sitting down quietly to wish you all the traditionary compliments of the season. . . . We all spent Christmas day together as usual in London Terrace. . . . The prettiest feature of the season was Mother's Christmas tree for the children, who were in ecstasies of delight, and insisted even upon perching on the branches to get as near to it as possible. Night before last was devoted to a brilliant little party for the children Hatty and Carry,—a very handsome and successful affair. I did not go, my wardrobe presenting only the alternative of bogy or bride, either black silk or a too dressy white silk, but Robert and I feasted on some of the remains last night, on our roundabout way home from Mr. Everett's lecture at the Academy of Music, and had a near and satisfactory view of the spun sugar beehives and candy castles surmounted by nougat cherubim, which graced the occasion.

A. H. W. to G. and E.

8 BREVOORT PLACE, JANUARY 7.

My Dear Girls:

I have only time before mailing hour for a short letter, but must tell you how pleasantly Hatty's and Carry's little party went off last night. . . . Maillard sent up at eleven a very handsome little supper. . . . Bessie and Mr. Merchant came in the afternoon to dinner, which was hardly over and our dresses pitched on when the company came. Miss Tilly Dawson was the prettiest girl here, and Charley Johnson was made happy all the evening by an introduction to her. I think Zenie Smith [Arixene Southgate Smith, who married Charles after the war.] was the next prettiest. She came with two young friends staying with her, and Minnie Worthington brought the sweet young fellow she is engaged to; and there were the McCurdy girls and Helen Skinner, and Lilly Lusk and Tom Perkins, and Frank Bond, and Mr. Stagg, and the Cryders and McKeevers, and Bucks, etc., etc. Supper was so delayed that I don't know how we should have got on if it hadn't been for the man Charley had engaged to play the piano, and they all danced, and you can imagine that it was not a slow time when I tell you that I! figured in a Virginia reel. Some of Charley's chums were agreeable young fellows, young Marsh, the son of G. P. Marsh, and others. Charley himself had been on the bed all day with a sick headache, but brightened up when the evening was half over, and in spite of his lame hand, dressed himself quite elaborately with a roman scarf for a sling and came down. . . . Chaplain Wrage goes to Washington to-night and will take you a hundred hymn books in German, which I bought at the Methodist book concern. They will do to give away when you come across a German soldier in the hospitals. . . . Did you know that the Boston Tract Society has an agent and a depository in the Post Office Building, Washington?

. . . The box of books for Joe, directed to Alexandria, Virginia, went off yesterday. Cousin Sarah Coit has sent us her one pair of stockings, her giant pair, that she says she has knit, and knit, and knit on, and seemed to make no progress. . . . Young Crosby begged, the other night, for whatever mittens we or our friends might have this week, to make up 120 pairs for Frank's artillery company of regulars. Did you know how many of the Crosby family are in the army? You saw Frank Stevens, who has a Lieutenancy at last, in Pratt's Ulster Guard. Then Schuyler Crosby is in the Regular Artillery at Fort Pickens. Floyd Clarkson is Major in a cavalry regiment at York, Pa. Rutgers is somewhere else, etc., etc. Charles Wainwright is Captain of a battery in General Cooper's Division on the Lower Potomac.

Little May has been fairly launched in school life, and Mary says she doesn't know which has raised her in her own importance most—going to school or going to the dentist's, to have ever so many fillings put into her little back grinders.

. . . We have had intelligence of Aunt Adela Newton, who tried to go through the lines to protect her property in Charleston. Somebody told Amelia Bailey that they had seen a lady from Richmond, who had lately seen Mrs. Newton and daughters in that city. They had passed our lines at some point not stated, had travelled by private conveyance and reached Richmond after every hardship and difficulty, wandering at one time three days in the woods—lost. I want Mother to write a few lines to Aunt A. to go by Fort Monroe and flag of truce. It would get South in course of time if it was short and not treasonable. . . . Dr. Buck came in last night and re-vaccinated Hatty and me. He says if Georgy wants to be vaccinated he can send on a little quill with pure virus (Union virus, as Joe says) from here. There is much small-pox and considerable alarm about it here as well as in Washington.

Mother to G. and E.

8 BREVOORT PLACE, TUESDAY EVE.

My Dear Girls:

The question of my going on to Washington has been agitated for some time past, yet I do not seem to come to any decision about it; not but that I would dearly love to look upon your faces again, and enjoy ever so much being with you, and seeing for myself all your goings and doings. Independent of all this, however, I confess I have no desire to visit Washington, and unless I could make myself useful there, and in every way a comfort to you, I think I am more in my place at home. Your uncle Edward was here this morning, and threw cold water on the movement, said it would be madness to run any such risk, as Washington was full of small-pox and typhoid fever. Now I write this evening to ask you what you think of our going on at present; whether there is really so much sickness as to cause any alarm. Do you want us? will it be a comfort to you to have a little visit from me? I do not ask these questions because I have any fears myself, but I am not willing, after your uncle's remarks this morning, to run any risk in Charley's or Hatty's going. I feel now that it will all rest upon what you say about it. . . . The report here this morning said twenty-five hundred cases of small-pox in Washington! This evening it has come down to eighty. . . . My eyes failing last night, I left my scrawl to finish to you this morning. We have had our breakfast, cold turkey (not boned), hot biscuits, and fish-balls, and the girls are gathered round the front parlor fire with the newspapers, reading items, and discussing the times; Charley is directing Elizabeth about his cushions for the chair he has carved and made, and I am scribbling this in the dining-room, feeling an occasional pang when I look up and see a horrid stranger, John by name, in the pantry, instead of the old faithful servant, William. You don't know how much I miss him in a thousand little things. This fellow is a perfect snail, never gets through with anything, and of course half is not done at all;—an Irish drone and tobacco chewer.

Poor William's occasional spree was really preferable. . . . I have nothing to say to begin another sheet with, but to send you my love and a Mother's blessing. Give Joe his share in both.

Yours lovingly.

Small pox was more or less prevalent about Washington at this time, and one of the sad cases, entirely characteristic of war, was that of G. R., a private in the 19th Indiana, cared for earlier by G. and E. in the Patent Office Hospital. He went safely through camp fever, measles and rheumatism, to die at last of small-pox in a lonely camp hospital in the outskirts of Washington, among strangers.

C. C. W. to G. and E.

BOSTON, JANUARY 13TH.

Dear Girls:

I dare say you will expect a letter from me while I am in Boston. . . . I find it exactly as I left it three years ago, only warmer. It used to be the coldest place imaginable, but the heated term seems to be on, so there is no skating and no talk of it. The Sanitary Commission occupies all the ladies, and in the spare time they work for the contrabands. Mrs. Huntington Wolcott is entirely devoted to it. She keeps thirty poor women in sewing and runs I don't know how many machines. Mattie Parsons, too, has come out in an entirely new character and fairly slaves for the cause, besides taking care of two families of volunteers in Mr. Stackpole's regiment, left destitute. They say she recruited a fourth of his company and knows every man in it. They are all devoted to the "Captain's lady," and swear to bring him safely home to her. . . . I went out to Cambridge on Saturday to review the scenes of my youth—three years ago—at the Prof. Agassiz' School. Alas! the former familiar faces that were wont to flatten their noses against the law school windows no longer beam upon my path; they are married and gone, and I am sorry to say the best are in the rebel army. The undergraduates look very small and the college grounds don't seem as classic as of yore.

E. to J. H.

WASHINGTON, '62.

We have made an engagement with Rev. Mr. Kennard, a young Baptist clergyman here, to visit the jail with him, where the poor contrabands are imprisoned on suspicion of being runaway slaves, or for debt. We have the Marshal's permit, secured through a friend. . . . We made our visit; it is a wretched place, but the contrabands are better off than the convicts, though many of the poor creatures are almost naked. There are twenty men and boys and a few women, all runaway slaves. We gave them socks, shirts, drawers, etc. and shall go again. The women were very glad to get the sewing we had arranged for them.

Mrs. Thomas Gibbons, mentioned in the following letters, was one of the distinguished Hopper family of "Friends"—strong abolitionists and managers of what was called the "underground railroad." Through their efforts many wretched hunted colored people were landed safely in Canada. Mrs. Gibbons was busy in the war from the beginning, and all her life long, with serene determination, waged her own war against evil wherever she encountered it.

From A. H. W.

J. C. called here yesterday bringing Mrs. Thomas Gibbons to see us. She told me much that was interesting, and disgusting too, about her experience at Fall's Church; the brutality of the regimental surgeon, etc. She and her daughter go on again the 24th of this month, and unless they hear something to the contrary will ill go to the same regiment, the 23d New York Volunteers. She had thought of writing to Georgy; wished I would do so, and see if she could learn from any of the assistant-surgeons, at the office, from the Commission, or from the army officers, where she would be most needed. They want to go where people are least liable to help, and where there is most to do. We are to have some towels, little books, etc., ready for her. . . . Mrs. Gibbons said that Horace Greeley was greatly distressed at the course of the *Tribune;* he was sick at *her house* three weeks with brain fever, this autumn, the result of disappointment, etc., etc., in the paper.

E. W. H. to J. H. in Camp.

JANUARY, '62.

To-day we are going out to look up some nurses for Will Winthrop's regiment, and then to the Senate. I forgot to tell you a pretty story we heard the other day from Mrs. Gibbons, our Quaker lady friend. She is a very sweet, kind old lady, and she and her daughter have been out at Fall's Church getting the hospital there into working order, and showing them how to nurse and cook for the sick, and, thanks to them, one poor fellow who was dying was nursed back into the right road and is now nearly well enough to go home with his father, who, meantime, had been sent for. He, a plain well-to-do farmer from Western New York, was so overcome with gratitude to Mrs. G. and her daughter, that he entreated the young girl to go home with him and be his daughter!—"He would do all in the world for her and she should be an equal sharer with his son in the farm of 300 acres," and it was said (Mrs. Gibbons told us) in the most delicate, genuine way, without any allusion to the young Lieutenant and probably without the least idea of "making a match." Of course the young girl declined, and then he went to the mother to ask if she hadn't other daughters like herself for whom he could do something to show his gratitude. Isn't it like some old ballad? . . .

The management of the jail was before the Senate yesterday and we heard the discussion, and left just before the bill was passed, requiring the release of all persons not committed for crime, which means, principally, the contrabands. Mr. Grimes, the chairman of the Committee on District affairs, abused Marshal Lamon roundly for his bad management and his insolent exclusion of congressmen from one of the institutions which it is their duty to supervise. G. sent Senator Dixon a note asking if, while the subject is before Congress, something can't be done about separating children committed for petty crimes, from hardened criminals. . . . There ought to be a reformatory school attached to every jail.

E. to J. H.

January 28.

My only letter by the mail last night was from Major Crane, about some of the patients of his Division who came down the Potomac in a wretched condition on a canal boat some time ago. He is going to do his best to find out who is responsible and prefer charges, and he wants us to help. Don't mention this, as we shall do it as quietly as possible, but also as thoroughly. . . . We hear every now and then of some new abuse among the surgeons, regular and volunteer,—for instance: Mr. Hopkins told us of one poor fellow of a Vermont regiment who was brought to the hospital in Alexandria with typhoid fever, having *both feet frozen* and one of them eaten by rats! It is too horrible to think of, but I tell you that you may understand why we feel so strongly on the subject. Good old Dixie hearing of the story went at once to McClellan and told him, and he sent an officer to find out all the facts and bring the responsible person to justice. . . .

The Miss Schuylers went down with us to Alexandria to-day and we showed them through the Hospitals, much to the delight of the nurses.

We have gone into the pension business too! and are going over to Mr. Wrage's camp to arrange about getting the necessary papers for a poor woman who is applying for a pension and wrote to G. about it. We knew her and her husband here in one of the hospitals and she has the most implicit faith in G's power and influence.

The end of January Mother and Hatty went on to Washington under Charley's escort for "two or three weeks," which lengthened out into three months with G. and E., and proved a great delight to all.

E. writes January 29, '62:

Mother, Hatty and Charley arrived last night in the middle of the storm and mud. Mother is now writing at the table with me, while H. is gazing admiringly at a group of Irish Brigadiers at the door. Charley is out somewhere, and is to meet the rest of us in the Senate Chamber at noon. We are cosily settled and having a very nice time. The roads are almost impassable owing to melting snow and frost and incessant rain. J.'s last ride back to camp the other day was very hard. He and the General floundered about in mud "like unfathomable chewed molasses candy," and stumbled against the stumps till darkness overtook them before they reached camp. Reports are brought in of private carriages abandoned along the road, and one—Mrs. Judge Little's—was fairly dragged in two by a government team which tried to haul it out of a hole. J. says we must not think of coming out to camp.

E. W. H. to J. H.

JANUARY 30TH.

The only thing of interest I have to tell you is of a very nice call we had last evening from: General Williams (your friend Seth). He got Miss Wilkes to bring him round and introduce him, and told us he had long wanted to call on us and offer his services. He hoped we would call on him for anything he could do for us, and said if I would send my letters to you up to Army Headquarters he would send them out at once by the orderly who comes in every day. So I will begin to-day by sending this one. They say that General Williams is as good as gold, and as modest as he is good. Miss Wilkes, who came with him, asked us all to spend Friday evening with them to meet a small party of Washington people and a few strangers. "Mrs. McClellan would be there and they hoped to see the General too," and I suppose the Franklins and Porters, and our friend General Williams and other "officers of note." Don't you want to come in? We shall go, as it will be a nice chance for Mother and Hatty to see the notabilities and will be pleasant for all. . . . How dismal it is again and how wretched the camp must be!

Our pleasant acquaintance with General Williams—the Adjutant-General of the Army of the Potomac throughout the war—lasted all his life. A year later than this first call Charley was assigned to duty on his staff as his personal aide, at Headquarters of the Army. General Williams held a position of immense responsibility through all the fearful years of the war, and died insane, at its close.

E's Journal.

FEBRUARY 1.

We all went to the Wilkes's Friday evening—a very pleasant little party. General McClellan could not come, but there were five other generals, FitzJohn Porter, Stoneman, Barry and Butterfield; also Commodore Shubrick, Commodore Wilkes, Judge Loring and family, the Prussian minister and family, and a good many lesser lights. General Seth Williams was the most modest man in the room, in plain skimpy citizen's clothes.

February 4th. Mother and all of us went down to Alexandria to visit the hospitals,—Charley provided with camp bed, blankets, etc. to go out and make Joe a visit. Joe met us in Alexandria with the General, and a spare horse for Charley. . . . Saturday afternoon Joe came in from camp riding "Lady Jane," but, poor creature, she took cold again on the boat, was dangerously ill all Sunday and died early Monday morning, kneeling on her fore-knees "as though saying her prayers," George Carr said. He and J. and the doctor were with her all Sunday, but could not save her. Joe had brought her from her comfortable stable at home to carry him through the war.

One of the alleviations of the situation at the Ebbitt House just at this time was the coming in now and then of the family cousin William Winthrop, from his camp near Washington, or an occasional jolly, not to say audacious, note from him.

William Winthrop to G.

HEADQUARTERS, BERDAN'S U.S. SHARPSHOOTERS, FEBRUARY. *Dear Mrs. Brigadier:*

For why should we not say so, when we know it will be so? Why this timidity of expression in time of war? . . . What is age, time, aeons, space, blood, prejudice, quite-another-arrangement-made-by-your-mother, or any other triviality? . . .

I LOVE wedding cake. . . .

P. S. THE NIGHT CAPS. Doctor Snelling had just come up from the hospital tent, after making his evening rounds, anxious and disturbed because of the want of *just such!* On account of the gale, the fires couldn't be well kept up; but the patients could keep warm in bed *as to bodies. Heads,* however, were unprotected; and the Doctor had instructed the nurses to capitate the men with their stockings, in want of night caps. Just then I entered the tent with your caps. All was gladness. You quieted minds, warmed heads, perhaps saved lives! I say there is a singular patness, appositeness in your composition. . . . Even the woman to whom my affections are irrevocably pledged might learn a thing or two from you. What more can I say?

This from a tent and with coldest fingers. I don't repine. Yesterday half the tents were blown down, but the cherub left mine standing. . . . Having immediate use for blankets for sick men, I send down *Burr* of my Company for the three or four which you said last evening I could have. Our surgeon says that the colored women nurses will be welcome. You say you will "send them out." If you can't, please inform bearer to that effect. When they come let them report to Dr. Marshall, Surgeon of the 1st Regiment Sharpshooters. Trusting you are blithe, I am, etc.

P. S. I address the envelope to you by your maiden name.

E. to J. H.

FEBRUARY 13.

I have nothing more than the usual "all right" to tell you, but you must always have that. We ought to congratulate each other on the good news from Roanoke Island and Tennessee, which quite thrilled us all yesterday. We were out at Will Winthrop's camp when the boys cried the "Star" and the victory, and we heard the particulars first from Mrs. Captain Rodgers, who came here directly from Mrs. General McClellan's. Mrs. McClellan described to her, her husband's delight when the news came. He flung his arms over his head, and, fairly radiant with glee, pronounced himself the happiest man in Washington, "and the General, you know," his wife says, "is such a quiet man usually. I have seldom seen him more excited." . . .

We managed to get out to Will Winthrop's camp yesterday without an upset, but (so Mother thought) at the peril of our lives! What will she say to the Virginia roads on the way to your *camp?* She is overwhelmed with pity for the poor men and officers. When we left, Will tramped some distance through the mud to show us a better way out, and we were immensely entertained at his manifesting his tongue in his cheek (behind Mother's back) when he found the road worse than he thought, remarking, "Why! this is quite a godsend. I had no idea of finding such a good highway."

. . . This morning George Carr has been out on horseback to take Will some cake and candy from Mother, to make up for a well meant but bad cake we took him when we went ourselves. . .

We hear New York is overflowing with cheers and jubilees for the victories, and in Philadelphia the celebration was the best of all, for they took steps at once to raise a fund for the orphans of the soldiers killed in that battle and to found a "Soldiers' Home" for all maimed and helpless volunteers when the war is over.

E. W. H. to J. H.

FEBRUARY 18TH.

We have just packed and despatched Charley for Baltimore and Fortress Monroe, and are now writing notes of introduction for Mr. Vincent Colyer, who is to join him at the Fortress, and if possible take him with him to Roanoke and Port Royal. I have given him a note to Mr. Withers, and G. will write one to Dr. Bacon, and I only wish we had some jolly little things to slip into the envelopes too. Mr. Colyer is to take down a quantity of stores for the hospitals. Charley also has a large trunk full. We hear from private sources that the sick of the Burnside expedition have suffered terribly for actual necessities—water to wash with, and food to eat, and this six weeks after the expedition had started!

Charley was at the War Department yesterday just after the news came of Grant's success at Fort Donelson and Mr. McClure described McClellan as coming in "pale with excitement" to rejoice over the victory a moment with Stanton before going to work again.

February 21. We went yesterday to the Navy Yard and were very much interested in all we saw. They make 15,000 Enfield rifle and musket balls in every twelve hours, or 30,000 while (as now) they work day and night! They also turn out 800 rifled and other cannon balls a day, and three rifled brass cannons a week, besides the ordinary work of a ship-yard and naval station. Our usual luck attended us, for we fell in, by mere chance, with a young naval officer whom Hatty had met in Rome, and he took us about and, best of all, showed us all the *rebel flags* which are to be presented to Congress, so we had an opportunity, which probably no other

outsiders have had, of trampling them privately under foot. The flags of
Fort Donelson and Fort Henry were there—fresh and new and without
the trace of a bullet hole—those taken from Roanoke and Hatteras, and
the famous *palmetto* one which was replaced by the Stars and Stripes at
Hilton Head. There was also a pretty little company flag made of choice
silk and embroidered by ladies' hands.

Later. . . . News from Charley. "Inside of Hatteras inlet, just going up
to Roanoke Island." The voyage had been rough and wretched but he was
well and happy.

We had no letters of interest yesterday except one from Carry, which
Mother enclosed to Charley at Roanoke Island. She gave a very funny
account of a wretched swollen face she has had. The Doctor recommended
a leech, so they sent for one, but were completely at a loss to tell its head
from its tail, and finally with many pokes from a hairpin (a new use) they
wriggled it into the tube and trusted to Providence to turn it right end up!
During the process, however, she was foolish enough to faint dead away,
and no sooner had she revived than Miss Parsons did the same. And Carry
wanted to go as army nurse!

E's Journal.

WEDNESDAY, FEBRUARY 26.

Encouraged by several windy days, which were likely to dry the roads,
we ventured out to J's camp for the first time since early in January, to
show it to Mother and Hatty. The roads were unexpectedly good, the only
really bad places being near the camp. J. had dined, but gave us a nice and
hearty after-lunch, and Mother enjoyed the experience very much. While
we were there the general order arrived placing the army in readiness to
march at very short notice. Four wagons are allowed to each regiment, and
quartermasters are to see that they are not heavily loaded: the men to carry
knapsacks and blankets and the little shelter-tents large enough for three
or four men to creep under. The order cast a gloom over our little visit, but
the effect on the troops was very different. As we sat in J's tent we could
hear the cheers ringing through the camps as the order was read—three
times three and a tiger.

Just before this J. H. had mailed a little box of trailing arbutus "from camp" to J. S. W. and this acknowledgment came back.

Arbutus from Camp, near Alexandria
Sent by Capt. J. H., 1862.

"Thank God for Spring!" I said;
While no one watches, through the gloomy hours
She walks the weary earth with noiseless tread
And fills the graves with flowers.

And, holding in my hand
My Soldier's message, in its leaves I read
Through winter-sorrows of a weeping land
A dawn of Spring indeed!

Dull, sodden leaves o'er-strown,
Then, tears of rain, and then, these flowers for me.
The wild war horses tread the blossoms down
And set the sweetness free.

So get me flowers again
Dear Soldier;—not alone of Hope and Spring,
Flowers of full Summer, through the crimson rain
And battle thunder of the stormy plain,
Close on their blossoming!

Red roses, flushed and bold,
Red victor-roses,—sea-blue bells wide blown
That ring for joy the river-edges down,
And white Peace-lilies with the spike of gold
That clasp the perfect crown.

           J. S. W.

A. H. W. to G. and E.

MARCH.

Dear Girls:

May is busy concocting things for a fair she and Bertha hold to-day, for the benefit of our BRAVE VOLUNTEERS. Papa and mamma and aunties are to buy the things, and May is to spend the money in little books, the first day she is well enough to come over. Robert asked me to say that he sent a box of books to Eliza's address, Ebbitt House, for some hospital library. They were chiefly English reviews, which were too good reading to give to any of the recruiting camps here, and he thought in a general hospital there would always be *somebody* who could appreciate them. I was glad to get Charley's second letter and wish he could hear from us.

Perhaps these winds will dry the roads and enable you to go comfortably at least to Joe's camp. It is too bad to have Mother leave Washington just as March winds prepare the way for McClellan's advance. I am ready, mind you, Georgy, to wait for McClellan just as long as he desires. Only I think unless he *threatens* the enemy in some way, and thus keeps them cooped up, he may wake up some morning and find them all flown southward and he left, stuck in the mud. I don't see why he couldn't have done on the Potomac last December what Halleck has just done on the Tennessee.

I shall take great interest in the working of the educational and industrial movements among the blacks at Port Royal. A large party of teachers, with supplies of various kinds, seeds and sewing machines, etc., went out in the Atlantic. Some of the lady teachers are known to us through friends, and though the whole arrangement has been matured very rapidly, it seems to be under judicious oversight. Jane has a venture in it. She went into the office to collect information and to offer help, and was levied on for eight neat bed-spreads, which she purchased at Paton's. We can imagine the lady teachers reposing on their camp cots, in those distant islands, under Jane's quilts. . . .

I wish I could feel that the end of the war will see, (as Prof. Hitchcock said on Sunday), in all this wide country "not a master, not a slave, only all Christ's Freemen."

Jane and I get along famously, as independent as two old maids. We are not even troubled with evening callers, but sit each in our armchair with a foot-stool, a cup o' tea and a newspaper, and shall be very much "put out of the way" if Mother comes home from Washington. We write begging her not to think of it again. Her duty and pleasure are both to be with you, and I don't want her to have a moment's uneasiness about the thought of separation, even if she stays months.

J. S. W. to G.

MARCH 10, '62.

Theodore Bronson has just called to say that he saw Mr. Woolsey (Charley) in Baltimore last night all well. He saw his name in the papers as bearer of despatches and wondered whether he really had any, or if it was a sort of passport. I am glad if he has been able to do any service, but I should not like him to go into the army.

E. to J. H.

MARCH 12, '62.

Charley has come back safe and sound via Baltimore from Roanoke, with rebel bowie knives, "shin-plasters," etc. He is ready to keep with us or go South when we go. He brought up parcels and letters from General Burnside for friends in New York, and took them on personally at once.

Mother, or "Moremamma" as all the grandchildren called her, and Hatty, were still with G. and E. in Washington, having a most interesting inner view of the city's daily war life. Mother kept up with the advance of the war in all parts of the country, and her little journal of events, as she wrote it from day to day, is kept among the family papers as a precious possession.

Georgeanna Woolsey, 1862
Woolsey Papers, Ferriday Archives

CHAPTER SIX

The Army Advances

SATURDAY, MARCH 8TH.

The item this morning is that Colonel Davies was confirmed yesterday by the Senate as Brigadier General, so J. is now Colonel of the 16th by unanimous choice of the officers, and will take command at once.

Mr. Robert S. Hone to E. W. H.

NEW YORK, MARCH, 1862.

Dear Mrs. Howland:

Mr. Russell has just been in my office and wishes me to say that he has just left Governor Morgan, who informed him that he had to-day signed Joe's commission as Colonel of the 16th Regiment, and that he was delighted to hear the very high terms in which the Governor spoke of Joe. With congratulations, I am, etc.

He writes by the orderly that he has been with General Slocum to see the regiment pitch their new tents in the valley of Four Mile Run.

March 9. A day of great excitement, for beside the news of the evacuation of Leesburg and the capture of Cockpit Point battery, we have the great naval fight at Fortress Monroe.

The great demon ship, the Merrimac, came down from Norfolk toward Newport News and attacked our ships Congress and Cumberland, destroying both. She split the latter in two and sank her, and burned the Congress to the water's edge. The Minnesota meantime was aground and perfectly useless, as well as several others of our vessels.

This ended the first day's fight—a victory for the rebels and a terrible disaster for us; but early this Sunday morning, when the Merrimac came out again, expecting to finish her little affair by defeating the Minnesota and then running out to sea, she found the new Ericsson iron-plated steamer, the "Monitor," all ready to receive her. From 8 A. M. till noon the two fought hand to hand, their sides touching, and then the Merrimac was towed off towards Norfolk, supposed to be in a sinking condition, while the "Monitor" was unhurt. The submarine cable from Fortress Monroe was laid just in time to bring the news. The cable was finished at 4 P. M. and the news flashed over it at 7.

G's Journal.

MARCH 10.

All strange rumors come on Sunday. Josepha Crosby, Hatty and I went down to spend the afternoon at the Patent Office Hospital. During the week the camps had been emptied of convalescents, sent north to recover, and their places in the hospitals were occupied by others. The Patent Office is full again; four rows of beds and very sick men in them. I stooped down between two 8th New York Cavalry men in their little cots while they told me that their regiment had moved off silently on Saturday night. Coming away, I hurried up to Mrs. Captain Rodgers' house and heard the story of the Merrimac fight. The first intimation they had of it was in church on Sunday morning, when, during service, a messenger came in and was seen to whisper something to General Meigs, who immediately left the church. A little while later General Totten was summoned, and then a Commodore somebody, by which time the congregation was in a state of suppressed excitement miserable to bear. Dr. Pine preached an unusually long sermon, and finally the people rushed out and heard the bad news.

While I was talking at the door with Mrs. Rodgers a four-horse ambulance was standing at McClellan's door, and we sat down on the steps intending to see who got into it, and which way it went, a determination shared by plenty of other people on their way from church. At last a servant brought blankets, and McClellan and Franklin got in and started on their way over the Potomac; and then I came home, and presently Colonel McClure came in and told us that Heintzelmann, with whom he had been sitting an hour, expects to move in the morning and that Manassas was reported evacuated. Contrabands brought word of it to

Kearney's quarters; he made an armed reconnaissance and discovered the truth; word was sent to McClellan, and his ride on Sunday P. M. was in consequence. Mrs. Rodgers came in as we were in our petticoats, getting ready for bed, and confirmed it all.

E's Journal.

We went to bed in a state of great excitement and were awakened early Monday morning by a knock from George and a note from Joe saying it was all true. He wrote at 2 A. M., having been up all night. They had just received their marching orders—the brigade to leave at 5 A. M., the rest of the corps at 9. I sent George over at once with a note to J., and he found him on horseback just starting, the regiments formed and ready, and the General and staff in their saddles, all off for Fairfax Court House, which they reached, J. writes me, at 5 P. M., all in good spirits, having borne the march well. The rebs have abandoned both Centreville and Manassas falling back, the *"Star"* says, as far as the Rapidan and Gordonsville—whether by panic or by a preconcerted plan, is unknown.

J. writes the climate at Fairfax C. H. is lovely and the air dry, pure and very sweet, but the country is utterly desolate, houses burnt or pulled to pieces, fences gone, and the inhabitants, tents, except a few miserable negroes, fled.

G's Journal.

MARCH 11.

So the great move was made, the thing we had been looking forward to for so many months. The entire army was in motion, troops on the other side the river advancing, troops on this side taking their place. All day Monday and far into the night regiments marched over the bridges into Virginia,—50,000 over the Long bridge, they say, and to-day we drove up to the Chain bridge, and they told us 15,000 crossed there yesterday. We walked down towards the Long bridge to-day; crowds of people were collected on 14th street to see the move. As we crossed the canal, mother, Charley and I, swinging along with the rest, three large army wagons brought up the rear, marked T. E., carrying the telegraphic apparatus for the Engineers, and the wires must have been laid last night, for this morning General Williams had the announcement from McClellan (who slept at Fairfax Court House), that our troops are in possession at Manassas.

G's Journal.

MARCH 12.

The most extraordinary movements are taking place. While I write the 85th Pennsylvania is scattered about at rest on 14th street, having just marched back from the other side of the river. The 14th New York Cavalry, dismounted and serving as infantry, marched up before them; wagons filled with baggage, blankets, canteens, etc., have followed them. It is reported now that all the regiments are ordered *back again,* and Edward Walker tells us that the roads on the other side of the river are all lined with them returning

MARCH 13.

While we were cooking some arrowroot in our parlor for a Vermont private, sick in this hotel, Joe came in, back from Fairfax for a ride. The officers had been all over the old battlefield at Bull Run, McDowell crying, and all of them serious enough. The rebel works at Centreville, Joe says, are splendid, as formidable as any of ours about Washington. Their winter quarters were capital log houses, enough to accommodate 100,000 men. The burial ground was near at hand, and not far away a field of hundreds of dead horses. The works at Manassas were very slight, mounted in the most conspicuous places with logs of wood painted black. The rebels had been evacuating for some time, but, at the last, left in a sort of panic, leaving dead bodies lying beside coffins, and quantities of food, clothing and baggage of all kinds, some of it fired.

E's Journal.

MARCH 14.

One of General Franklin's aids has been in to say that his Division is now marching into Alexandria and is to *embark* on Saturday or Sunday, down the Potomac. . . . We went down to Alexandria and took lodgings at Mrs. Dyson's, on Water street, for over Sunday, and two more wretched or longer days I never passed. Through a drenching storm McDowell's corps was marched back from Centreville, 35 miles, and arrived at dusk, cold, hungry, wet to the skin, to find no transports ready and no provision made for their shelter or comfort. The city was filled with the wretched men, many crowded into the market stalls and empty churches, others finding shelter in lofts or under sheds and porches, and some, we know, sleeping in the open streets. In the market they had large fires, but with soaking knapsacks, no dry clothing to put on. In one place, the loft of a foundry, where Chaplain Hopkins found shelter for one company, the steam which rushed out as he opened the door was as that of a laundry on washing day. The poor fellows suffered from hunger as well as cold and fatigue, for on Sunday all the stores were closed. Whiskey could be had, which Moritz and G. and H. distributed among tired and wet volunteers on cellar doors. Some of them actually begged for bread or offered to sell their rings and trinkets for food.

It was a wretched and heart-sickening day and shook our confidence in McClellan or McDowell, or whoever the responsible person may be. We sent Moritz up to Washington for a half barrel of socks Aunt E. had just sent on and took them to the churches where the soldiers were quartered, and distributed them among the eager and grateful men. The men were lying on the benches and floors, and in the baptistry of the "Beulah Particular Baptist" and the Presbyterian secesh churches, and we stumbled about, holding the end of a candle for light, distributing socks. All ours were soon gone, and Chaplain Hopkins went back to the hospital, and telling the steward to *protest*, so that *he* might be shielded from blame, deliberately took ten dozen pairs from the store closet and distributed them. The two long useless marches with nothing accomplished, no shelter and no food, have shaken the unbounded faith in McClellan. Congress has been debating a bill displacing him; the *Star* says it was withdrawn to-day. *Our* soldier, Joe, and the 16th, were not in that wretched plight but were kept in bivouac out of the town. Joe took final command of the regiment that Sunday morning.

E's Journal.

MARCH 21.

A damp, drizzly day, but I wanted to see Joe in camp once more, and we went down to Alexandria, where Mother and Hatty distributed a lot of sweet flowers to the poor fingerless, one-armed and broken-legged fellows in the hospital, while I went on.

Joe has only had command of the regiment these few days and I found him extremely busy reorganizing and getting it into condition for the advance. Each man has been thoroughly inspected and all deficiencies in clothing, etc., are being filled. He keeps the officers busy, has an informal class of instruction for some of them, and has been issuing orders for arrangements on the transports, precautions against fire, etc. I only stayed a very little while. On our return boat from Alexandria we had a chance to see *eleven* of the transports start down the river crowded with troops, the men cheering and tossing their hats. It was a fine and striking sight as the boats, densely packed with volunteers, moved out from the docks, the sun lighting up the sails and colors of the schooners and steamboats, the signal flags nodding and bobbing, and the bands playing lively tunes, while the crowds on shore cheered in response.

We met the Berdan sharpshooters marching down to embark, and shook hands with Will Winthrop and Capt. Hastings. As we drove into town, McClellan (looking old and care-worn) and Franklin passed us, going out to the army.

G's Journal.

MARCH 20.

We have been getting some stores to-day for Will Winthrop. They are at last delighted by the order to join Heintzelman. Twenty to thirty thousand men have gone in the transports already. Will's black mess-boy came in to us and took out a basket with enough for the voyage. Have been up to see Charles Bradford, son of Captain Woolsey Hopkins' sister, at Columbian Hospital, and have sent him jelly, oysters, etc. Nice young fellow and pleased to see us.

From Mother's Journal.

SATURDAY, MARCH 29.

To camp again. Snow-storm. Stayed at Mrs. Bright's cottage Saturday night and drove up to camp on Sunday. Service in hospital tent, Dr. Miller, of the 16th, and Dr. Adams, of the 5th Maine, officiating. Communion—about thirty soldiers and several officers partaking. Heavy and continual thunder, with everything outside covered with snow—a singular combination of summer and winter, and rendering this interesting occasion still more strange and impressive. Stopped Sunday night again at the Brights', a clean and comfortable cottage at the head of Cameron Lane. All around us were the tents *d'abri* and other tents, and hundreds of men without any tents at all, bivouacking on the hills and in the fields and swamps everywhere; one cavalry regiment had arrived and their tents were pitched while we were out at the 16th. The camp fires at night were a new feature to me, and strangely did they loom up in the darkness, bringing to view groups of soldiers gathered round them;—hundreds of these fires in all directions.

E. W. H. to Chaplain Hopkins.

WASHINGTON, D. C., APRIL 1ST, 1862.

Dear Mr. Hopkins:

I send some *Independents* with the "Rainy day" in them. We mentioned that you liked the verses, and Abby sent these on for you to distribute among your patients.

We spent last Sunday near Alexandria glad to be storm-stayed on many accounts, one of which was the opportunity it gave us of going to service in the 16th, the first communion service since Mr. Howland took command. It was pleasant to see the little "church" assemble in a hospital tent in a Virginia field.

Chaplains Hopkins to E.

ALEXANDRIA HOSPITAL, APRIL 5TH.

My Dear Mrs. Howland:

Yesterday was one of the brightest, pleasantest days I have known for a long time. The wards were more inviting, and the men more cordial than usual. All day I seemed to be in the right place at the right time, and by a glad intuition, to discover the avenues which were unfortified and the doors which were unbarred. I have told you this because I am fully convinced that it was owing wholly to the good start that you gave me by that early morning visit. By some skillful adjustment, which I failed to notice at the time, you left me in tune. . . .

Please thank your sister Abby for the bundle of *Independents*. They were very welcome and I gave them away, each with the charge: "Be sure and read the Rainy Day in Camp." Did I tell you that I read it after each of my services last Sabbath? and I think that it did more good than all that went before it. The men listened in perfect quiet. I feel sure that, if I could have looked up myself, I should have seen tears in the eyes of more than one who had been "skulking in the rear."

Mary had written a number of verses for the soldiers, and they had been printed as leaflets, each one floated over by the flag in red and blue, and distributed widely among the enlisted men. The first of these was:

A Rainy Day in Camp.

It's a cheerless, lonesome evening
When the soaking, sodden ground
Will not echo to the footfall
Of the sentinel's dull round.

God's blue star-spangled banner
To-night is not unfurled
Surely *He* has not deserted
This weary, warring world.

I peer into the darkness,
And the crowding fancies come:
The night wind, blowing northward
Carries all my heart toward home.

For I 'listed in this army
Not exactly to my mind;
But my country called for helpers
And I couldn't stay behind.

So, I've had a sight of drilling,
And have roughed it many ways,
And death has nearly had me,—
Yet I think the service pays.

It's a blessed sort of feeling—
Whether you live or die—
You helped your country in her need
And fought right loyally.

But I can't help thinking sometimes,
When a wet day's leisure comes,
And I hear the old home voices
Talking louder than the drums,—

And the far, familiar faces
Peep in at my tent door,
And the little children's footsteps
Go pit-pat on the floor,—

I can't help thinking, somehow,
Of all the parson reads
About that other soldier-life
Which every true man leads,

And wife, soft-hearted creature,
Seems a-saying in my ear,
"I'd rather have you in *those* ranks
Than to see you brigadier."

I call myself a brave one,
But in my heart I lie!
For my country, and her honor,
I am fiercely free to die;

But when the Lord, who bought me,
Asks for my service here
To "fight the good fight" faithfully,
I'm skulking in the rear.

And yet I know this Captain
All love and care to be:
He would never get impatient
With a raw recruit like me.

And I know he'd not forget me;
When the day of peace appears,
I should share with Him the victory
Of all His volunteers.

And it's kind of cheerful, thinking,
Beside the dull tent fire,
About that big promotion,
When He says, "Come up higher."

And though it's dismal—rainy—
Even now, with thoughts of Him,
Camp life looks extra cheery,
And death a deal less grim.

For I seem to see Him waiting
Where a gathered heaven greets
A great victorious army,
Marching up the golden streets.

And I hear Him read the roll-call,
And my heart is all a-flame
When the dear, recording angel
Writes down my happy name!

—But my fire is dead white ashes
And the tent is chilling cold
And I'm playing *win the battle,*
When I've never been enrolled!

E's Journal tells of a quiet day in camp before another advance by the regiment:

We were on the point of driving out here yesterday when a telegram came from J. saying he was coming in. It was with his camp wagon this time, to carry out various things—new guide colors for the regiment, stationery, etc., and his new Colonel's uniform "with the birds on it," as Moritz says. Suddenly it occurred to me to come out to camp too. So I put up my things hastily and J. drove me out, sending James ahead on "Scott" to order another mess tent put up for me and have the fire made. It was our first drive together since Joe entered the service nearly a year ago. "Fairfax," the pony, jogged along at his ease and we didn't reach here till after dark. Camp-fires along the road and over the hill-sides burned brightly and picturesque groups of men gathered round them, cooking and smoking. The 16th, when we reached it, seemed like a little village of lighted and well-kept streets. James soon got supper for us and when the fire was burning we felt as serene and comfortable as possible. The *"Evening Star"* and the printing of a lot of postmarks with the new regimental stamp, filled the evening, and then, building up a good fire and getting under the piles of blankets Surgeon Crandall had sent in, I slept soundly and warm till "reveille" just after sunrise. After reveille came roll-call, then the sick-call on the bugle, then breakfast for the men, then guard-mounting at eight, then our breakfast. After this J. went out to drill the battalion and I wrote letters, had a call from General Slocum, and sent General Franklin the flowers I had brought him; by which time the drill was over. The day was delicious, warm, soft, spring-like, and fires were oppressive. The evening parade was an uncommonly nice one. General Slocum, Colonel Bartlett and J. reviewed them and the men looked finely. The white gloves and gaiters Joe has given them greatly increase the neat appearance, and the band is quite another thing. "Coming through the rye" is no longer played as a dirge.

The new colors were all brought out and the effect was very pretty, as they were escorted out and back and saluted by all the officers and men. After parade came a game of base-ball for the captains and other officers, and in the sweet evening air and early moonlight we heard cheerful sounds all about us as the men sang patriotic songs, laughed and chatted, or danced jigs to the sound of a violin. There is a nice little band of stringed instruments in the regiment, and Joe sent for them to come and play for me in the tent, and then it was proposed to adjourn to General Franklin's Headquarters and give him a serenade. This with a call on Col. Bartlett in his patriotic tent, hung with American can flags, finished the evening. We went to bed, tired, but as peaceful and unwarlike as could possibly be. . . . At 3 A. M. we were suddenly roused. The brigade was again under marching orders, to leave at ten o'clock for *Manassas* once more! This was the meaning of the vague rumors we had heard that our division was not *to sail* after all.

I built up the fire and dressed and after a cup of tea at 5.30 said goodbye. Our peaceful little time was over.

April 7. A note from J. tells of the regiment's safe arrival at Manassas, where they are camped. The General had complimented J. on moving his regiment better than any of the others.

G. and E. had "enlisted for the war," which they did not understand to mean staying comfortably housed in Washington, while the army marched to danger and death. So when the orders came for the advance of the Army of the Potomac, they definitely determined to go too, in some way or other, and not to allow themselves to be kept back even by dear J. H.'s concern for their comfort and safety, feeling sure of his consent when the right moment came. G. writes to him:

Will you, dear Joe, seriously think about our going when and where you go. . . . The distress of having you away and in the greatest danger—hours and hours, probably days—beyond our reach, would be infinitely harder to stand than any amount of cold, hunger, or annoyance, and the knowledge that Eliza was in such a state of mind would make you quite as unhappy as the thought that she might be hungry and cold. . . . We want to be within one hour's ride, at most, of the battlefield, and to be there ready for the battle if it must come. When it is all over what possible use would there be in our coming on? There will always be some roof of a barn at any rate that would give us shelter enough, and where we could stay if there was fighting. It was bad enough to go through Bull Run here in Washington. Nothing can be more miserable than a second such experience. . . . You only laugh when I talk to you, so I am obliged to write.

E. to J. H.

. . . I feel it to be my right and privilege to follow you, not only for my own satisfaction in being near you, but because we know we can be of great use among the troops in case of sickness and danger. We can follow you in the carriage, keeping within reach of you in case of need, and with George and Moritz we can be sufficiently protected anywhere in the rear of our army. I trust to you, dear, to do all you can to forward our plan, and I am sure you will not leave us in doubt and indecision longer than you can help. . . .

The impression seems to be that a great battle will take place in the neighborhood of Yorktown very soon. In view of this, think of the criminal neglect of the medical department in not having any hospital arrangements made there or at Fortress Monroe which begin to be sufficient! One of the doctors of the Sanitary Commission writes that on his arrival there he found already 500 sick men without beds to lie on. The Commission have fitted up one large hospital on their own account, and have sent for supplies to be forwarded immediately, and we have this morning set a large amount of sewing going—bedticks, etc., to be forwarded to Old Point as soon as possible. There are so many sick and so few to take care of them that Dr. Robert Ware of the Sanitary Commission has had to undress and wash the men himself. And this is *before* a battle.

A. H. W. to G.

NEW YORK, APRIL, '62.

I notice what you say of bed sacks. The Sanitary Commission furnished thousands to the Burnside Division for its hospitals at Roanoke. Charley says not one of these was ever filled or used, there not being a wisp of hay or straw or moss or anything, except what was brought there for forage. The men all lay on the board floors. At Fort Monroe it *might* be easy to send down from Baltimore ready-made mattresses, or the material for filling, but I question whether anyone on the spot would take the trouble seeing them applied. You could mention the instance of Roanoke to the Sanitary Commission to prove to them that mere *sacks* are not enough.

Yesterday when I came in from Mary's, found "Robert Anderson, U. S. A." 's card on the table again. John said he bade him say General Anderson called in person to thank Miss Carry Woolsey for the flowers. . . . James Gibson writes from Belfast that "England did not want war with America, and special prayer meetings for peace were held"; but wasn't it Earl Shaftesbury who refused to attend, saying such an act would place him in hostility to his government? If England did not mean war, why did she fly to arms in that indignant and indecent haste! Why did Lord Palmerston suppress the nature of the despatch from Seward, read to him by Mr. Adams, and even allow it to be contradicted in his organ the *Post?* No; *two things* will always stand on record as showing the hostility of the governing class in England toward America in its life and death struggle;—this hurry to make a *casus belli* of what ought to have been a question for diplomacy to settle; and that first great wrong done us in the outset, when the English ministry, while Adams was on the railway train, the very day he was on his way from Liverpool to London, last May, hastened to declare the North and South equal belligerents. They confound the law-power and the law-breaker; they call the police and the burglar brother-rogues. . . .

It is just as Mr. Scharff's father said at the very beginning of the war, "Well, John, I don't know what part England will take in this matter, but I am very sure of one thing, it will be the *meanest* part, possible." . . .

Eliza's lovely home at Fishkill was all this time shut up and desolate, but the grounds were in the hands of their neighbor, Mr. Henry W. Sargent, who kindly undertook the work Joe had to give up for the war. He planted the place, selecting trees and superintending the work day after day. The little rise in the lawn north of the house he named Mars Hill, and there Mr. Thomson, the farmer-in-charge, set up a flag-pole and kept the colors flying, though the house stood empty.

C. C. W. to E.

APRIL 8TH.

Dear Eliza:

We have made our little visit to the W's at Fishkill, and the first thing after dinner drove over to your place. . . . Every one says it is very much improved, and the trees that are being set out are very fine ones and add to the general air of elegance. . . . I must tell you how beautiful too your greenhouses looked, lots of flowers and very beautiful ones, and two large boxes have come down this week for Mother, and been arranged in rustic baskets, etc., and make us look very popular to the seven usual evening callers; last night they were admired by Messrs. Beekman, Shepherd, Goddard, Denny, Bronson, Frothingham and Dorus W., and each gentleman tried to look conscious to the others, while I looked so to all. . . . Returning from Fishkill we found Sarah Woolsey here, and she is now sitting on the sofa reading the news. Uncle Edward has just gone, and Jane and Hatty are off at the hospital. Abby is very down in her mind about the Merrimac, and thanks fortune (secretly) there is always something to be melancholy over. . . .

Sarah drove out one morning to see Aunt E., who entertained her with abusing Abby for her political opinions! She said the *Tribune* was not a paper for Christian people, particularly *females,* to take, and that as long ago as Rutgers Place times Uncle E. had warned us against it. "I read it myself, it is true," she said, "but then the curious eye and ear must be satisfied!" Capital reason for doing what a Christian "female" should not do!

J. S. W. to Mother in Washington.

THURSDAY EVENING.

Dear Mother:

Your letter, or rather G.'s, E.'s check, etc., arrived this morning, with the important item inscribed, as usual, on the flap and disfigured in opening. We are very sorry to hear that Hatty doesn't get on faster. Perhaps if, instead of a "good old soul" of a doctor, she had an enlightened young one, she might get sooner rid of her sore throat. I believe much more devoutly in modern than in ancient doctors.

Sarah, Abby, Carry, Miss Parsons, Charley and Robert have all gone to the "Reception" of the Cumberland's men to-night. It was time to show some interest in them. The Chamber of Commerce has got this up. I hope it will be a success. You remember the officer calling to the half-drowning men, "Shall we give her another broadside, boys?" and the "Aye, aye, sir," and the final volley, as the water rushed in at the portholes. We have had two visits lately from Prof. Hitchcock on the subject of a ladies' committee of visiting; auxiliary to the gentlemen's committee of the New England Soldiers Relief Association. He asked us to collect some names of ladies willing to serve (visiting only), and we have enrolled six or eight: Mrs. Gurden Buck, Mrs. H. B. Smith, Miss Annie Potts, Margaret Post, etc., etc. I fancy there will be little to do really, as there is a resident superintendent and wife, and, I believe, nurses, in the house corner of John St. and Broadway. You will see the details of the are arrangement in the papers. . . All the flags are out again for the Western victories and the Western heroes. Col. Bissell, the officer who *made a river* 12 miles long to flank the rebel position, is Mrs. Dr. Parker's brother, a man of extraordinary energy and perseverance. . . .

Mrs. Bacon told Sarah that Frank had 700 sick men under his care and made a point of seeing every man every day, so never wrote, leaving that business to Theodore. We sent, him and Mr. Withers each, another bundle of papers by the last mail.

Sarah Woolsey to G.

New Haven, April.

I spent one delightful day in New York with Jane at the New England rooms, where everything is nicely prepared for 300 men. The superintendent has time during intervals to rush down stairs and compose puffs on Jane, which he publishes in the newspapers next morning! The day we went down, we had the luck to fall upon the first wounded soldier of the season, and, though he was not very sick, Jane went to work in the most approved way, and you should have seen her with her bonnet off, her camel's-hair shawl swung gracefully from her shoulders and a great-pocketed white apron on, making tea over a spirit-lamp and enjoying it all so thoroughly. The Newbern hero was fed with sardines and oysters and all sorts of good things, and face and hands washed by Jane's little paws so nicely. . . . Don't say anything when you write home, for Jane is rather huffy when we talk too much about it, since her appearance in the public prints. Did you see the letter from a soldier in the hospital, describing Jane, and using the celebrated sentence which, as she says, leaves no doubt as to the identity: "I dare not mention her name, but she is beautiful."

William Winthrop to G.

Berdan's Sharpshooters,
Camp Before Yorktown, April 11, 1862.

Dear Cousin:

Your welcome and full letter brought joy and facts. . . . As for us, we are sitting down before Yorktown, as yet untaken. The enemy retreated before us, first from Great Bethel, then from the extensive entrenchments at Smithville, two miles beyond. Yorktown is their stronghold; the works are understood to extend pretty much all the way across the Peninsula to the James. They have some forty guns on the works now facing us.

On the 5th, we saw something like war. As the head of Porter's Column—*we* are that head—emerged from the wood and rose upon the open land which forms a gradual natural glacis to the batteries, we were saluted with shell after shell, and all day the shell and round shot and rifle bullets cracked and boomed and whizzed about us. *We,* as usual, skimmed the *crème de la crème* being posted as skirmishers, as well under cover as we could get, about three-fourths of a mile in advance of the main army, and one-half mile in advance of our own artillery. We lost two and had four wounded during the day, and it is most unaccountable that our loss was not twenty times as great; for the horrid, detestable music of shot and shell and ball was almost continually tingling our ears. One of the killed was in my own company—Phelps. I had him buried next day—a sweet Sunday—and laid the green turf neatly over the mound. . . . By the way, I think of you and Eliza as I see the little hospital flags hung out from all the more respectable farmhouses. . . .

General Porter said in a note of commendation on our regiment, read on parade, that the enemy "by their own admissions had begun to fear *us* and provide against us as far as possible." This praise has rather turned the head of our Colonel. *Moi,* I have been too cold, too weary, too wet, too unslept, too unwashed, to feel conceited or proud. Further, our teams have not yet come up with the officer's baggage, so I am without mutations of raiment, or have to depend on strangers for the same; also am only one-half blanketed. But these are minor ills, for which, no doubt, our lovers are pitying us more than we deserve as they sit in their boudoirs far away.

The brandy and things which you sent me, just before going off, were very valuable. I had a few swallows of the liquor left in my flask a few nights since on picket, and it proved worth more than so much liquid gold. A soldier of the 2nd Maine, on picket with my men, was struck by a ball which broke his leg. He crawled through the rain and cold of that miserable night, half a mile, on his hands and knees, to the reserve picket, and was just fainting when I came in with your brandy treasured up for just such a moment.

The weather is now fair and warm and delicious. I walked through the woods this A. M. before reveille, to the sandy beach of York River, and saw the sun come up out of the sea; and watched our gunboats, which are ready to co-operate when the right moment comes. I hope we shall not be cheated out of a good battle.

Since the sailing of the great expedition from Annapolis, F. B. had been on active duty with the troops on the coast of South Carolina and Georgia, and at the reduction of the two forts at Port Royal, and of Fort Pulaski, April 11th. At the siege of the latter he was on duty with the battery nearest the fort, and was requested by General Gilmore to keep an account of the shots fired from our batteries and from the rebel guns within the fort. Here he stood in a scarlet lined cloak with Gilmore's long, shining double-barrelled field-glass in his hand for two days,—a fine mark for the enemy. After the fight he went about the fort with the rebel officer who surrendered it, and who said, as they came to a big gun, "I commanded here, and sent a large number of shots at a man who stood at the corner of that cistern, and wore a cloak, and had some long shining thing in his hand. I wonder if I hit him!"

General Franklin's wife to E.

APRIL 12.

My dear Mrs. Howland:

Last night (late) I was informed as a *great secret* that General Franklin's Division *was* to go to General McClellan after all! I was wondering when

I awoke this morning if I might not go and tell *you*. . . . General Meigs was one of the authorities given for the truth of the report—so I think we may believe the good news. . . .

I have a favor to ask, which is, if you decide to go down to Alexandria to try and see your husband on his way through, will you let me know? as I would like very much to go too.

I feel as if it would be a great comfort to see them before they start South.

Love to your mother and sisters. It is truly a mercy from above to have the Division relieved from the *false position* they were placed in, and now we have only to pray for their safety.

Yours aff'ly,

ANNA L. FRANKLIN.

G's Journal.

ALEXANDRIA, APRIL 15, '62.

Saturday morning we had private information that Franklin's Division was shipping down the river, and we packed our bags at once and with Mrs. Franklin came down to the Dysons' Cottage, Alexandria. . . . Dyson's two slaves, Harriet and her mother, have run away, for which I sing songs of thanksgiving. . . . The 16th and all the others have arrived and are camping under Fort Elsworth, their old ground.

At the street corner coming down here, we found ten men struggling with one of their comrades of the 5th Maine, who had just fallen in a fit; about a hundred had collected to shut off the air and double him up, with his knapsack still strapped on his back. We asked the crowd to do what they ought to do for him, till we were tired; and then we pushed them aside and went in ourselves, had a strong sergeant keep the crowd off, put the man on his back with his clothes loose, bathed his head and poured brandy down his throat. E. went to a near hospital, but they would not take him in. So we put him in his blanket for stretcher, and started him off with bearers to the Mansion House, while the crowd dispersed, one woman saying, "Poor fellow, he is fighting in a good cause, and ought to have a dose of ipecac."

Mother to G. and E. in Alexandria.

EBBITT HOUSE, MONDAY EVENING, APRIL 15 OR 16, '62.

Dear Girls:

We have just had a call and salute from Joe's manservant James, who wished to know if we had any "word for Mrs. Howland in the morning." What with your three devoted "Mercuries" we seem to keep up a pretty constant intercourse, which is very cheering. . . . I was at my lonely tea this evening when suddenly I heard a sepulchral voice at my shoulder saying, "How is Miss Woolsey, Madam, this evening?" It was "me" young Augustus on his way out from the table behind me, where I had not noticed him. "You seem to be quite alone. I will be happy to take my breakfast with you, if you will permit me!" I was horror stricken at the idea of having either of your chairs occupied by anyone to whom I should feel called upon to do the agreeable. . . .

I shall be *very late* unavoidably to-morrow, so that he will eat and go before I get down. This seems to be a favorite little attention with our gentlemen friends here—"taking breakfast with you!" . . . Only think of my missing another call from Mrs. McClellan and her mother. I had ventured out on a stroll by myself, to get my cap, which I didn't get, and to bring Hatty a tumbler of ice cream, which I *did* get, and she enjoyed it very much with some fresh ladyfingers. This woman is not to be relied on, the cap was not done, and I shouldn't wonder if she is taking the pattern instead of clear-starching it. I continued on to the avenue, bought Hatty a pair of gloves, looked in at one or two stores for something extremely pretty and cheap for a spring dress, but was not successful in finding it. The sun was very hot, and I was glad to get back again. . . . How in the world are you all accommodated in that small house? . . .

So, after all, you mean to go, if you can, to Fortress Monroe. I am sorry for one thing—you will be so much more inaccessible to your family, almost beyond our reach, as *only* those belonging to the army will be permitted to go there. Nevertheless, I will make all the enquiries you name, and although *my* heart will break, will speed you on your way. Plague take this war! Hatty is better, but misses her other two nurses, and I do not believe has any confidence in my cooking; she acknowledges, however, grudgingly, that the beef-tea "tasted good," and the arrowroot was excellent, though I saw her afterwards pouring in a double quantity of port wine, I having already seasoned it with sherry.

After   Tea.

I have seen Mr. —————— by particular desire in the parlor,—waylaid him, tied him down and pelted him with questions—as to the facilities, etc., of reaching Fortress Monroe at this present time. He gave no encouragement whatever as to your getting there; said he was quite sure that no passengers were allowed to that point and none on the Baltimore boat. . . . You had better not set your hearts upon such a plan. Would you not be quite as near, and hear as readily, in New York? We should be so glad to have you there with us. But I do not urge anything; all I can say is take care of yourselves, as you are very precious to your
Mother.

We were pulling every possible wire to get permission to go to Fortress Monroe, and Mother was aiding us. General Franklin lent a hand too, but all failed.

General Franklin to Brigadier General Thomas.

Headquarters 1st Division, 1st Corps,
Army of the Potomac.

My dear General:

Mrs. Howland, the wife of Colonel Howland, of the New York 16th Regiment, desires to be presented to you in order that she may get permission to join her husband, who is in my Division. I beg that if you can do anything to assist her in obtaining her very natural wish, you will do it, and I will consider it as a favor done to me.

Mrs. Howland is by no means an idler when she is with the soldiers, but has really done more than any other lady of my acquaintance in adding to the comfort of the sick as well as those in health. I therefore believe that it will be for the interests of the service that she should have the permission for which she asks.

Very respectfully yours,
W. B. FRANKLIN,
Brig. Gen. Com. Div.
Brig. Gen. L. Thomas,
Adjutant General U. S. Army,
Washington, D. C.

General Thomas, however, failed us; his general orders prohibited all passes.

C. W. W. to G. M. W.

NEW YORK, APRIL, '62.

Dear Georgy:

Your letter to me came this morning about the facilities for (or rather the hindrances to) getting from Baltimore to Fortress Monroe. . . . Cousin William A. tells me all authority on General Dix's part to grant passes to anyone has been suspended. . . . he has refused all—the Vice-President's son among others. . . . If *he* cannot give us passes *no one can* unless we can be smuggled through on one of the transports from Alexandria down the Potomac. . . . Fortress Monroe is crowded to overflowing, though I know you would be satisfied with a square inch per man if you could only get there (minus hoops). . . If I get letters that *will* take us by the transport to-morrow morning, I will telegraph you and come on immediately.

Cousin Margaret Hodge to G.

PHILADELPHIA, APRIL, '62.

My dear Georgy:

I feel a great interest in dear Eliza and yourself, and also in your dear mother, and all the family, knowing how anxious you must all be about Joe. I do wish you could get to Fortress Monroe, or, as you say, to the Hygiea Hotel. . . . We had a letter this morning from Lenox, dated from on board the steamer Welden, which Dr. Smith has chartered to fit up as a hospital ship for the Pennsylvania wounded. You know we have 50,000 at Yorktown, at least so say the papers.

Lenox seems much pleased that they have the steamer, as it makes them so independent, and enables them to go where they may be most needed, without troubling any one. Dr. Smith's plan is to have a building on shore for a hospital, and the steamer can convey the wounded to it. Some of the doctors are to attend to their removal from the field, while some are to take charge of them on the steamer, and the remainder to receive them at the hospital. . . . Lenox was just going off to Cheesman's landing. He is very much interested in all he sees; has visited the Monitor and been all over it, and also he had been over the fortress and visited several camps.

It is a great trial to part with him, but he has wanted so long to do what he could for the cause that it is a great gratification that he can go now without interfering with his duty to his father. The lectures are over, and he can spare him better than he could before, though even now Lenox is a great loss to his father. . . .

My love to your dear mother and Hatty, and say I am still looking for their promised visit, and shall count on their coming here on their way home. We have Lottie and baby here now, for a little visit, but I have plenty of room for all.

From H. L. Hodge

FORTRESS MONROE, APRIL 19TH, 1862.

Dear Georgy:

We were summoned to Yorktown, and about twenty of us left Philadelphia yesterday morning. We passed on the Bay this morning many transports bearing, as I suppose, Franklin's Division. I presume that Joe and myself were not far apart. He goes, however, if report be true, to the opposite side of York River. They brought down here some wounded yesterday; they are under the care of Surgeon Cuyler and are comfortably located.

We have come only in anticipation that we may be needed, and may therefore remain a short time or for a long while, according to circumstances.

On April 17th the 16th had finally started from Alexandria on the steamer Daniel Webster. No. 2, with Franklin's Division, to join McClellan on the Peninsula.

J. H. to E. W. H.

STEAMER DANIEL WEBSTER, APRIL 18.

I have a chance to send a boat ashore to get a mail and so can say good morning to you. All the steamers are lying in the stream two or three miles below Alexandria receiving their "tows."

There are about a hundred schooners and barges to take down. We tow four. All's well. The boat is very crowded, but the men are more comfortable than I supposed they would be and are behaving admirably. The work of getting them well on board was a hard one. I have 820 officers and men on this boat and the four schooners. The sick are doing well; the change of air and rest are curing the dysentery. I do not know where we are going.

NEAR FORTRESS MONROE, SUNDAY, APRIL 20.

No orders. The boat is becoming very dirty and cannot be cleaned as she is so crowded that there is no place to put any number of the men while cleaning is being done. The decks are swept and *shoveled* once or twice a day, but need washing. The regiment is behaving well. I have had to punish only one man since we left Alexandria, but have made an example of him for smuggling and selling liquor.

We had a nice little service a short time ago and the chaplain is repeating it in different parts of the boat, as it is not safe to assemble the men in any one part where even a couple of hundred could hear. The men were very attentive. The more I see of the regiment the more highly I think of it. I am sure the old 16th will always behave creditably.

YORK RIVER, APRIL 22.

Here we still lie awaiting orders, without a word of news and nothing to do. The boat is so crowded and dirty that life is becoming intensely disgusting, yet there does not appear any prospect of getting away. Last night there was heavy firing towards Yorktown and we could see the flashing of the guns; but we do not know what it was.

April 24. Yesterday, at last, I landed the regiment, having asked permission to do so and have the boat thoroughly cleaned. Having picked out a piece of level ground at the head of a little bay where there are lots of oysters, I got a stern-wheeler and sent the regiment ashore by companies, and got all fairly into camp before sunset. I put the major in command on shore, keeping my headquarters on the steamer, and had the work of purification begun as soon as the hold was cleared.

I saw Franklin yesterday, and he asked after you and ours. I took the steamer's quarter-boat last evening and serenaded the old chap with our stringed band. He seemed pleased and the music sounded very sweetly on the quiet water.

I suspect Commander Rodgers is the right sort of man for the Galena. I heard a story of him to-day. Some one said to him, "Your iron plates are too thin; their thickness should be at least four inches." His reply (some-what profane) was, "What to h—— do I care about their thickness,—my business is to go up York River and shell the enemy."

J. S. W. to G.

NEW YORK, APRIL 25, '62.

. . . I always have a little talk with Col. Betts coming out of church, he keeps out such a sharp eye. He predicted all that business of the sub-division of McClellan's command and the Rappahannock department exactly as it fell out. He predicts now—(he laughs and says of course he only guesses)—*no* desperate fighting at Yorktown. He thinks there will be some bombarding but *no* storming of the works; that the great battle at Corinth, now imminent, will occur before a battle at Yorktown, and will probably greatly demoralize the rebel cause. . .

Cousin William Aspinwall has just sent us in an interesting letter from Lieutenant Greene, giving his experience on the Monitor in the voyage and fight. He is only 18, and was in command for a little while after Worden was blinded. I have been down several days this week to the New England Association, and have succeeded in doing nothing with considerable éclat. We have had only eight or ten transient lodgers, have had some droll incidents, have made a few beds and a few cups of tea, got great glory in the newspapers, and that is all. Don't think I am going into a minute account, for I have no idea of it. Indeed there is none to go into. The ladies committee does not work altogether smoothly, and I think there will be some further attempt at organization with a responsible head. W—— B—— looks in occasionally and does nothing. M—— P—— tries to come the heavy patronizing over me with entire want of success. . . . The house is admirable, and the patients (if there are any) will be splendidly taken care of. If you know any New England men coming home invalided, and who want to rest over a night or two (most of them will not do it), send them to us.

A. H. W. to Mother.

NEW YORK, APRIL 26TH.

My Dear Mother:

We are all bright and well this fine morning. Jane and Charley have gone to the Philharmonic rehearsal and Carry is practicing some of her old music on the piano, in a way to make you, who love to hear it, happy. Mr. Prentiss came in last night to see us, looking well, but queer, as he always does in a black stock. He had been hard at work moving his books, and did not intend to go to prayer meeting, and evidently didn't suppose *we* had gone, or he wouldn't have come to spend the evening with us. He told us much that was pleasant and funny about his visit in Washington, which, short as it was, paid him well, he thought, for going. He hopes E. and G. will get their wishes and go to Fort Monroe, as they are in a state of mind to be fretted and troubled if they don't. . . .

Very few of the wounded brought by the Cossack from Newbern were landed here. . . . All were crazy to get home, all full of spirits and fun. The five or six who were carried to the N. E. Relief only fretted at having to spend a night longer on the road. The man with both legs gone smoked his pipe and read his newspaper. His chief anxiety was to go into New Jersey by a certain train. . . . Five or six ladies were at the rooms, Jane among them, yesterday, a lady apiece and several men to each volunteer. . . . No wonder it dazed an Irishman just released from four months imprisonment in Richmond. "Begor," he said, "I can't pay for all this!" . . .

Jane says there is nothing much for the present set of ladies to do, except to rearrange the piles of shirts, etc., on the closet shelves—changing them about from the way she had fixed them! They immediately proceeded to that work, and each new set of ladies will have *that*, at least, to occupy them. As for the Park Barracks, a portion of them have been scrubbed and whitewashed, the bunks taken down, neat iron beds all made and put up. Mrs. Mack is to live there as Matron, and, for the purpose of a mere halting place and infirmary, it is as good an one as they could have, though too many ladies were on hand, switching things over with their hoops, giving unlimited oranges to men with the dysentery, and making the sure surgeons mad. There were, beside, half the medical students in the city, all staring and eager for jobs;—no difficulty in the men's having all, and more than all, the attention they want. One good thing Mrs. Woodruff did, at Mrs. Buck's suggestion,—sent over to the Astor House for a steward, and through him ordered a good dinner brought in of tender beef, fresh eggs, etc., for the twenty or thirty New York and New Jersey men who were resting there. It will be charged to New York State, which supports the Barracks. . . . We have Lloyd's map of Virginia hung under the front parlor picture of the Virgin, along the back of the sofa, and we sit there and read the papers and study it.

E. to J. H.

WASHINGTON, APRIL 26.

Mr. Knapp, of the Sanitary Commission, has just been over and offers to take a note for me when he goes to Yorktown to-morrow. We like him so much, and shall be in communication with him all summer if we succeed in going down, *and we are very likely to go!* Mr. Knapp said the Commission had been speaking of us and hoping we might be able to go, and that, if they found women would be allowed, they themselves would be very glad to have us under their charge, and would manage to get us there. We mustn't call it "our luck." It is something far better, and I for one shall be truly grateful to God—and the Commission. Mr. Knapp asks as a special favor that we will keep him informed of our movements.

A smiling providence opened the door wide for us at last.

The hospital steamer Daniel Webster. Photograph about 1862.
National Library of Medicine

CHAPTER SEVEN

Simply Eyes & Hands

E. W. H. to J. H.

MONDAY MORNING, APRIL 28.

Where do you think I am? On the "Daniel Webster No. 1," which the Sanitary Commission has taken as a hospital ship. We are now on the way down to Cheeseman's Creek, near Ship Point, and when you receive this we shall be lying just there. Saturday afternoon the gentlemen of the Commission, Mr. Olmsted and Mr. Knapp, came over to see us, and to our great surprise and pleasure proposed to us to come down with them in the ship as "nurses at large," or matrons, or what not—to do of course all we can for the sick and wounded men in the approaching battle. They had telegraphed to Mrs. William P. Griffin and Mrs. Lane of New York to come on at once, and go too. We only had one night's notice, as they were to leave early Sunday morning, but we accepted the offer at once, and here we are! We four are the only women on board except a colored chambermaid, but there are 30 or 40 men nurses and hospital dressers, and several members of the Commission—Mr. Olmsted, Mr. Knapp, Mr. Lewis Rutherford, Mr. Strong, Dr. Agnew, Dr. Grymes, etc. They have two boats, this and the Elm City. The latter is to be a receiving ship and permanent floating hospital, and this one the transporting one, in which the wounded will be carried at once by sea to New York, Philadelphia, or Baltimore and Washington, as the case may be. It is an old ocean steamship, and used to run on the Aspinwall route; is stanch and sea-worthy, but now wretchedly dirty. A dozen stout contrabands are at work night and day scrubbing and cleaning, and, as they finish, the whitewashers and carpenters succeed them, and by degrees it will be put in good condition. . . .

I saw Mrs. Franklin the night before we started and have a note for the General. We left our little dog Mopsey with her. . . . If you are still off

Ship Point we shall be very near each other. . . . There is a P. O. station at *Cheeseman's Creek* to which please direct your letters to me, care of Fred. Law Olmsted, Hospital Ship of Sanitary Commission.

G. to Mother.

FLOATING HOSPITAL, DANIEL WEBSTER.
CHEESEMAN'S CREEK, APRIL 30, '61.

The sail down the Potomac to Aquia Creek, where we anchored for the night, was extremely pretty. Just as we started the little gunboat "Yankee" passed up, bringing, all on a string, five rebel craft she had just taken in the Rappahannock.

Late in the afternoon we passed the stone fleet, eight boats all ready to sink in the channel, in case the Merrimac should try to run up the Potomac. The rebels having taken up all the buoys, we had to come to anchor at dark. Sunday, the first day, was gone. As for us, we had spent it sitting on deck, sewing upon a Hospital flag fifteen by eight, and singing hymns to take the edge off this secular occupation. It is to be run up at once in case we encounter the Merrimac. Just as we anchored, a chaplain was discovered among the fifty or sixty soldiers on board—men returning to their regiments, and in half an hour we got together for service and an unprepared discourse exhorting the Sanitary Commission to works of charity! The contrabands all came in and stood in a row, so black, at the dark end of the cabin, that I could see nothing but eyes and teeth; but they sang heartily and everybody followed them.

H. R. W. to G.

EBBITT HOUSE, APRIL 27.

Everybody was delighted with what you left in Washington for the hospitals. Some of the jellies and wine (I found a whole box of it left without orders), and some shoes, I took over to Georgetown to Mrs. Russell, who was just out of all. Mother is going about the room indignant still at the Bank, and "expects to have every policeman in the city tapping her on the shoulder to know the facts of the case." We try not to miss you, but yesterday was *very* like Sunday, much more quiet and Sabbath-like than when you were here; to-day we have had the bank excitement to keep us busy.

The "bank excitement" is the little incident recounted in the *Evening Star* as follows:

A Cool Operation.—This morning, Mrs. C. W. Woolsey went to the Bank of the Metropolis to draw the money for two checks of a hundred dollars each. Unacquainted, apparently, with business of the sort, she stepped into the bank, and instead of applying at the counter, presented them to a person who was standing at a desk outside, and returned to her coach. This person presented the checks to the paying teller, who refused to pay because they lacked Mrs. Woolsey's endorsement. He took a pen and went out to the coach and returned with the checks properly endorsed. They were paid, and the fellow made off with the money, leaving the lady minus.

The man had just the right business manner, not too polite—stepped out without his hat as if he had left his desk to oblige a lady. He was thanked for his courtesy, and left "right sudden" with the funds.

It was hardly fair in us to run Mother on this winding up of her triumphant career in Washington, which city, as she indignantly said, she "left, under the full recognition of several of the Metropolitan police?"

A. H. W. to G. and E.

New York, April 28.

My dear Sisters:

Mother's letter of Sunday morning, giving the startling intelligence of your having gone off suddenly to Fort Monroe, came before breakfast. Since it was your very earnest wish, and, as Mr. Prentiss tells us, you might have chafed at being held back—why I am glad you have gone. But it seems to me a very trying position for you: you will work yourselves sick. Joe will be the *most* surprised person, and I don't believe he will approve of your being on a hospital boat. It is very satisfactory that Mrs. Griffin is on board; as long as she stays you will not need either man or woman protector. . . . Georgy's letter to Charley came with Mother's. He will see to the wire camp-beds, and we will put the other stores, your hats, etc., etc., all in a trunk and have them ready for the first opportunity. If you write for Charley he will take them on at once. . . . It is strange that Mr. Olmsted should have had you in mind, without having known of your desire to go. It shows that, as Georgy says, "Heaven had opened the door." ... Our best love to you two dear brave girls; you are doing what you love to do, and I hope will take care of yourselves as well as of the soldiers.

A. H. W. to J. H.

APRIL 30.

We had a very pleasant visit the other night from Charles Johnson, of Norwich, just returned from Port Royal. He went down as Allotment Commissioner from Connecticut and had pretty good success. He was particularly indignant about the chaplain of the Connecticut —th who had made a "handsome thing" all along out of the men whose money he received for being forwarded to their homes. He charged them a commission, and then by buying drafts on New York, which are at a premium in Bridgeport, Connecticut, managed to make his one per cent net.

Charles J. arrived out the day of the bombardment of Fort Pulaski and was among the first visitors after its surrender. It was curious, he said, to see the extra defenses prepared by the rebels; heavy timber blindages against the casemates and quarters, all round the fort inside, sodded six feet deep with earth dug from trenches with which the whole parade was criss-crossed. These ditches were already two feet deep with the green, slimy water which had oozed upward through the soil. . . . He said that the 7th Connecticut, now garrisoning the fort, were a pale, peaked, sick-looking set, but every man of them as proud as Lucifer, and he came home with a higher idea than ever of the energy and spirit of our troops. One night he and Colonel Terry and Dr. Bacon couldn't sleep on account of the mosquitoes and heat, and they agreed to bring out the letters left behind by the rebel prisoners, which had to be examined and sent some day to Savannah by flag of truce. There were more than a hundred; some very laughable specimens of course, but some well written and sensible. About thirty were written in one hand, by some officer for his different privates I suppose, and every one of them began, "We have met the enemy and we are theirs!" always winding up with the earnest advice to their friends, to quit Savannah. . . .

Mr. Prentiss has lately spent a week in Washington, in company with Dr. Stearns and Professor Schaff. Everywhere they went, of every great man, Professor Schaff asked his stock question—whether the social and political conquest of the South was not to be more difficult than its military conquest. He received very characteristic answers. President Lincoln thought—perhaps, yes—but it wouldn't cost so much money!" Mr. Seward said, decidedly, "No!" and then trotted himself out, most obligingly, in a dainty little sort of oration, using one of his fine figures in illustration. "You are like President King," he said, "who was greatly concerned here, last week, about the dome of the Capitol, how it was ever to be finished, and whether it would bear the weight of the figure of Liberty that is to be placed on it, and how the figure was to be got up there, etc. I don't *know* how it is to be done, but the engineers know. The plans were all made to accomplish just that result. The dome was built for the figure, and this figure cast to be in harmony and size with it, and the pulleys and ropes are all agreed upon; and though it is a long way from the ground, where the statue lies now, to the top of the finished dome, I *know* that the work will be done, and *the figure of Liberty shall yet stand on the top of the Capitol.*" . . . Mr. Chase was not so eloquent or philosophic. He thought we ought to "do our present duty and leave the future to Providence," which perhaps was the best answer of all; and putting the three together Professor Schaff was well satisfied with the argument and quite willing to be laughed at by his friends for his pertinacity in asking the question.

From E's Journal.

S. S. DANIEL WEBSTER.

Just before sunset, last night, we passed the mouth of the York River, and could see our gunboats and a fleet of some four hundred sloops and schooners lying a little way up it—among them *our* fleet, Franklin's Division, still lying off Ship Point. We made our way in among them and dropped anchor just off the Point within a stone's throw of the rebel barracks, now used as a hospital for our men. After dark we could see the lights of the fleet all around us like the lamps of a great city on the shores of a harbor, and these, with the camp-fires on shore lighting up the horizon, and the little row-boats darting about, dashing up phosphorescence at every stroke of the oar, made the scene a magical one; while the bugle calls and regimental bands on the different boats increased the effect. Joe's boat, the Daniel Webster No. 2, lies further away from us up towards Cheeseman's Creek. . . .

G's Journal.

Next morning Mr. Olmsted hailed the steamer which carried the 16th New York, to "let the Colonel know that his wife was on board among the nurses." He received an acknowledgment from the Colonel in the form of a check for one thousand dollars for the Sanitary Commission, and what was still better, Mr. O. said, a note of hearty appreciation of the Commission's work for the soldiers. Joe soon came over to the steamer himself, and Lenox Hodge, who was with a Philadelphia detail of surgeons on the steamer Commodore, also came on board.

G. to Mother.

MAY 1, '61.

We are in sight of the abandoned rebel quarters at Ship Point, now used as a hospital, on low, filthy ground surrounded by earth-works, rained on half the time and fiercely shone on the other half, a death place for scores of our men, who are piled in there covered with vermin, dying with their uniforms on and collars up, dying of fever. Of course there is that vitally important thing, medical etiquette, to contend with here as elsewhere, and so it is:—"Suppose you go ashore and ask whether it would be agreeable to have the ladies come over, just to walk through the hospital and talk to the men?" So the ladies have gone to talk with the men with spirit lamps and farina and lemons and brandy and clean clothes, and expect to have an improving conversation!

While we are lying here off Ship Point, New Orleans has surrendered quietly, and round the corner from us Fort Macon has been taken. What is it to us so long as the beef tea is ready at the right moment? We have been getting the beds made on our side of the cabin; only 25 are ready, but in two of them a lieutenant and private of the 16th are lying brought over from the shore yesterday—Eliza's game. She has taken them vigorously in hand, stealing clean clothes from the Wilson Small and treating them to nice breakfasts and teas. Dr. Haight, of New York, has just put his head in to know if Miss Woolsey has any rice ready. "No. She has used it all up on the man in the bunk-ward, with the dysentery." Ask the cook—cook won't boil it; so Miss W. lights her spirit lamp and boils it, and boils it. She has her reward—two men, each with his little plate of it—Was it good?—"Yes, beautiful."

E's Journal about this time.

Before we were up this morning, Joe came over to the Webster to ask us to go down to Fortress Monroe for the day with him, General Slocum and Colonel Bartlett of the 27th New York. Finding I was not likely to be wanted, I accepted gladly, Georgy preferring to go over to Ship Point again. The sail down was only about two and a half hours, and we came upon the fleet almost before we knew it. A great deal of shipping was lying off Old Point Comfort, and in the midst lay the "Minnesota," and the "Vanderbilt," with her great steel prow, prepared to meet and run down the Merrimac; and just off the Rip Raps we saw the "Galena," the "Naugatuck," and the "Monitor." We landed at once and began our sight-seeing with a great space covered by some three hundred enormous cannon lying side by side like giant mummies in Egypt. Then we went directly to the Fortress itself unchallenged, and meeting Captain, now Colonel, Whipple, A. A. G., were taken to his nice little house and office just put up within the pretty enclosure of the fort, and then to General Wool's headquarters. The old General was alone and very polite, said he remembered Uncles Gardiner and Sam Howland, and took me for a daughter and therefore Joe's sister. He read us the despatches he was just sending to Washington announcing the fall of Fort Macon and the retreat of Beauregard from Corinth to Memphis. He insisted on taking us through his pretty garden and gave me a lovely bunch of lilacs and tulips, jonquils, wall-flower, etc., which the old gentleman picked himself (mostly without stems) and presented with very gallant little speeches.

Captain Whipple took us over the moat and on the ramparts, and to the wonderful water battery where the great guns stand ready to belch forth at any moment on the Merrimac or any other enemy. The monsters "Union" and "Lincoln" stand by themselves and point towards Sewall's Point. Even the lighthouse is on its guard and has its faces towards the enemy darkened with canvas.

Got back to the ship all right and found nothing had occurred.

A. H. W. to G. and E.

NEW YORK, MAY 1ST, 1862.

My Dear Girls:

Never were two creatures pounced on and whirled out of sight more completely than you. Fate seems to descend and wrap you from the vision and the reach of your family, and every event only carries you farther off. Do write us when you can and help us to realize what and where you are! . . . We hear from Mrs. Buck or somebody that the Daniel Webster is expected here the last of this week, on her first trip with wounded and sick, but I should hardly think it could load so soon. Is it to come through the canals, as the "Richard Welling" is coming with the Vermont wounded? Perhaps we shall see you too! That will be famous if you come on in her to New York. . . . We have got sponges, lots of towels, doylies, castile soap, etc., etc. together, and are all ready to put them up and send them to you at any moment. If you find you don't need them on board, keep them for the use of the 16th. We *must* do something for that, as *our* regiment. . . .

There are three times as many ladies as are needed at the hospital, 194 Broadway, and Jane's work finished, she will not go again. . . . Mrs. Buck, Jane and Miss Caroline Murray are to have Thursday each week as their day at the Park Barracks. Young Dr. Schauffler *lives* there, and the notice is posted all over the city, so that disabled soldiers returning (singly sometimes) may see it and know that there is rest for them and surgical treatment, all freely provided, and Mrs. Stetson of the Astor House, who is one of the committee, engages to have beef tea, broth, gruel, etc., always ready in case they are called for, and to have *any* delicacy quickly prepared.

H. L. H. writes:

SHIP POINT, MAY 3, '62.

Dear Georgy:

The 8th Illinois Cavalry arrived several days ago. They are disembarking to-day. Cannot the Daniel Webster take the sick off from Ship Point? They will be doing a great service if they can.

G's Journal.

MAY 4.

Mr. Olmsted decided to do it, and the "D. W." sailed with 190 sick from the deserted camps within a range of some miles—eighteen, the poor fellows say who were jolted down to the shore over corduroy roads. The loads began arriving at 5.30 this morning, and we refitted the state-rooms which had been made up twice already, all along of the men nurses turning in and rioting in boots in the nice clean beds. No objection to the "relief-watch" lying down gently on the outside of the beds, but why should they pull out the under-quilts and pin them up for state-room doors? E. and I discovered all sorts of candle ends tucked away or stuck in cakes of soap, with every facility for setting the ship on fire—also the work of the men nurses.

Mrs. Griffin and Mrs. Lane were, meantime, in the pantry getting breakfast for the sick.

G. to Mother.

OFF SHIP POINT.

It was the Wilson Small (a little steamboat chartered by the Commission to run up the creeks and bring down sick and wounded), that came alongside with our first patients, thirty-five in number, typhoid cases, from Ship Point, who were slung through the hatches on their stretchers. . . . We women arranged our days into three watches, and then a promiscuous one for any of us, as the night work might demand.

After breakfast, Sunday, on the Webster, we all assembled in the forward ward, and Dr. Grymes read the simple prayers for those at sea and the sick. Our poor fellows lay all about us in their beds and listened quietly. As the prayer for the dying was finished, a soldier close by the doctor had ended his strife.

We crawled up into our bunks that night amid a tremendous firing of big guns, and woke up in the morning to the announcement that Yorktown was evacuated! Franklin was in McClellan's tent when the news came, and he says McClellan did not know what to make of it.

A little tug has just passed, calling out to each transport to be ready to move in ten minutes if the order is given; probably to go round to Yorktown, and be ready to push up the river in case our men advance. A tug from Baltimore came alongside just now with contrabands and workmen for the "Ocean Queen," which the Commission has secured, and E. and I will probably go over to her this evening.

A. H. W. to G. and E.

My Dear Girls:

We have received this morning your letter of Monday and Tuesday (Georgy's) written at intervals and mailed off Ship Point. What a strange life you are leading on board a hospital ship, sewing hospital flags, dispensing medicines, etc., etc. You two have always been together in the queerest and most varied circumstances, and in all parts of the world, from the heart of the Mammoth Cave to the top of the Pyramids of Egypt, in peace; and now, in war. You did not inclose the ward-list, but "Dr. Woolsey," we feel confident, is a joke on Georgy. She deserves a title of the sort, I am sure. You thought of everything it seems, even to a flat-iron. . . . We seem to be sitting at home impotent and imbecile. It costs us no trouble to order home a few pieces of mosquito bar from Holmes', or a few dozen towels from Milliken's—and even these are sitting under the piano waiting. We have screwed the bandage-roller on again, and the little table stands with strips of cotton and pins and labels just as it stood one year ago, when Georgy fired away with it day after day,—between the folding doors of the parlors.

Mother came home yesterday from Philadelphia, leaving Hatty at the Hodge's. Aspinwall, wife and baby are there. We think Mother looks well. She brought a few of Joe's photographs. What a keen, alert, decided look he has, as becomes a Colonel and a man who has done a year's military duty! Soon after Mother, came Mary, Robert and May to dine and spend the night. This happened very nicely, as it was Mother's first evening at home after Washington.

What great events are happening! Awhile ago, two such things as the fall of New Orleans and of Fort Macon in one week would have crazed us with surprise and delight. We are almost *blasés* in such matters. . . . It is a good joke and commentary on the southern doctrine of "State rights" that the Governor of North Carolina has been arrested in Richmond, Virginia for "Unionism"!

From H. L. H. (sent on board the hospital ship to G.)
Cheeseman's Landing, Friday.

Dear Georgy:

I hope to see you and Eliza to-day. . . . We received all the wounded from the assault on the lunette alluded to, except one too badly hurt to move (who has since died, they tell me) and a few so slightly injured as to be retained for future service. The "boys" here say that Thomas Archer, your servant's brother, did not belong to their Company H, but to Company A, and that he was among those left behind on account of his injuries being slight.

So far our patients, with hardly an exception, have been a superior class of men, and it has been a great pleasure to attend to them.

Dr. Tripler was here yesterday, and I was glad to hear of the probable removal of not only the 200 sick at Ship Point, but of 400 scattered elsewhere, to Boston, New York or Philadelphia.

Mother to G. and E.

New York, Sunday p. m.

My Dear Girls:

I have an unexpected opportunity of writing, or rather of getting my letter to you. Dr. Gurden Buck was telegraphed this morning, through the Sanitary Commission, to leave for Yorktown on board the "Ocean Queen," and he is off for Baltimore at 5 o'clock this p. m., to take ship there. In the meantime just as we came in from church, a telegram arrived from you, dear E., to Charley, asking if he would like the "Clerkship" of the "Daniel Webster," and if so to come on. . . . Charley accepts the clerkship, and will be ready when the "Daniel Webster" comes here. Right upon the top of this excitement of a telegram from Yorktown to us! comes another to Mrs. McClellan at the 5th Avenue Hotel, telling her that Yorktown has been evacuated by the rebels, leaving all their large guns, and much else besides! The newsboys are out already with their extras, and the Aspinwalls are at the door wishing to know why we don't unfurl our flag! which is all rolled up round the stick. Cousin William has been in to tell us of the news direct from Mrs. McClellan, and the whole city is at once commencing its rejoicings. How eagerly we shall look for your account, and how anxious to know what your movements will be. Why are they telegraphing for so many surgeons from here, and Philadelphia, and other towns, when there has been no battle, as we understand? I suppose the army is to push on after the retreating rebels. . . .

I wish I were down there with you, and have a great mind to offer my services to Dr. Buck as head nurse or matron of the "Daniel Webster." . . . Jane has gone off with her Sunday treat to the hospital, of jelly and oranges; Abby and Carry have gone to church again, and Charley is out making enquiry about the boats and trying to find out whether the "Daniel Webster" is expected here, and *when*.

Your things are all ready to go by him, and we have offered Dr. Buck any stores he may wish. We have piles of elegantly rolled bandages which he may be glad to have.

J. S. W. to J. H.

8 BREVOORT PLACE, 3D MAY, CHI ALPHA NIGHT.

So you three have met again, Georgy, Eliza and the Colonel. . . . It must have been a jolly meeting for you all on the floating Hospital, and Eliza says you showed symptoms of illness immediately on seeing the comfortable beds. But it is rather a perilous position for the girls. It is no longer *visiting*, but *living*, in an atmosphere of infection, day and night, typhoid, rubeola, gangrene, and what not. They will be in for anything going, and the service in a crowded transport will make terrible draughts on the sympathies of all concerned. We hear surmises that the Daniel Webster will come round to New York. If so, I sincerely hope the girls will come in her if possible, if it is only for a day. What an excellent thing to have these boats systematically provided, and to have *ladies* on board. It will go far to humanize the horrid vehicles. Heavy reproaches belong *somewhere* for the want of foresight and humanity in the government arrangements of the kind. I have seen it. Send your sick men, if you have any, on a Sanitary Commission transport. Fully *half* the complaints about the Vermonters of Lee's Mills are strictly correct, and half are half too many for toleration. The men are in comparative paradise now in "our" (!) hands, though one or two will die in consequence of careless treatment,—Government doings. Somebody says of the barbarisms of the Chinese Tae-Pings: "if you want to complete the picture, transfer them to America and prefix the adjective Red."

We have been having a Chi Alpha (the Clergymen's Social Club) for Mr. Prentiss, while he was moving. I say "we" although *our* participation was through the key-hole alone. The last of the mild elderly gentlemen has taken his hat and cane, and the family have rushed down and wildly consumed vast quantities of sandwiches, chicken salad, and the loveliest fried oysters! Don't you wish you had some? . . .

One of the entertainments, not edible, was a "James Projectile," weight 58 lbs., brought in the self-sacrificing and gallant hat box of Chas. Johnson, sent by Frank Bacon as a receipt in full, I suppose, for the few little matters we have sent him from time to time,—filled and covered with the red brick dust made by the great breach.

The slave shouts in the barracoon
As through the breach we thunder!

But never, Chas. Johnson says, *never* was there such a disgusted set of men as the Connecticut Seventh, when the white flag went up; they had set their hearts on storming the place, and everything was ready. He went through the casemates with F. B. on his rounds among the patients, his own and those left to his care by Colonel Olmsted, and gave us a very interesting picture of the scene, too long and circumstantial to write out in a letter. He was very much pleased with Dr. Bacon, "so exactly the man for the place," he said; so utterly cool, so gentle, and so untiring in care and patience.

One young fellow they came to, had lost his leg, and the Doctor was trying to soothe him to sleep without an anodyne—"What part of Connecticut are *you* from?" asked Charles J.; "I'm a Georgian, sir. Yes, sir (kindling up), I fired the last gun from this fort, sir!" "Yes," said the Doctor quietly, in his mesmeric way, "he stood by his gun till a shot dismounted it and hurt him. But try now to go to sleep, and if you find you cannot, I'll give you something to help you." "O, if I could have one drink of milk, Doctor!" "I'll see; perhaps I can get you a little." So he gave the candle (in a bottle) to Charles, and was gone for a quarter of an hour, coming back with a little milk in the bottom of a cup, which the young Georgian eagerly swallowed. The story is getting too long—and there were two or three others to match—but what I observe is, that a man of less fine fibre, instead of taking up the talk of the poor Georgian, would have "improved the occasion" to him.

Did you notice that to-day, in the transactions of the Board of Brokers, when the "Government Sixes touched par," for the first time since the rebellion, that the brokers were all on their feet in a minute giving three tremendous cheers? . . . Mother seriously announces just here, that two of the tea spoons, used by the clergymen this evening, are missing, and mentions the name of Rev. Dr.!

Sunday.—A day of great events. At 1 P. M., Cousin William came in to tell us he had seen a man who had seen a man (literal) who had read McClellan's telegram to his wife, announcing the evacuation of Yorktown. The man, once removed, was Barlow, and Mr. A. considered it perfectly reliable. At two the extras were out in a swarm, and Colonel Beats and one or two others came in most kindly, bringing papers and congratulations. It is a blessed respite in our anxiety about you, for we were afraid of a severe battle if there had been any battle at all. It is good news for all who have friends in the army. . . . It becomes us at any rate now to thank God and take courage and draw a much longer breath than we've drawn for a month.

Apropos of your Uncle Frank's "improving the occasion" at Fort Pulaski—he *did* improve it in giving the *rebel surgeon* a mere rebuke. "Good-bye, my poor fellows," the surgeon had said, "I don't know what will happen to you *now*. I shall have to leave you to *this* gentleman." "You need not have any apprehensions, sir," F. B. answered; "these are not the first wounded Georgians I have had to care for;" and then he told him of the wounded rebels he had looked after at the battle of Bull Run. The fellow melted at once and said those men and Colonel Gardner came into his hands directly from F. B.'s, and he had heard of the kindness shown them.

E's Journal.

ON THE YORK RIVER, MAY 5.

Before we were up this morning, though that was very early, the army fleet (including Joe's transport) was off up York river to cut off the retreat of the rebels. Our last load of sick came on board the Webster this morning early, and by nine o'clock she was ready to sail for the North, so G.

and I, with Messrs. Knapp and Olmsted, and our two doctors, Wheelock and Haight, were transferred by the Wilson Small to the great "Ocean Queen," lying in the bay. We sailed up to Yorktown, standing on deck in the rain to enjoy the approach to the famous entrenchments. Gloucester Point alone, with its beautiful little sodded fort, looked very formidable, and the works about Yorktown are said to be almost impregnable. The rebels left fifty heavy guns behind them and much baggage, camp equipage, etc.

A. H. W. to G. and E.

NEW YORK, MAY 7TH, 1862.

My dear Girls:

I hadn't time to write a long letter, but must send off a note to say that the Daniel Webster came to the dock at dusk yesterday. Charley went down at once, thinking there was a possible chance of your being on board, or at all events, some of the 16th sick. Mrs. Griffin, who came up to care for the men, had gone, and several of the officers had landed, but the men were to remain till morning. . . . I am thankful you were not on board, for your own sakes. *Five men* died and more are dying today, and will die in the act of being landed. . . .

McClellan's despatches to-day are not very hopeful. "He will do the best he can—"the "rebels out-number him greatly," "are fighting fiercely; will contest every inch of the way; strongly intrenched," etc., etc. Yesterday he called it a "brilliant success." . . . Your letter, Georgy, to Charley, of Saturday and Sunday, is received this morning. It furnishes us the missing links in the story, and will instruct Charley whom to apply to about his duties and his passage, etc. We felt that your telegram, with merely your signature, did not authorize him to go aboard and assume duty. . . . Mrs. Griffin sent us your penciled note as soon as she landed, with one from herself, saying she had left you well—"lovely and active," I think were her expressions. She asked if I knew anything about Mrs. Trotter's decision as to going to the front. The latter was here yesterday. She said she should love dearly to go, but she believed she couldn't, her mother couldn't spare her just now.

Later. . . . Charley went down yesterday and saw Mr. Strong, and was inducted as *Purser* of the ship Daniel Webster. Mr. Strong gave him a sum of money, and he has been on board to-day paying the medical cadets and the contrabands. Came home just now for a lunch and has gone down again to finish. He thinks he may have to sleep on board. The vessel is not cleaned up or ready yet. . . . They *may* get off to-morrow afternoon. Mrs. Trotter is to send up to-night to see what we have heard. She is going to join the Daniel Webster on its return trip.

E. W. H. to J. H.

MAY 7TH, '62.

My dear Joe:

Down in the depths of the Ocean Queen, with a pail of freshly-made milk punch alongside of me, a jug of brandy at my feet, beef tea on the right flank, and untold stores of other things scattered about, I write a hurried note on my lap, just to tell you that we keep well, but have been so busy the past 48 hours that I have lost all track of time. You had scarcely left us the other day when our first installment of sick came aboard—*150 men*—before anything whatever was ready for them. We had only just taken possession of the ship, as you saw, and not an article had been unpacked or a bed made. With two spoons, and ten pounds of Indian meal (the only food on board) made into gruel, G. and I managed, however, to feed them all and got them to bed. They have come in the same way ever since, crowded upon us unprepared, and with so few to do for them; and we have now nearly 600, and more coming to-night. . . .

Until to-day we have had only our small force who were detached from the Webster, and I may say without vanity that G. and I, and the two young doctors, Wheelock and Haight, have done *everything*. We women have attended to the feeding of the 400 or 500, and those two young fellows have had the responsibility of their medical care! Last night, however, a large party of surgeons, dressers and nurses arrived from New York, and though to-day things have been frightfully chaotic, they will settle down soon and each one will have his own work to do. . . . G. and I look after the special diet and the ordering of all the food. Beef tea is made by the ten gallons and punch by the pail. I was so busy yesterday morning that I didn't know when you left, and only saw the last of the fleet far up York river.

G's Journal.

Lenox Hodge happened to have come over from his hospital station on shore to call on us, just as the first patients arrived for the Ocean Queen, and, being the only doctor on hand at the time, was pressed into the service. He superintended the lowering into the forward cabin of all the very sick. He told us to have wine and water ready for the weakest, and I in the front cabin, and E. in the back, went round with brandy and water and gave it to every man who looked faint. By the time this was done, the gruel was ready, and it was good to see how refreshed the poor fellows were. E. and I were almost alone at the time these first men came. Messrs. Olmsted and Knapp were away on business, and the two young doctors had gone ashore; we should have been completely at a loss without Len. Tug after tug followed, and 800 men were put on board in the next three days.

G. to Mother.

"OCEAN QUEEN."

It seems a strange thing that the sight of such misery should be accepted by us all so quietly as it was. We were simply eyes and hands for those three days. Strong men were dying about us; in nearly every ward some one was going. Yesterday one of the students called me to go with him and say whether I had taken the name of a dead man in the forward cabin the day he came in. He was a strong, handsome fellow, raving mad when brought in, and lying now, the day after, with pink cheeks and peaceful look. I had tried to get his name, and once he seemed to understand and screeched out at the top of his voice, John H. Miller, but whether it was his own name or that of some friend he wanted, I don't know. All the record I had of him was from my diet-list, "Miller, forward cabin, port side, No. 119, beef tea and punch."

Last night Dr. Ware came to me to know how much floor-room we had. The immense saloon of the after-cabin was filled with mattresses so thickly placed that there was hardly stepping room between them, and as I swung my lantern along the row of pale faces, it showed me another strong man dead. E. had been working hard over him, but it was useless. He opened his eyes when she called "Henry" clearly in his ear, and gave her a chance to pour brandy down his throat, but he died quietly while she was helping some one else. We are changed by all this contact with terror, else how could I deliberately turn my lantern on his face and say to the Doctor behind me, "Is that man dead?" and stand coolly, while he listened and examined and pronounced him dead. I could not have quietly said, a year ago, "That will make one more bed, Doctor." Sick men were waiting on deck in the cold though, and every few feet of cabin floor were precious; so they took the dead man out and put him to sleep in his coffin on deck. We had to climb over another soldier lying up there, quiet as he, to get at the blankets to keep the living warm.

From the "Ocean Queen" we, with the rest of the Sanitary Commission Staff, were transferred to the "Wilson Small," which became from this time our home and Headquarters' boat.

A. H. W. to G. and E.

8 BREVOORT PLACE, SATURDAY.

My Dear Girls:

How little we know where you are and what worlds of work you are doing. It is hard to keep still, I know, where so much ought to be done.... Yesterday Charley and the Webster were to sail and we had a carriage and all went down with the traps—box of brandy, trunk of towels, etc., bundle of air-beds, bundle of fans, and a basket with a few eatables—some fresh eggs which had just arrived from Fishkill, and three or four bottles of ale, which I hope Eliza will drink; she sometimes used to take a glass of it at home. As for Georgy, I do not expect to have her take anything of that sort, after what mother tells me of the fate of the boxes of claret you took to Washington. One box was still unopened, and, so far as *she* knew, Georgy had never touched a drop. . . . We found Mrs. Trotter on board. The other ladies soon came—Mrs. Griffin, Miss Katharine P. Wormeley, Mrs. Blatchford and Mrs. H. J. Raymond. . . .

The vessel is a fifth-rate bed-buggy concern, I should say, and the hold where the men were put seemed miserable in spite of your pains, but for which it would have been *very* forlorn. Charley was so busy running hither and thither that we hadn't much chance at him. I was sorry we had not packed a great hamper of cooked food for him and Mrs. Trotter. Another time we will do better. They expect to be back by Wednesday with as many sick as they can carry, and judging from the number they brought packed on the Ocean Queen, they will stow them with deadly closeness. We saw Dr. Grymes and liked his looks and manner. He startled us by telling us that the Ocean Queen was coming up the bay with over a thousand sick, *four hundred typhoid cases.* Couldn't do without *you,* he said; "only ladies down there to come—of course they are on board." Mrs. Griffin, too, was convinced of it and sent back by us a big bundle of tins she had bought for Georgy. We left the Webster at four, when they were to sail at any moment, and drove down to the pier where they said the Ocean Queen was to lie. She was not due till six, so we came home. What with the news from West Point, Virginia, *without details,* and with the idea that you were the only women on the Ocean Queen to see after the nurses and the sick, and Charley's departure, we were sufficiently sobered and excited, a compound of both. This morning Uncle Edward reports us the *Herald's* news from West Point, that it was only a skirmish and that the loss of the 16th was two killed, beside wounded. . . .

At ten o'clock Dr. Buck landed on the Ocean Queen, came up to his house and sent us word that you were *not on board.* This morning he has been in for a moment, and says you were indefatigable and indispensable at the front; far more useful in staying than in coming up, that he didn't know where you went when you left the Ocean Queen, but that you were "all right" with Mr. Olmsted somewhere, and taken care of. . . . Eleven hundred, Dr. Buck said, came on the Ocean Queen. So many of them are *virulent fever* cases, men who must die, that there is great perplexity what to do with them. The City Hospital, North building, is fast filling up, and the air is so infectious that Mrs. Buck thinks it unsafe to enter it. The Commissioners propose that these new cases should go to Ward's Island. The government barracks on Bedloe's and Riker's Islands won't be ready for some days, and I dread having the Daniel Webster or some other transport bring a thousand more before these have been decently housed. . . .

Mother has driven out to Astoria with Uncle E. Carry has gone to Park Barracks with flowers and cologne sent from Astoria, and Jane is at the City Hospital with oranges for fever men. *She* goes into the fever ward, considering it duty, and undertakes too much for her nerves, but you needn't tell her so. Carry and I are going this afternoon to see a "Mr. Woolsey," who was sent to St. Luke's, sick of fever.

A. H. W. to G. and E.

FRIDAY, MAY 16.

We have hundreds of dollars sent to us to spend "for the soldiers." Mr. Wm. Aspinwall, for one, sent Jane a cheque for $250. Now how shall we lay it out, so as to be most useful? Dr. G. said it made him heartsick, as it would us, to see the destitution and suffering of those men brought in at Yorktown. It makes me heartsick to think of it, and the only comfort is in knowing that if the condition of the men is horrible as it is, what would it be if nothing were done—if there were no Sanitary Commission. Take away all that voluntary effort has done for the army and what light would the government appear in before the world? Shamefully inefficient and neglectful!

Dr. Grymes shook Mother warmly by the hand to-day as we went on board the Daniel Webster, and said, "We can't do without your children. We fight for them down there, to know whether they shall go up on the boats or stay at Yorktown, but on the whole, they are more useful where they are. Your son, too, is very busy and is indispensable." I hope you will all three manage soon to be together and have the comfort of each other's help, and keep each other in check from doing too much. Jane says she has awful dreams about Georgy, that the other night a message came that she was ill with hasty typhoid fever followed by paralysis from over-exertion! There, Georgy, is a catalogue of evils for you.

Uncle Edward is ready to do anything on earth. He sent by the Daniel Webster 75 canton flannel shirts which he thought would be useful for typhoid men brought in from camp. Up here, he says, they are sure to be taken care of after a while. He bought also eighty dollars worth of cotton pocket handkerchiefs, half of which I sent by Mrs. Trotter; etc., etc. He brought here for Jane to dispose of six jugs of very old port wine, each half a gallon, which he had decanted himself. Jane says *that* shall be distributed under her own eye. . . .

We sew *your* red flag, I suppose it was, that you spent Sunday in making, flying at the peak of the Daniel Webster. . . . After the hundred canton flannel bed gowns were all made they told us they were too long for sick men and too heavy for fever patients. . . . Mother is extremely anxious to go on one of these trips of the Daniel Webster, and urges my consent! I generally evade the subject, for I think it would be too severe service. Don't you need step-ladders for climbing to upper berths? Have you got them?

We, G. and E. had, by Mr. Olmsted's orders remained on the "Wilson Small" instead of going North, in order to help in the reception of wounded men from the front, the fitting up of the hospital transports and the trans-shipment of patients. Some of the twenty women who had just arrived from New York went up in charge of the Ocean Queen and other transports as they filled up.

We were all assigned to duty by Mr. Olmsted wherever he thought we fitted in best, and his large printed placards put up on the steamers gave orders for the "watches" and hours for "relief," meals, etc., etc., so that the work went on as in a city hospital.

G's Journal.

WILSON SMALL, MAY 7, 62.

The Merrimac is out; and the Monitor and Naugatuck are fighting her. The Galena has run up the James towards Richmond. We are lying along the dock at Yorktown quietly, where four days ago the rebels were ducking themselves in the water.

Franklin's division has moved up to West Point with large reinforcements, and has been fighting at the point of the bayonet. Captain Hopkins steamed alongside this morning and called out the news, just down from West Point, on business, in the Mystic. Two of the 16th are killed, and Captain Curtis wounded in the chest.... We took on board the Small 20 to 30 from this fight. Had beds made on the cabin floor, and each man carefully put into a clean one as his stretcher came aboard, Captain Curtis among them. Several were amputations, and two died on the boat. Everything was done for them; beef tea and brandy given, and a capital surgical nurse was in charge. It was pleasant to see Mr. Olmsted come quietly into the cabin now and then. I would look round and he would be there sitting on the floor by a dying German, with his arm round his pillow—as nearly round his neck as possible—talking tenderly to him, and slipping away again quietly. He only came when the ward was quiet, and no one round to look at him.

E's Journal.

MAY 14.

I can't keep the record of events day by day, but last Friday we came down again from West Point to Yorktown, and G. and I went to Fortress Monroe on two hospital ships, G. on the Knickerbocker with the sick of Franklin's Division, and Miss Whetten and I on the Daniel Webster No. 2, with two hundred of the Williamsburg wounded. Since the day of the battle they had lain in the wet woods with undressed wounds. Some one had huddled them on to a boat without beds or subsistence, and then notified the Sanitary Commission to take care of them; and we were detailed to attend to them on the way to Fortress Monroe, with basins, soap, towels, bandages, etc. We washed and fed them all, Moritz going round with buckets of tea and bread. The poor fellows were very grateful, but we had a terribly hard experience. One man had lost both legs and had one arm useless, but was as cheerful and contented as possible. Colonel Small, of the 26th Pennsylvania, was wounded and lying in the dining room. Just before midnight I went in to see Colonel Fiske, sick with typhoid fever, lying on the bare slats of a berth with only his blanket under him and a knapsack for a pillow. We made him tolerably comfortable and left him much happier than we found him.

Sunday morning the sick were all carefully removed by Dr. Cuyler to the shore hospital at Fortress Monroe, and we ran back to Yorktown, where we found Charley, just arrived on the Daniel Webster from New York, transferred to the Small.

From Mother.

8 BREVOORT PLACE, MAY 13TH.

My Dear Girls:

I have just come up to my own room from breakfast, and from the reading of your most welcome and satisfactory letter, my dear Eliza, written off West Point; and now before anything calls off my attention, or any visitors arrive to "sit the morning," I have seated myself to thank you both, Georgy for her's of the 8th, received on Saturday, and yours E., this morning. It is very thoughtful and kind in you to write at all, and I wonder how you can do it in the midst of *such scenes!* and yet how miserable it would be for *us* if we did not hear directly from your own pens of your welfare. I am as much and more at a loss than yourself where to begin to tell you all I want to say. . . . Miss H. and a lady friend were ushered in upon me this morning, the latter wishing to know *all* the particulars about the *position* of lady nurses down at Yorktown, and what was particularly required of them, as she had started from home with a "strong impulse" to offer her services. All I could tell her was that "a desire to be useful, plain common sense, energetic action, fortitude, and a *working apron,* were some of the absolute essentials!—not to be a looker-on, but a doer—to take hold with a good will and a kind heart. She left with a feeling that perhaps she could be quite useful without going down to Yorktown! I have no doubt she can. . . . Charley must have seen you before this. He will tell you all about his getting off and our being on board with him. He took a quantity of things for himself and you girls, which I hope you may find useful. I told him to help himself from the long basket, and use anything he wanted for himself or others on the voyage. The fruit, I was afraid, might not keep. The fresh eggs were from Fishkill, especially for you, E. I long to hear from Charley all about his trip, and I wonder much whether he will come back in the boat or stay behind. I think it will be better, perhaps, for him to make the trip back here, and then return to stay with you. But this you will, of course, arrange among you. . . . So you have both seen Fortress Monroe, and landed, in spite of Stanton and his strict rules! I am glad of it. You are certainly highly favored girls, and I must give way to a little motherly feeling and say you deserve it all. You cannot imagine what our anxieties have been since the commencement of McClellan's move to push the enemy to the wall. The evacuation of Yorktown took us by surprise, and somehow or other we do not seem to get up the proper degree of enthusiasm about it. The subsequent doings, with the destruction of the much dreaded Merrimac, have not called forth the jubilant demonstrations throughout the community here that I supposed such news would produce. They seem to be waiting for the *occupation of Richmond* to burst out with a joyous and prolonged expression of their feelings. Think of our troops being so near the desired "on to Richmond!" We can scarcely realize all that has happened since our parting that Sunday morning. Oh! how lonely and sad I felt when I turned away from the window to the empty room, and the deserted little beds in the corners at the Ebbitt House. But Hatty and I *made the* most *of each other.* I did not leave her that day. . . . A young gentleman sent in his card last evening,—Julian T. Davies—and followed in. He came to see Mrs. Howland, as her name and Miss Woolsey's were mentioned as having; arrived here in the Ocean Queen. Mr. Hone had called for the same reason, and Mrs. Russell, I believe. Young D. said the report that Colonel Howland was wounded went up one aisle of the church in Fishkill, and immediately after, the *contradiction* went up the other, but he called to know *what* we had heard from you. You cannot tell what a relief and comfort your letter this morning gives us. I drove out on Saturday to Astoria with your Uncle E. Took an early dinner there, and then went up to Mary's and sat with her till six o'clock. Found her perfectly well, and the children lovely. . . . Abby mails you the daily papers constantly; they must be taken by other eager hands. Do let us know if any men from the 16th are brought here. We would like to find them out. Jane is untiring in her visits and attentions at the Hospitals—Abby at her shirt-making and cutting out for others to make, and doing all sorts of good things in the intervals, and doing all the running for the family generally. We cannot prevail on her to take time or money to buy herself a spring bonnet or dress. My love to Charley. I do not write him, as he may be on his way back. Hatty is still in Philadelphia. I am so glad you have Lenox Hodge at hand. It is a real comfort to think of it—tell him so, with my love. Give a great deal of love to our own Joe from us all. We shall be so anxious now to hear all the time. We grasp at every paper. . . . Farewell, dear girls, with a kiss to each, and to Charley two, if with you. We look anxiously for the Daniel Webster. Dr. Buck came and told us all about you—exalted praises!

A. H. W. to G. and E.

MAY 14.

My dear Girls:

Since Mother wrote you yesterday the Daniel Webster has come in again. Fred Rankin called last night with a message from Mrs. Trotter, whom he met in the street on the way from the steamer to take the cars for home. He told us that Charley had stayed down at Yorktown. It may have been necessary for him to do so, in the service, or at the request of the Sanitary Commission, but we feel disappointed that he did not finish up the round trip and return in the steamer. . . .

"Capture of Richmond" has been cried every day for a week by the "Express; 4th Edition" boys!

Mrs. Trotter sent word that she had a very pleasant and satisfactory trip and should sail again on Friday; that most of the men improved on the voyage. They were *all* to be landed at 194 Broadway, F. Rankin thought. Among them, in the newspaper list, we see *Capt. Parker, Co. D, 16th New York.* Carry has just started down town, and a boy with her, carrying a quantity of flannel shirts for convalescents and some cotton ones for the City Hospital. She will stop at all the depots, the Hospital, Park Barracks and 194, and at the two latter will enquire for Captain Parker. She has stuck some handkerchiefs and cologne in her pocket, and I think delights at the prospect of sallying forth unwatched to "find some wounded soldiers." . . . Last night Mother made a white flannel shirt, which has gone down to be put in use at once. She sighs for the quiet of Washington and the companionship of G. and E., whom she *admires,* and who, she is afraid, are making themselves sick. . . .

Do take care of yourselves and let us know what *we* can do. I am having long, white, flannel hospital shirts made, and have bought and sent off all I could find at the employment societies of cotton night-gowns and red volunteer shirts.

Charley's hurried letters from Headquarters of the Sanitary Commission no doubt gave the account of his arrival and his work as purser on the Daniel Webster, and as clerk in the Quartermaster's Department later. We have nothing left but an occasional mention of letters as received. Aunt E. among others says, "Charley's long, interesting letter reached us to-day," and in a letter of F. L. Olmsted's to the Rev. Dr. Bellows his name occurs in this paragraph:"

OFF YORKTOWN, MAY 15.

It is now midnight. Knapp and two supply boats started five hours ago for the sick at Bigelow's Landing. Two of the ladies are with him; the rest are giving beef tea and brandy and water to the sick on the Knickerbocker, who have been put into clean beds. Drs. Ware and Swan are in attendance, aided most efficiently by Wheelock and Haight. Mr. Collins is executive officer on the boat, and *Mr. Woolsey, clerk,* taking charge of the effects of the soldiers.

And later from Miss Wormeley:

"We all take the greatest interest in Charley's letter. He writes well, just what he sees and thinks about and throws genuine light on other accounts."

G. to Mother.

STEAMER KNICKERBOCKER.

If my letter smells of "Yellow B." sugar, it has a right to, as my paper is the cover of the sugar-box. Since I last wrote I have been jumping round from boat to boat, and Saturday came on board the Knickerbocker at Mr. Olmsted's request, with Mrs. Strong and some others, to put things in order, and, privately, to be on hand to "hold" the boat, which had been made over to the Commission, over the heads of the New Jersey delegation. Dr. Asch was on board, and we had the New Jersey dinner table abolished and 56 Sanitary Commission beds made on the dining-room floor that night. The 200 wounded and sick brought down to Fortress Monroe under our care were transferred to the shore hospital, where we stole some roses for our patients on the Small. Saw regiments embarking for Norfolk, which surrendered the next day. Saw Mr. Lincoln driving past to take possession of Norfolk; and by Tuesday had the boat all in order again, with the single exception of a special-diet cooking-stove. So we went ashore at Gloster Point and ransacked all the abandoned rebel huts to find one, coming down finally upon the sutler of the "Enfants Perdus," who was cooking something nice for the officers' mess over a stove with *four* places for pots. This was too much to stand; so under a written authority given to "Dr. Olmsted" by the quartermaster of this department, we proceeded to rake out the sutler's fire and lift off his pots, and he offered us his cart and mule to drag the stove to the boat and would take no pay! So through the wretched town filled with the debris of huts and camp furniture, old blankets, dirty cast-off clothing, smashed gun-carriages, exploded guns, vermin and filth every-where, and along the sandy shore covered with cannon-balls, we followed the mule,—a triumphant procession, waving our broken bits of stovepipe and iron pot-covers. I left a polite message for the Colonel "Perdu," which had to stand him in place of his lost dinner. I shall never understand what was the matter with that sutler, whose self-sacrifice was to secure some three hundred men their meals promptly.

We set up our stove in the Knickerbocker, unpacked tins and clothing, filled a linen-closet in each ward, made up beds for three hundred, set the kitchen in order, and arranged a black hole with a lock to it, where oranges, brandy and wine are stored box upon box; and got back to York-town to find everybody at work fitting up the "Spaulding." I have a daily struggle with the darkeys in the kitchen, who protest against everything. About twenty men are fed from one pail of soup, and five from a loaf of bread, unless they are almost well, and then no amount of food is enough.

One gets toughened on one's fourth hospital ship and now I could stop at nothing; but it is amusing to see the different ways taken to dis-cover the same thing. Dr. McC.: "Well-my-dear-fellow-is-anything-the-matter-with-your-bowels-do-your-ears-ring-what-'s-your-name?" Dr. A.: "Turn over my friend, have you got the dia*ree*?" Dr. A. was in a state of indignation with Miss Dix in the shore hospital at Yorktown. She has peculiar views on diet, not approving of meat, and treating all to arrowroot and farina, and by no means allowing crackers with gruel. "*Them* does not go with this," as Dr. A. gracefully puts the words into Miss Dix's mouth.

Interior of a Hospital Transport
Harper's Pictorial History of the Great Rebellion

CHAPTER EIGHT

The Working Sisters

E's Journal.

MAY 17, SPAULDING. STEAMING UP YORK RIVER.

We have just been transferred to this big boat, while the Wilson Small goes for repairs. This boat will accommodate four or five hundred men in bunks, now being put up by the carpenter and filled with mattresses stuffed by the "Lost Children" who are garrisoning Yorktown....

May 18. My entry was broken short by the arrival of 160 men for the Knickerbocker, and we were once more very busy. They were all fed,—numbered, and recorded by name, (Charley's work), and put to bed. Next morning arrived 115 more, for whom the Elizabeth with Miss Wormeley, Miss Gilson, and two men of the staff had been sent up Queen's Creek—tired, miserable fellows, who had been lying in the wet and jolted over horrible roads. There was another tugboat full, too, and Mrs. Griffin and I took charge of both till the men were moved into the Knickerbocker.

We are now steaming up towards White House, all on deck enjoying the sail except Mr. Knapp and Charley, who are unpacking quilts for the bunks now ready.

G. to Mother.

MAY 19.

We are lying in the Spaulding just below the burnt railroad bridge on the Pamunkey. It is startling to find so far from the sea a river whose name we hardly knew two weeks ago, where our anchor drops in three fathoms of water, and our ship turns freely either way with the tide. Our smoke stacks are almost swept by the hanging branches as we move, and great schooners are drawn up under the banks, tied to the trees. The Spaulding herself lies in the shade of an elm tree, which is a landmark for miles up and down. The army is encamped close at hand, resting this Sunday, and eating its six pies to a man, so getting ready for a move, which is planning in McClellan's tent.

E. writes

Half a mile above us is the White House naming the place, a modern cottage if ever "white" now drabbed over, standing where the early home of Mrs. Washington stood. We went ashore this morning, and with General Franklin and his aides strolled about the grounds—an unpretending little place, with old trees shading the cottage, a green lawn sloping to the river, and an old-time garden full of roses. The house has been emptied, but there are some pieces of quaint furniture, brass fire-dogs, etc.; and just inside the door this notice is posted:—Northern soldiers, who profess to reverence the name of Washington, forbear to desecrate the home of his early married life, the property of his wife, and now the home of his descendants. (Signed)
A GRANDDAUGHTER OF MRS. WASHINGTON.

Some one has written underneath in pencil, "Lady, a northern officer has protected this property within sight of the enemy and at the request of your overseer." It is Government property now, and the flag waves from the top, and sentinels pace the piazza.

After wandering about the grounds General Franklin sent for General FitzJohn Porter, who, with General Morell and their staffs and Will Winthrop, whom we met by chance, came back to the Spaulding with us and were treated to clean handkerchiefs, cologne, tacks, pins, etc., from our private stores. General Seth Williams also made a long, friendly call on deck, during which we dropped half a mile down the river and anchored.

Mr. Knapp has gone down to bring up the rest of the Commission fleet, and White House will be our headquarters for the present.

The Army of the Potomac was all this time advancing, and McClellan was at New Bridge, within eight miles of Richmond, his base of supplies being White House on the Pamunkey, a feeder of the York River; and there the hospital fleet assembled and the Sanitary Commission established its headquarters on the line of the railroad running to Richmond.

Our forces held the road, and trains of wounded, and men dying of fever from the swamps of the Chickahominy, arrived at any and all hours.

A. H. W.

NEW YORK, MAY 19, 1862.

My Dear Children:

I am writing in a book-store down town. . . . We had a famous letter on Saturday from you, Georgy, and another, half Eliza's half Charley's. I did not discover at first at what word one broke off and the other began. Your adventures are like those of the fox and the goose and the bag of corn. I hope you will all come together after awhile, perhaps have done so already, as both these letters were directed in Charley's handwriting. Charley himself ordered your *Tribune* transferred to our house, and it is coming regularly. I have all the numbers from May 1, and I understood Mother that she had in one of the trunks all the numbers up to that date. . . . Baskets of flowers, vegetables, mushrooms, butter, etc., came down on Saturday from Fishkill. . . .

I have bought all the shirts I could find at the employment societies. . . . Do you need grey or red *flannel* shirts. You may as well say out and out what your observation decides is needed, and don't be mealy-mouthed as to asking, or in mentioning quantities. We can as well send hundreds as dozens, except that it takes a little more time to collect them. Money is no barrier, of course. If all we can do is to *send* things for you to make useful, do let us send enough! and do you use up fast enough. . . . Thomas Denny & Co., Mr. Aspinwall, Robert, and others have just made their money over to Jane, "for you and your sisters to spend in any way for the soldiers," and they all refuse to say what we shall buy or precisely how much shall be used here or sent there.

You remember I said Carry had gone down in search of Captain Parker, of the 16th. She picked out the handsomest man in the barracks, with pale complexion and long blonde beard, but he was in bed, undressed and fast asleep.

The lists had not been made out, and no one knew if that were he.

She had no flowers—nothing but a soft old cambric handkerchief which she cologned and laid on his pillow, but she had to come away without finding out who he was. . . . You must send any wounded officer to our house, using your discretion of course about it—those officers who have been used to refinement, and who need care. We should be very glad to entertain them and take care of them as they pass through the city, above all any officer of Joe's regiment. Captain Curtis must certainly come to us when he is well enough to move. . . .

Jane has gone to the City Hospital this morning with her usual illustrated papers and pots of jelly. The mortality in the North house, where the fever patients are, is very saddening. They hardly seem sick at all, but they die. She takes down things one day to a man, and next day he is dead. Five or six is the daily number. . . . Good-bye, dear girls and boy.

From H. L. H.

ON BOARD HOSPITAL SHIP "WHILLDIN,"
CHESAPEAKE BAY, MAY 21, 1862.

Dear Georgy:

We are again on the Bay on our way to join the army. I was very sorry that we moved up to Queen's Creek for the wounded of Williamsburgh before Eliza and yourself examined the Commodore. For a few days we were very busy. Some 1,500 wounded men passed under our charge.

I was home for a day or two and saw Hatty. Mother enjoyed her visit very much. I send this to you, though I do not know where you are, simply to announce that I hope soon to see you. As we both have the same object in view, may we arrive at the *same spot again,* no matter where that may be.

E. to J. H.

FLOATING HOSPITAL, SPAULDING,
OFF WHITE HOUSE, MAY 22.

We are to go on shore presently to see what we can do for the large field hospital there. Two of our doctors, Ware and Draper of New York, spent the day yesterday trying to organize it and make the men tolerably comfortable. They furnished from the Commission nearly a thousand mattresses, secured them fresh water in hogsheads (which they were entirely without) and saw that all who needed medicine got it. System and food seem to be the great wants, and to-day we ladies will attend to the latter take them supplies and show the hospital cooks how to prepare them. There are 1,200 or more sick men there, and until the Commission took hold they were in a most wretched plight, lying on the damp ground without beds, without food or water, and with little or no care. . . . I hope you take all necessary precautions in this wretched climate. *Don't give up your quinine.*

Later.—Directly after I wrote you this morning Georgy and I went to the shore to breakfast the men we had dinnered and teaed yesterday, and there we had a little house nearby, which Dr. Ware had found, nicely cleaned out for a hospital or resting-place for the sick when the other overflows. The floor of one of the rooms up stairs is six inches deep in beans. That makes a good bed for them. . . . Meantime Mrs. Griffin and the others got this boat in order for sick, and this afternoon fifty odd have been brought on board. To-morrow it will fill up and leave for New York.

G. to Mother.

STEAMER SPAULDING.

The Spaulding is bunked in every hole and corner. The last hundred patients were put on board to relieve the over-crowded shore hospital late last night; stopped at the gang plank, each one, while Charley numbered all their little treasures and wrote the man's name. Though these night scenes on the hospital ships are part of our daily living, a fresh eye would find them dramatic. We are awaked in the dead of night by a sharp steam whistle, and soon after feel ourselves clawed by the little tugs on either side of our big ship, and at once the process of taking on hundreds of men, many of them crazy with fever, begins. There's the bringing of the stretchers up the side ladder between the two boats, the stopping at the head of it, where the names and home addresses of all who can speak are written down, and their knapsacks and little treasures numbered and stacked. Then the placing of the stretchers on the deck, the row of anxious faces above and below decks, the lantern held over the hold, the word given to "lower," the slow-moving ropes and pulleys, the arrival at the bottom, the lifting out of the sick man, and the lifting into his bed; and then the sudden change from cold, hunger, and friendlessness to comfort and satisfaction, winding up with his invariable verdict, if he can speak, "This is just like home."

The Spaulding being all ready was now started northward, and the "staff" moved back to the Small once more, from which they were busy day and night receiving the sick and wounded, fitting up hospital ships, and starting them to northern ports.

A. H. W. to G. and E.

MAY.

My Dear Children:

Doesn't Charley want something? Mother is racking her brain to think what it can be, as he no doubt does want something, going off in the hurry he did. She is afraid, too, that he is exposed to illness—running risks from the climate, from contact with soldiers' clothing, from the atmosphere of the hospital ship, etc., etc.

Yesterday, Jane, Carry, Mrs. Buck, and Col. Bliss and a few others, started from Park Barracks for Bedloe's Island on a committee of investigation. They chartered a little steam tug at ten dollars an hour, and went from the Battery, not staying very long, and quite enjoying the trip. They found the hospitals extremely comfortable. Some sick in the brick barracks, and some in three large hospital tents, close on the shore, with the sea breeze driving through them, and the waves rippling up close by. The men they saw were as pleased with their accommodations as could be, and everything looked ten times better ventilated and more hopeful than at the City Hospital, for instance. They have about a hundred men on Bedloe's Island, mostly from the Ocean Queen, and not many now are alarmingly ill. The ladies took down four large baskets of oranges, jelly, towels, etc.—some of the abundant supplies that have been pouring in at the Park Barracks—and we are to get together next week some books for a library. Jane says she has seen what does her heart good at the City Hospital—some tidy, sensible, once-upon-a-time-fashionable ladies, nursing men every day in the fever wards—Mrs. Charles Strong, Miss Irving, and four or five others; they went down and offered their services, which were accepted—such was the great number of sick, and the necessity of an immediate increase of nurses; and they go down every morning at seven and go away at seven, taking their meals down there. Hired nurses, men, watch at night. Here was an excellent chance to put some of the port wine Uncle E. sent us, into use. Jane came right up for a jug and put it in Mrs. Strong's charge, and it has been of inestimable use already to some of the patients. These ladies must have served a week or ten days now, and will continue daily. They do everything for the men, under the direction of the doctors, administering food and medicine. It is really most praiseworthy and delightful, and, as in the case of your young doctors whom you like so much, gives you a better idea of human nature—*their* human nature, at all events. I cannot say so much for the young doctors of the New York Hospital as you do for yours. They made a strike the other day for increase of salary, writing the Trustees quite an impudent letter, reminding them what advantages the State now offered to volunteer surgeons at Yorktown, etc., and requesting an immediate answer. They did have a very immediate one. The gentlemen assembled next morning and sent the young doctors word that they could have just so many hours to pack up and quit,—an answer that astonished and mortified them. You see it was very mean, for it was just when the largest number of sick that the house could contain were being brought in. The Trustees intended to increase the corps of surgeons, but *that* these residents would not listen to, "they were fully competent to do all." . . . Jane went down this morning with Mrs. Professor Hitchcock, Mrs. Smith, and Mrs. Buck, to take their turn at 194, but found that the last week's committee and their friends to the number of twenty, were so firmly established still, that they refused all hints about "relinquishing the keys," being "tired of the service," etc., etc.; "Oh, no; we are as fresh and interested as possible:" and indeed they were, though they were at the rooms until one last night, when Colonel Howe chartered an omnibus and sent them home. They had received all those who came yesterday afternoon by cars from Baltimore, and had worked faithfully, and hated to give up to the new set.

A. H. W. to E.
Dear E.:

The returning Spaulding takes to you 12 Boston rockers, 6 boxes of brandy (if it gets there), 1 package of mosquito bar (getting very scarce), a bundle and a basket, and chewing tobacco, for Charley to distribute! . . .

Tell him the 22d marched in splendid order; their own uniforms and long yellow leather leggings. The cheers and fireworks and interest all along the line were as great as the 7th ever elicited. Carry and Charles Johnson sat on a stoop on Broadway, till ten o'clock night before last, to see them pass. We hear that they are ordered to Harpers Ferry.

J. S. W. to a friend in Europe

MAY 23, 1862.

We all talk politics now. I asked a wide awake cousin to-day, "What do you think about England now?" "England? England?" was the answer, "I had entirely forgotten that there was such a country!" . . . Our English friends sent us Mr. Gladstone's speech. Mr. Gladstone is a fair representative Englishman, and a man whom everyone must respect; but hear him! the same mysterious incapacity to understand us. Hear his excuse for England's lack of sympathy. He says an expression of sympathy with us would have alienated six or ten millions who *might have become* an independent nation! But why alienate, for their sakes, eighteen or nineteen millions *already* an independent people? Because the friendship of the rebel section (granted independence), was better for trade. How the shop shines through! Then he uses the false analogy of the rebels of '76, etc., etc., and that is the best they can do. But at the same time I honor the fortitude, and pity the sorrows of Lancashire, and don't despair of even "sympathy" when Bright and Stuart Mill live and lift up their voices; though it seems sometimes as if Great Britain had wantonly thrown away the friendship of this country, between the South, which hates her because she has not yet broken the blockade, and the North, which distrusts her intentions. Probably there is no other question on which both sections are so completely agreed. . . . I think I must have done my little duty by the affairs of the nation, and descend from these topics to the comparatively ridiculous items of personal narrative. We are connected with one or two organizations for receiving the disabled volunteers on their way home, . . . helpless, wasted gaunt, fever-smitten, worn-out men. It is the old story; camp sickness immensely in excess of wounds. A great many have died at the city hospitals, and a great many are still here, slowly going, or slowly recovering. We do what we can. There is nothing they need or fancy, they cannot instantly have, but it is heart-breaking work; I feel as if I had been wrung

out and dried: and how nobly the men behave! I *must* testify to their
patience and sweet humor through everything, dying in torment with a
smile in their eyes and grateful thanks on their tongues; praying for their
country and *their nurses* in their last delirium. I could tell you twenty stories, but I'll only tell one. Private Jones, hurt mortally in the charge on
the rebel rifle-pits at Lee's Mills, and forced to have the bad regimental
surgeon's work done over again here, showed great fortitude, the tender-
hearted surgeon told us, during the dressing of his wounds. We repeated
the surgeon's praises to him and asked him if he really found it easier than
he feared. "O, no!" the dear boy said, "it was *very* bad, but I saw the tears in
the doctor's eyes, and do you think I was going to let *him* see how much he
hurt me?" My head and heart have been so full of these things that they
will come out through the inkstand. The "boys" have a great deal to say
about the "mean whites," and several of them have told me emphatically
that they consider them much less worthy of freedom than the negroes.
Sergeant Eaton tells me "their faces are dirty, their clothes are dirty, and
their conversation exactly matches their dress." . . . Mrs. Howland and
Georgy, who are in the transport service on York River, say no praise can
do justice to the untiring and tender carefulness of the volunteer doctors.
They speak very highly of Mr. Olmsted, who directs it all, finding, as they
say, continual comfort in his administrative genius.

They explored the forsaken works at Yorktown, and saw the wreck and
the indiscriminate, wanton destruction of the flight. They saw many tin
plates left with bits of pork upon them, and nasty tin cups with dregs
of coffee, but almost every plate and cup they saw, was slashed with an
axe. Here and there all through the camps were stakes driven with the
warning, "dangerous," graves of torpedoes and other infernal apparatus.
Charley saw one in a water-jug. He is volunteer purser, and he and the
ladies go from one transport to another, as they are wanted. . . . The siege-
approaches, or whatever they call them, are killing work for the men. I
asked a wan, crippled creature at the Park Barracks last week if he had
been in battle. "Oh, yes," he answered, "in many battles, but I fought them
all with a shovel."

Mary's fifth little girl was born at Astoria, May 24th, '62. Various
names were proposed for the "bright little thing with dark steel colored

eyes":—Bella ("horrida belle" Jane said) among them, but she was generally known as "Pamunkey," Abby writes, "that being a household word at the time. When she was old enough however, she was, in honor of her Aunt G., who was doing hospital work, taken in from Astoria to the chapel of old St. Luke's Hospital on Fifth Avenue and 54th-55th Sts., and baptized by her father's old friend Rev. Dr. Muhlenberg, "Georgeanna,"—Sarah Woolsey being god-mother. The record is in the books of the hospital chapel, no doubt.

One of the favorite relics to send home from the front used to be shot and shell picked up on battle fields. Carry seemed to feel less grateful than we expected for those forwarded to 8 Brevoort Place, from the immediate front of the Sanitary Commission.

C. C. W. to C. W. W.

FRIDAY MORNING.

Dear Charley:

We live in mortal fear of the projectiles going off, the grape shot exploding, and the cannon balls doing something else equally unpleasant. There is no reason why we should not set up an armory, we have such a variety of arms. But really the grape has never been used and I see nothing to prevent its suddenly igniting; at all events, I don't mean to hammer on the nail at the top, which I firmly believe to be a fuse. The day it came Mr. W. was calling and, though I was deeply interested of course in what he was saying, I could not help hearing the conversation that went on in the entry between mother and the city expressman, whom mother took to be a soldier from the Daniel Webster and treated accordingly, gave him half a dollar (12½ cents being the price) and, not exactly invited him in to dinner, but offered him some there! . . . We have a quantity of things to send to the girls on the return hospital transport. Uncle Edward sent here yesterday 100 shirts, some to go to Eliza, and 1,000 pocket handkerchiefs. . . . Mother and I went to the Park Barracks yesterday in Jane's place. There is a system of passes now, and no lady can get in without one, except myself, who go and come freely and no questions asked,—I don't know why, unless there is a natural dignity and committee expression in my face that no one is discerning enough, except the admitting policeman, to see. . . .

Write when you can and tell us all you do. We still direct Cheeseman's Creek.

From Mother.

8 BREVOORT PLACE, FRIDAY MORNING.

My dear Girls and Charley:

All your notes and letters are of thrilling interest to us now, and though we think it very kind of you to take a minute even for us, in the midst of all that is going on around you, we are craving enough to cry for more, more. I was a little disappointed not to see you, Charley, by the Daniel Webster, but I am not surprised at your staying behind.

I meant to have given more time to my pen for you, but spent all day yesterday at the Park Barracks, nailing blue cambric over wooden clothes-horses for screens around the men's beds, a very tiresome job, and I came home used up, and went to bed at once. This morning I feel all right again. My quiet three months in Washington and a drive out, instead of a dragging walk every day, has spoiled me for the distracting noise and cares of New York, or else I have grown old and feeble! I want very much to slip into Jane's place at the hospitals if she will let me, for she is breaking herself down. It is not half so pleasant here in these places as it was in Washington or Alexandria, as you could go in there amongst the soldiers and talk with them, and give them, yourselves, the clean handkerchiefs, all cologned! and the books and papers, etc., but here you are not allowed to do this; can only be admitted to the committee room by ticket. . . . This system is carried to a hateful excess. . . . The greatest quantity of goods and food and drink and everything you can imagine is constantly being sent in—people send them here (to No. 8), too. Our front entry is literally filled up now with immense bundles and packages of shirts, draw-ers, stockings, shoes, everything. One item is one dozen boxes of cologne from your Uncle E. . . . Abby has *bought out* several industrial societies in shirts and drawers. Charley, I saw one poor soldier walking off yesterday with what I instantly recognized as one of your old shirts I had given to Mrs. Buck. she said he was so proud of his plaited bosom! They prefer old fine ones to new cotton without bosoms or stiff wristbands. And they all ask for neckties to wear home, so I am going out this morning to buy a great lot of them. . . . Carry is writing to you, dear Charley, and Abby is

scratching away to some of you. Pico and Mac are yelping and ravenous for breakfast. . . . Do come up for a run one of these days, but not to take turns in night-watches on board with the sick, in a crowded cabin. I want you to have a little rest and some fresh air. . . . Did Charley find the gimlets and corkscrew? I stuffed such little things in where I could find room, for his stateroom. I should judge he had not much room to hang a coat from the looks of his den on the transport when I saw it. With ever so much love to you all, and the earnest wish that you would *send for me,*—I want to go down exceedingly—
YOUR LOVING MOTHER.

E. W. H. to J. H.

FLOATING HOSPITAL,
OFF WHITE HOUSE, MAY 27.

Still not a word from you for a fortnight now. I am beginning to be very hungry,—not anxious, only *hungry,* for letters. I only hear in indirect ways that our division was near the Chickahominy a day or two ago and was ordered to march into Richmond the next morning; and again yesterday that the whole army was to move in light marching order, leaving wagons and tents behind the Chickahominy. I dream about it all, and wonder, but *know* nothing. . . . We moved to the Knickerbocker from the Small and found a great state of confusion consequent upon having the Elm City emptied into it. . . . The event of this evening is the return of the old Daniel Webster, which we all look upon as a sort of home. . . . Dr. Grymes always invites us over "home" when he arrives in it, and we had a very nice dinner with him to-day. He rose as we came in and said, "I give you welcome where you have a right." Mrs. Trotter returned in the Webster and Mrs. Baylies, Mrs. Bradford and Miss Mary Hamilton came down from New York this time. The two latter are to stay, and be replaced on the return trip by some of our force who want to go home. The Webster brought us more bundles and stores from home and lots of letters and papers.

Captain Curtis of the 16th, who had been a patient on board our Headquarters boat the "Small," since his wound at West Point, went up in one of the transports to an Alexandria hospital. He found there our friend Chaplain Hopkins, still hard at work among the sick and wounded. The following letter from the chaplain is inserted to show the success of our effort to have hospital chaplains appointed by the government. Mr. Hopkins received his commission and was under military orders from this time.

ALEXANDRIA, JUNE 3D, 1862.

My dear Mrs. Howland:

As you may have noticed, the bill for hospital chaplains has become a law. . . . After several ineffectual attempts to see the President, I at last gained access to him yesterday, to ask the appointment of a hospital chaplain in my place, and found his excellency in a most genial frame of mind. He was fairly exuberant; told funny stories! volunteered the remark that he "was afraid that fellow Jackson had got away after all," etc., etc. He told me that he had that very day appointed a man to help me—Bowman, he believed. "A very good man, isn't he?" Mr. B. had been condoling with him on the loss of his son Willy. My application he seemed to be most favorably impressed with, endorsed what I had to say on the back of it with his own hand, rang for Mr. Nicolay, and—I say it with pain, but not without hope—*had it filed away.*

The moment Richmond is taken I shall apply to be removed there, and shall hope to join you and Miss Woolsey in many an excursion into the to-be historic environs. How you ladies can preserve calmness and elasticity of spirit I do not understand, but I know that you do.

On May 30 and June 1, '62, the terrible battle of Fair Oaks was fought.

The Commission had had a new Hospital tent pitched on shore at White House, near the railroad landing, for a kitchen and store-house, and we women took charge of it, feeding nearly all of the three or four thousand men who were brought down from the battle-field. The Commission established a bakery, and 100 fresh loaves were stacked on our tent table daily.

G. to Mother.

JUNE 3.

The trains of wounded and sick arrive at all hours of the night, the last one just before day-light. As soon as the whistle is heard Dr. Ware is on hand and we are ready in the tent, blazing trench-fires and kettles all of a row, bright lights and piles of fresh bread and pots of coffee; tent door opened wide, the road leading to it from the cars dotted all along the side with little fires or lighted candles. Then comes the first procession of slightly wounded, who stop at the tent door on their way to the Hospital boat, and get cups of hot coffee and as much condensed milk as they want—these followed by the slow moving line of bearers and stretchers, halted by our man, Wagner, detached from the Duryea Zouaves, and the poor fellows on the stretchers have brandy, or wine, or iced lemonade given them. It makes but a minute's delay to pour something down their throats and put oranges in their hands, and saves them from exhaustion before food can be served them, in the confusion that reigns in the regular Government boats! When the worst cases have been put on board, the rest are sent to the twenty Sibley tents pitched for the Commission along the railroad, and our detail of five men start, each with his own pail of hot coffee or hot milk, crackers, soft bread, lemonade, and ice water, and feed them from tent to tent. For these men no provision has been made by the Government, and they are left on our hands, sometimes three days at a time. They would fare badly but for the sleepless devotion of Dr. Ware, who works among them night after night, often until two or three o'clock in the morning.

Without exception, the Government boats so far have been inadequately provisioned, wretchedly officered, and in a general state of confusion,—Dr. Agnew calls it "damnable."

One Government boat, which had been lying here waiting for wounded for a fortnight, would have left this morning, crowded with suffering men, without food (except hard-tack), but for the Commission; without a cup, or a basin, or a lemon, or a particle of lint, or bandages, or old linen, without clear water for bathing, and without an ounce of beef,—though their official report had been to the Commission that they were "all ready." One man had been without nourishment all day until an hour before his shoulder was taken off. Then the surgeon hurried over and asked us to take him beef tea and egg-nogg, and I crossed the coal barges and fed him myself, and two others; this after the doctor had himself told me that they needed no help. This is just where the Commission comes in—kettles of soup and tea with soft bread and stimulants are sent from the tent kitchen, and with them go cups and spoons and attendants to distribute the food. It is just the same with lint and bandages, and splints, all of which the Commission supplies freely.

We fed from our kitchen 600 men for two days on two of these Government "all ready" boats.

Some of the hurried notes in the small blank books we carried about with us (G's tied to her belt) are characteristic, and somewhat mixed at the distance of 36 years.

78 pillow-cases, and 4 mattresses. Whiskey for 10, brandy for 4. W. T., 48th Ga., Co. D. C. G., both legs; handkerchiefs, arrowroot, bay-rum. V. W., shoulder off, 17 Cedar St. E. D., lowest berth; Waters, top berth.

And in the midst of it this note:

To Mrs. I.

3 Milligan Place.

My dear Mother:
You must not be anxious about me as I am not wounded, only sick. I was not in the battle because I was not strong enough to hold my gun. The battle began Sunday while I was in bed. We had to jump up and take our arms. I asked the lieutenant to let me fall out; he said I might, and stay there. The rebels came right up to the pits. Our men began to retreat very fast, and one came and told me to get up or I would be taken prisoner. So the doctor sent me down in the woods. Three nights I had nothing to cover me, slept just under the dew. The doctor put me on the cars and I was brought to White House. I am lying now in better condition and being better taken care of.—Beef essence, tea, oranges! Etc., etc. etc.

We used to say:

> "In the great history of the land
> A lady *with a flask* shall stand."

A. H. W. to G. and E.

Georgy's letter of the 23d, written on the Spaulding from White House, came in this morning at breakfast, which is more prompt than usual. It tells of the proposed opening of hospital tents ashore, and *two thousand* sick ready to put into them at once. Why the Commission should have had to work long and perseveringly to accomplish this, I don't know. . . . The accumulating number of sick is frightful, especially when we remember that hundreds probably die unknown on the roads, literally from starvation and exhaustion. . . . *God's* curse, and not his blessing, is evidently on the whole country now, and will be while such pro-slavery policy as we have had is persisted in, and such burning sins as the Fugitive Slave Law gives rise to are perpetrated on the very Capitol steps at Washington.

Here is Banks, the embodiment of "success," which is his motto, his command pursued and scattering; the Baltimore & Ohio road and the termini of those other important communications, all abandoned. Mobs in Baltimore, panic everywhere, and we just where we were more than a year ago; the *7th Regiment ordered off this afternoon* for the defense of Washington. . . . Why, the war proper hasn't so much as *begun* yet. . . .

Later:

Carry took Jane's turn at Park Barracks yesterday afternoon. They have gone lately on alternate days and as Carry is very chatty with the men and very communicative when she comes home we hear a great deal of funny talk and pleasant incident. She helped get tea for them last night at 194. Smoked beef and boiled eggs, tea and toast and butter, all on little white plates, and each man served on a separate little tray at his bedside, if he was weak and in bed.

A. H. W.

NEW YORK, JUNE 2D, 1862.

My dear Girls:

Charley's letter of Thursday came in this morning. He explained to us his system of numbering and sorting the men's luggage, etc., which interested us very much, and shows us what his duties are in some of their details. We are glad the nutmegs and lemon-squeezers happened to fit in a gap. What else can we send? I hope Moritz, with the rockers and brandy, will all arrive safely. Do you want more air-beds? . . . Dorus Woolsey has been in for a final goodbye this morning.

He will get a furlough as soon as possible, for his business affairs hardly allow of his being absent so soon. The 7th, 22d and 37th are doing police duty at Baltimore. I mean they are the military guard of the city. . . . Rev. J. Cotton Smith went too as chaplain. The night before, he tried to make a speech to them in the regimental armory, but was cheered so that he had to stop. "Go on, go on!" they all cried, and he managed to make himself heard, and said "On the whole I won't go on now; all I want to add is that I am *going on to-morrow!*" at which there was tremendous cheering again.

Night was made hideous with *Herald* extras, screamed through the streets between eleven and twelve. We waited till this morning, and got the news in the morning papers of that horrible battle, and what is worse—that *in*decisive battle. It has shattered the strength of McClellan's army—what poor creatures were left in it, after all the sickness and fatigue of the march—and has accomplished *nothing.* . . . Charley says that 3,900 men of Casey's division were lost on the march. God help them and their families, who can only know that they died like dogs on a roadside with fatigue and hunger This makes four full regiments out of a division which only had ten to start with. No wonder it was overborne and broke line and scattered! Never accuse such men of cowardice.

We are much worked up this morning with this news of our disaster, and with the information that North Carolina slave-laws are re-enforced and Colyer's black schools disbanded by government direction. What Government that commits such an act, can expect anything *but reverses* to its arms!

Worst of all, as far as *our* petty little hopes and interests are concerned, here is the order promulgated this morning, by which General H. B.

takes supreme military command of all sick and wounded arriving here on transports. They are to be unloaded at Fort Hamilton and Bedloe's Island, and the ladies' game at Park Barracks and at 194 is blocked. B. is a regular of the regulars as to primness and military order, and personally has no more heart than a mustard seed. . . . Jane has gone down this morning full of wrath, to kidnap Abbott, of the 16th, if possible, and send him to his friends in Maine. She wants to get a ticket transferring him to 194 Broadway, when, if necessary, he can be "lost on the way," and whipped into a carriage and down to the Fall River boat! . . . All these volunteer efforts at comforting and clothing the men must come to an end. Fort Hamilton is too far out of the reach of ladies with oranges and clean pocket handkerchiefs' unless they hire a tug at ten dollars an hour, and go through all the formalities of military passes.

A little later E. writes to J. H.:—

I enclose some comments about Casey's division, and we all agree here that justice was not done to the men. It is surely hard enough to lose as terribly as they did without being reproached for cowardice. Abby says in a late letter—"Anna Jeffries came on from Boston yesterday in the train which brought many of the Daniel Webster load, scattering them all along at or near their homes. One gentleman was asking another whether Casey was of Rhode Island or Connecticut, when a wounded soldier cried out from some seat nearby, overhearing Casey's name—a cry of anguish and anger—'They didn't run! they didn't run!' He tried to stagger to his feet, being wounded in both ankles, and then added—'I can't stand, but I tell you they only broke, they didn't run.'"

H. L. H. to G.

PHILADELPHIA, JUNE, 1862.

Dear Georgy:

Once more our paths have separated. . . . Upon my return with the wounded from the battle of Fair Oaks, I received an appointment to a large hospital (1,500 beds) now building in West Philadelphia. I will live at home, but will be *there* a part of each day.

The Pennsylvania delegation to which, as you know, I was attached when at the White House and elsewhere, has been dissolved.

H. R. W. to G. and E.

New York, June.

Dear Girls:

I write more for the sake of sending a letter by Dr. Draper, than because there is anything to tell you about. . . . I think Abby looks miserable and needs rest. I don't believe even you, "the working sisters," as Dr. Ferris calls you, do as much as Abby does, for there is certainly something that pays in giving nice little things to soldiers and having them so grateful to you and seeing them get well under your care,—there is an excitement in it all which cannot be got out of homely unbleached cotton, yards and yards and hundreds of square yards of shirts. . . .

Think of my having a chance of becoming a nurse up at the Mott Hospital in Fifty-first street. Mrs. Ferris offered me a place of that kind, out of consideration for my merits and the one hundred dollars Uncle E. had given them the week before, but I foolishly gave in to the family row. They had me laid out and buried twenty times over of malignant typhoid, diphtheria, and other ills which flesh is heir to.

. . . Carry is engaged in finding a summer retreat for the family. . . . The combinations absolutely necessary are: sea and mountain air, a place near the city with speedy communication, and no New Yorkers.

I send Charley's wine, Dr. Draper having offered to take anything for us.

We must give you a little breathing place. Your Aunt Abby's dark views for the country, with her eyes persistently kept on the Army of the Potomac, were not justified to anyone willing to take a wide sweep of the horizon. McClellan was not our only general, happily. All round the edges of the map of the rebel states, inroads were being made, and the army and navy at large were giving us hope and courage. Admiral Foote had reconnoitered the Mississippi for a long distance. Garfield (later President) had successes in Kentucky. Hatteras, N. C. was occupied, and a provisional loyal governor congratulated that state "on its salvation." General *Grant* had taken Fort Henry, on the Tennessee River, and Fort Donelson with 15,000 prisoners. Roanoke Island was captured off North Carolina by the army and navy. Springfield, Mo. was taken. Mitchell (professor of Astronomy in Dudley Observatory) was in charge of the troops who took and occupied Bowling Green, Kentucky. Pope in Missouri had captured three Generals, 6,000 prisoners, and 100 siege-guns. Nashville, Tenn. was evacuated and held by the U. S. troops. Columbus, Kentucky, saw another sight, "the national flag raised where the rebel colors had been hauled down. And on April 11th Fort Pulaski, off Georgia, had surrendered to the National guns fired from Tybee Island, and the 7th Connecticut (F. B. included) had taken possession of it.

On April 26, Farragut had captured New Orleans, and the *Mobile Register* about this time announced to its readers, "The enemy is raging along our lines on coast and frontier." Better than all these was the action of both houses of Congress, abolishing slavery in the District of Columbia.

These were some of the victories since '62 began. So that although there was sorrow enough, and discouragement, we were on the whole, running our race with a bright look ahead.

E. W. H. to J. H.

OUR SHORE TENT, JUNE 5TH.

. . . I am very glad of the chance of sending you a note by Quartermaster Davies, who has just looked in at our tent door and been fed with coffee and bread and oranges, and seated on a box-end and generally well treated. . . .have captured a darkey from the country who brought fresh butter for sale this morning, and promised peas and strawberries for tomorrow! We have had pine-apples and bananas from New York and fresh eggs from Fishkill! which Moritz brought down, and which I wish you could share with us. He reports everything looking lovely at home and descants largely on the sunshine and sweet air and the pleasure of sitting on the piazza. . . .

I write with chattering all about me, for Mrs. Griffin and G. and Drs. Ware and Haight are sitting on boxes and barrels talking and laughing and enjoying the respite we are having. We are both well: also Charley, who is doing good service, is very cheerful, and thrives on it.

The quartermaster waits. The only thing I think of to send you is some fresh bread,—I also put in a package of concentrated beef tea for two or three 16th men who I hear are very sick, and some farina, arrowroot and handkerchiefs for the same. . . .

Only 100 wounded came down this morning, and have gone on the State of Maine, which is in beautiful order for them. We fed about 600 yesterday, three meals each.

G. to Mother.

JUNE 6, WILSON SMALL.

We have on our boats nine "contraband" women from the Lee estate, real Virginia darkeys but excellent workers, who all "wish on their souls and bodies that the rebels could be put in a house together and burned up." "Mary Susan," the blackest of them, yielded at once to the allurements of freedom and fashion, and begged Mr. Knapp to take a little commission for her when he went to Washington. "I wants you for to get me, sah, if you please, a lawn dress, and a hoop skirt, sah." The slave women do the hospital washing in their cabins on the Lee estate, and I have been up to-day to hurry them with the Knickerbocker's eleven hundred pieces. The negro quarters are decent little houses with a wide road between them and the bank, which slopes to the river. Any number of little darkey babies are rushing about and tipping into the wash-tubs. In one cabin we found two absurdly small ones, taken care of by an antique bronze calling itself grandmother. Babies had the measles which would not "come out" on one of them, so she had laid him tenderly in the open clay oven, and with hot sage tea and an unusually large brick put to his morsels of feet, was proceeding to develop the disease. Two of the colored women and their husbands work for us at the tent kitchen. The other night they collected all their friends behind the tent and commenced in a monotonous recitative, a condensed story of the creation of the world, one giving out a line and the others joining in, from Genesis to the Revelation, followed with a confession of sin, and exhortation to do better; till—suddenly—their deep humility seemed to strike them as uncalled for, and they rose at once to the assurance of the saints, and each one instructed her neighbor at the top of her voice to

> Go tell all de holy angels
> I done, done all I kin.

Just as they came to a pause, the train from the front with wounded arrived—midnight, and the work of feeding and caring for the sick began again. Dr. Ware was busy seeing that the men were properly lifted from the platform cars and put into our Sibley tents. Haight was "processing" his detail with blankets, and our Zouave and five men were going the rounds with hot tea and fresh bread, while we were getting beef tea and punch ready for the sickest through the night. By two o'clock we could cross the plank to our own staterooms on the Wilson Small.

E. to J. H.

FLOATING HOSPITAL, WHITE HOUSE,
SUNDAY, JUNE.

We are having a delightful quiet Sunday—such a contrast to the last few days. A hundred and fifty men, to be sure, came down last night, but unless we have two or three hundred we think nothing of it nowadays. We are going for a walk, and Dr. Jenkins of the Commission is to have service for us under the trees. We have almost lost sight of Sunday lately in the press of work.

There are large bunches of laurel and magnolia in our parlor-cabin and dining room, and the air is full of their fragrance.

Miss Dix spent last night with us, but is off now.

Carry writes Charley June 6:

We were surprised and pleased to see your letter in the *Post* last night, and sent out and bought up all the copies in the neighborhood, and have mailed them to James Gibson (Ireland) and elsewhere.

C. W. W. to New York Evening Post.

SANITARY COMMISSION, FLOATING HOSPITAL, PAMUNKEY RIVER.
OFF WHITE HOUSE, VA., MAY 31, 1862.

The work of the Sanitary Commission, as connected with the army of the Potomac, is just at this time, as you doubtless know, a most important and indispensable one. More than two thousand sick and wounded men have been shipped by the Commission to New York, Washington and Boston during the past month, and it is safe to say that the lives of hundreds have been saved who would otherwise have died in camp and on the march.

The vessels used by the Commission are chartered by the government, and are first-class ocean steamers and Sound boats. They are supplied with all the necessary hospital apparatus at the expense of the Commission, and are furnished, so far as possible under the circumstances, with every convenience for the transportation of the sick, who are too often victims of neglect in regimental sanitary regulations. If your readers care to know something about the detail of management on board a hospital ship, let me give them briefly the program of a single day's routine—a routine in the case of the majority on board, let them remember, of inevitable and monotonous suffering or sleepless pain.

Four bells,—but the day does not begin then, it is only a continuation of yesterday and the day before. On a hospital ship night and day are alike to all hands, and "on duty" for a nurse means only his "watch," whether it comes at noon or midnight. Dr. Someone is medical and military chief, and every well man on board, except the ship's officers and crew, is subject to his authority. His command consists of four or five surgeons and physicians, a commissario-quartermaster, a purser perhaps, a varying number of volunteer nurses, eight or ten contrabands, and from one hundred to four hundred or five hundred sick men, according to the capacity of his vessel. On the ocean steamers the greater number of bunks are between decks, and roughly built of secession lumber, in tiers of three ranged on either side the length of the ship, and a double row down the centre. On this deck also are a dispensary, with an apothecary to preside, and a room or space reserved for the exclusive use of the lady nurses.

The sick are divided into several wards, each with a ward-master, generally a medical student, and the watch is arranged by the medical chief—the twenty-four hours being divided into three watches, of six hours each, and two dog-watches, of three each. Let us divide all the doctors and nurses on board into two squads, or reliefs, called A and B. Squad A relieves squad B at seven in the evening; B goes to bed and quickly to sleep until one o'clock, when it relieves A; A turning in until 7 A. M., when it relieves B again, and so on. The dog-watches in the afternoon reverse the order, so that neither squad may have the same hours of watch two successive nights. The satisfactory arrangement of these watches to all parties concerned is no small matter.

The bulletin at the main stairway displays a record of the ward arrangements for the day, the hours of the house diet, the most explicit directions in case of fire, and more than the usual number of warnings with respect to the use of lights in the cabins.

By far the most formidable part of the work is getting the sick men on board and then landing them. The steamer lies out in the stream, and the sick men are in their camp hospitals on shore, it may be several miles inland, or perhaps left exhausted on the roadside, in the advance. A day or two ago thirty-six men arrived on the shores of the Pamunkey who had fallen off from the army, in this way, unable to proceed from fatigue and exhaustion. They said they had walked fourteen miles since midnight, and had had no food for three days. When they applied at the Government tent hospital at White House for food and shelter they were told that there was no room for them, and that they had better look along the shore for a hospital ship. In this condition they fell into the hands of the Sanitary Commission, were transferred to the Spaulding, and were speedily fed, clothed, washed and convalescent. Up to the 29th instant General Casey's division had lost in this way three thousand nine hundred men since leaving Yorktown.

The difficulty is to get the sick men from the land to the floating hospital—from the hands of the government to the Sanitary Commission. Convalescents can walk and in some measure help themselves. The sick must be lifted, (and not always with the tenderest care,) first into an ambulance, then jolted to the shore (even ambulances jolt in Virginia, those vehicles that offer every facility for accidental death), then put on a tug to be taken out to the steamer.

On the Sound boats the process of embarkation is comparatively easy, as the decks are low. In the case of an ocean steamer a tackle is rigged from above, fastened to a fixed frame into which the stretcher and all are placed while on the deck of the tug. The tackle is then hoisted, with the sick man and his effects, to the upper deck. Before being lowered to the receiving doctor below, who assigns him to a berth, all his baggage, including his gun and blankets—new blankets being furnished him—is taken from him and firmly tied together. His rank, name, regiment, company and post office address are noted down, and a number assigned to him and a corresponding number pasted on his baggage. In this way his baggage is cared for, and much confusion, which without some such system would prevail, is avoided. [This was Charley's work.]

Necessarily, now and then, a blanket or pair of shoes loosely packed, or a likeness carelessly put in the haversack, is lost or unclaimed. Occasionally a soldier, much to his chagrin, may be obliged to carry home some one else's gun, new, perhaps, from the factory, instead of his own trusty rifle that has shot, to his certain knowledge, at least half a dozen rebels. Jones, of the Third Maine Cavalry, who is stout, may be obliged to put up with a coat belonging to Jenkins, of the Tenth Indiana Infantry, who is slim, etc.; but, in the main, the men have their baggage returned to them intact at the end of the journey.

A detail of men sometimes accompanies the sick, who are employed as nurses. When every bed is filled and order begins to come out of the seeming chaos, a meal is served to those who need it, the gangway is lowered, the whistle blows, and the ship, with its strange cargo, is in motion for New York or Washington. The doctor makes his rounds, giving particular directions about the sickest, and the watch begins. Down the York river, round the cape, and so, with the flag of the Sanitary Commission waving at the mast-head, out to sea. Convalescents, who are well enough, smoke their pipes on deck, and in picturesque groups talk over the wonderful scenes they are leaving, or discuss the superior merits of their several regiments.

Up stairs, we are a lot of soldiers off duty, on a pleasure trip down a peaceful little Virginia river. Down stairs, how different! Occasionally a death occurs on the passage (though the proportion is very small), and a vacant bed in the long line marks the soldier's last resting place while living. His knapsack and gun are taken by some friendly hand to be returned to his family, and thus the soldier ends his fight—sadly, yet in a noble cause; his heroic aspiration crowned so soon with their utmost result.

A dark side there must necessarily be, but a bright side is by no means lacking. Chloride of lime and the lady nurses contribute largely to the brighter half. Whitewash and women on a hospital ship are both excellent disinfectants. Men are nurses of the sick only by study and experience, women by intuition. A man can dress an ugly gun-shot wound or prescribe for a typhoid case better, perhaps, than a woman, but a woman's hand must knead and smooth the bed that supports the wounded limb, or much medical science may go for nought. Masculine gruel, too, nine cases out of ten, is a briny failure; but gruel, salt-tempered by feminine fingers, is nectar to parched lips.

Creature comforts abound in the presence of lady nurses, and from their culinary retreat between decks come forth at all hours of the day a sizzling sound as of cooking arrow-root; armsful of clean white clothing for the newly washed, and delicacies for the sick without number, sometimes in the shape of milk punch, or lemonade squeezed from real lemons, some- times a pile of snowy handkerchiefs that leave an odorous wake through the wards. Again, a cooling decoction of currants for the fever case near- est the hatchway, or a late *Harper's Weekly* for the wounded man next him, (who to his surprise and delight recognises his last skirmish, though feebly reduced to the consistency of printer's ink, with his identical self in the foreground), or oranges, cups of chocolate and many a novelty, but never a crumb of hard tack, (unless in the pulpy disguise of panada,) or ever so faint a suggestion of too familiar salt pork. . . .

Suffice it to say that the services of the ladies who are here as nurses of the sick are invaluable to the Commission and duly appreciated by the battle-tried and camp-worn soldiers. A simple word of sympathy or encouragement from a genuine woman is sometimes more potent to cure, than brandy or quinine from the hands of the most skilful physician. The kind looks and deeds of our nurses, and their kindlier words go straight to the hearts of the sick men and bring them nearer home by many a weary mile. We have other bright features, too.

Of articles contraband of war there are several specimens on board. They are always jolly and grinning, and ready for the hardest kind of labor, and breathing a "mudsill" atmosphere has not made "sour niggers" of them. Strange as it may seem, too, at uncertain intervals, they even make use of an ejaculation peculiar to that genus of article in a sportive and jocular yelp: "Yah! yah!" says Aaron to Jim (not Moses) "dis yer's a heap better than Massa Coleman's"; whereupon James performs an affirmative comedy of "Yah, yahs," and looks all teeth. Moreover, these men seem to take kindly to the wages (!) that are paid them from time to time, and especially on these festive occasions are they exceeding lavish in their dis- play of ivory, and blithesome to a degree passing strange.

A little while ago I witnessed the novel spectacle of an "article" earning his living. Six weeks ago he was an "indefinite" article—a chattel—a non-entity; now sole proprietor of his own muscle and able to convert the sweat of his brow into legitimately-gotten shining metal. He was rolling a barrel of northern pork aft, and I saw him halt three several times on his march to the kitchen, in order to execute a *pas seul* from his favorite plantation jig. It was a march of triumph to him, for he knew that every revolution of his barrel rolled out for him at least the fraction of an expected dollar, the just recompense of his free labor, and his ungainly "juba" was only the natural overflow of his exuberant glee upon attaining at length his long-denied manhood. There is a "down East" smack and flavor in this their first taste of freedom that seems to be peculiarly grateful to the contrabands, and which I doubt if prolonged years of tasting will expunge.
C. W. W.

J. S. W. to G.

Charley's letter to the *Post* was quite a success and I advise him to continue his communications. The Vanderbilt, Government Hospital Ship, got in last night at six or seven, and will be emptied to-day, I suppose. There has been a great and general muss on the whole subject (of course) between General B—— and Satterlee and their underlings, parties of the first part,—and all the State agents and volunteer doctors, parties of the second part, the old fight between regulars and volunteers—conflict of authority and efforts to sustain small personal dignities at the expense of everything else. In the mean-time however, the patients, contrary to the usual course, have *not* suffered very much, as the public have had pretty free access to them and their wants have been supplied. Now, all transports are obliged to anchor in the stream and report to the regular quartermaster. . . .

The Vanderbilt is the first arrival under the new regime and we shall see how it works. As much flourish of authority as they like, if it only shows fruit in the comfort of the patients, a subject on which I have misgivings. Fort Hamilton is the new depot; that and Bedloe's Island. We went to the Island on Friday and found things improving. A few weeks ago Dr.

Agnew (I think) or one other of the Commission went down and found the doctor drunk, the stewards on leave given by themselves, and the fever patients dying of neglect. He, whoever he was, cruised about the Island, found ten pounds of beef, cut it up and made broth himself, and spent the night feeding the sick men. They have got a new surgeon now, but I think the steward steals. One reform at a time.

We are determined, we "females," to make the place much too hot for him if we can *prove* anything. But how many weak-minded sisters there are! I never realized before how few people in the world are *really clever* and how very few are capable of "taking the responsibility." I have also discovered that there is nothing like philanthropy to bring out the quarreling propensities. Two young gentlemen called yesterday and asked for Charley, expressing great surprise that he hadn't got back, as they saw him driving his horse a day or two ago. They might have mistaken the man, but they appeared confident on the subject of the horse. So, Charley, Mr. Coles may be guilty of some black-hearted treachery. My mind always misgave me that Wilson's men went out o'nights with Nelly Bly. *What* is the news from Joe and the 16th? We search the papers in vain to find his where-abouts. Yesterday in the *Herald*, in a chance letter, was this, "General Franklin, in crossing a brook to-day, got mired in the soft earth banks and was thrown, but instantly emerged unhurt, dripping, puffing and laughing." That is the only public news I have seen of the Division for ten days. *Where* are they?

Tioronda
Home of Eliza and Joseph Howland
Woolsey Collection, Ferriday Archives

CHAPTER NINE

An Important & Useful Place

E. W. H. to J. H.

WILSON SMALL, JUNE 7TH.

The Commission has sent out to establish a camp hospital at Savage's Station on the railroad about twelve miles from here, a depot for supplies, and a little encampment of twenty tents or more as a resting-place for sick and wounded stragglers, and a kitchen to feed the sick from as they pass by. Mr. Rogers and Mr. Holman are the agents of the Commission there, and Mrs. Fogg. It is a nice thing, and will greatly decrease the sufferings of the poor fellows. . .

We have no news from you to-day. 250 more wounded came down last night, mostly rebels, and are being cared for on the "Louisiana." Georgy has just been giving them clean handkerchiefs, and our dear Mrs. Griffin has come in, blooming, from her rounds, saying she has had "a delightful morning." The rebels are very badly wounded, and so have better care than our own men; for the worst cases, whether Union or rebel, have the best treatment. They ought to be impressed by the kindness they receive, and many of them are. I offered wine and water to one fine, manly-looking fellow who was carried on a stretcher past our tent, and he answered gently, "No, sister; thank you; I don't want any." Another little Georgian was "so sorry to give Georgy so much trouble" when she took him a pillow. . . . If only I could see you now and then! Tell me when you write what you mean by the *swamp*.

The "swamp," by which, and in which, the army of the Potomac was operating, was the deadly Chickahominy to which so many thousands were sacrificed.

241

While we were lying at White House in the Wilson Small, one day, Mr. Olmsted came to G. with the statement that "young Mr. Mitchell of New York, who had come down to help in the Commission's Quartermaster's department, was ill on the supply boat Elizabeth." G. went across the plank to him at once, and found a most attractive six or seven feet of future brother-in-law cramped into an uncomfortable little hole of a cabin. This was E. M.'s first introduction to the family; he was looked after a little, and sent home in a returning hospital ship to recruit. Mr. Olmsted had his father's private instructions to keep him out of the army.

A. H. W. a little later, writes:

Mr. Mitchell called yesterday afternoon to say good-bye and to offer to take anything to Georgy. Dr. Agnew had sent for him in a great hurry to go back as quartermaster on the Elm City. He had promised to go back on three or four days' notice, and had hoped to spend those at the seaside, where his physician had told him he ought to go. We had nothing for Georgy,—the Elm City lying at Jersey City, it would not have been convenient anyhow—but Carry took to his house in 9th street a letter to Georgy, and a large bundle of candy for himself.—(C's first present to her future husband).

J. S. W. to G. and E:

SUNDAY, JUNE 8TH.

Dear Girls:

Being at home from church on account of the rain, I may as well do the next wickedest thing, write a letter. I have given up trying to get ahead of Abby, but am able to cut in now and then when she is out of town. With great exertion we got her off with Mother for a few days in Norwich. . . . We sent up after them Georgy's pencil note telling of your being at the railway terminus feeding the wounded in transit. I envy you from the bottom of my heart, but it is also my opinion, kept pretty much in that sacred receptacle, that you are killing or will kill yourselves. It is not only the positive fatigue, but the awful drain on your sympathies, and the excitement, etc.—you will be wrung out and dried—yellow and gray, if you ever get home at all. I have no doubt Abby will be horrified to hear that you are at the White House Station; and all your softening of your labors for family use does not take us in in the least. However, as I said, I envy you, and I respond to the little song you are no doubt singing out of Maud,

>"What matter if I go mad,
>I shall have had my day."

Dr Agnew says that he is "not using too strong terms when he says the government's neglect of its wounded is damnable." . . . The St. Mark is to go down, probably, on Wednesday. We will send the few things you mention by her, and hope to hear in the meantime of something more that you want. Dr. Bellows goes in her. It seems to me that some people with money are not half waked up to the need of giving it in this cause. I alone, could name a dozen who don't seem to know or care anything about hospital matters. *Poor* people give a great deal—dozens of plain men and women come with clothes, provisions, etc., to the different barracks, but many of the better able ones neither come nor send. By and by their day of opportunities and grace will be over.

Hatty writes:

JUNE 10.

We shall send you the things you ask for by the steamer St. Mark to-morrow, and hope you may get them, though I have my doubts as to Charley's wines making a sea journey safely with government employees on board ready to drink them up. William Hodge has just walked up the street with me, says Lenox has come back for an appointment in one of the government Hospitals in Philadelphia.

E's Journal.

WILSON SMALL, JUNE 13.

Little to do. As we were sitting in our parlor-cabin Wednesday, trying to keep cool, Joe ran up the stairs into the midst of us. Everything was quiet at the front and in the regiment, and General Franklin told him "he would rather have him come than not." He and Captain Woolsey Hopkins rode the twenty-five miles down together, over roads more frightful than they ever were near Washington. We took them into the Commission for the night in spite of the new rules excluding outsiders. As there was little to do, we ran up the river in the evening, in the "Wissahickon," past the broken bridge and Colonel Ingalls' encampment and the lily pads, far up into the moonlight.

Later. . . . It was Friday night our stampede happened. We were all quietly at work in our tent on shore (having fed a hundred or more sick men), preparing for the night, when a wounded soldier came by with the news that the train which was just in had been fired into by rebel cavalry near Tunstall's Station, about three and a half miles from White House. One man was killed, and six or eight wounded, but the train pushed on and gave the alarm. We felt no fear whatever for ourselves, but I was very anxious to hear of J.'s safe arrival in camp the day before. A peremptory order from Quartermaster-General Ingalls came to Mr. Olmsted: "Put your women behind the iron walls of the Spaulding, and drop down below the gunboats."

Edward Mitchell went up to headquarters to see if there was no mistake, and came back with the message: "Drop down below the gunboats at once, and look out to keep clear of vessels floating down, on fire." So we reluctantly hurried on board the Small with all the staff, (except Drs. Ware and Haight, who stayed with the sick on shore) and skedaddled ignominiously. Once moored alongside the Spaulding, Mr. Olmsted came back in a rowboat for news, and found all the camp followers, teamsters, sutlers, railroad and barge men organizing in companies, and arms and ammunition serving to them. Edward Mitchell, who had volunteered for this duty, had a company.

The sickest men from the tents were all taken on board the Small, a detail of twenty-five doctors and men from the Spaulding acting as bearers.

It was now after midnight, but we made up about forty beds, got beef tea and punch ready, and about thirty, including the wounded from the train, were made comfortable. They were to have been transferred to the Spaulding, but a new order prevented this, and Saturday morning we once more took our old place at the White House wharf. Simultaneous with the attack on the train was one on the forage landing, a little above here on the Pamunkey, where two hundred government wagons were burnt, forage destroyed, and several of the teamsters killed. A schooner was also burnt, and we supposed the light of it to be that of a burning bridge. The scare has blown over.

A. H. W.

8 BREVOORT PLACE, JUNE 17TH.

My dear Charley:

We had just been reading in the *Times* about the scare at White House when Georgy's letter arrived. We have read it aloud over the breakfast table, and are now going to enclose it to Mary and Carry at Astoria, that they, too, may have the private version of the affair. It was a bold and very clever dash of the rebels; just what might have been expected, however. They are up to all sorts of thievish, daring things. . . . It would not have been out of place for you all to have been much *more* frightened than you profess to have been. Georgy's letter, in fact, we presume, was prepared for *home consumption*. She always tries to "draw it mild" for our benefit; is always having a lazy, lovely good time, perfectly well, and in the best of spirits, and as to the scenes of suffering about her, not caring a bit; has to pinch herself, I dare say, to see that she isn't stone—thinks she "hasn't any heart," etc., etc. Tell her, of course she hasn't, or won't have soon—it's *ossifying*, that, or something kindred, is what all surgeons die of—suppressed emotion. Tell her we insist on her coming home for a few weeks; now that you are with Eliza, she has not that excuse for staying.—Eliza, of course, we cannot induce to leave, it would be useless to try. Tell Georgy her known imprudence in overdoing herself, her known obstinacy about precautionary and remedial measures, impel me to insist on her taking a northern trip and a little rest just now. . . . Mrs. Gibbons goes back to her Winchester hospital next Monday. I am going up to see her, hear some of her tales and offer what supplies we have on hand. She and her party were obliged to fly for their lives when the rebels drove Banks out, lost on the way their three trunks, containing all their clothing, and Mrs. G. was without a bonnet. They have been very busy sewing up a new outfit, and I hope won't be interfered with again, though Jackson threatens another raid up the valley with 70,000 men as soon as the harvests are ripe. . . . I have saved our only piece of news till the last—the engagement of Pussy Wheeler; make Georgy guess who to. . . . It is Dr. Ceccarini, the Italian oculist, an accomplished man and skillful surgeon. . . . Mother says, "Tell

Charley how glad I am always to get his letters, and tell him that when he cautions Georgy on the subject of health, to be sure to be prudent himself." You are in a most useful and important place, and we would all rather have you there than in any part of our army.

Mother to C. W. W.

NEW YORK, JUNE, '62.

My dear Charley: Here are lots of scraps for you. Our basket is just going off to the steamer. I hope you will enjoy the gingerbread. We are all anxiety for further accounts since the battles of the last few days. The paper this morning states two deaths on the Knickerbocker of poor wounded men. What trying scenes again for you! I agree with you in all you say of Georgy's health, but know that persuasion is useless. You ask about coming home. We do not *need* your aid in getting out of town, however pleasant it would be to have you. There is no prospect of our going at present; we have no place in view at all. . . . Have the rebels cut the telegraph lines, that we get no news from the army? Where are you all to rendezvous now that the White House is given up? Some of the movements seem so mysterious to us—such as this, and the falling back of McClellan's army to Savage's Station, and some other strange doings. I hope it will all come out right. Do take care of yourself and the girls. I am so much better satisfied to have you where you are, than with the 22nd. Your Cousins William and Anna have been on to Baltimore to see Lloyd; they are greatly distressed at the idea of his being sworn in, even for three months! . . .

Farewell dear boy. Mother's love and blessing to you.

Northern hospitals in many places were all this time filling up with wounded from the front, and women were volunteering as nurses in them also. The following letters show what was being done at the New Haven General Hospital, years before its Training School for Nurses was organized.

S. C. W. to G. M. W.

NEW HAVEN HOSPITAL, JUNE.

I have been so very busy that my conscience does not reproach me at all for not writing. A fortnight ago our wounded came—240 of them, all dreadfully neglected and needing attention of every kind. I cannot just this moment recollect the name of the ship which brought them, but there was only one surgeon on board to care for them, no nurses and hardly any provisions; the wounds of many had not been dressed for nearly a week when they got here, and seven or eight died on the passage. For the first few days most of them were placed in tents on the hospital grounds, but since then the new Barrack Hospital has been finished, and all except about twenty very bad cases are quartered there and doing very well. They would not let any young ladies enter for the first three or four days, the sights and sounds were too bad for them. Such was the enlightened decision of the excellent incapable in charge, but Friday I worked my way in, and since then have been there nearly every day, taking charge of the linen room and giving out clothes, etc. to the men. At first everything was in dreadful confusion, but gradually our department is getting into order, and in the course of three or four days will be thoroughly systematized. A good old lady and myself are to take turns in presiding over the clothing supplies, and as she is rather inefficient and feeble, I hope to take a very big half of the time. The small corner they give us as a store-room was yesterday all shelved and cup boarded under my direction, and will be capable of holding three times the supply it did before. . . . I go up at nine and stay till seven, and all day long the nurses are coming after sheets, and shirts, and bandages, and rags, and towels, and soap, and the men stopping at the door to ask for trousers or coats, and in time I hope to get the true tailor's measure in my eyes. Such fine, manly, patient fellows as they are. Many of them, almost all, from Michigan and Pennsylvania and New York; not one Connecticut man among them. From the linen room one can organize little rushes into the wards to see special cases, etc., so it is not to be despised even though not as satisfactory as the actual nursing would be. Just outside of our long wooden barrack is a small wooden kitchen, and there Harriet Terry and Rebecca Bacon preside over the diet for the special cases who cannot eat the hospital rations, and if one looks in there about twelve, such a smell of good things greets the nose as it does one good to experience; and arranged on the table are such nice little messes all labelled and numbered—such brown crisp toast and savory chops, and smoking beef-tea, and little messes of this and that; and later the great trays come in and carry them off down the long entry, and so, many poor fellows are made comfortable. One building, which holds eight wards, and comprises four tents full of sick, is all well managed, orderly and thriving, with good paid and excellent unpaid nursing; but in the main hospital where the housekeeper has control, it is all mismanagement, confusion and waste; really sickening to see. The men are doing pretty well though, and all of them are so happy and grateful for the care taken of them. A very nice man from the 105th Pennsylvania, for whom I was writing a letter yesterday, told me to tell his mother not to feel anxious about him, for he was cared for just as if he was at home, and had everything he desired.

S. C. W. to G. M. W.

LINEN ROOM, NEW HAVEN HOSPITAL,
JUNE 26TH, '62.

My dearest G.:

A lull in business gives me a chance to write a few lines to you and tell you how glad I was last night to find your letter waiting for me when *I* got home from my day here. . . . What wonder that you have not written when I have never found time to write until after ten o'clock at night. . . . One of my pets here among the men is sure that you and Eliza are the ladies who were in a large tent on shore at White House, and brought him some bowls of bread and milk and swigs of strong drink of some kind. He was so interested to make sure of the point that I promised to bring up your picture for him to see and compare with his recollections. . . . The Surgeon-General has written to Dr. Jewett to say that he hears such favorable accounts of the state of affairs here that he is going to send 300 of his worst cases for us to care for. Inspector-General Hammond is coming on Saturday to see with his own eyes, and we are to be swept and garnished for his benefit. Mrs. Hunt ("H. H.") helps me here often; mends clothes by the hour and comes for three days during the week to write letters for the men. . . . My fortnight's experience here convinces me that I could soon acquire the art of keeping, not an "Hotel," but a small country variety store. There is the same run of customers, the taking of stock, the arranging of the goods, the sweeping-up and closing of the shutters at night. My stock comprises almost everything—shirts and collars, cravats and suspenders, coats and trousers, vests and shoes, handkerchiefs, sheets, pillows and pillow-cases, rags, bandages, soap, thread, needles, tape, buttons, combs, brushes, hats, fans, cotton wadding, water beds (2), stockings, oranges, lemons, bay rum, camphor, stationery, towels, dust-pans, brushes and mosquito netting, and this morning a woman bolted in, saying, "Is it in this room that the *corpse* is?—they tell me that it is in this end of the passage, and I thought I should like to see him!" I didn't happen to have one, however, and she seemed quite aggrieved. . . . Jenny is somewhat better, and the baby lovely as can be. . . . She is a dear little puss, and one of the great obstacles to my entire devotion to my country.

From Edward Mitchell.

WHITE HOUSE, JUNE 20, 1862.

My dear Father:

Heavy firing in the advance this A. M. Since writing to Fred, I have had no time to write another word. Sitting up late that night, I was waked up, with Drs. Jenkins and Haight, to go ashore for 24 hours at 3 A. M. In consequence of being routed out at this unusual hour, yesterday was spent, so far as leisure hours were concerned, in deep sleep. . . . I now write to thank you for your kind expressions of regard for my health, and of love for me; and for your desire to see me with you once more. . . .

My health—it is excellent. . . . And so far it has been possible to find an assistant, who though stupid to an extent and lazy, is willing to go twice a day to wait an hour or more for commissary stores;—it would be perfectly disgusting to me. . . . I doubt much if Mr. Olmsted will be willing to let me go home for some months at least. The staff is now well organized, and the departure of one would throw very much labor on another who would not understand it at all. This is especially so in my case. The drawing of rations requires much care, and to know what stores the Commission has, and where they are, one must be continually among them. . . . *You* were right about the rebel cavalry, not I. It was very bold. Gen. Stuart commanded. In case *we* had been called out, I had intended to use only the bayonet and to creep round if possible on the flank of the enemy and charge at my own time—have lain in ambush, in other words. I think Sawtelle would have been willing to allow me my own way, for as he was a regular, he of course placed not much reliance, if any, on such a Falstaff army. . . .

Olmsted has a deal of tact; as much as a woman. Also much shrewdness and a very quiet manner. In some characteristics he reminds me a little of you, or rather what you would have been if you had been called more actively into public life. . . .

A battle is *predicted* to take place in three days, by Capt. Sawtelle; time will show.

The Webster and Spaulding go to New York. Dr. goes in charge of the latter. In my capacity of aide I delivered his sailing orders to him. He may be a very nice man and an excellent physician, but he has an unquench-able and unalterable desire to spread himself and his authority. I received instructions to *bully* him into staying on board in case he should attempt to come back to the White House! Some funny things occur here!

I regret immensely that I will be unable to be present at Neil's com-mencement. I would rather loose $50 than not to be there. . . .

E. to J. H.

WILSON SMALL, JUNE —.

This morning I have your Sunday note with the charming little poem. Who wrote it? Be sure and tell me. It *is* a poem, and though entirely unde-served, I value it very much indeed.

Poem by a Lieutenant of the 16th N. Y., dedicated to E. W. H.
TO MRS. JOSEPH HOWLAND.

From old Saint Paul till now,
Of honorable women not a few
Have quit their golden ease, in love to do
The saintly works that Christ-like hearts pursue.

Such an one art thou, God's fair apostle,
Bearing His love in war's horrific train;
Thy blessed feet follow its ghastly pain
And misery and death, without disdain.

To one borne from the sullen battle's roar,
Dearer the greeting of thy gentle eyes,
When he aweary, torn and bleeding lies,
Than all the glory that the victors prize.

When peace shall come, and homes shall smile again,
Ten thousand soldier hearts, in Northern climes,
Shall tell their little children, with their rhymes,
Of the sweet saint who blessed the old war times.

E. to J. H.

JUNE 20.

I am much entertained by the regiment's vote of thanks to *me* for the hats with which I had nothing whatever to do. [J. H. had himself ordered straw hats for the 16th, to help guard against the intense heat of the Chickahominy swamp, and gave them in E's name.] . . . Quartermaster Davies has gone off with an order for the delivery of the musical instruments, and you will probably receive them to-morrow. Let me know if they are good ones. I have a "Psalm of the Union" for you, which I will send by the Quartermaster—a composition of old Mrs. Hill's, Mother's opposite neighbor. It is sent to you with her compliments. "She always expresses her emotions in harmony."

We ran down at daybreak yesterday to Yorktown to see the floating hospital, the "St. Mark," just arrived from New York with Drs. Agnew, Draper, Carmalt, and others on board. . . .

Later—The Small came back during the evening, and brought Dr. Agnew and Dr. Carmalt (Annie Woolsey's brother-in-law), and a number of the St. Mark's force, to go out to the front to-day. We all spent most of the evening in the tent, with the front curtains down and the back ones open to let in the blaze of the camp fire, over which on the pot-hooks hung the kettles of tea and coffee and soup which were preparing for 200 or 300 sick who were expected down on the trains. Nearly 500 came before morning and were provided for. The Commodore is fitting up and will leave for New York to-morrow. . . . Another party, the third of Congressional picnickers, came down to-day, but were refused transportation to the front by General McClellan's orders. I rejoice in it. . . . Won't you tell

Dr. C. to pin the *name and address* of all his sick men somewhere about their clothing, if he has to leave them, and however *little sick* they may be. So many men come down and die here without name or token, and then—so many families are left in sorrow and suspense.

G. to Mother.

JUNE 22.

The Commodore, government boat, lies at the dock nearly full. Sixty Sisters of Charity had arrived yesterday and to-day, and were to be established at the White House and work at the General Hospital—on shore. They came down unexpectedly by some one's orders and would have done good work, but now they sat on their large trunks on the Knickerbocker's deck, forbidden to stay by the Padre, who was in a high state of ecclesiastical disgust at not finding full provision for them on shore, including a chapel! I labored with the old gentleman upon the unreasonableness of expecting to find confessionals, etc., on a battlefield, but to no purpose. There sat the Sisters clean and peaceful, with their sixty umbrellas and sixty baskets, fastened to their places by the Padre's eye, and not one of them has been allowed to come over and help us to put the Commodore in order. So our staff went to work among the 500 patients. We asked for basins; there were none on board this government vessel. We secured all we needed from the Commission's stores, however, and before the boat started that night, the sickest men were fed and washed, and beef tea and punch enough made to last the worst cases till they reached Fortress Monroe. We wrote all the names and home addresses of all the sickest who might be speechless on arrival and pinned the papers inside their pockets. The Sisters now gladly took hold of the work and returned to their convents, as nurses on this hospital steamer.

E's Journal.

WILSON SMALL, JUNE 23.

A very anxious day. An orderly from Brigade Headquarters brought word from Captain Hopkins that Joe was ill and unable to write. I at once put up a basket of stores for him—bedsack, pillows, sheets, arrowroot, etc., etc., to go by the orderly, and Charley telegraphed Generals Slocum and Franklin to know the truth, while Mr. Olmsted arranged with

Captain Sawtelle for a pass to take me to the front to-morrow morning. My mind was relieved, however, by the telegraphic answers and better accounts, and I have given up the idea of going out.

June 25th. General Van Vliet says that if I want to go to the front at any time and will send him word, he will have his wagon meet me and take me over to J's camp. This morning Dr. Bigelow came back to our boat from the front.

June 26th. Running away down the Pamunkey again as fast as we can go, escaping from Stonewall Jackson!

All night the wood choppers were at work cutting down the woods at the White House to give the gunboats a chance to command the land beyond, and just now as we passed, the banks were shorn and the pretty little place laid bare. The pickets had been driven in, and Jackson was supposed to be close at hand. Eighty wounded were brought down last night and put on board the Knickerbocker. Twelve more and a few sick came down this morning The Whilldin follows us, nearly full of sick and wounded.

The rumor to-day is that all communication with the front is stopped, to conceal an advance of our army.

June 28th. We went as far as West Point followed by a train of schooners and barges running away like ourselves. There we lay through the evening and night, watching for the flames of burning stores at White House which did not burn, and for booming of guns which did not boom—without news or orders, until after dinner, when we turned and ran up the river again in search of both. Near Cumberland we met the Arrowsmith with Surgeon Vollum on board, who hailed us and told us all we yet know of yesterday's action at the front.

Colonel Vollum then pushed on to Washington for medical supplies and we kept on up here to White House again.

We little knew at the time that "yesterday's action at the front," to which E. alludes so quietly, was the desperate battle of Gaines' Mill, June 27, 1862, the first of the terrible seven days' battle before Richmond. It was in this action that J. H. was wounded at the head of his regiment. His commanding officer (General J. J. Bartlett) said, in his official report of the battle:

The enemy were slowly but surely forcing back the right of the entire line of battle. At this juncture I ordered forward the 16th New York Volunteers, Colonel Howland commanding. From the position of the regiment it was necessary to change front forward on first company under the most terrific fire of musketry, with the shells and round shot of two batteries raking over the level plain, making it seemingly impossible for a line to withstand the fire a single instant. But with the calmness and precision of veteran soldiers the movement was executed. . . . To Colonel Joseph Howland I am indebted for maintaining the extreme right of my line, for nobly leading his regiment to the charge and retaking two guns from the enemy. Whatever of noble moral, physical and manly courage has ever been given by God to man, has fallen to his lot. Cheering his men to victory, he early received a painful wound, but with a heroism worthy of the cause he has sacrified so much to maintain, he kept his saddle until the close of the battle.

Lieutenant-Colonel Marsh of the 16th was mortally wounded in this engagement at Gaines' Mill, and apart from the Colonel and Lieutenant-Colonel, the loss of the regiment in killed and wounded was 260 men, rank and file, fully one-quarter of its effective force on that day.

It was "for gallantry at the battle of Gaines' Mill, Virginia," that the rank of Brigadier-General by brevet was later conferred on J. H. by the President of the United States.

When the battle at Gaines' Mill was all over and Joe began to realize his own fatigue and wounded condition, he dismounted and lay down under a tree not far from the field, and presently fell asleep. He did not know how long he had slept, but it was dusk when he was waked by something soft touching his cheek, and rousing himself he found it was his war horse, old "Scott," rubbing his nose against his face. He had got loose from where he was tied and had looked for his master until he found him. Joe was not ashamed to say that he cried like a child as he put his arm round the dear old fellow's neck.

He brought him home and rode him after the war until he grew to be old and no longer sure-footed. Then his shoes were taken off and he was turned out to grass to have an easy time and nothing to do the rest of his life. After a little, however, he moped and refused to eat and was evidently dissatisfied with life. So Thomson came to Joe and said, "Do you know, Mr. Howland, I believe old Scott would be happier if he had *something to do.*" And accordingly, although he had never been in harness in his life, he was put before the lawn-mower, and to do active light farm-work. The effect was excellent; he grew happy and contented again, and proved to be one of the best working-horses on the farm for several years.

It was Scott's last shoes as a saddle-horse, when he was turned out to grass, that we mounted and hung in the office at our Fishkill home.

The news of J.'s being wounded reached us at White House through a telegram kindly sent the morning after the battle by Dr. McClellan, Staff Surgeon at Army Headquarters, as follows: "The Colonel has a slight flesh wound. He is in my tent, and will be taken good care of until he can be sent down."

At almost the same moment communication with the front was cut. We telegraphed for more details, in vain. The rebels were upon us. Stoneman sent in word that they were in sight. We stayed as long as they would let us and then went off into the dark, taking what comfort we could in the one word, "slight."

G. M. W. to Mother.

WILSON SMALL, JUNE 28.

The telegraph wires had been cut just as we received the news of Joe's wound, and a mounted messenger announced the enemy at Tunstall's. Stoneman's cavalry were worrying them till we were all safely off, when he would fall back, and the rebels would walk into our deserted places. So we steamed away, watching the moving of the last transports, and the Canonicus (Headquarters' boat for the army officers at White House), with Colonel Ingalls, Captain Sawtelle, and General Casey and staff. The most interesting thing was the spontaneous movement of the slaves, who, when it was known that the Yankees were running away, came flocking from all the country about, bringing their little movables, frying pans, old hats, and bundles, to the river side. There was no appearance of anxiety or excitement among them. Fortunately there was plenty of deck room for them on the forage boats, one of which, as we passed, seemed filled with women only, in their gayest dresses and brightest turbans, like a whole load of tulips for a horticultural show. The black smoke began to rise from the burning stores on shore (fired to keep them from the enemy), and now and then the roar of the battle came to us, but the slave women were quietly nursing their children, and singing hymns. The day of their deliverance had come, and they accepted this most wonderful change with absolute placidity. All night we sat on the deck of the Small, watching the constantly increasing cloud of smoke and the fire-flashes over the trees towards the White House, as we moved slowly down the river.

The Wilson Small, with the whole fleet of hospital ships, made its way to Fort Monroe, and lay waiting for news from the front, cut off from all communication with the army and our own special part of it, Joe.

During this time the seven days' fighting before Richmond took place. The line by the York River was abandoned, and the army made its fearful and humiliating retreat across the Peninsula, through the deadly Chickahominy swamps, fighting and retreating upon the James, as a change of base. On July 2nd the gunboats headed by the Galena pushed cautiously up the James from Fortress Monroe, followed by our headquarters boat, the Wilson Small, to Harrison's Landing. Our retreating army had reached that point almost at the same moment, and to our joy we saw the flags flying as we neared the shore.

Arrived at Harrison's Landing, the Sanitary Commission at once began establishing its depot of supplies and made ready to receive the wounded. Almost immediately Joe was helped on board the Small. He had been brought across the Peninsula, wounded, and ill with Chicka-hominy fever, in a headquarters' ambulance—a very painful experience in itself—but he was safe now, and *with us*.

Mother to C. W. W.

JUNE 29 OR 30.

Your last letter this moment come! We know not what to think. Dear E., what a heroine she shows herself. This slight wound may be the means of saving Joe from greater danger, as he *must* now *lie by*. Dear boy, how sad we feel about him. Our best love to him when you can. How very anxious

we are to hear more. Thank you and G. for letters. We feel thankful it is
no *worse* with Joe. Let this feeling keep up all your hearts. Our dear love
to Eliza; I am rejoiced she is so brave. I wish I were there to help take care
of Joe. Let us hear at once all you know.

Mother to E. W. H.

JULY 3 '62.

My dear Eliza:

What times you are living through! in the very midst, too, of everything
as you are!—and how dark, very dark, it all looks to us this morning as we
read the last "reliable" accounts from the army before Richmond! Think of
six days' continuous fighting. When I looked over the list of horrors, my
first thought and exclamation was, "just think what Joe has been spared!"
I really look upon his "slight wound" as the greatest blessing which could
have happened to us all, and I am thankful for it. It may have been the
means of saving his life. Abby is writing you, but I put in my own words of
tender love and sympathy. . . . I rejoice that Charley is at hand with you.

A. H. W. to E.

JULY 3.

Georgy's letter sent ashore at West Point came this morning; Charley's
came yesterday. Both are postmarked Old Point. We learn of Joe's wound,
and trust it may be no more than you describe it, and that his previous illness will not be against his recovery from this fresh drawback. We shall be
extremely anxious to learn all particulars. No doubt if any one is well taken
care of, he will be, as he is so near his General and other army friends. But
what are the thousands and thousands of our poor wounded to do, cut off
from railroad transportation, left in a swamp, without supplies? We see by
the morning papers that hundreds from the fight on the *left* were carried
to the banks of the James River, where were neither supplies or surgeons
or transports. Some were huddled on a government tug, but who can tell
the distress and disorganization that attends such a reverse as ours. Not a
word of intelligence have we had since the last date, Saturday evening, on
our right, and nothing from the left for days and days. The city has been
full of wild and gloomy rumors, which may well fill us with doubts and
anxiety. . . . I hope you have all had enough of McClellan at last.

Captain Curtis stopped here a few moments yesterday, on his way back to the 16th. He went by the 5 p. m. train. "Not well enough to go, as a man, but well enough as an officer," he said. Joe will be glad to feel that he is at his post once more, in his own absence. I hope you won't let Joe worry about his regiment, though I do pity the poor men now. . . .

We are thankful, as you are, Eliza, that Joe is safe from the desperate fighting we have had for six days and the worse that is to come. Everything looks like a terrible reverse. It leaks out that our loss in two days was ten thousand, including, I suppose, Porter's fight on the right. The call for three hundred thousand volunteers shows, as I have seen all along, that so far from ending the war on the 4th of July, we should only have to begin it all over again. Well! we must be thankful that as a family we have been so mercifully spared so far. The papers are not allowed to publish a word, and as *good* news is never held back, we are left to the wildest and gloomiest rumors. How many families must be in painful suspense. There were twenty calls here yesterday: Rockwells, Aspinwalls, Johnsons, etc., all happening in, all much concerned, and all sending much love. General Porter lost eighteen pieces of artillery we see, in that horrid fight and retreat at Mechanicsville and Gaines' Mill. Thank God that Joe came out of it so well. Jane has seen at the New England Relief several of the 7th Connecticut, wounded at James Island lately; Corporal Hooks and Private Cook and others, who all spoke in the warmest terms of the bravery and kindness of Surgeon Bacon, who was in the very front, taking care of the men, lifting them out of danger, etc. Corporal H. had had his arm amputated, but so well was it done, that he says he never has had a sensation of pain in it from the first moment. The surgeons say that all the surgery on these 7th Connecticut men was splendidly done.

Corporal H. sent home eleven dollars to his mother out of thirteen. He laughed a loud laugh when Jane said to him, "Your arm was too much to give to those rebels, wasn't it" "Law! they might have the other and welcome, if they'd only let me go back!" He had promised to write to Dr. Bacon, but asked Jane if she wouldn't do it for him; "he hadn't got used to having only one hand, and couldn't hold the paper steady."

We shall not keep a very merry Fourth anywhere in the North to-morrow.

One of the hospital duties of all the nurses at the front was writing letters home for the sick and wounded men, and sometimes the sad work of telling the story of their last few hours of life. That such letters helped to comfort sorrowful hearts, the following answer to one shows. The soldier was mortally wounded in the seven days' fight, and in E's care on the hospital ship.

To Mrs. Joseph Howland.

JULY 2ND, 1862.

Madam:

Your letter of the 26th ultimo, conveying the mournful intelligence of the death of R. P., was received on Monday, the 30th ult. . . .

Until I received your letter, I had indulged the hope he would survive the injury; and had—not ten minutes before it was delivered to me—been informed by a lady, whose son is in the same division, that he was wounded, and that the other members of the company were preparing to send him home. This information, with a knowledge that he was of a robust constitution, and perfectly healthy, induced the belief he would recover. . . .

Madam, that letter of yours, although it was a messenger of death, when it was received by those who were being tortured by alternating thoughts of hope and fear, was like the visit of an angel; for it relieved their minds of a torturing anxiety.

I am requested by R's father to let you know that he is utterly unable to express his gratitude; that the only way he feels able to compensate you is by offering his heartfelt thanks.

Madam, the occupation which it appears you have chosen, that of alleviating the condition of those who are in affliction, is for its labor paid in a still secret way, which is not fully appreciated by any, except they be like you; for I doubt not, that on receipt of this, (when you will have known that you have been instrumental in conferring a lasting favor,) a lady of your nature will feel she is somewhat repaid.

A. H. W. to E.

8 BREVOORT PLACE, SATURDAY, JULY 5TH, '62.

My dear Eliza:

Georgy's and Charley's letters from Harrison's have just arrived, the last date being a postscript Thursday, July 3, which brings us into close correspondence again you see. These letters have relieved the painful anxiety that began to possess us, about Joe's condition and whereabouts. We thought perhaps that if his wound were really slight, he had been tempted to rejoin the regiment, and had shared in that horrible battle of White Oak Swamp. . . . Mother says that if it is Charley's *desire* to stay a little while longer, she consents; he is evidently so useful, that she should not have the heart to insist on his coming back. As for Georgy, if you leave her behind, we shall never forgive you. She *must* come. Mother cannot stand the anxiety much longer, nor can Georgy bear the constant strain. By-and-by, perhaps, if necessary, she could go back; *now* she must come home with you. We should be better pleased to have Charley and all once more together, at the end of this battle-year, and before we all begin on other years of separation and distress. Have C. come too. Poor, poor Colonel Marsh! mortally wounded at Gaines' Mill. What a mercy it would have been had he been killed on the spot. . . . We shall never know all that this week of desperate fighting has cost us; our dead and wounded being left behind, or crawling painfully along in the trail of the retreating army. Here and there an officer picked up in a passing ambulance, as Joe rescued the four you speak of. Our great, beautiful "Army of the Potomac," dwindled down to an exhausted handful. . . . *Fifty* thousand in all destroyed by fever and wounds, in McClellan's brief campaign! No wonder if the President has hesitated to send more troops to be used up in swamps, when so little was being done to show for it. . . . Any fool might have known that Beauregard and the bulk of his army had come to Richmond; but then our generals are not even fools, but something less if possible. . . . It may be God's will to destroy this nation by inches. It is certainly the devil's will to put dissension into the hearts of our leaders, and blundering darkness into their minds. God overrules all evil, even this, I suppose, to his own glory. I have no question that this and all other defeats are intended to drive us, as a nation, to a higher moral ground in the conduct and purpose of this war. As things stand, the South is fighting to maintain slavery, and the North is trying to fight so as not to put it down. When this policy ceases, perhaps we shall begin to have victory, if we haven't already sinned away our day of grace.

I don't know who kept Fourth of July yesterday; there was not much for public rejoicing though many families had private mercies and deliverances, like ours, to be thankful for. Hatty and Carry went with the Bucks to Bedloe's Island, with a tug load of ice cream and cake, and flowers, and flags, and a chest of tea, forty quarts of milk, and butter, and handkerchiefs, papers and books, to set out a long table and give a treat to two hundred in hospital there. To their distress they found that H—— B—— (malisons on him) had ordered away the day before, back to their regiments (via Fort Monroe I suppose), all who were strong enough to move about. They cannot possibly carry their knapsacks or guns, and must go into hospital again from relapse.

The forty convalescents left on the Island had a glorious feast, the doctor giving his full consent that even the twelve sick ones, in bed, should have as much *ice cream* as they wanted. Mr. Lasar, the singer, and one or two others, went about twice in the course of the day, from tent to tent, singing patriotic songs and hymns, winding up with "Lord, dismiss us," by particular request of the men; and then the men escorted the whole party, after tea, back to the tug, with three cheers and overwhelming thanks. Each man had at least a quart of ice cream, Carry thinks, and each a glass of Catawba wine, and a good slice of cake, and no doubt there will be many made sick, and the ladies will be blamed as the cause.

If you have a hold on Hammond, do get him to look into the hospital rations in the hospitals here: Bedloe's and David's Islands. There seems to be no "special diet" provided—nothing but coffee (no tea), dry bread and stew, rank with onions and white with grease. I have written to the ladies at New Rochelle, begging them to take David's Island in hand, and open a "ladies' kitchen," a "gruel kitchen," as Sarah says theirs in New Haven is called. But they say the surgeon looks with disfavor on the visits of ladies, and they feel "satisfied that the men are *well* taken care of." . . . They will find out by-and-by that surgeons and hospital stewards are not all angels in uniform. . . .

People kept coming yesterday, having seen Joe's name in the newspaper lists, and to-day we have notes of inquiry from all directions. . . .

Edward Walker's account of the fight at Gaines' Mill agrees with the *Tribune* reporter's—black masses of men coming upon our guns with *orderly joy* determined to take them, and falling under our fire in solid blocks, others pressing forward to fill the gaps.

The Daniel Webster was now filling up again with wounded and sick taken on at Harrison's Landing,—J. H. among them,—and, with Eliza as hospital nurse-in-charge, it sailed July 5th for New York. Charley and G. stayed on a little longer, till the army fell back towards Washington.

A. H. W. to G. at Harrison's Landing.

8 BREVOORT PLACE, JULY 7, 1862.

My dear Georgy:

Eliza and Joe came safely through yesterday (Sunday) morning. Jane and I were just going to the front door on our way to church when their hotel coach drove up. They had a pleasant voyage, only Joe says (in joke) *he* was neglected—Eliza and Miss Lowell directing their attention to other men! . . . Joe hobbled up on his broom-stick for a crutch, and we swarmed round, having so many questions to ask that we didn't know where to begin, and so were silent. Some broth and sangaree were quickly served and relished. I should say that Charley's telegram from Washington came Saturday afternoon, and gave us notice enough to send out and get what extra supplies we needed. . . . Mother and Uncle E. drove right in from Astoria, and Joe has had the story to go over a great many times.

A. H. W. to G.

8 BREVOORT PLACE, NEW YORK, JULY 10TH, 1862.

Eliza, Joe and Jane have gone off this morning to Fishkill. . . . Joe's place here was in the long lounging-chair by the front parlor window, while we received ordinary folks whom he wouldn't see, in the dining-room. He has worn a full white suit of Charley's, which Hatty happened to lay her hands on, and went off in it this morning, home, via Newburgh. . . . He did not mean to go till this afternoon, but got a letter yesterday from Mr. Masters (who has been one of the callers here) written in great haste, and full of excitement. It was to Eliza, saying that the people of Fishkill were so full of enthusiasm for her husband, that they were bent on having a demonstration on his arrival, which he knew would be contrary to Eliza's taste, and injurious to Joe's health. He therefore advised that they should change the hour and way of their proposed coming, and if they would telegraph him to Newburgh—*under an assumed name* (isn't it funny?)—he would be there to receive the message and would let Thomson and Moritz know! ... We think it a shame to disappoint the people so much, but Joe *would* get up at five this morning and leave the house at six, with his sword, etc. done up in a brown paper parcel. He thinks if there is such enthusiasm, he ought to be able to turn it to account for *recruiting*. It is really pleasant to know that the country people have such a spirit—for the cause. It is a good sign. . . .

The farmer, Mr. Thomson, wrote me a letter of thanks for mine to him, describing Joe's wound, etc. He said there had been "such reports in Fishkill as never was. Some had it his nose had been shot off, and some, his *jaw,* and the story was 'Mrs. Howland was pris'ner,'" etc. Great discussions took place in the church porch on Sunday, whether his moustache would grow over such a very bad scar, and Mr. Masters was so besieged for details that he ended by reading from the pulpit part of a letter of Carry's to Mrs. Charles Wolcott.

The neighbors have all been in, or sent in to offer their services to us and our wounded hero, having watched him get out of the coach that Sunday morning. Carry was so intent on watching the Hills from her window, and so desirous that they should all be ranged at their front windows, looking, as they *were,* that I believe she missed seeing Joe get out herself! . . .

Did anyone tell you of your friend Mr. Mitchell's call the other night? He brought your note and was very pleasant. We had no candy for him, but he drank iced lemonade. His father won't let him enlist, so you may see him back again. Jane recognized him as some one she had seen at Philharmonic rehearsals fifty times or more.

Mrs. Trotter writes G. about this time: "John met Edward Wright (of the army) to-day. He spoke in the highest terms of Mr. Howland. He says he is the idol of the regiment, and there is not a man who would not do anything for him. I trust his reward will be as great as the sacrifice."

E. W. H. to G.

New York, July 7th, '62.

Dear G.:

I am just going out to get the things you need, and so cannot report in advance as to their loveliness. Will make a pencil list at the end if I can. I shall send two "Agnews"—one for Miss Wormeley. It is very nice to be here, but I am overwhelmed with the luxury of everything, and lie in bed measuring the height of the ceiling "in a maze like." . . . Strange to say they (Mother particularly) seem quite contented to have you stay, that is they think you did right, though they are very much disappointed at not seeing you. . . . We had a very good voyage, perfectly smooth and fine, and delicious nights. The men were mostly very slightly sick or wounded, and the principal occupation was dressing them up in clean clothes, including gorgeous linen bosomed shirts, of which there were lots. There were only half a dozen very sick—one of whom died;—one consumptive of the 5th Maine sent to me for "just a little piece of meat to suck," and was profoundly grateful to "Lady Howland," who, he told one of the nurses, had been in his regiment "thousands of times." Lieutenant Hill was dressed up in Joe's second suit and has them on now at the Brevoort House, where Mrs. Van Buren was hovering over him yesterday when I sallied round with some grapes and some old linen for his arm. I have some lovely flowers for him to-day, which I wish you of the Wilson Small could share. I think of you all, all the time, and pine for you. Give my love to the staff, particularly Miss Wormeley, Mrs. Trotter, and dear Mrs. Griffin, who has probably joined you by this time. Write me all the details, and all you want. I hate to be clean while you go dirty. The pile of filthy things I am sending to the wash would, however, console you. To-day is hotter than any we had on the Pamunkey. Love to Charley.

E. promises on the first page of this letter to send on "two Agnews": an explanation is in order. The red flannel shirts of the Garibaldian troops used to be called Garibaldis when adopted as part of a lady's outfit, after the Italian battles. When Dr. C. R. Agnew came down to the front in a delightful black and white flannel shirt, the eye of the shabby-looking G. was fastened upon it, and she made bold, cut off from all supplies as she was, to say to the departing Doctor, *"Please* give me your shirt for my own wear." He did, and from that time we wore "Agnews."

E. to G. M. W.

FISHKILL, JULY 13.

Except for seeing how much good the rest and the home scenes are doing Joe, I would much rather be at Harrison's Point. He is improving nicely. His wound is not healed yet, but the inflammation has all gone and it looks better every day, . . . and but for a good deal of debility and shakiness of leg and hand, he would be quite himself. . . . Did they tell you of the demonstration the village people had prepared, and how we had to change our time of coming and telegraph secretly to Mr. Masters at Newburgh in order to escape it? They had actually arranged to take the horses out of the carriage and drag Joe home themselves. Fancy the struggle we should have had, to maintain an expression of mingled gratification and humility all through the three miles!

Joe received the other day the company reports of the 16th's part in Friday's battle, and their simple story is exceedingly touching—all of them speaking particularly of the coolness and cheerfulness of the men. Lieutenant Corbin, who wrote the little poem, makes out the report of Company C, which in its quaintness and simplicity reminds one of the old days of knight errantry. "Four of my men," he says, "fell dead *fighting bravely and pleasantly."* Company C, you know, is the color company, and of them he says, "The colors, which my company had the honor to guard, *were safely kept,* though they bear many an evidence of the hot fire in which they stood." The reports are nearly all equally simple, and one captain says, speaking of the order to cross and reinforce Porter, "This seemed highly pleasing to the boys, and with elastic step we took up our march for Gaines' Mill." Joe says they came out of the fight, too, with equal bravery and cheerfulness, and he got a smile from every man he looked at that day.

They all seem to want him back again, and his great anxiety is to be with them.

C. W. W. to J. H.

Wilson Small, Harrison's Landing,
Saturday, July 12th.

Dear Joe:

I saw, to-day, your adjutant, surgeon, and quartermaster; the former is much better, he says, and is going home in a day or two. He reports the 16th in good condition and in excellent spirits. This is unmistakably the case with the whole army. Exhausted and disappointed they naturally are (or were), but they have never lost heart, and the morale of our army is as good as ever. Having but little to do on the boat I have been on shore about the camps for a day or two, and have got a good idea of the strength of our position. It seems to me impregnable even without the earthworks we have thrown up at the weakest points. With these, we are very strong and can surely hold our own. Taking Richmond, however, is quite a different thing.

Send us the "Fishkill Standard" containing the account of the "ovation," and do not stand too long poised on one leg when you harangue the assembled multitude from the Tioronda balcony.

Georgy is going home soon, and perhaps myself. Love to E.
Yours affectionately,   *C. W. W.*

Sarah Woolsey to E. W. H.

New Haven, Tuesday Night.

I am just home from a very hot day at the New Haven Hospital, and so glad to find Jane's note with the news of your arrival that I must write a line before going to bed to tell you of it. And thus our week of suspense ends, and while so many thousands are straining eyes and hearts towards the bloody Peninsula, we may draw a long breath and refresh our thoughts with a picture of our dear Joe safe and resting his "honorable scars" amid friends and comfort and home and peace. . . . Do you know that one of our hospital cases here, on seeing your *carte de visite* the other day, recognized you as the "lady who gave him some very nice wine as he lay on a stretcher at White House, and bowls full of bread and milk afterward"—upon which he quite took on over it. He is one of the
"Ten thousand soldier hearts in Northern climes."

. . . Dr. Frank Bacon is here, having come up on a twenty-day furlough to recruit himself. I have not seen him but hear that he looks wretchedly—utterly broken down by overwork.

The James Island fight occurred early in June, '62, and in the official report of the general commanding, F. B.'s regiment is singled out for mention: "The 7th Connecticut moved up in a beautiful and sustained line." "The 7th Connecticut had been on very severe fatigue duty for three days and three nights." "The 7th Connecticut advanced in the open field under continued shower of grape and canister." "The medical officers were unwearied on the battlefield and in the hospital."

After this service F. B. went home on sick leave. Later he resigned from the 7th Connecticut, passed the examination for the Corps of Surgeons of Volunteers, and was assigned to duty in charge of the Harper's Ferry Hospital.

Here he found a large accumulation of army supplies and a hospital in what he considered an exposed position. On reporting this to Washington and recommending its breaking up, he received prompt orders to carry out his own views, and had the satisfaction of getting the patients and supplies safely off on the last train, before a rebel dash captured the place. He writes to J. S. W. that if he had continued the hospital at Harper's Ferry he should have wanted a select party of ministering angels, and asks whether we write M. A. after our names now, "after the manner of a mature female in the Harper's Ferry laundry, who sent up a requisition with 'D. R.' after her signature, and on a demand for explanation said 'daughter of the regiment, sir, which I have been adopted by the 109th.'"

F. B. was then assigned to duty in Washington on General Casey's staff, to examine outlying camp hospitals and break them up when expedient, and to overhaul new regiments and their doctors as they came in. Here, a little later, having got permission to join the troops at the front, he had the miserable experience of marching in from the second battle of Bull Run with the Army of the Potomac, defeated again on their old first field.

Katherine Wormeley
USAMHI

CHAPTER TEN

A Blessed Exile

W HILE WAITING for the army to make some move, G. ran up to
Washington with Mr. Olmsted and Charley, on the Small, to
secure more hospital supplies, and took news so to Mrs. Franklin of her
husband the General, at Harrison's Point.

A. H. W. to E.
                            8 BREVOORT PLACE, JULY, '62, FRIDAY MORNING.
Dear E.:

Enclosed are a lot of letters for you, Georgy's own among them. . . . She
describes their doings at Washington, voyage, etc., and says the best thing
Mr. Olmsted did was to get Meigs to give him fifty hospital tents, each
holding twelve patients. Also to get him to promise to send the old tents
stored since last winter, enough to shelter fifty thousand men. Our poor,
wretched army, she says, "lies tentless and blanketless at Harrison's Point,
smitten by sun by day, and moon by night, and it only makes her cry to
hear them cheer." . . .

General Franklin to G., sent on board the Small at Harrison's.
                            CAMP NEAR HARRISON'S BAR, JULY 10, 1862.
My dear Miss Woolsey:

I am exceedingly obliged to you for the trouble you took in bringing
me the two bundles, and for your kindness in presenting me the tea and
the sherry. The round bundle I am happy to say contained straw hats and
white sugar, and the other, musquito bars. My wife knows my tastes too
well to send me cakes. The tea and sherry were particularly acceptable, and
General Smith and myself have tested the qualities of both articles with
very high approbation.

I am glad that you saw my wife and that you thought she was braver than her sister army ladies. I see from her letters that she is cheerful and looks on the bright side of things. If I have time or opportunity I shall be very glad to call to see you.

I hope that you hear good accounts of Colonel Howland. Please give him and his wife my kind regards when you write.

Truly your friend,

W. B. FRANKLIN.

A. H. W. to G.

JULY 11TH.

Dear Georgy:

Your letter arrived this morning—letters I may say, enclosing multitudes for Eliza. We have forwarded them to her at Fishkill.

Dr. Carmalt was here last night. Does not go back on St. Mark. Mrs. Dr. Jenkins was here this morning to see Eliza, who had seen her husband. She is pretty and pleasant. . . .

General McClellan's "caution," Georgy, has ruined the country. It is too expensive a policy. We are bankrupt already.—Stewart, and Lord & Taylor began yesterday to give change to their customers in postage stamps;—handed Carry a tiny envelope stamped U. S. 50 cts., in change for something, which she in turn handed out in payment for a piece of ribbon at Aitkin & Miller's, all right, no words exchanged. So we go! Aspinwalls and Uncle E. blue as indigo. Don't know what to do about our property and their own too. I would give every dollar of *mine* if it would end this accursed war and slavery to boot.

In July, 1862, Cousin William Aspinwall sent to the War Department his check for $25,296.60, his share of the profit on a contract for arms purchased by Howland & Aspinwall and sold to the Government.

The Secretary of War ordered that "the thanks of the Department be rendered to Mr. Aspinwall for the proof which he has furnished of the spirit which animates the people of the United States and the assurance given that its citizens prefer public welfare to private gains."

This was true of a large proportion of the people, if there *were* contract swindlers and speculators, to our grief.

G's Journal.

JULY 12.

Lying off Harrison's Point in sight of the hospital on shore to which we went the other evening. The fifty tents we brought from Washington are going up and are partly filled—men on cots, and not very ill. The place is to be used as a rest for a few days for men who can then join their regiments. The Medical Department is greatly improved, and the Sanitary Commission, who were chiefly instrumental in putting in the new Surgeon-General (Hammond), who in his turn has put in all the good new men, finds its work here at an end, and might as well retire gracefully. Four thousand sick have been sent north from Harrison's. Soup, and food generally, are being cooked all the time, without the aid of the Sanitary Commission, and they would leave now but for the flag of truce sent in by Lee to arrange for the bringing away of our wounded left behind in the retreat. The transports are under orders.

Commodore Wilkes is here in charge of the gun-boat fleet, and Captain Rodgers sent his small boat for us the other day, and took us all over his vessel and then over the Monitor and the Maratanza. The Galena was full of cannon ball holes. The Maratanza gave me a piece of the balloon found on the rebel gun-boat Teaser. It was made of the old silk dresses of the ladies of Richmond, forty or more different patterns. They gave me, too, the signal flag of the little imp. We went over her to see the damage the shell did her, bursting into the boiler and disemboweling her.

The army is quiet and resting, and the surgeons of the regiments have been coming in constantly to the Sanitary Commission supply boat with requisitions for the hospitals. We are giving out barrels of vegetables. The Small will run up the river and be ready to fill a gap in bringing off our wounded prisoners, and it will be a comfort to do something before going home ignominiously. The last two weeks of waiting has been wearing to us all, and Miss Wormeley is a fascinating wreck.

Edward Mitchell, having been asked for some account of his later connection with the Sanitary Commission, sends us this modest résumé of what was a laborious and important service for two years and a half.

"You remember that Mr. Olmsted assigned me to duty rather as a personal aid on his staff of assistants, and, when I parted from you on the James River, he took me with him to Washington some time in July, 1862. Soon after I was sent to the front with a wagon-train of Sanitary Commission supplies, for one of the Corps of Pope's Army, then engaged in the "Second Bull's Run." Returning to Washington, I was sent with a train of fresh supplies for the Army of the Potomac, as far as Antietam, in September. In November or December, 1862, I was ordered to sail with the Banks Expedition, destination unknown. On reaching New Orleans and reporting to Dr. Blake, who was in charge of the Sanitary Commission there, I was put in charge of the store-house, receiving and issuing supplies until the Spring. In March or April, 1863, I was started out with a wagon-train to accompany an expedition through the Teche country and to Baton Rouge. At Baton Rouge I established a depot, supplying the hospitals there and the hospital boats coming down the Mississippi, until after Port Hudson was taken. In the winter of 1863 I was dispatched to Matagorda Island to receive and distribute potatoes and barrels of pickles and sauer kraut to the troops under command of General Napoleon Jackson Tecumseh Dana, who, when some one complained to him of his Commissary in general terms, asked, "What charge do you make against him?" and being answered somewhat vaguely that he was "generally unpopular," replied, "I would not give a d—m for a popular Commissary."

In the Spring of 1864 I was ordered to proceed to Alexandria with two assistants, and a large assortment of various stores, and establish a depot there for the use of the "Red River Expedition," which was composed of General A. J. Smith's troops, who came down the Mississippi and united with General Banks' army. After returning to New Orleans I resigned from the United States Sanitary Commission, but went with General Smith up the Mississippi, and, either at Cincinnati or Nashville, meeting Dr. Newberry of the Western Branch of the United States Sanitary Commission, I, at his request, spent some time at Murfreesboro, Chattanooga and Knoxville in the service of the Commission. In the autumn of 1864 I returned to New York and the Columbia College Law School, but for many years after, I was constantly stopped on the streets by men, quite unknown to me, who begged me to "take a drink," insisting that something distributed by me had saved their lives.

Somewhere about July 14, 1862, Charley and G. must have gone home from Harrison's Landing, probably in a returning hospital ship. The record is lacking—Sarah Woolsey's letter of July 22 being the first mention of it. She had been serving all this time at the New Haven Hospital.

S. C. W. to G.

NEW HAVEN, AT THE BARRACK HOSPITAL. July 22.

When the family leave you a little gap of time, write me one line to make me feel that you are *really* so near again. I cannot help hoping that if you go back, there may be a vacancy near you which I can fill. The work here is very satisfactory in its way, but is likely to come to an end before long if the decision about "Hospitals within military limits" is carried out. . . .

This is Sunday, and I have been here since half past nine—it being about 5 P. M. now . . . It has not been very Sunday-like, as I've mended clothes, and given out sheets, and made a pudding, but somehow it seems proper. Mary would laugh if she knew one thing that I've been doing—distributing copies of "A Rainy Day in Camp" to sick soldiers, who liked it vastly. I had it printed in one of our papers for the purpose. To-morrow I am going to change employments—take Miss Young's place in the kitchen, and let her have a day's rest, while Mrs. Hunt supplies mine here. Meantime as a beginning I must go and heat some beef tea for a poor fellow who hates to eat, and has to be coaxed into his solids by an after promise of pudding and jelly. . . .

P. S.—Have come back from service and administered the beef tea, though it was an awful job. The man gave continual howls, first because the tea was warm, then because I tried to help him hold a tumbler, then because I fanned him too hard, and I thought each time I had hurt him and grew so nervous that I could have cried. Beside, there is a boy in that tent—an awful boy with no arms, who swears so frightfully (all the time he isn't screeching for currant pie, or fried meat, or some other indigestible), that he turns you blue as you listen.

The whole staff of the Wilson Small seems now to have scattered and "fallen back," on Washington. The letter of July 21 is from Miss Katherine

P. Wormeley. She and Mrs. William P. Griffin had been delightful friends to us. We were the four "staff" women on the Wilson Small through the whole Peninsular campaign. Miss W. came home on our old hospital ship the Daniel Webster, in charge of her last load of wounded from the Peninsula, Mrs. Griffin remaining at Hampton Roads in a receiving hospital for some weeks longer.

Miss Wormeley to G.

NEWPORT, R. I., JULY 21ST, '62.

Dear Georgy:

How did you take to civilization? I got along perfectly till I was caught going off the boat without paying my fare. Captain T's mother was on board, which was a capital thing, and induced him to behave himself. I found intimate friends on board who were dear to me because they escorted me to supper. Georgy! if you ever take passage on the Metropolis, go down to supper for my sake and imagine how it affected me. My friends rather apologized for their desire to go down; for my part all I could do was to conceal my disappointment at not being able to eat everything. It seemed to me there was everything good that I had ever heard of, ending with peaches and ice cream.

I put the wounded captain into an express wagon (the nearest thing to an ambulance) and got home myself at 4 o'clock, to be finely cackled over by Mother. The next day the town called on me, beginning, like a Fourth of July procession, with the mayor and clergy. The next day I stayed in bed till after visiting hours. By-the-by, isn't a bed delicious? I can't believe it is the same mattress, the same blanket and sheets that I had before I went away. Of course you know that Dr. Wheaton with 1,700 men are here (six miles from here). Excursion boats run from here and from Providence to the camp. It is the fashionable drive, and the dear creatures are all female sutlers with baskets of *pies* and cakes and pickles and sweetmeats. Colonel Vollum is here. I have sent him word that if I can do anything sensible with authority I will, meanwhile I do not intend going near the camp. . . . I am truly sorry that Colonel Howland's furlough is shortened. Fanny Russell told me about it, and we spent all the time we were together in adoring "Mrs. H." I have said one hundred times "I will tell that to Georgy," but behold I have forgotten everything. Yesterday was a happy day to me, the dear little chapel was so peaceful and full of love and praise. I thought of Mr. —— as I sat there. . . . No large mind doubts God or the excellence of life with Him merely through looking at the mean lives of others.

Good-bye, love to Mrs. Howland and C. W. W.
I am yours faithfully,
K. P. Wormeley.

J. H. kept up constant communication with the 16th and his commanding generals, always in the hope of going back, in spite of all discouragements.

Gen. Henry W. Slocum writes to him:

HARRISON'S LANDING, JULY 19, '62.

My dear Colonel:

Yours of the 16th has just come to hand. I am sincerely glad that you are doing so well and I shall be rejoiced to see you back. I think the major is doing well, but there is nothing like having the head present. Still I hope you will not think of returning till you are *fully* recovered. If you come back feeling weak, you will be obliged to leave again. This climate is very debilitating and nearly all the officers, even the strongest are affected by it. . . . My advice to you is to remain at home until some move is made here.

As to your conduct and that of your regiment on the 27th, I hear but one opinion—all speak in terms of praise, the strongest terms.

General Franklin told me to say to you that you must not come back till you are well. He (Franklin) is about half sick. I am in the same condition—too sick to be worth much and too well to go home. . . . Remember me to Mrs. Howland and tell Miss Georgy that her favor has been received and that I will "follow them with a sharp stick" as requested.

Yours truly,
H. W. Slocum.

By July 22 Joe could not be kept away from the army, and only half well, he started back, probably in a hospital return boat, to the regiment at Harrison's Landing. It was, however, only to break down again. The

Historical Sketch of the 16th, prepared for their reunion at Potsdam in 1886, says: "Colonel Howland visited the regiment for the first time since the battle of Gaines' Mill. His suffering was plainly seen, and the men showed their love for him by going to his tent and relieved each other's guard, so that everyone might take him by the hand."

E. writes him from Astoria, July 23:—

Dear Joe,

It is the dull twilight of a dull November-like day and I am afraid you have had a cold, dreary passage. Once at Harrison's Landing, however, cold weather will be better and healthier for you than not. I suppose you must have arrived to-day. . . . Georgy and I drove out yesterday with Robert, found Mary well and the children asleep. To-day we have had the full benefit of them within doors and have fought with the little rebel Bertha and played with the strange child Una, and studied the fascinations of the little new baby, most of the time. Georgy is an unusually sweet, bright little baby, and Una is a real beauty. Bertha's affectionate greeting was: "I throw you in the bushes, and pull your head off for me dinner."

The Elizabeth at Harrison's Landing is the Sanitary Commission store boat and has plenty of hospital clothing and supplies, and the Medical Director's boat has plenty of farinaceous food, farina, arrowroot, etc. . . .

E. and G. meantime were planning to join the hospital service again, and keep near Joe, under the Sanitary Commission auspices.

Frederick Law Olmsted to E. W. H.

U. S. SANITARY COMMISSION,
NEW YORK AGENCY, 498 BROADWAY.
NEW YORK, 25TH JULY, 1862.

Dear Mrs. Howland:

I have just received your note of the 22d.

It is expected that the "Euterpe" will leave here on Saturday for Old Point, there to "await orders." Dr. Jenkins writes me that Dr. Cuyler changed his mind and his orders about the use of the hospital vessels two or three times a day, and he could form no plans. . . .

I hope some decided and tangible line of work may be determined on. At present everything remains as when we left James River. . . .

The Commission would, of course, be glad to have you and your sister take passage upon the returning hospital ship if you wish; and you can do so without placing yourself under any obligation to remain upon her. You could, upon arrival at Fortress Monroe, determine, by consultation with Dr. Jenkins, whether you could find duty at Berkely. Most respectfully yours.

Early in August J. H. broke down once more with malarial fever and was sent home by the army surgeons, this time not to return to the regiment, and our going to the front was given up.

E. W. H. to Mother.

FISHKILL, AUGUST 15.

Dear Mother:

In answer to my letter Dr. Draper came up yesterday noon and stayed till this afternoon. . . . The visit was part professional and part for pleasure and was satisfactory in both ways. He finds Joe improving, though more slowly than he had hoped, but he says he must not think of returning to camp. That if fever got hold of him again he would stand very little chance of recovery. It would permanently break down his constitution, if it was not immediately fatal. . . . It is very disappointing. He hoped to gain fast enough to go back the end of this month, and is greatly depressed about it, for he has made up his mind that under the circumstances it is great injustice to the regiment and to Major Seaver to continue to hold his commission, getting the credit as it were, while the Major has all the care and responsibility. He wishes to do only what is most for the interests of the service.

J. H. resigned from the service by the advice of Dr. W. H. Draper of New York, whose medical certificate stated that he was suffering from extreme nervous exhaustion and debility, and was unfit for duty. The resignation was received by his superior officers with expressions of great regret, and letters full of affection poured in upon him.

General Bartlett, commanding the brigade, writes:

HEADQUARTERS 2D BRIGADE.
SEPTEMBER 4TH, 1862, "CAMP FRANKLIN," VA.

Dear Howland:

I received your papers just as we were embarking at Newport News, and you cannot imagine how badly I felt at the thought that perhaps we should never be associated together in the field again, and perhaps never again see each other. We all agreed that you ought not to come back, all seemed actuated by the same feeling of love for you and all expressed their sorrow that you would no longer be with us. . . .

The old 16th are still "A. No. 1."

General Bartlett writes again:

HEADQUARTERS 2D BRIGADE,
NEAR BAKERSVILLE, MD. OCTOBER 1ST, 1862.

My dear Howland:

I enclose to you the acceptance of your resignation and honorable discharge from the service.

I had much rather it had been your appointment as brigadier, for I don't believe the service can afford to lose many such officers, and yet I would rather see you recover your health and strength than to be made a major-general, myself.

On the 14th of August—McClellan's attempt to reach Richmond via the Chickahominy swamps having proved a disastrous failure—the transfer of the army to Washington began.

Lieutenant Robert Wilson of J. H.'s regiment wrote home at the time a letter which might easily have come from any regiment in the Army of the Potomac. "Six days' march," he says, "to Newport News, choking with dust, parched with thirst, melting by day and freezing by night, poorly fed and with nothing but the sky to cover us. You can judge of our exhausted condition when I tell you that six miles before we reached the camp at Newport News the 16th Regiment, N. Y. Vols., numbered only 184 men in the ranks, though men straggled in, so that there were 400 in the morning, *and the 16th is no straggling regiment.* Next day embarked on transports and arrived at Alexandria, sorrowful and humiliated when looking back over a year and finding ourselves on the same ground as then. The debris of the Grand Army had come back to its starting place with its ranks decimated, its men disspirited, its morale failing, while the thousands who sleep their last sleep on the Peninsula demand the cause of their sacrifice."

The retreat from the Peninsula was almost immediately, (August 29, '62,) followed by the "Second Bull Run" disaster, which again filled the Washington and Alexandria hospitals to overflowing and taxed the hospital workers to the utmost. Chaplain Hopkins, still on hard service in Alexandria, writes:

Office Of General Hospital,
12 o'clock Sunday Night.
Alexandria, August 31st, 1862.

My dear Mrs. Howland:

These days are more terrible than any thing the nation has yet seen, and their horrors are at our very doors. Yesterday we sent 375 men to the north, and 433 to-day, and yet to-night we have opened a hall where, strewn on the floor, without even blankets, lie scores of wounded men unattended, with rebel lead festering in their bodies, but thankful for even that accommodation. Many of them came all the way from the battlefield in horrid army-wagons after lying in the rain and mud upon the field through the night;—patient, unmurmuring men. The best of New York and Boston blood oozes from their undressed wounds. I have just come from doing all that I could for them and am resting for the next train, which we momentarily expect at the foot of Cameron Street. . . . You have seen all this at Harrison's Landing, but in my wildest dreams, when I first reported to you in Washington, I never thought of such scenes. Through all the wards confused heaps of torn and dirty clothes and piles of bloody bandages, tired attendants doing their best to make comfortable the poor fellows torn and mangled with shot and shell in every imaginable way. Things now, from what I hear in the hall, are coming into order, several surgeons having just reported themselves to Doctor Summers, besides large numbers of citizen attendants from the departments in Washington and from this city, too.

By the time this reaches you the papers will have informed you that last night the main part of our army on the left wing was compelled to fall back on Centreville. This morning the whole army was concentrated there, utterly disorganized, with the exception of Sumner's Corps and some other fresh troops just arrived. They formed in front with their splendid artillery, and the rest of the army began to gather itself up for fresh encounters. The fight began again at three o'clock this afternoon, and men who left there at four o'clock say that it was going against us. God grant that the tide may have since turned.

Don't apprehend our capture here, for the forts have been fully manned and supplied with ammunition; besides, we are going to whip them on the present battlefield to-morrow. I hear the whistle of the expected train with wounded and must stop this hasty letter.

The tide did turn. Chaplain Hopkins' prayer was answered. The "fight which began at 3" the afternoon he wrote, ended with the repulse of the rebels by McDowell, and our troops rested that night at Centreville. There was a drop of comfort for H. H.'s poor men in the knowledge, later, that their courage and suffering had not been all in vain, though the poor army was again, after all its frightful losses, just where it stood in March, six months before.

Chaplain H. H. to G.

ALEXANDRIA HOSPITAL, SEPTEMBER, 1862.

My dear Miss Woolsey:

In great haste I write to say that to dispense anything which will do the bodies of these poor sufferers good will be a most welcome task. . . . Outside of the house, at the Mansion Hospital, we fed 1,100, 1,900, 2,100, and 1,600 patients passing North on successive days, so that those inside suffer some lack of care and of good food. Last night 75 came in from beyond the lines by flag of truce. I thought I had seen weary and worn-out human beings before, but these bloody, dirty, mangled men, who had lain on the battle-field, some of them two and three days, with wounds untouched since the first rude dressing, and had ridden from near Centreville in ambulances, were a new revelation. We cut their clothes from them, torn and stiff with their own blood and Virginia clay, and moved them inch by inch onto the rough straw beds; the poor haggard men seemed the personification of utmost misery. But some of them were *happy*. One nobleman who attracted me by the manliness of his very look in the midst of his sufferings, when I spoke to him of the strong consolations of a trust in the Saviour, threw his arms about my neck and told me, weeping, that for him they were more than sufficient. Some of these fellows I love like brothers and stand beside their graves for other reasons than that it is an official duty. . . .

It was for such heroic sufferers as the "nobleman" described by Chaplain Hopkins that Mary wrote these verses:

> "MORTALLY WOUNDED."
> I lay me down to sleep,
> With little thought or care
> Whether my waking find
> Me here—or THERE!
>
> A bowing, burdened head
> Only too glad to rest
> Unquestioning, upon
> A Loving breast.
>
> My good right hand forgets
> Her cunning now;
> To march the weary march
> I know not how.
>
> I am not eager, bold,
> Nor strong,—all that is past!
> I am willing *not to do*,
> At last, at last!
>
> My half-day's work is done,
> And this is all my part:
> I give a patient God
> My patient heart;

And grasp His banner still
Though all its blue be dim
These stripes, no less than stars,
Lead after Him.

Weak, weary and uncrowned,
I yet *to bear* am strong;
Content not even to cry,
"How long! How long!"

Mr. Lincoln's call for 300,000 more troops was being answered. All over the country camps were being formed and boys drilled in all the pleasant villages of the land. Mother and all of us went to rest awhile, after Charley and G. came home, in Litchfield, and watched the drilling and recruiting.

A. H. W. to H. G.

LITCHFIELD, SEPTEMBER 3, 1862.

My dear Hatty (Gilman):
I should like you to see the beautiful camp of the 19th C. V. here before it is all broken up. We are to have a flag presentation from Mr. Wm. Curtis Noyes, and a religious farewell service was appointed to be held to-day in the Congregational Church. Good Dr. Vail will pray, I dare say, as he did on Sunday: "God bless our 19th Regiment, the colonel and his staff, the captains, and all the rank and file." . . .

The calm air, the physical comfort and peace we have here, make mental peace easier I suppose. We cannot be too thankful, we say to each other, that we are not in New York, heated and tired and despondent. It is infinitely sad, all this desperate fighting and struggling; this piecemeal destruction of our precious troops, only to keep the wolves at bay. But how well the country is going to bear it! I suppose these poor, innocent, confident new lives will be in the thickest of the fight at once. They will have their wish! be put to the immediate use for which they enlisted. . . .
I grow stony and tearless over such a *mass* of human grief. I am lost in wonder, too, at the generalship, the daring and endurance of the Southern

army. We are to fight it out now, even if it becomes extermination for us and them. . . .

A camp for sick and wounded had been established at Portsmouth Grove, near Newport, R. I., and as a matter of course it appealed to Miss Wormeley, its near neighbor. She was allowed only a short rest before earnest request came to her to take charge of the nursing there. We were all hankering for our active life in the thick of the fight. Mr. Olmsted used to say:

"My heart's in the Pamunkey."

G. to E. W. H.

LITCHFIELD, CONNECTICUT, AUGUST 26, '62.

Miss Wormeley had a nice note from Mr. Olmsted which she sent me to read and which I, returned to her—all about "the staff" on the Wilson Small—complimentary, but saying that he wonders at himself for having been at the head, and never could attempt to say how he felt towards all those who were associated with him. She wrote to ask his opinion about accepting the directorship at Portsmouth Grove Hospital. . . . I can't find her note. It told me that the Surgeon-General, Hammond, had been to see her and had asked her to take the lady directorship. She hesitated and he sent the surgeon-in-charge to see her, who wouldn't take "no" for an answer; said he liked women, and agreed at once to write for Dr. Robert Ware. He did write, but the Dr. could not be found. [Dr. Ware volunteered for service further South, and died there of fever contracted on duty.]

She asks what I think about it. I advised her to take it, and if she could not live in the hospital, to go out several times a week, and keep her paw on it, and insist upon order and system in the housekeeping department and kitchen arrangements. I hope she will, it is too good a chance to miss, and it is certainly a great compliment from the Surgeon-General.

The interchange of letters between Miss Wormeley and G. ended in an agreement that they should join hands again for hospital work at Portsmouth Grove, and as G. made bold to propose your Aunt Jane and Sarah Woolsey as co-laborers, all three of them were given the chance they coveted. Miss Wormeley's plan for organizing will give you an idea of your aunts' duties thirty six years ago.

Miss Wormeley to G.

NEWPORT, SEPTEMBER 5TH, '62.

My dear Georgy:

I found the new surgeon inclined to one woman for each ward (wards or barracks, of sixty men in each). I hunted him out of that idea however. Everything in the domestic management of the hospital being left to me, I shall *gently* avail myself of the courtesy. Now then for your advice. My ideas are these. Please give your decided opinion on them. To give five wards, sixty beds to each ward, to the superintendence of five friends—you, your sister, cousin, H. Whetten, and a lady here whom I esteem and consider efficient. Under these I should put one, two, or three women nurses, as occasion may require. These five ladies would he responsible for everything connected with their wards, *in general.*

You know what general supervision means,—cleanliness, beds, linen, due washing thereof, etc., etc., in all of which the women under you should do the actual work whilst you see that they do it. . . . I want to have *the men* intelligently looked after, as only a lady can. I should therefore wish that the ladies should go round with the surgeons *invariably*—to make short notes of each patient's treatment, medicine, and diet. Medicines I should want her to make sure were properly and timely given. The special diet lists ordered by the surgeon I should wish to be handed in to me as soon as practicable. I shall put a special diet kitchen at each end of the Barrack St. with a female cook in each, whom I shall attend to myself. . . .

This is in general a sketch of my ideas. What do you say? Will you come? . . . I want to point out to you that no ladies have ever *been allowed* to come into a *U. S. General Hospital* in this way—much less warmly requested, and thanked, and confided in, as *we are,*—for of course it has nothing personal to myself in it; it is General Hammond's first cordial reception and experiment of ladies in hospital, and is in consequence, as he told me, of the grateful sense he had of what we did at White House.

Now as to our own living there. A house is building for us, to be finished by the 12th of this month. It has bedrooms for all the female nurses, a dining-room for ditto, an office for me. We shall have to carpet our own rooms, and adorn them as we see fit; the Government supplies the common necessities of a bed, etc., for the nurses in general

I should want to have you with me at the start. Can you arrange to come? . . .

Write me at once, please. What a vile place you are in; the mails take a week to go.

A. H. W. to H. Gilman.

LITCHFIELD, SEPTEMBER 22.

Charley is trying for a Lieutenancy in one of the new regiments, and Governor Morgan has promised, as all governors do, to "see about it." This is going to be a great drain on Mother's spirits and strength, if the application succeeds, and will bring us all continued personal interest and anxiety.

Georgy was telegraphed ten days ago to come immediately to Newport to a great military barrack hospital.

On September 17th the fierce battle of Antietam was fought by the Army of the Potomac,—a drawn battle, little better than a defeat for us; and though the rebels retired there was no following up on our part, and no result worth the enormous loss of life.

And now the moment had come for the war-measure Mr. Lincoln had held in reserve. The Government had been fighting to uphold the Government, and announcing all along that if the abolition of slavery proved needful to that end, then slavery should cease.

On September 22, 1862, Mr. Lincoln issued a preliminary proclamation declaring that in all States found in rebellion on January 1, 1863, slaves should "thenceforth and forever be free." Congress, however, delayed to take the action urged upon them by the President, until the time limit expired.

J. S. W. to a friend abroad.

8 BREVOORT PLACE, N. Y.

October, 1862.

The fighting at Cedar Mountain and Gainesville and on futile fields of Manassas, the mysterious ups and downs of commanders, the great invasion scare, the mean dissensions and the sad delays, have kept us constantly agitated, the more so that we were in the tauntingly still and sweet country, where the newspaper train was sure to fail in great emergencies. There was a time,—I confess it because it is past, when your correspondent turned rather cold and sick and said "It is enough!" . . . and when my sister Abby, (who acknowledged the Southern Confederacy when the rebel rabble got back unpursued across the river from Winchester), went about declaiming out of Isaiah, "To what purpose is the multitude of your sacrifices; your country is desolate, strangers devour it in your presence." . . . We came out of that phase, however, at any rate I did, and concluded that despondency was but a weak sort of treason; and then with the first cool weather came the Proclamation, like a

> Loud wind, strong wind, blowing from the mountain,

and we felt a little invigorated and thanked God and took courage. . . .

In Litchfield we followed with great interest the growth of the 19th Connecticut recruited in that county, all the little white crumbs of towns dropped in the wrinkles of the hills sending in their twenty, thirty, fifty fighting men; Winsted, Barkhamsted, Plymouth companies, and companies clubbed by the *very* little villages, marching under our windows every day to the camp ground. Almost all the young men in Litchfield village have gone; the farmers, the clerks in the shops, the singers in the choir. Who is to reap next year's crops? Who is to sow them? Everyone spoke well of the new recruits. There was not a particle of illusion for them. They understood very well to what they were going; disease, death, a common soldier's nameless grave. They made themselves a new verse to the marching song:

> A little group stands weeping in every cottage door,
> But we're coming, Father Abraham,
> *three hundred thousand more.*

General Tyler went over to Danielsonville to look at a company just raised in that town, and was waited on to know if another company would be accepted. "If it is here this time to-morrow," he answered in jest. *It was there*. It is not altogether a question of bounty. A fine young fellow came into our hotel a day or two after the bounty-giving ended, to inquire the way to camp. Charley asked him, "Why didn't you come before the pay stopped?" "That's just what I was waiting for," he answered; and a dozen men went from the village to whom the bounty could offer not the slightest inducement. The Congregational clergyman told us he looked over the growing list of names with tears, knowing what good names they were and how ill they could be spared. But the 19th Connecticut is no better than a hundred other regiments. There are very few men in the 18th Connecticut who are not persons of weight and value in their community, cousin Mary Greene says. And see how they fight! Look at the Michigan Seventh at South Mountain. The Michigan Seventh was two weeks old. And yet it is coming to us from over the sea that we can't get men, and if we do they will run! . . .

The generalship and fighting of the rebels is also certainly very fine—corn-cobs and no shoes are pathetic when one forgets the infamous cause. . . . Their "obsolete fowling-pieces" go off with considerable accuracy, says a malcontent at my elbow.

When we came to town last week the streets seemed full of anxious and haggard faces of women, and when I caught sight of my own face in a shop glass I thought it looked like all the rest. The times are not exactly sad, but a little oppressive. . . . G. and I cannot stand it any longer and we are off to-morrow. We are in the government service now and entitled to thirteen dollars a month! (At the Portsmouth Grove Hospital, as assistants to Miss Wormeley.) We are going into exile—a blessed exile.

S. C. W. to G. at Portsmouth Grove.

New Haven, October, '62.

And now for Miss Wormeley's delightful letter; my dear, it sounds too good to come true, all of it, and yet I can't help thinking that Providence smiles on the scheme and will bring about papa's consent. . . . We shall have it working beautifully in a short time, I see—and oh, G., what a happy winter we shall have! . . . Abby remarks in her last to Mary—"Sarah's going and Jane's (!!) I regard in the light of an agreeable fiction, but it will do for them to play at for a little while." . . .

I shall be ready any day after Monday.

A. H. W. to G.

NEW YORK, OCTOBER 6TH.

Jane wishes me to tell you that she leaves here by the same route that you took for Portsmouth Grove, on Wednesday, 8 A. M. She has sent word to Sarah to meet her on the train at New Haven. . . .

Charley proposes that you shall call your house the (H)'Omestead, in compliment to F. L. Olmsted.

Charley's determination to join the army, in the field at last had its way, and Mother's letter gives us the first news of his commission. Mothers in those two years had learned that sons were first of all defenders of the flag, and joining the army had come to be a matter of course in families where any sober view of life was taken.

Mother to G.

LIBRARY, No. 8., THURSDAY, OCTOBER 2D.

My dear Georgy:

I was charmed to get your pencil note this morning. . . . An hour after you left for Portsmouth Grove, Charley arrived at the door in his wagon, Pico and all, very sorry to have missed you. . . . Oh, Georgy, I do miss you greatly: in the parlor, up stairs, in my bed, morning, noon, and night, and my heart craves you all the while.

Charley has had a letter from Governor Morgan telling him he can have a lieutenancy in an Irish brigade, Colonel Burke. He has gone off this morning full of business, and says he shall accept it at once. There are so many other positions in which he might serve his country that I should have preferred for him! . . . Do let us hear as often as possible, dear G. Tell us just how you found things, and what you have forgotten—your *flask* for one thing. Make my regards acceptable to Miss Wormeley, and always love your loving Mother.

E. W. H. to Chaplain H. H.

DECEMBER, '62.

Charley, you may have heard, has gone into the service as lieutenant in the 164th, but he was detached at once for staff duty and is aide to General Burnside and a member of good old General Seth Williams' mess—*just where we would most like to have him.* We have heard from him up to Saturday morning, the day of the battle, and are not yet *very* anxious about him. . . . Georgy and Jane are hard at work at Portsmouth Grove, terrors to evil-doers as well as good friends to those who need it. They and the other ladies have effected many reforms and won the respect and confidence of all concerned except the mutinous convalescents and the lying stewards, whom they pursue like avenging fates.

We were very glad to hear of your work after those dreadful days of the "Second Bull Run." . . . I write principally to ask what I can do to help you take care of the wounded. . . . You know I want to do all I can now that I am unable to be there myself. You must call upon me freely.

On November 8th McClellan had been relieved of command and Burnside had superseded him. On December 13 was fought the first battle of Fredericksburg, with the rebel Lee victorious. Few or no letters mark these anxious months.

And so the second year of the war came to an end without any sound of public cheer or private rejoicing. There is no mention in the letters of Christmas fun, even for the children, while our poor defeated Army of the Potomac was huddled into Fredericksburg with the loss of 13,000 men. As a family we were again scattered, some of us in hospital work and Charley in the field. One window, though, was opened Heavenwards, since for three million slaves, across the blackness of a civil war

"God made himself an awful rose of dawn."

Jane Stuart Woolsey
Woolsey Collection, Ferriday Archives

CHAPTER ELEVEN

Our Beloved Bohemia

On the 22nd of September, 1862, a gleam of light had shone, the President had issued his preliminary proclamation of emancipation; and now on January 1st, 1863 came the announcement of full liberty to the captives.

Extract from the Proclamation.

"I, Abraham Lincoln, President of the United States, by virtue of the power vested in me as Commander-in-Chief of the Army and Navy of the United States, . . . and as a necessary war-measure, . . . do order and declare that all persons held as slaves (within the states in rebellion) are, and henceforward shall be free."

The passage by Congress of the 13th Amendment to the Constitution followed, extending emancipation to all parts of the United States and its territories.

A. H. W. writes, January, '63:

I improved yesterday to my satisfaction in reading the President's proclamation "The Lord reigneth, let the earth rejoice!"

And so *Abby's* war had ended in victory: ours was carried on for more than two years longer.

The second year of the war closed with Charley's commission for active duty in the field. He must have left at once; two mutilated scraps from a note of Hatty's are the only record. All else is lost.

"Charley appeared just now in full Lieutenant's uniform and looks so tall and brave that I should scarcely know him."

And,

"Charley did not get off this morning; a young scamp of an aide was walking about here in town, with papers directed to Charley in his pocket, and C. spent the day in trying to find him."

The only letter at this time in Charley's handwriting is from the front, to Eliza, January 14, 1863, reporting the 16th New York.

"The camp is in a pleasant place near White Oak Church. The General and I have established a friendship; he is not too much of a Brigadier for a young cuss of my size. The chaplain took me to see the hospital—new tents, nice large open fire-place, and but five sick men."

Jane, Sarah Woolsey and G. were meantime nicely established at the hospital six miles from Newport, R. I., with a jolly little thin board house built for the nursing staff; their rooms 10 x 10, furnished from home with every comfort, and work fairly begun.

J. S. W. to A. H. W.

PORTSMOUTH GROVE, JANUARY, '63.

Dear Abby:

This morning in the grey (I don't know how she managed to be up and seeing) Sarah looked in at the ventilator and announced, "Girls, there's a big black steamer off the hospital dock.—The soldiers have come!"

She proved to be the Daniel Webster with 290 men from *Fredericksburgh,* many of them! There she lies at this writing, two o'clock, no tug having been got up from Newport, and the tide being so excessively low that she can't move in. They have boarded her in boats however, and report the men very comfortable—short, delightful trip from Fortress Monroe, plenty to eat and no very bad cases on board. . . . Everything is ready for 450. Clean wards, clean beds, clean clothes and the best of welcomes. Georgy and I, who have the medical division, will not profit much. We shall get the sulky old "chronics" and "convalescents," and Sarah and H. Whetten will have all the surgical cases; but we shall go to see them all the same, and they shall have all our stores, soft towels, jelly and oranges.

Shingling the barracks goes on bravely. I think things will be all so much finished to the satisfaction of Mr. *Jefferson Davis*, by spring, that he will perhaps retain us in office! . . .

7 P. M. The men are all safely landed, housed and suppered, and all the surgeons are busy dressing wounds. They must work all night. The men are bright as buttons and jolly. Tell Harriet Gilman that her shirts are blessing *Fredericksburgh men to-night.*

Dr. Edwards, surgeon-in-charge, in the handsomest way offers to turn *out* anybody we wish and put *in* anybody we wish, so if you know of any first-rate candidates amenable to female influence, forward us their names.

The boxes of home supplies now had Portsmouth Grove Hospital as their principal destination. The following is one of the letters in return for supplies:

The games, as well as the slates, which came in the boxes and barrels, are a great delight. I have just been over to see Fitch and set him up at a *solitaire* board. He was all over smiles, and pegging away with his game in bed.

With another gift of tools, the boys in Ward 20 knocked up a nice little bagatelle board with glass balls and a cambric cover. Ward 6 went over to inspect and imitate. They came back disgusted; "would scorn to play on such a thing; would have a board on which a lady could dance a horn-pipe, if she pleased." Highly improbable that any one would please to do that, but I promised them that if they would make a first-rate board, they should have all that was necessary. So they went to work, and the result was a beauty. The table is seven or eight feet long, covered with scarlet flannel, and with turned balls and walnut cups, and the men of the ward have enjoyed every minute of its existence for the past month. I have never gone in when there hasn't been a crowd round the table pushing balls or keeping count, and I really think that the health of the ward has improved under the treatment.

Money spent in lemons for bronchitis, oranges for fever patients, mittens and socks for "convalescents" (who have to go on guard in puddles of snow-water) and in games and tools for wretched, bored, half-sick, half-well, wholly demoralized men, may not seem a great investment to the givers; would not seem so to me, if I did not live in a general hospital, and know where Government munificence stops and where private beneficence may to advantage begin.

The meals in our hospital mess-hall are nicely served and well cooked. At the beating of the drum the "convalescents" form in line, and march, by wards, into the long hall, where three lines of tables, each 250 feet long, are set. Last night, when we inspected the supper, there were shining tins up and down the tables with a very large portion of rice and molasses, hot coffee and plenty of bread for each man, and many little pots of butter and jam came in under the Braves' arms, out of their home boxes, to help garnish the tea.

This morning I was invited by a soldier to join him in a banquet over a box from home; "and all I want beside," observed he, "is a little gin." "It is very lucky for you that there was none," was my answer, "or the whole box would have been confiscated." "Confiscated indeed!" returned the Brave; "I should like to see *that* thing done. I'm none of your cream and chocolate men. I'd carry the case up to Abraham himself!"

The other day Miss —— was washing a boy's face very gently. "Oh!' said he, "that reminds me of home"—(Miss highly gratified); "that's like my sister; she often did that for me. *My eyes! wasn't she a rough one!* She'd take off dirt, and skin too, but she'd get the dirt off."

G. to J. H.

P. G. HOSPITAL.

Thank you, my Colonel, for the doughnuts and comic papers. They are just what the men prize most, and under every pillow I shall establish a little nest of both! . . . I always accompany a "Life of Headley Vicars" with a piece of chewing tobacco. . . . We are going to have a chapel in two weeks. At present it consists of eight holes in the ground and a tolerable fishing pond, but in one fortnight this will be a church and will stand next door to our house, leaving us no excuse for staying at home in the evening. We have embraced the puddles all along as argument against "protracted meetings." . . . Jane and Sarah and H. Whetten have just been relating their refreshing experiences for the day, in the next room. Miss Wormeley is down stairs getting up her official correspondence with the Surgeon and Q.-M. General. The diet tables are all made out and consolidated for tomorrow, and several reproving notes to wardmasters sent in to meet them at breakfast; and now, nothing comes except the usual burglar and as much sleep as this howling, driving storm will let us have. . . .

From J. S. W.

PORTSMOUTH GROVE.

My dear Cousin Margaret:

Now that I have been long enough in this place to have learned tolerably well my topography, the names and titles of my coadjutors, how to make out my diet books, etc., . . . I can take breath (and "my pen" as the soldiers always say in their letters) to say that we are well and more than contented with our present position. . . . Georgy already has her "department" almost completely organized and supplied, and develops daily an amount of orderly foresight and comprehensive carefulness which would astonish one who has watched her somewhat erratic career from childhood. I, who have always rather held myself up to her as a model of the non-spasmodic style, find myself in secret and in reluctance borrowing ideas of *her*. She has found her work certainly, at least at present. . . . We are nine miles away, as Sarah pathetically observes, from a spool of cotton, and of course this has its effect. There was a time when Newport made it a sort of fashion, and curious crowds infested the wards with plum jam and cucumbers, but now "the season" at Newport is over and the supplies in a measure fall off. . . . We are fortunate in having a good and active young man for a chaplain. He has a large and very attentive audience on Sunday and at daily evening prayers, and it is quite refreshing to hear the full soldiers' chorus in all the good old hymns. Last Sunday two soldiers were received into the church and baptized. Mr. Proudfit is a Presbyterian. . . . As to our house, it would not be fair to call it a shanty, as the doctors have taken so much pains or pleasure in fitting it up. . . . The outer walls are double and filled in with paper shavings (I believe), and this, with large stoves, will keep us warm; perhaps *too* warm some fine windy midnight. "Wooden walls" keep out all enemies according to the old song, but they don't keep out voices, for there is Georgy saying (I can hear it as if she were at my elbow), "I shall never be able to settle down into the conventionalities of society after the wandering life I have led these five years. Once a vagabond always a vagabond; I shall marry an army surgeon and go out to the frontier!" . . . Miss Wormeley, our chief, is clever, spirited and energetic in the highest degree—a cultivated woman, with friends and correspondents among the best literary men here and in England, John Kenyon and the Browning family for instance,—a great capacity for business and not a single grain of mock sentiment about her. . . . One good thing has happened to-day. Miss Wormeley is made agent of the Sanitary Commission here, with sole authority to draw and issue supplies, and we are to have an office full of comforts for the men at once. . . .

P. S.—All the barracks are to be plastered, large bath-rooms and steam wash-house to be built immediately, bad men turned out and good ones put in. "The kid begins *to go*," and I can see by candle-light it's halfpast midnight and time I was dreaming an hour ago.

A little item of interest for those of us who find "washing-day" a nuisance now, turns up in G's ward note-book—the washing-list for her barracks:

    120 sheets.
    60 shirts.
    70 towels.
    60 pillow-cases.
    Ditto drawers and socks.
    6 washing-machines, 300 pieces to each.

1,800 pieces for her wards weekly. We were pretty clean, you see.

What the children played in those days is shown by the following little letter:

Little May Howland to G.

NEW YORK, JANUARY, 1863.

Dear Aunty:

Did you get my letter I wrote you from Moremamma's? You must come home now and nurse me, I have the chicken pox. . . . The children play that one is you, and the other Aunt Jane, and they play that the logs of wood are the soldiers. They get bits of ribbons for cravats. I am going to crochet a pair of slippers for the soldiers. I may as well scratch out that I have the chicken pox, for the doctor has just been here and said that I can go out. . . .

A. H. W. to G.

Charley sends his "regrets" from Headquarters for the Bond wedding. We get his letters with wonderful despatch. A letter written Saturday *night* delivered here by twelve on Monday! General Williams had reached Falmouth again and will be very busy. The four grand divisions being abolished, the eight corps commanders report directly to Hooker, which doubles the work of his A. A. G. Charley is to have an office tent and one branch of the business to be assigned specially to him. General Williams will employ several such aides or clerks. . . .

I have ordered for you ten copies of the *Independent* for three months, ten of the *Methodist* and ten of the *Advocate.* . . .

Our service at Portsmouth Grove lasted only about five months. Sarah was the first to be called home, the family greatly alarmed over an outbreak of smallpox of the worst variety, with a number of deaths among our men. S. had to obey the call, leaving me (G.) in charge of her wards and this scrap of a note: "Number 41 ought to have soda-water and egg beaten in wine every day—Eastman, near the door; be good to him and to D. and C. and M., and read the Pickwick Papers to the poor fellow who blew himself up with gunpowder."

S. came back for a little while, later, but our "staff" was broken up; Jane and I yielded to the home demand, went back to New York and did not return.

S. C. W. expressed our common sentiment: "Civilization is even more revolting than I supposed, and I pine all the time for our beloved Bohemia."

G. writes to mother from Fishkill: "If you have any difficulty in deciding what we shall have for dinner, the Surgeon-General's diet-table for each day will be found among my papers; what is good enough for our soldiers will be even too good for us."

Portsmouth Grove was before long turned into a convalescent camp.

Charley was all this time at the headquarters of the army, assigned to duty on the of Adjutant-General's staff. He has kept some of his original dispatches, sent to General Burnside from the fighting front at the *first battle of Fredericksburg,* because, as he says, he "was so green and young at that time." He writes: "The first time I went under fire I had a tremendous responsibility put upon me, to send back half-hourly reports to the commanding general, Burnside, of the way the battle was going. Later I had a thousand other quite as important duties, but this *first* plunge into the uproar of a great battle I can never forget." And *we* had been quieting our anxieties with the idea that "aides at headquarters were never much exposed!"

We have two or three of these hasty dispatches in Charley's handwriting:

HEADQUARTERS ARMY OF POTOMAC,
APRIL 30.

Major General Howard:
I have the honor to enclose to you the accompanying statement concerning the position and forces of the enemy.
Very respectfully,
Your obedient servant,
CHAS. W. WOOLSEY,
Lt. and A. D. C.

Copy of telegram:

The Major General commanding directs that General Sedgwick cross the river as soon as indications will permit, capture Fredericksburg, with everything in it, and vigorously pursue the enemy.
(Signed) BRIG. GENL. VANALEN.
Per CHARLES W. WOOLSEY, A. D. C.

Then a list of countersigns for the month under Hooker, and best of all, a copy of this original paper written by Charley June 4th:

Major General Meade, commanding 5th Corps.
General:

I have the honor of transmitting to you herewith a copy of a telegram just received from the President respecting sentences of Daily, Magraffe and Harrington.
(Signed) C. W. W., A. D. C.

—and Charley had the pleasure of hurrying to Meade's headquarters with the *reprieve* of these men from sentence to be shot. These are among the very few papers connected with Charley's position at head-quarters which are now in our possession, many others having been lost in the Morrell fire.

Memorandum by C. W. W.

While in camp before Fredericksburg, "Snowden," the Seddons' house, was in full view on the other side of the river, inside the rebel lines. When the town was taken by us a guard was stationed at the house for its protection, but the people in it were suspected of signaling, by lamps at night, to confederates in our (then) rear—the side of the river we had left. I was sent to Mrs. Seddons with a letter containing a word of advice to her in this connection—it was probably a threat of very severe punishment if anything further occurred to excite suspicion. I do not remember seeing the letter, but I took her reply, which she wrote while I waited. It is very plucky and to the point, unswerving in her loyalty to the rebel cause, and has quite the story-book smack to it.

Here it is:

I, Mrs. Seddon, utterly deny and challenge the proof that any signals of *any kind* have been made from this house "to parties on the other side of the river."

While Federal guards protect my property my hands are bound to refrain from serving a cause to which I would willingly sacrifice my life, but not my honor.
Respectfully, MARY A. SEDDON.

SNOWDEN, MARCH 13, 1863.

The term of service for which thousands of men had enlisted was now ending; the old army organization was expiring by its own limitations. There were in this army, as in all others, mercenaries and shirkers, but the bulk of the volunteer forces was of splendid and steadfast purpose. Early in the war this was seen with many of the three months' men; for example, the 2nd Connecticut, F. B.'s regiment. They kept their faces to the foe, and though their time was more than up, and they might have gone home with honor before the First Bull Run fight, they marched as a matter of course into that disaster, many of them never seeing again the wives and mothers who had believed the days of danger and separation ended. The spirit of the veterans of two years is shown in the history of the last few days of *our* 16th New York. Its time of service expired May 10, 1863. The terrible Chancellorsville campaign was its last and severest test, a few days only before the regiment was mustered out.

Lieutenant Robert P. Wilson of the 16th, at this time Captain and A. A. G. on the brigade staff, wrote:

I did not think we were to be attacked. It was so late, we were all so tired, the day had been one of such constant fighting, that I could not believe another engagement imminent; but as I was returning towards the General I saw him take off his hat in rear of a New Jersey regiment and cheer them on. The whole thing flashed upon me at once. I drew my sword, and felt that *the test had come*. . . . I never felt prouder than when I saw the brave men of the 16th—each one of whom I knew—steadily advancing through the woods to what we knew was all but certain death. Their term of service nearly expired, their lives dearer than ever now, their hopes of home strong; yet, flinging all these aside, thinking of nothing but duty and honor, they coolly dressed their line and as willingly entered the woods as if friends instead of foes lay behind. . . . For a moment we were irresistible and the rebels ran, but now from behind the rifle-pits in our front, which we had thought unoccupied, there rose up like magic a fresh line and into their very hearts at pointblank range poured the deadliest volley I ever saw. Our whole line melted before it. . . . The *brigade* when rallied was a sad sight: 687 men were gone, and but a remnant of each regiment was left to tell the fearful tale. . . .

E. W. H. to A. H. W.

MAY 9, 1863.

Dear Abby:

The loss of the 16th alone is placed at 20 killed, 83 wounded, and 64 missing—probably badly wounded and left behind. A frightful proportion: nearly half I should think. What a little handful are left to come home next week!

Colonel Woolsey Hopkins, Assistant Quartermaster-General of Division, writes at this time to E. W. H., on the disbanding of the division.

STAFFORD COURT HOUSE, VIRGINIA,
MAY 9TH, 1863.

My dear Mrs. Howland:

This has been a sad day to me. We were ordered to a review of the 1st division at 2 P. M. We rode silently and slowly to the field, and then down the front, stopping at regiments of 200 and 300 men General Slocum would make some remark to the Colonel, and move slowly on. Thus we passed the infantry and artillery. The General then ordered all the commanding officers to the front, where he very feelingly addressed them; thanking them for their services, and urging them to encourage their men. . . .

There was a sad, proud look, in men and officers, as of those who had just looked death in the face, as he seized companions on the right and left of them. The tattered flags riddled by bullets brought tears to my eyes, and that choking sigh that came when I saw the 16th without our dear Colonel.

One of the last acts of the 16th N. Y., before being mustered out of service, was the presentation of a superb sword, with sword belt and sash, to their old Colonel, J. H., "as a mark of their regard for him as a man, a Christian, and a soldier."

At the same time the enlisted men of the regiment, of their own motion, sent to E. W. H. a beautiful folio copy of the Bible, very valuable in itself and made still more so by the addition in binding of a full list of the donors' names.

The following letter, written while the regiment was still at the front, accompanied the gifts:—

Headquarters 16th N. Y. Vols.
Camp Near White Oak Church, Va.,
April 25, 1863.

Col. Joseph Howland.
Dear Sir:

The officers of the Sixteenth New York Volunteers desire to present you with the accompanying sword as a testimonial of their appreciation of the gallantry and ability displayed by you while in command of the regiment during the Peninsular Campaign.

The enlisted men of the regiment, feeling that Mrs. Howland has laid them under a deep debt of gratitude by her many contributions to their comfort and by philanthropic labors in the hospitals, send the Bible for her acceptance.

Very respectfully,
W. B. Crandall,
Pliny Moore,
R. W. Wilson,
Committee.

J. S. W. to a friend in Europe.

Washington, May 25.

We have just been spending a month in Washington, my first visit since the war, and the city certainly looks like war-time, the white tents showing out of the green of all the hills, headquarters' flags flying above all the remaining bits of wood, and everywhere on the highish places, the long, low, dun banks of earthworks you get to detect so soon, looking like a western river levee. Then it is strange not to be able to go in the ferry-boat to Alexandria, or take an afternoon drive across the bridges into the country, without producing a document which sets forth over your names in full,—men and women,—that your purpose is pleasure visiting, and that you solemnly affirm that you will support, protect and defend the Government, etc., against all enemies, domestic or foreign, etc., any law of any State to the contrary notwithstanding, so help you God. It was odd, too, at the opera one night, to see an officer of the Provost Guard come into the theatre between the acts and accost the gentlemen in front of us: "Sorry to trouble you, Major; your pass if you please"; and so, to every pair of shoulderstraps in the house. Then there are the great Barrack hospitals and the dwelling-houses turned into hospitals, the incessant drum-beat in the streets and the going and coming of squads of foot and horse, the huge packs of army-wagons in vacant lots, the armed sentinels at the public buildings, and all the rest of it. Washington certainly shows the grim presence. It is a calumniated city in some respects. It is as bright and fresh this springtime as any town could be. The sweet, early, half-southern spring is nowhere sweeter than in the suburbs of Washington; on the Georgetown Heights, as we drove with Dr. Bacon up the river-edges to the Maryland forts or the great new arch "Union" of the new aqueduct, or down the river-edges by the horrible road, or went on a little breezy rushing voyage in a quartermaster's tug to Mount Vernon to see Miss Tracy, the lady who lives all alone with the Great Ghost,—all these little excursions are most charming. . . .

But some days of our visit were dark ones,—the three or four inevitable days of doubt and lying despatches at the time of the Chancellorsville battles; then the days when the truth came partially out (Mr. Sumner told one of our party last week that it has never yet come out); then the days when the wrecks drifted in, hospitals filled up and our hotel, being a quiet one, became almost a hospital for wounded officers. In the evening we used to hear the tugs screaming at the wharf; soon after, carriages would drive up, a servant get out with one or two pairs of crutches, then a couple of young fellows, painfully hoisted upon them, would hobble in. Some were brought on stretchers.

Then one day came our friends, Frank Stevens, 1st New York, shot through the knee, and Captain Van Tuyl, shot through both legs; then Lieutenants Asch and Kirby, one, arm gone, one, leg gone; then Palmer and Best of the 16th, etc. Stevens was left on the field at Chancellorsville, taken prisoner, sadly neglected. But it is astonishing to see the cheerful courage of these young men. I went to see Captain Bailey, 5th Maine, with superfluous condolences. "In six weeks I shall be in the service again; if they can't make me a marching leg I'll go into a mounted corps; you don't suppose I call *that* a 'disability'!" pointing to where his right leg used to be;

lying, pale and plucky, encouraging three other more or less mutilated men in the same room with him; and much more in the same strain, like the music of Carryl, "pleasant and mournful to the soul."

We saw a long train of rebel prisoners come in, not by any means, I am bound to say, ragged or gaunt or hungry-looking; dirty, of course, with queer patchwork quilts in many cases for blankets; some without shoes, some without hats, but fighting men, not starvelings, every one of them. Our friend Major Porter came up on the tug with one detachment. They opened their haversacks and ate their rations, which consisted in every case of crackers and sugar. One young fellow brought his blanket and spread it by Major Porter, to take a nap, saying, "Would you please wake me up, sir, when we pass Mount Vernon? I'd like to take off my hat when we come to the place where Gentleman George Washington lived." . . .

None of us know much about the retreat and the "reason why." The President was anxious and restless in those days, and went down to the tugs two or three times to see and talk with wounded officers. Georgy met him by chance one morning in the White House garden, and found him greatly changed since last summer. He was walking slowly, eating an apple, dragging "Tad" along by the hand and gazing straight before him, afar off,—older, grayer, yellower, more stooping and harassed-looking. . . .

Jane's letter, given above, happily contains also extracts from one of Charley's, after the Battle of Chancellorsville. He writes May 8th:

We have forced the enemy out of their works and made them fight us in the open, but instead of their 'ignominiously flying,' *we* have retired in good order to the other side of the Rappahannock, and are in our old camp again, bitterly regretting that we pulled down our chimneys when we went forward. And why did we come back? Nobody knows. It was *not* the storm, for when the order was given it was fine weather. Our position was strong. Everybody thought we could hold it for any length of time. I have been on the go of course, day and night; no rest for the A. D. C. On Thursday night (April 30) I was sent to Potomac Creek to look for a missing battery; then to the bridges to report progress; was on duty the rest of the night opening despatches, and back and forth all next day with orders to Gibbon. At 11.45 Saturday night I delivered to Sedgwick General Hooker's orders to cross the river at once, march on Fredericksburg, capture everything in it and march by the flank road to Chancellorsville. The night march began immediately. At 10.30 next morning I found Sedgwick in one of the houses in the town and gave him the General's order to attack. He charged on the heights splendidly. Later in the day I took the order to General Gibbon to hold the town, and then went to Sedgwick, three miles beyond the town, to report progress.

He was resting on the hills we have been looking at all winter. I reported to General Hooker up the river. The General said to me, "Mr. Woolsey, you will remain with me and take in all despatches that come." So I saw only Meade's fight, and was favored with communitions from "Father Abraham," (who knew very little of what was going on); from Peck, who ought to have walked into Richmond, and from corps commanders. On Tuesday night the army re-crossed about dark, the General started off suddenly and the staff scattered. He was just in time, the Rappahannock was rising, the pontoons shifting. I had to jump my horse from the last boat and wade him 20-30 feet, quite deep. The crossing of the artillery and infantry was tediously delayed.

After some search I found General Hooker on the back porch of a little house high up on the river's bank; the front rooms were filled with wounded. There were only three or four men with him; he looked very dejected and sad. The wet troops outside were toiling by in the mud and dark, in full retreat. The General and Butterfield nodded in their chairs before the fire. It was a melancholy sight. The General sent me repeatedly to report from the bridges. 'Tell them,' he sent word, with great solemnity, 'tell them that the lives of thousands depend upon their efforts.' All night and all the early morning the troops came slowly in. It was with great difficulty that I could stem the crowd on the bridges to get back with messages to Meade, who was covering the rear. He expected to be harassed, but I do not know of a shot being fired.

We are all very much disappointed, but do not believe that we are demoralized. I have heard hard things said of Hooker. Some of the headquarters men use his name in a way that ought to be punished as rank insubordination. The congratulatory order is the subject of many sarcastic remarks. On authority I may state that this army will be filled up with conscript men, and I am disposed to think that Providence never intended

the A. P. for anything but an army of observation. Let Hitchcock succeed
Halleck and Dan Sickles Hooker, and I think we may all go abroad to live,
with a clear conscience."

About this time President Lincoln left Washington to visit the commanding General at Headquarters, going by steamer to Aquia Creek.
Charley, who must by this time have received his first promotion as
Captain, was detailed to escort the President to the front, and arrived
at the banks of the Potomac with a headquarters' ambulance and a fine
led horse in charge of a lieutenant and guard. He met Mr. Lincoln,
presented his credentials, offered the ambulance or horse, and asked for
orders. "Well, Captain," the President said, *"You* be boss," and seated
himself in the ambulance, where by his side Charley had the honor and
pleasure of a friendly talk during the long drive back to the army headquarters.

F. B. having been on duty as Chief Medical Officer of Provisional
Brigades for months in Washington, was now, in the early part of June,
'63, relieved from this duty, with orders to report to General Banks,
commanding the Department of the Gulf. General Casey, on whose
staff he was while in Washington, thanked him for his services in
a highly complimentary general order, and he left for New Orleans,
where he organized and took charge for nearly a year of the great
St. Louis Hotel Hospital. After this he was made medical inspector,
and then medical director of the department. He resigned late in the
summer of 1864, after nearly four years' service, to accept the Professor-
ship of Surgery in Yale College. The following letter was written in '63
while he was still in charge of the New Orleans Hospital:

F. B. to G. M. W.

JULY 6TH, 1863.

My present experiment is trying whether I am equal to that American
standard of ability "to keep a hotel,"—the St. Louis Hotel, to wit. It is
a fine building over in the French quarter of the city. Chocolate-colored
old gentlemen with white moustaches, much given to wearing of nan-
keen and seersucker and twirling of bamboo sticks, (whom tortures could

not compel to speak three words of English, nor a general conflagration drive across Canal street into the American region,) prowl thereabout, and scowl French detestation at the interloping Yankee as he passes in and out of their national hotel. The rattle of dominoes, upon marble tables in *cafés* all about, is incessant, and on Sundays rises almost to the sublime.

The St. Louis was a good hotel, but makes a bad hospital. I remonstrated as stoutly as I could against its being taken for the purpose, but, with a fixity of will which I would have preferred to see exercised in some other direction, the order came for the St. Louis to be a hospital, and for me to be Surgeon in charge. So now, making the best of it, though my rooms are mostly small and my passages narrow, I have a superb marble entrance with two big lions, one *dormant,* one couchant, "to comfort me on my entablature." . . .

The labor of starting the Hospital has been immense, . . . for nothing about the house that could be disordered, from the steam-engine in the cellar to the water-tanks upon the roof, was in working order. . . . On the 16th I had to receive a steamboat load of patients, all of the poor fellows wounded, from Banks' second assault of Port Hudson; hourly, for the past week, we have been painfully expecting another such arrival from his *third.* . . .

Thank Heaven, the patients have done well! I am going to send as many North on furloughs as possible, convalescence is so slow and uncertain in this climate.

How wonderfully cheerful these wounded men always are! You should see one of our pets, a young fellow about twenty-one years old, from a New York regiment, Kretzler by name. Right thigh amputated, right forearm the same, shell wound as big as my two hands in the left thigh, ugly wound under the jaw, scratches about left hand and arm. He never complains of anything, takes all the beefsteak and porter we can give him, insisting on helping himself to the latter and drinking it from the bottle. He sits up in his bed a large part of the time, smoking his pipe with an expression of perfect serenity. When I ask him how he does, it is always "bully," with a triumphant air. Passing near his room the other day, I heard him singing "The Star-Spangled Banner" in a robust style, with the remark in conclusion, "There, guess them Rebs won't like that much," alluding thereby to a lot of hulking scoundrels of Texans, prisoners, wounded at Donaldsonville, and lying in a room within ear-shot of him, as well as to some female visitors of theirs who, having no longer the salutary fear of Ben Butler before their eyes, were making their sympathies a little too apparent. This kind of cats I pretty uniformly exclude now, and as a consequence, when they find themselves baffled, I have some highly dramatic interviews with them, almost at the risk of my eyes, I sometimes feel.

I reluctantly confess that I am subjugated and crushed by a woman who sings The Star Spangled Banner copiously through all the wards of my hospital. . . . She weighs three hundred pounds. She comes every morning, early. She wears the Flag of our Country pinned across her heart. She comes into *my* room, my own office, unabashed by the fact that I am the Surgeon in charge, and that an orderly in white gloves stands at the door. She looks me in the eye with perfect calmness and intrepidity. She takes off her sunbonnet and mantilla and lays them upon my table, over my papers, as if they were rare and lovely flowers of the tropics. She knocks off three of my pens with her brown parasol, worn out in the joint, and begins to exude small parcels from every pocket. . . . She nurses tenderly, and feeds and cries over the bad cases. Poor Martin Rosebush, a handsome, smooth-faced, good boy from New Hampshire, desperately wounded and delirious, would start up with a cry of joy when she came, and died with his arms around her neck, calling her his mammy.

Jerry Cammett, a peaceful giant, grown as they grow them in Maine, with pink cheeks, bright-yellow beard, and handsome blue eyes as free from guile as a baby's, lies with his right thigh amputated. After each visit she makes him, I hear the effect it has upon Jerry in about three hours of steady quiet whistling to himself of funny, twiddling Methodist hymns. Of course I do not encourage the visits of this creature with the Flag of our Country and the National Anthem. On the contrary, they encourage me.

So do those of "Olympe, sare, natif to ze citie." She is a stately, sybilline old black, or rather brown woman, everything in her appearance indicating great age, except her intensely black and glittering eyes, which still show the fire of youth. She wears a most elaborate turban of Madras handkerchiefs, a dress of fine and exquisitely white muslin, handsome pearl drops in her ears, and around her wrinkled neck a string of large beads of that deep yellow, almost tawny gold, which comes with ivory and palm-oil from the African coast. She brings little parcels of extremely nice lint, small pots of jelly, and bottles of orange-flower syrup, all made, she would have me know, with her own hands in her own house; this she says with great dignity, and shows me how carefully she wraps them up so that the Confederate ladies, her neighbors, shall not know that she brings them to Union soldiers. I fancy that if one should sit down with this old lady, and, in French, talk oneself into her confidence, she would prove immensely entertaining and instructive.

Captain Charles Rockwell's appearance was a very pleasant surprise to me. I hoped that he would be assigned to duty in the city here, but, the day after his arrival, he was ordered up to Port Hudson. . . .

JULY 10TH.

P. S. Let us have a season of felicitation over Vicksburg and Port Hudson, from both of which we have got the good news since I stopped writing.

The rage and incredulity of the Secesh are really comical, and fill my soul with an infinite peace.

Now send us good news of what cometh to Lee of the wicked raid, and all may be well.

United States Sanitary Commission, Gettysburg
Frank Leslie's Illustrated Newspaper

CHAPTER TWELVE

Three Weeks at Gettysburg

T HE ARMY OF THE POTOMAC, after the wretched retreat at Chancellorsville, had lain, along the Rappahannock, scouting here and there, burning rebel sloops and bringing in "contrabands," till Lee, who had not followed up his victory at once, put his forces in rapid march up the valley for the invasion of Pennsylvania, part of his army reaching and occupying Gettysburg June 26.

The Army of the Potomac made quick marches to overtake the enemy, but by the 27th of June were only a little to the northwest of Baltimore. At this point Hooker was relieved from command, on June 28, and Meade put at the head of the Army, which he at once put in motion.

Charley continued always with General Seth Williams, but was in every action assigned to duty on the commanding General's staff. He was transferred in this way to duty as "aide" to General Meade on the field, for the frightful battle which was approaching. On the night of June 30th the two armies faced each other in the immediate vicinity of Gettysburg, and on July 1st the fight began,—one of the decisive battles of the war.

It had been raging for three days. We at home knew that Charley was in the thick of it, and were most anxious and ready to believe the worst, when a telegram to me (G.) came from our old commander, Mr. F. L. Olmsted, saying, "If you are going to Gettysburg let me know." We jumped at the conclusion that *he* knew of bad news for us from Charley, and Mother and I started at once to go to him, "Uncle Edward taking us as far as Baltimore. There the news reached us that Charley was safe, and the rebels, repulsed at every point, were, at that date, July 4, in rapid retreat towards the Potomac, which they reached and recrossed July 13th, with the loss only of their rear guard of 1,500 men captured. They left all their dead and dying in our hands at Gettysburg. 7,000 of the dead of both armies were buried on the field at once; and all buildings on the hillsides and in the little town, both private houses and shops, were full of wounded men. That July 4th saw also Pemberton's entire army of 31,000 surrender to Grant at Vicksburg; and Charley was safe! So it was a day always to remember with wonder and solemn thankfulness, though with horror at the suffering and distress all about us.

A month later I wrote a little account of our three weeks stay at Gettysburg to F. B. in answer to his New Orleans letter of July 6th, already given.

G. M. W. to F. B.

FISHKILL, AUGUST 6, '63.

Mother and I were in Gettysburg when your letter came, having hurried on immediately after the battle, under the impression, due to a mistake in telegraphing, that Charley was hurt; and, being on hand, were fastened upon by Mr. Olmsted, to take charge of a feeding station and lodge for the wounded men. So there we were, looking after other people's boys, since our own was safe, for three weeks, coming as near the actual battle field as I should ever wish to. You know all about that fighting, how desperate it was on both sides; what loss, and what misery; the communications cut, no supplies on hand, no surgeons, or so few that they were driven to despair from the sight of wretchedness they could not help,—20,000 badly wounded soldiers and only one miserable, unsafe line of railroad to bring supplies and carry men away. We were twenty-four hours in getting from Baltimore to Gettysburg, when in ordinary times we should have been four. This was the only excuse I could think of to give the wretched rebels who, two weeks after the battle, lay in the mud under shelter tents, and had their food handed them in newspapers: "I am sorry, my man; we are all distressed at it; but *you* have cut our communications and nothing arrives."

Never say anything against the Army of the Potomac again, when so few of our men, after their marching and fasting, overtook and overcame Lee's fatted twice-their-number. I saw but very few who were *slightly* hurt among the wounded, and we fed all the 16,000 who went away from Gettysburg. So brave as they were too, and so pleased with all that was done for them—even the rebels. We had our station with tents for a hundred, with kitchen, surgeon and "delegation," right on the railroad line between Gettysburg and Baltimore, and twice a day the trains left with soldiers,—long trains of ambulances always arriving just too late for the cars, and no provision being made to shelter and feed them except by the Sanitary Commission. We had the full storehouse of the Commission to draw upon, and took real satisfaction in dressing and comforting all our men. No man of the 16,000 went away without a good hot meal, and none from our tents without the fresh clothes they needed. Mother put great spirit into it all, listened to all their stories, petted them, fed them, and distributed clothes, including handkerchiefs with cologne, and got herself called "Mother,"—"This way, Mother," "Here's the bucket, Mother," and "Isn't she a glorious old woman?"—while the most that *I* ever heard was, "*She* knows how; why, it would have taken our steward two hours to get round; but then she's used to it, you see;" which, when you consider that I was distributing hot grog, and must have been taken for a barmaid, was not so complimentary!

Then those rebels too, miserable fellows; we hated them so much when they were away from us, and couldn't help being so good to them when they were in our hands. I am, or should be, angry with myself in that I felt worse when Lieutenant Rhout of the 14th South Carolina died on my hands, singing the Lutheran chants he had sung in his father's church before they made a soldier of him, than when E. C. writes me that "Amos" was their oldest son, and that she and his father were over sixty. . . . I am glad we helped those rebels. They had just as much good hot soup, when our procession of cans and cups and soft bread and general refreshment went round from car to car, as they wanted; and I even filled the silver pap-cup that a pretty boy from North Carolina had round his neck, though he was an officer and showed no intention to become a Unionist. "Yes, it was his baby-cup," and "his mother gave it to him;" and he lay on the floor of the baggage car, wounded, with this most domestic and peaceful of all little relics tied round his neck. We had lovely things for the men to eat—as many potatoes and turnips as they wanted, and almost "*too much cabbages*"; and custard pudding, and codfish hash, and jelly an inch high on their bread, and their bread *buttered*—"buttered on *both* sides," as the men discovered, greatly to their amusement one night, considering that the final touch had been given when *this* followed the clean clothes and cologne,—"cologne worth a penny a sniff." "I smell it up here," a soldier called to me, poking his head out of the second story window, while I and my bottle stood at the door of his hospital.

If at any time you would like to swear, call your enemy a Dutch farmer—nothing can be worse, or, if he is a man of decency, make him feel more indignant. The D——— farmers of Gettysburg have made themselves a name and a fame to the latest day, by charging our poor men, who crawled out of the barns and woods where they hid themselves after they were wounded, three and four dollars each for bringing all that was left of their poor bodies, after defending the contemptible D——— firesides, down to the railroad. We found this out, and had a detail from the Provost Marshal to arrest the next farmer who did it, and oblige him to refund or go to prison. The day before we came away a sleepy-looking, utterly stupid Dutchman walked into camp, having heard we had "some rebels." He lived five miles from the city and had "never seen one," and came mooning in to stare at them, and stood with his mouth open, while the rebels and ourselves were shouting with laughter, he "pledging his word" that "he never saw a rebel afore." "And why didn't you take your gun and help drive them out of your town?" Mother said. "Why, a feller might a got hit;" at which the rebels, lying in double rows in the tent, shook themselves almost to pieces.

It was a satisfaction to be in Gettysburg, though I confess to a longing to shut out the sight of it all, sometimes. The dear fellows were so badly hurt, and it was so hard to bear their perfect patience; men with a right arm gone, and children at home, and no word or look of discontent.

The authorities want us to go back again, and look after the special diet in the new and fine General Hospital for 3000 men, too sick to be moved. We can't do so, though, as Jane and I have promised to spend the winter at Point Lookout in the Hammond Hospital. Look with respect upon your correspondent; she is at the head of the Protestant half of the women's department of that hospital. The Sisters run half the wards, and I expect to have fun with their Lady Superior and to wheedle her out of all her secrets, and get myself invited out to tea. Why shouldn't she and I compare notes on the proper way to make soup? I will call her "Sister," and agree to eat oysters on Friday,—(they are particularly fine on the Maryland shore).

It will be rather jolly down there, particularly as the surgeon in charge is delighted to have us come, and we shall ride over him just as much as your dear old women, black and white, do over their particular conquest. As for gardens of oranges, and flowers—well, we shall have beds of oysters, and, as it is a military station, there will be a band there to keep up our spirits; which reminds me to give the Baltimore fire-man his due, who, being one of our friends at Gettysburg, secured two bands before we came away and marched them down to camp to serenade us, which they did standing at the mouth of the long tent and refreshing themselves afterwards with gingerbread and punch, unmindful of the fact that the jolly Canandaigua "delegation," finding its fingers inconvenienced by the sugar on them, just dipped their hands in the claret and water without saying anything! It will be a long time before Gettysburg will forget the Army of the Potomac. Their houses are battered, some of them with great holes through and through them. Their streets are filled with old caps, pieces of muskets, haversacks, scraps of war everywhere, and even the children fling stones across the streets, and call to each other, "Here, you rebel, don't you hear that shell?" and one babe of four years I found sitting on the pavement with a hammer peacefully cracking percussion caps from the little cupful he had. . . .

What a good thing the public burying of the colored Captain has been, down where you are in New Orleans. Send me some more accounts of your hospital.

I have your great-grandmother's little note book, Una,—kept while at Gettysburg, with such entries as these:

"*Myers:* Wrote a letter to his father for him; only son—leg badly wounded."

"*Chester Gillett:* Wrote to his brother; right leg wounded on the 1st of July, amputated on the 8th."

"*Henry Rauch:* Lieutenant, Rebel Army—Came into the tent July 16th, died 17th; his father is old and blind."

"*Young Sloat:* Died of lockjaw; wrote to his mother."—You can imagine what a tender letter that was, from a mother to a mother.

23,000 rebels were wounded in those four July days, and 13,713 loyal men.

I (your Aunt G.) being urged, wrote later a little pamphlet giving Mother's and my experience at the front, and called "Three Weeks at Gettysburg." It was meant to "fire the hearts" of the sewing circles, which, all over the country, were keeping up the Sanitary Commission supplies. The Commission ordered 10,000 copies for distribution, and I went off to Point Lookout Hospital, leaving Abby all the work of getting it printed.

A. H. W. to Harriet Gilman.

FISHKILL, JULY, 1863.

It took so long for letters to come from Gettysburg, and Mother and Georgy had so little time to write, that we didn't hear often. They have come *themselves* at last; arrived Tuesday, midnight. . . . Georgy came up here this noon, and we have been sitting together talking over all the strange scenes in those tents by the railroad, where 16,000 men have been fed and comforted in the last three weeks. Just imagine Mother in a straw flat and heavy *Gettysburg* boots, standing cooking soup for 200 men at a time, and distributing it in tin cups; or giving clean shirts to ragged rebels; or sitting on a pile of grocer's boxes, under the shadow of a string of codfish, scribbling her notes to us.

She has many a memento of that strange battle—one, of a rebel lieutenant who died in her care; and a score of palmetto buttons from rebel coats—dirty but grateful, poor wretches; etc. . . . They say that the *women* of Gettysburg have done all they can, given the wounded all that the rebels had not taken, and have boarded the Sanitary and Christian Commission for nothing. At one house, where Mother and G. got their dinner one day, the woman could not be induced to take money. "No, ma'am," she said, "I would not wish to have *that* sin on my soul when this war is over."

We may go to Brattleboro for a month. But if Charley holds out the hope of his coming home, it won't be worth while to go away. We have not heard anything recently from "the army,"—I mean *our* modest portion of it in the form of Charley. He and all of them I am sure must be mortified at this escape of Lee at Gettysburg, scot free. He lost many men, but so did we. Pennsylvania is safe from "the invader"; but, dear me, our army has begun the hateful scramble all over Virginia again.

Charley wrote that "Halleck urged forced marches after the retreating rebels and an immediate attack, as he had positive information that Lee was rapidly crossing the Potomac." Charley adds, "but we have had nothing but forced marches since we left the Rappahannock, and we *know* that Lee *isn't* crossing and cannot cross rapidly." [He did, though.]

The enormous losses of the war now made a draft necessary to fill up the depleted regiments. Many thousands of the discharged two-years' men reenlisted for the war; but idlers, and the evil-minded, resisted. There were serious outbreaks in Boston and other cities, but in New York the disorders were outrageous. Mother and G. were still at Gettysburg at that time; Abby and Jane away from home, and Hatty and Carry alone in the house. C's letter seems written in haste with a poker:—

C. C. W. to A. at Fishkill.

10TH ST., NEW YORK, MONDAY, JULY 13, 1863.

Dear Abby:

It has come—resistance to the draft! The city is in a tumult and Uncle Edward wishes us to go out to Astoria in the 6 o'clock boat. The regulars are all out and the streets are full of rioters. The gas house on 23rd Street is blown up and 10th Street full of black ashes,—our door-steps covered. They say they will blow up the powder-mill in 28th Street, where the Gilmans live, and we have told them (if they will) to come all here. Hatty G. was in a minute ago, and Mr. Prentiss. There has been a great noise in town all day. The carriage is waiting, but I was afraid you would feel anxious. We would like very much to stay, but Uncle E. insists.

C. C. W. to A.

ASTORIA, JULY 15TH, 1863.

We left in such a hurry we had no time to leave directions for the servants, except to close the house early, and be very particular about fastening the doors and windows. . . . While driving out here we heard distinctly the cannon at Harlem. We have had no real trouble here from the mob, but were *threatened* last night and the night before. About two hundred men and boys, principally from Harlem and the upper parts of the city, were careering round the village. They went to Mr. M——'s, and made him come out and speak against the draft, and announced their intention of visiting Messrs. Wolcott, Woolsey and Howland among others. Groups of them were gathering in the afternoon as we drove through the village. Uncle Edward was a good deal excited as night came on, and had a man placed in the stable with directions to cut the horses loose should any alarm be made. Robert had his carriage, or rather his horses, harnessed and ready to pack the children in. Uncle Edward had a pile of fire-arms loaded and placed conveniently near the window. Aunt Emily put her rings on and her valuables in a safe place, and we pocketed our purses and laid Mother's camel's-hair shawls, which we brought with us, where we could easily seize them in case of sudden chill, caused by the draft! . . . But nothing turned up, and things have quieted down. The militia regiments are (five of them) coming home; the 7th has already arrived.

Hatty adds:

One of the Ball & Black firm came the next morning to ask Uncle E. if he could hide some treasure on his place. He lives in 86th Street and his house had been threatened. Uncle E. said he might take his three or four trunks through the woods to the "black lodge," but of course it was at his own risk, as no one was to be trusted on the place. They were all kept safe in Margaret's hands, and he came back and got them in a few days. Isn't it shameful that the fiends should have sacked Mrs. Gibbons' house?—everything destroyed and all her little things carried off. Uncle E. is perfectly indignant and in a state of suppressed rage at the Irish, but he agrees with Aunt E. in not allowing a word said against them at table, or within reach of any of the servants' ears.

Mrs. Gibbons was a victim to the low pro-slavery roughs, the dregs of the democratic party in New York, round whom all the worst elements of the city rallied. She was too well known as a pronounced abolitionist to escape. She had been, as she wrote Abby a few days before the riot, six months at Point Lookout Hospital, "a long time for a person of my age"; adding that she must come back where she "could enjoy home, and work too." Her "home" was gutted by the mob!

Joe at once went down from Fishkill to New York, to offer his assistance to the authorities, at the time of the riot. His train was surrounded at Manhattanville by a crowd with clubs, searching for soldiers. Being in citizen's dress, with his uniform in a portmanteau, he escaped, crossed a field and found a place at the nearest stage-line on top of an omnibus crowded with roughs, one of whom clapped him on the back and said, "You're a fancy looking sort of a chap; what would *you* pay for a substitute?"

Joe turned and looked at the man, saying, "I don't need to pay for a substitute, I went myself," and then, by a happy inspiration recognizing the unmistakable look that old soldiers, even bad ones, brought home from the army, added, "Do you know I believe I have seen you before! weren't you encamped on Cameron Run in the winter of '61?" Sure enough, he had been, with the Irish 68th, and they fell into old-time army talk till, presently, the rough threw his arms round Joe with a half-tipsy hug, and said to his fellows, "Take good care o' this gen'lman, he's a partic'lar frien' o' mine."

As they got near the city some row down a side street attracted the attention of the gang, and they all climbed down from the omnibus and disappeared. Then the driver turned and said to Joe, "Well, you had a *mighty narrow escape,*" adding that they were one of the roughest gangs in the city and capable of any crime.

Little Georgy Howland's peaceful christening in the Chapel of St. Luke's was a pleasant picture connected with the old building in 1862. In 1863 the hospital saw a different sight. The riots reached even that sacred spot. One hundred beds were at the time filled with wounded soldiers. The first alarm was the burning, that morning, of the Colored Orphan Asylum, corner of 5th Avenue and 44th Street, by the mob. At noon a stentorian voice called from the basement of St. Luke's, "Turn out; turn out by six o'clock, or we'll burn you in your beds!" "as a huge, hatless laborer, with his sleeves rolled up to the armpits, bare-breasted, red with liquor and rage, strode up and down the hall."

But a wounded rioter (shot, with a brick-bat in his hand), was about this time brought by a crowd to the hospital door, promptly admitted, and kindly cared for. Dr. Muhlenberg, leaving the man's bedside, went down alone to face the crowd, going right in among them, "in simple dignity," and telling them that to every wounded man needing help those doors were freely open;—"would they threaten this house with fire and storm?" Cries of "No, no; long live St. Luke's," came at once, and the crowd formed themselves into a vigilance committee, and protected the hospital from all harm.

The Rev. Dr. Muhlenberg, at the head of this great charity founded by himself, was an elderly man then, with a noble face, white hair and wonderful dark eyes. As he braved alone that howling mob of men and women, and by his personal magnetism quieted their rage, it was like the picture of the working of a miracle by a mediaeval saint.

Mother and G. came home after the riots from Gettysburg and longed for their hospital life again. Georgy did not long keep out of it.

G. M. W. to Mother.

FISHKILL, AUGUST 5.

Dear Mother:

Thank you for your nice note which came last night. . . . No wonder you regret Gettysburg. You will be gladder all the time that you went there and did what you did; and you will be ready to give me great praise, I hope, when I tell you that I have given up all idea of going back there, and have accepted in place of it Mrs. Gibbons' offer of the position she is giving up at Point Lookout Hospital; securing, before I go, the month you want me to have in the country, as we need not go to the Point before September. After the intense satisfaction you have experienced at Gettysburg, you cannot, my dear and patriotic Mamma, be otherwise than delighted at the prospect before us, while you must regret that I cannot also pull the special diet of Gettysburg through. Mrs. Gibbons will, I suppose, have got all things about straight at the Point, so that with little effort we can keep them going. It will be an easy and pleasant position; better, "till this cruel war is over," than sitting at home thinking what we *might* be doing. The surgeon in charge is "delighted" to think that we will come. . . . I shall hanker for our old life at Gettysburg and wish you and I were going back to run the new concern. However, there will be the satisfaction of taking the wind out of the "sisters'" sails. I dare say they will have made headway during this interval, and when I arrive with three feathers stuck in my head, "O won't I make those ladies stare." . . . We shall collect at home once more, Charley and all, before the winter, as you will not of course go to Brattleboro now till he arrives. . . .

Charley came North at this time on short furlough, and the family were reunited for twenty days before scattering again, Jane and G. to Point Lookout Hospital, Charley to the front, and Mother and the other home ones to rest, in Brattleboro, Vermont.

The Army of the Potomac had followed the retreating rebels from Gettysburg south again into Virginia, and by July 31st both armies were again on the Rappahannock, where cavalry raids and skirmishing all along the lines went on.

E. W. H. to Mother.

FISHKILL, AUGUST 24.

We ought soon to hear from Charley, and if Mr. Hopkins' rumor is true we may feel at ease about him for the present, for Meade won't attempt a movement without the conscripts. Do you see that Charley himself is one, although in the service already? Let us know how he got down to camp after his furlough with all his traps, and send us all his letters. . . .

Mrs. Gibbons remained after all at Point Lookout, and we were quickly established in our half of the Hammond General Hospital and "supplies" were laid in. One list is before me of the twenty boxes and barrels received from home and the twenty-four Boston rocking chairs. These we found mines of comfort wherever we went.

The Point was a delightful place, the Chesapeake Bay and the Atlantic Ocean meeting and rolling in opposing breakers at our feet. Every morning we watched our little darkey tuck up her skirt and take her bucket and her chance of catching a wave or two for our bath tubs, and all day the salt wind was a spur to work. Ten women nurses reported for duty to Mrs. Gibbons.

The Brattleboro Hospital was also full of returned soldiers, and Mother, who was longing for Gettysburg, took a little consolation in visits there.

A. H. W. to H. Gilman.

BRATTLEBORO, SEPTEMBER 17.

I hope soon to hear of the girls' arrival at Point Lookout. Georgy wrote us of her night at your house and how good you all were to her and to her *soldiers* too.

Mother is much interested in the hospital here and has been up several times; is interested in the worst way, that is, without the opportunity of doing anything. The wards are thrown open every afternoon from two to five, but visitors are few, and even the kind words she can take, and those of other ladies from this house, seem valued. The men said, "You are so different, ladies, from *some* that come here, who only walk through and stare at us as if we were wild beasts." One man was almost convulsed at seeing Mother, and, with tears, would hardly let her hand go. "I knew you, ma'am, the minute you came in. You were at Gettysburg, and were the first one that dressed my arm." And there the poor arm still lay, useless and swollen, and constant streams of cold water necessary to keep down inflammation.

The same wretched want marks this hospital as all others: the little attention paid to the food of the sick men. Typhoid patients are starving on pork slop, or eat smuggled cutler's pies of the toughest sort, from a craving for food of some kind. Some of those alphabets for "spelling games" which Mother took up were a great amusement to them, and to-day in the book-store Mother saw one of the soldiers trying to buy some more. None were for sale, but Mother promised him some, and at the printing office ordered, for a very little trifle, a hundred alphabets, which she will give them. . . . We hear that Joe was drafted in Fishkill, and as *colored!* the "colonel" before his name which the enrolling officer inserted, being so understood. He feels himself a thorough *black Republican* now. The villagers met him at the depot one day as he came up from New York and informed him he was drawn, and he had to make them a speech, telling them what an honor he should consider it, if he were well enough, to go, but he should find a substitute (which he has done, a "veteran"), etc., etc. They called out now and then, "That's so! that's right, we knew you would take a proper view of it!" . . .

When the substitute was ready to leave for the front, he came to say goodbye, "a little the worse for wear," and assured Joe with a beaming smile, "Kurnel, you're a noble man, and I'll exhonorate your name!"

A. H. W. to H. G.

We have had our first letters from the girls at Point Lookout, and everything promises pleasantly. The only grievance is the chaplain, whose face is "as hard as a wooden chair," and who looks as if he had fought through life, inch by inch. He is fanatically Episcopal, though his sermons were practical and good, and he has the melodeon (paid for by general subscription) picked up and carried off and locked in his own room after every Sunday service, that it may not be used at the Methodist prayer meetings which the men choose to have! Georgy says they have grand good singing, whether or no, without it. . . . There is a little of almost every phase of the war there, except the actual fighting. They have the prisoner's camp, the New Hampshire brigade to guard it, with their splendid drill, dress parades, officers' wives, hops, etc. There are the hospitals for each, the General Hospital, and lastly the large Contraband camp. Jane's first letter was long and interesting, as she was much at leisure, but we do not expect to hear at great length hereafter . . . Charley, always at Headquarters Army of the Potomac, writes us to-night that they have sent off two corps to West Tennessee, and that he thinks the ultimate use of the balance will be within the defences of Washington. Is not Rosecrans' crushing defeat a sad blow? . . .

J. S. W. to J. H.

POINT LOOKOUT HOSPITAL,
SEPTEMBER.

Eliza's help and all her little nice things were, and are, invaluable to us. . . . Things promise pretty fair here in every respect. The surgeon in charge is civil and ready to support us in everything necessary. The post is a queer one, hospital, military encampment, Contraband camp, rebel camp, Roman Catholic element and divided jurisdiction of Mrs. Gibbons and Miss Dix. Quite a mixture. We shall be involved in no gossip or small quarrels, but do our work as we find occasion, without partiality and without hypocrisy. . . . John, our man servant, is a nuisance. He interferes right and left, upsets everybody in a mistaken idea to serve *us*, and volunteers his views on all subjects. He would be in the guard-house in a week if he didn't go home to-night. . . .

Women were only recognized, in connection with the *regular army* service, as washerwomen, and were so entered on the payrolls, and detailed to the nursing department when needed. As Point Lookout was a regular army hospital, we were obliged by army regulations to be mustered in, and paid $12.00 a month. But we were hardly well established and in good working condition, when the following general orders were received and issued by the Surgeon-in-charge. The Point became a camp for rebel prisoners, and our connection with it ceased.

SURGEON-GENERAL'S OFFICE,
WASHINGTON, SEPTEMBER 26TH.

Surgeon Heger, U. S. A.

Sir: The Secretary of War has directed the transfer of seven hundred wounded *prisoners* from Chester, Pa., to Point Lookout General Hospital. . . .

Upon their arrival you will discharge the female nurses (both of Miss Dix's and Mrs. Gibbons' selection) reserving only one suitable person in low-diet kitchen and one in linen room. By order,
C. H. CRANE, *Surgeon. U. S. A.*

POINT LOOKOUT, MD., OCTOBER 7TH, 1863.
SPECIAL ORDER NO. 123:

The female nurses will be relieved from wards 6, 7, 8, 9, 10, 11 and 14, and they are strictly enjoined to abstain from any intercourse with the Prisoners of War.
A. HEGER, U. S. A.

CIRCULAR, NO. 17.
POINT LOOKOUT, OCTOBER 7, '63.

Miss G. Woolsey:

In accordance with instructions received from the Surgeon-General's Office, dated October 7th, 1863, the discharge of the female nurses on the

5th inst. refers only to their discharge from the *Hospital*, not from the service at large. . . . Enclosed please find certificates of pay.
By order of the Surgeon-in-Charge.
W. H. G., Assist. Surgeon.

A. Heger, Surgeon-in-Charge Hammond General Hospital:
Sir:
    I have the honor to enclose four duplicate certificates of pay, for myself and my sister, Miss Jane S. Woolsey. Will you be kind enough to make use of them for the benefit of the hospital fund?
G. M. WOOLSEY.

POINT LOOKOUT, MD., OCTOBER 7, 1863.

Madam:
    The transfer of the certificates of pay of yourself and sister to this Hospital is received, and in the name of those poor soldiers who shall enjoy the benefits of your gift, I tender you many thanks for it.
Very respectfully,
Your obedient servant,
A. HEGER.

    On our retreat from Point Lookout, via Washington, it was suggested to Mrs. Gibbons, who was with Jane and me at the Ebbitt House, that there was work to be done at the large barrack hospital established on the Fairfax Theological Seminary grounds near Alexandria; and through Mrs. Gibbons an introduction was secured for us to the surgeon, Dr. David P. Smith, who called to talk matters over with us. We followed up the conversation with an inspection of the hospital, and were put through a catechism by Dr. Smith as to what we thought we could do, if we came and took charge. The result was that he told us he should like us to try it, and we moved over the river and were installed as Superintendents of nursing, and quartered in the house of the Chaplain and his wife. Here Jane and I found ourselves in absolute control of our own department, and most cordially sustained by the surgeon-in-charge. An office was assigned to us in the Seminary building, where there was room enough for barrels and boxes of stores, a long table for office work, and a huge open fire-place where we kept a blazing wood fire, tempering it with a wide open window towards the hills and the distant view of the dome of the Capitol. The hospital filled up rapidly and supplies from home began to arrive.

J. S. W. to A. H. W.

Fairfax Seminary. Virginia,
Monday Night.

Please present my grateful acknowledgments to the Society for the barrel of shirts, etc., received Saturday p. m. They are always very valuable. Cases come up every day for such charities. Last night, for instance, a modest note was handed in at my door, signed Crawford, saying, "I am discharged for disability and am going a day's journey home in the morning. I have no means of procuring clothes and must leave the hospital clothes behind me; could you let me have a shirt?" Another man brought the note while "Crawford" waited at the foot of the stairs. I asked if he could come up. "Yes," the friend answered; "he ain't lame." So he came up to the door. It appears he was very modest; a tall, gaunt, bright-eyed man, not old, but with greyish hair. His left arm hung at his side,—elbow shattered and three-fourths of his hand cut out,—frightful looking; health broken, means of support all gone, but as cheery as possible. He got his shirt and a pair of socks besides, for which he was modestly thankful. Another man with one leg, got one, and a broken-down rheumatic at the High School another. . . . I shall give the woolen shirts to discharged-for-disability men, and poor men with large families. There was one such case I had almost forgotten—a drafted man, of the draft before the last—who has not been assigned to any regiment and can draw no pay or clothes. He got no bounty and came out, leaving seven children behind him. The chaplain knows his story and says he has done his duty bravely and cheerfully. . . . So *he* got a shirt. . . .

We are slowly working up new diet-tables.

J. S.W. to J. H.

Fairfax Hospital.

We are trying to get the regimental hospitals in the neighborhood—poor places at best—emptied into this or some other General Hospital. There is a great deal of bad sickness among the new recruits. Six men have died of typhoid malaria this last week in the 2d Connecticut Artillery, near here—new men all but one, but good healthy, decent, Litchfield County men. Some of the hospitals in Alexandria are to be broken up and the sick will probably be sent in to us. We hear more of the army via New York than in any other way. We had pressing invitations! to the Great Ball, to join a party in a special car and all that, which we think we see ourselves!

The country, the air and the weather are as sweet as sweet can be, with a sort of barren sweetness. You know what the country is. From our uncurtained windows' height we see the shining river and the bluish-purplish fields and shores end the trees still left standing, with the sort of look of spring, 'not now but presently,' in them.

I hope your lame leg has forgotten its bruises by this time, and you won't have to apply to Palmer. Three Palmer legs go up and down stairs daily under our ears, and do wonderfully well. The legs are heroic; the men are not—being addicted to poor whiskey and indifferent witticisms.

Your cheese is lovely and has already gladdened the stomachs of fifty braves. Eliza's rugs are very uncommonly nice and useful. They are the only vestige of carpet we have.

E's jelly is famous. It rejoices the heart of poor Clymer, a man with half his face torn away by a shell, one eye gone. He can only eat soft things, and thought "if he had some acid jelly it would taste first-rate." . . . Nothing we have to distribute can possibly go astray or be stolen.

I'll remember that G. owes $11.00 for a chair, which came safely. The man it was meant for, first, died last night, after a wonderful fight for his life.

Our Surgeon in charge at Fairfax, Dr. David P. Smith, had a lurking distrust of his "contract surgeons" and implicit confidence in his two women Superintendents, and the most friendly relations with them. I remember a "general order" which came to me one morning from his office: "The Surgeon in charge requests that his aide, Miss G. Woolsey, will report to him any case of smallpox she may find in the wards in her rounds;" and daily bulletins, such as the following, came to our office door:

My dear Miss Woolsey:

3 P. M.

I don't just see the force of your requisition for hatchets, unless it be to endeavor to let a little common and uncommon sense into the brains of "them officers?"

I send up my General Orders for your edification.

Mayn't I take my coffee with you this evening? Very respectfully.

G. to A. H. W.

FAIRFAX HOSPITAL.

To-day (Monday) the Pierson box has arrived. . . . I gave Nurse one of the two little brooms in it, with an exhortation to have a man detailed to attend to the little tables by each bed, and to brush them off with the nice new brush, every day. So that if the frantic little tables in Ward G improve, and banish their bits of bread-crumbs, dirty newspapers and stale tobacco scraps, it will be entirely owing to Mr. Pierson's broom.

Mr. Prentiss' note (with the extract from the *North American* about the Gettysburg tract) is amusing. However, I don't equal the celebrity of "A Rainy Day in Camp." Miss Dix has a standing *mis*understanding with the Surgeon in charge; in short, she hates him. He is a genius, a remarkable man in his profession. Miss Dix writes him a highly dignified note assuming command of him and his, and then, either to show her willingness to labor for him as a human being, or else to intimate that she considers him a fit subject for "tracts," she encloses "A Rainy Day in Camp." He told us of it! We told *him* nothing! We never let on!

Tell Mary that when *I* am used to box the ears of refractory surgeons, she may look upon me as an equal.

Chaplain Hopkins, whom E. and G. left two years before at his work in the Alexandria Hospitals, still toiled on with the utmost faithfulness, and now and then when a half hour of leisure came, galloped his pony out to the Seminary, and by our bright fireside made a link for us to home and civilization. He brought us good cheer, and we shared our supplies with him.

He was our most willing agent, shopping for us in Alexandria and Washington whenever we needed extras for our hospital, and we needed them in considerable variety and quantity. From a large package of hastily scribbled notes sent in to the Chaplain's hospital from our's, and full of commissions, these few will show what demands we made on our comrade in the service.

Dear Harry,

Don't forget to get me the boards for filing away all the hospital accounts, double, with elastic straps. The Surgeon in charge has, in the handsomest way, laid the hospital at our feet, and implored us to buy every thing, including the kerosene oil, and to keep all the accounts strictly, and save him all trouble. So send out some boards to keep the nasty accounts straight with. Also send me some note paper. *G.*

To the Same.

Will you be kind enough to ask at some beer shop, if you don't mind going to such places, what the price of porter is by the cask? I don't mean bottled stuff, but a cask full of the unpleasant thing, and whether they can get me some in a day or two. I don't want to ask the Sanitary Commission for any more, as they have sent me five casks already; and besides they are having a "convocation of women." Fifty delegates from the sewing circles, East and West, have assembled to talk it all over, and shake hands, saying "Courage my sister," or (which is quite as likely) to make faces across the table from East to West. Send me word about the something to drink as soon as you can. *G.*

To the Same.

If you have time, will you send me by the ambulance a box of brandy? We are ordered to receive 275 patients to-night from the A. P. —*G.*

Chaplain Hopkins to G. M. W.

ALEXANDRIA, FRIDAY MORNING.

Dear Georgy:

I take you at your word and send for the chairs and crutches. Nothing ever sent to the hospital did half the good that those two dozen chairs have done, which you and your Mother gave us more than a year ago.

These go to Fairfax Street and Wolfe Street. . . . With a good morning to Jane. In haste, Yours,
HARRY.

Rev. Henry Hopkins writes to me now, 36 years later, from his post, at the head of important religious operations in Kansas City:

No picture from any scene of my life is more vivid in my recollection than that of Jane, of beloved memory, as I saw her sometimes at Fairfax—her illuminated face with the wonderful eyes, and the wonderful smile, her fragile form wrapped in the ermine-lined cloak she used to wear. Do you remember the night when a sudden snow storm in the evening prevented my return to the city, and I slept on the floor in your office with your two ermine cloaks [they were rabbit, but never mind] for a covering—after the sentinel and I, making a chair of our hands, had carried you two through the deep snow to your house? And the afternoon, just before I left Alexandria for the field, when we three sat on the grassy slope south of the buildings, and you two gave me your blessing as I went to try the new scenes?

The further history of life at Fairfax, is beautifully given by your Aunt Jane in her pamphlet, printed for her own family, and called "Hospital Days." You have it. She remained in charge at this hospital till the close of the war.

Charley was in camp near enough to the hospital for us to get an occasional note on a mutilated scrap of paper, and to allow of mutual aid in emergencies, should they occur.

One morning in November, 1863, the poor boy hobbled into our office crippled, and suffering severely with inflammatory rheumatism. We tucked him up for the night by our bright fire, and next day I took him home to New York, where he was nursed by Mother back into what *he* considered good condition, and left for the field again, only half fit for it, as *we* knew.

That rheumatism has never left him.

Gentlemen's sons in those days left the soft beds and luxurious surroundings of their own homes, and went cheerfully out to lie down in mud puddles, to crawl at night under gun-carriages, or to spread their blankets under the sky in pouring rains, for such sleep as they could catch.

H. R. W. to Jane and G.

NEW YORK, DECEMBER 2, '63.

Dear Girls:

Charley's rheumatism is better and yesterday he walked without his cane. When he gets on the doe-skins (the triumphs of art that Mother is now at work upon) and his india-rubber knee-cap, I think he will be all right. At any rate, well or not, I suppose it is better for him to go to Washington, for he worries, now that the army is moving and he not with it, and his leave expired. . . . He is pounding away at a new camp-bed he is making. . . . I consider him a fit subject for the hospital, and to be doctored accordingly. . . . Our Church Sewing Society for the army had its first regular meeting yesterday. Abby is treasurer, and Mother, having been put into the president's chair, got out again, not liking the conspicuousness, and was immediately pounced upon for the purchasing committee.

E. W. H. writes:

Charley is doing up all his errands (very fatiguingly) and announces his intention of going back, leg or no leg. . . . We are waiting very anxiously now for every mail and the news from Grant and Burnside—and if Meade is also fighting, as last night's *Post* thinks, it would seem that the great crisis has really come.

I go to cut out army shirts.

There had been some heavy cavalry fighting along the Rappahannock about November 7th, and again on the 26th, and the rebels had been driven and 2,000 prisoners taken, but there was no following up of the victory. Charley, happily for us, was at home then and out of the horror of war; but at the front again, soon.

C. W. W. to J. S. W. at Fairfax hospital.

GENERAL MEADE'S CAMP,
NEAR BRANDY STA., DECEMBER 7TH, '63.

Dear Jane:

The train which left at 11 yesterday morning brought me through all right last night, by dark. A telegram from General Williams, sent to the conductor and meeting me on the train, said, in reply to one from me, that the ambulance would meet me at Brandy Station. The conductor had had some difficulty in finding me on the long train, but at the railroad bridge I heard "Woolsey" yelled at the door instead of "Rappahannock Station,"—which proved successful. I find that no movement of importance is on foot, and winter quarters somewhere (not here) confidently looked for this time. I hear a great deal said in justification of General Meade's retrograde movement. The War Department is entirely responsible for the failure of the last campaign,—having ordered it, but not allowing General Meade to attack in his own way. We might have had a great battle and carried the rebel position with very great loss, but nothing but the position would have been gained. The rebels behind their strong works could have been very little damaged and would have had only to fall back, if we had assaulted.

We are camped in the woods near John M. Botts' house, and are in this way shielded from the winds. There is no news.

Abby Gibbons with wounded soldiers at Fredericksburg, May 1864.
National Library of Medicine

CHAPTER THIRTEEN

God's Shadow Falls

B Y 1864, operations against Richmond having been practical fail-
ures, a general feeling of distrust as to the officers in command
prevailed, and the necessity for a reorganization was apparent. General
Grant's splendid victories at the West had given the death blow to the
rebellion along the Mississippi, and public opinion selected him for
supreme control of the National Army. He was called to that position,
and established his headquarters with the Army of the Potomac, in the
field, issuing his first General Order March 16, 1864.

Work for the soldiers was still going on all over the land, and in the
spring of this year all New York was given over, body and soul, to the
raising of money for the Sanitary Commission through a monster Fair.

Home letters sent to Jane and G. at the Fairfax Hospital were full
of it, and it helped as a distraction for thoughts which otherwise would
have been gloomy and anxious.

Mother to Jane and G.

8 BREVOORT PLACE, MARCH 9, 1864.

My dear Girls:

We are all sitting together at the round table, Abby looking over the old
letters from Point Lookout, and reading an incident occasionally aloud;
Carry composing an address on her Bloomingdale orphans for their May
anniversary. It is too amusing to have Caroline Murray and all those old
lady-managers deferring to our Carry on all subjects connected with the
asylum. . . . Mary is very much engaged in her arrangements for the floral
department at the Fair, and very much interested in it. All the ladies are
agog for novelties. They will be charmed with an occasional communication from the Hospital at Fairfax! We are to have a daily paper too, which

is to beat the "Drum Beat"—"The Fair Champion." Do send in poetry and prose and as many incidents as you can; get your doctor and the soldiers to send me an article for it, or letters for the Post Office. Send whatever you have to me, that I may have the pleasure of handing it to the committee on *literature!* Abby says, "Georgy, may I write out the German soldier boy's dream, or any other extract from your old letters that is not too stale?" I am sure you will say yes.

Abby is getting quite warmed up about the Fair; it is difficult not to feel so when everybody else is full of excitement about it. She is making a beautiful silk flag, a dozen or two of the new style of tidy-covers of muslin or embroidery edged with lace, beside lots of other little matters. Mary's idea of having garden hats of white straw, with broad ribbons, and their ends painted in flowers, is a pretty one, to be hung in her arbor of flowers. She is also painting a lot of little wooden articles. Every thing of hers is to be of the garden style. We find a use now for all our old flower baskets, rustic stands, etc., and a huge pile of them now stands ready to be carried to the flower department. My chair, the cover for which I was obliged to give up working, is under way, also three silk comfortables, all spandy new, none of your old gowns, lined with silk and beautifully quilted in scrolls and medallions by a Fishkill woman, and trimmed with ribbon quillings; also one dozen ladies' dressing-sacks of various styles; also, one India satin sofa cushion, one embroidered worsted do., four elegant toilette cushions, one doll's complete street dress, (even to an embroidered pocket-handkerchief), one doll's stuffed chair, and other articles "too tedious to mention," are all under way. I dare say we shall all do our full part, both in making and purchasing.

Mrs. Chauncey has already sold her baby house, Sarah Coit tells me, for five hundred dollars! Kate Hunt has received her Parisian purchases for the Fair, for which she expects to realize a very large amount; says she is furnishing things to the amount of a thousand dollars! Eliza is coming down to-morrow. . . .

H. R. W. to J. and G.

FISHKILL, SUNDAY.

My Dears:

We came up here last Thursday, and you may imagine it was somewhat of a relief to get Mother away from the everlasting Fair business that, for the last few weeks, has completely run her off her feet. . . .

New York is really in a disgusting state of fashionable excitement; nothing is talked of, or thought of, or dreamed of, but the big Metropolitan Fair! Mrs. Parker has her thousand dollar tea-sets to dispose of; Kate Hunt, her two hundred dollar curtains; Mrs. Schermerhorn, her elegant watches; and Mrs. Sombodyelse, the beautiful jewelry sent from Rome for the Sanitary Commission. . . .

Mary, and Edward Potter have been very busy with their floral department, and Mary has made some "sweet" things, one very pretty garden hat, a pure white straw with wide white ribbon streamers and a bunch of large pansies painted on the end of each, exquisitely painted, and to bring in thirty dollars or more. . . .

All the committees are at swords' points, of course; the Restaurant ladies wish flowers in their department, to which Mrs. George Betts, chairwoman of the Floral Committee, says "as sure as they do, I will have oysters on the shell in mine, and call them seaweeds." . . .

A. H. W. to Jane and G.

WEDNESDAY, MARCH 30TH.

I came from Fishkill yesterday afternoon with a trunk full of finished elegancies for the Fair.

They have put up a tremendous and expensive building in 17th Street, reaching from Broadway to Fourth Avenue, which we saw yesterday for the first time. It is a long barrack, with the end buildings one story higher, truss roof, huge oriel windows, and fine planed plank throughout. This is supplementary to the other structures on 14th Street. . . .

"Taps," Mary's army poem, is really coming to something. Robert sends word that he has an appointment this afternoon to go to see about the illustrations for it with Mr. Potter. If it isn't ready for the *first day* of the Fair, it will still be in time. A discharged one-armed soldier, James Nichols, 5th N.H., has offered himself very promptly, as salesman. . . .

E. W. H. to G. M. W.

FISHKILL, APRIL 26.

I am thankful the Fair is over, particularly on Mother's account, for she used herself up completely day by day, and would have given out entirely if it had lasted another week. Abby and Mary and in fact everyone who has had anything to do with it, is tired out, and there are still the auctions to arrange for and attend, and I have no doubt our whole family will help in them.

I wish we could have brought Mother again to the country, for it is delicious here and the spring is opening beautifully. Is there nothing you want in the way of wines end brandies, etc., in view of the coming campaign? There must be, and we wish to send it.

A. H. W. to Jane.

8 BREVOORT PLACE. SUNDAY.

We three girls had a glorious time on Thursday day afternoon, at a banquet given to William Wheeler's Battery. We came away enthusiastic in our admiration for him. Imagine this handsome, manly, gallant officer, loved by the men, cheered uproariously by them at intervals of five minutes all the afternoon, and *à propos* of nothing,—"Three cheers for Cap'n Will Wheeler." He is as free with them in the German language as in English. There was also a distribution of beautiful bouquets which the Wheelers had been busy tying up all the morning, 60 or 70—one for each man.

The Battery has re-enlisted for the war; their 30 days' furlough is up, and they go back to Tennessee.

Old Mr. Boorman, the Wheelers' uncle, made a speech *that* afternoon—feeble and pale and broken as he is. He told the men he "remembered the Captain as a baby, he remembered the Captain's *Mother* as a baby, and he remembered the Captain's *Grandmother* as the prettiest little girl they ever saw. She is not on earth now, I shall go to her soon, and—boys, if any of you ever desert that flag, I'll send Grandmother to haunt you all the days of your life!"

The Captain never came home. So many captains never came home. By August he had been killed, while his brother John, hungry and bare-foot, was a prisoner at Macon. Abby says, "how characteristic the history of these two young men is of the spirit of the times, and the conduct of the war."

At midnight, May 3d, '64, the Army of the Potomac crossed the Rapidan, and Grant's campaign against Richmond began. Charley as usual served as aide on the personal staff of the commanding General, through the frightful battles of the Wilderness Spottsylvania, Cold Harbor, and all that they involved. Fortunately, a few of his hurried notes to Mother, written on the field to quiet her fears, had been copied to send to friends, the originals (afterwards burned) being too valuable to risk in the mails. The first day's fight, of the twelve continuous ones in the Wilderness, was over, and at midnight, tired enough, no doubt, he writes:

C. W. W. to Mother.

FIVE MILES SOUTH OF GERMANNIA FORD,
MAY 5TH, 11.30 P. M., 1864.

Dear Mother:

To-day we have had probably the hardest fight of this campaign. The battle was principally fought after 4 P. M., (our troops attacking,) and raged until dark. Our losses have been great, for the fighting on both sides was desperate, but all goes well and Generals Grant and Meade are in good spirits and confident of completely finishing up the thing this time. The ground is the very worst kind for fighting, a perfect wilderness of dense forests and underbrush, where you would suppose it impossible for anything to get through. Hence there has been no opportunity for the use of artillery, the infantry has done it all. The cavalry also has been successful on the left flank, driving the enemy splendidly.

A despatch I took to General Meade from Sheridan about 4.30 this P. M. pleased him greatly, "The cavalry bricks are driving them; three cheers for the cavalry," he said. The lay of the land and the underbrush render it entirely unnecessary that the army headquarters A. D. C.'s should be up with the troops on the actual line of battle, and on this account scarcely any of us have been under fire. We communicate chiefly, you know, with the Corps headquarters, which are always in the rear. We have been going about all day, but shall have a good rest to-night, grateful to many a tired fellow. Of all the movements, of course, I can tell you nothing now. With Burnside and part of the Sixth Corps we shall have from 35,000 to 40,000 fresh troops to-morrow. Everything is working well, but

it is a matter of great regret to Meade's "company," his A. D. C.'s, that
we have seen, and can see, so little of the front. Carry's note reached me
this morning, when the musketry was very loud. Hooray for the American
Eagle! With much love to all.

Aff'ly, dear Mother,
C. W. W.

> FIVE MILES SOUTH OF THE FORD,
> FRIDAY, MAY 6, 1864, 5 A. M.

No mails go out, but I shall write each day. I wrote yesterday, but it
could not go. The infantry has begun again with light. Burnside will go in
to-day. We are sure of the best result with all these fresh men. Everything
is going well.

> MAY 7TH, 3 P. M.

This goes by a special messenger, and I cannot tell you more than that
everything is going well, and that I am all right. The enemy has fallen
back and the prospect is very cheering. The roads and thick underbrush
are such that the corps headquarters with which we aides communicate
must be farther to the rear from the line of battle than under ordinary circumstances, and on this account we can see but little of the fighting in the
front.

> MAY 7TH, SATURDAY, P. M.

All right along the lines, and with
Yours aff'ly.

> SPOTTSYLVANIA C. H., MAY 8TH, P. M.

The infantry fighting is over, for some time probably. We are apparently
pushing hard for Richmond, and all goes well. Don't have any fears for
my safety, for I have not yet been to the extreme front. No Headquarters'
aides are sent, and no mishaps as yet. This goes via train of wounded to
Fredericksburg.

Aff'ly,   C. W. W.

A. H. W. to Rev. Dr. Prentiss.

8 BREVOORT PLACE, THURSDAY, MAY 12.

My dear Mr. Prentiss:

The mail that has come through from the army has brought us, just now, a note from Charley, dated Tuesday, 10th, written, of course, before that horrible conflict began again Tuesday evening. How thankful we are—to hear so promptly—when so many are in suspense or grief. Here it is:

NEAR SPOTTSYLVANIA C. H. MAY 10TH.

To-day for the first time we are going to send a mail through if possible, via Fredericksburg. You have no doubt received some, if not all, the notes I have sent you, and the papers have given you an account of our successful advance. It is by no means probable that we could have got to Richmond without hard fighting. This we have had, but we have beaten the enemy back in each instance, and his army is very much cut up. Our own is rested and in good spirits and admirably disposed. There is no enemy on our right, and the cavalry are probably doing great damage to their railroad communication. The rebel cavalry have been plucky, but have invariably been driven with loss. You may expect to hear of the destruction of the rebel army very soon. Our scouts do good service and information has come in from the rebs which is very cheering. The weather has been delightful, except at times too hot for the infantry. With love to all,
C. W. W.

Another note says—on Monday:

Our losses have been large, in all the battles, but not extraordinarily so. The fighting has usually been only part of a day, and still through the thickest underbrush. We lose a great deal in General Sedgwick's death, but Wright is an able soldier.

C. W. W. (Copy.)

IN FRONT OF SPOTTSYLVANIA.
WEDNESDAY, MAY 11TH.

Dear Mother:

I have written you up to yesterday A. M. Last night at 5 there was to have been a general attack along our lines, but the report came in that the enemy was massing on our right and trying to turn it, and the attack was suspended. A sharp fight however took place before dark, when Upton distinguished himself, taking 1,200 prisoners and driving the enemy from a breastwork five feet high. There is now better opportunity for the use of our artillery and the batteries were firing sharply up to dark. As we cannot see the enemy's line, all this counts for but little, and is successful only as *demonstration*.

Burnside was engaged yesterday, during the day, but we could not hear his musketry—his guns we heard distinctly toward dark, coming from the enemy's rear, almost, Burnside having got well round on their right flank. General Meade, I think, does not consider it at all probable that the rebels would try to turn our right. To me, it seems the absurdest thing possible. The enemy to do it must withdraw troops from his right or centre, weakening his line too much, when ours is so long and so strong on our left.

Yesterday P. M. I took to General Meade the rumor that we had possession of Petersburgh, &c., &c. This was at once published to the troops, but cheering was strictly prohibited, as this would discover to the enemy our position. Since yesterday A. M., our right and left have advanced.

Our headquarters' staff are all right. General Grant camps near us and is on the field with us. He says very little and smokes a great deal.

Everything is quiet this (Wednesday) morning, except the skirmishers, and it is rumored that the enemy is falling back. All is going well.

Don't say "why don't they push into Richmond."

Wait and see!

I do not think I have said anything contraband.

Very aff'ly yours,

C. W. WOOLSEY.

Mother to J. and G. at Fairfax

NEW YORK, THURSDAY, MAY 12TH.

What awful carnage is going on from day to day, and what an immense amount of suffering, in the heaps of wretched wounded men. I am glad so many of our surgeons have gone on, but what are a dozen of them among thousands of sufferers? I do not believe they have anything like half enough for the demand. I wish *I* were a man! I would be there to do my little all, and I think I could beat some of those old fogies in dressing wounds, if not in sawing off limbs! Dr. Buck went on Monday to Fredericksburg [which on May 9th part of our army under Burnside occupied as an hospital].

We have more pencil notes from Charley—up to Tuesday 10th; after this the great battles of that day came off. All was well up to that time. I enclose copies of his notes. What terrific fighting there has been! and oh! the dead, the dead, the maimed, and worse than dead! and the desolate homes throughout the land. Peace and freedom dearly bought—if indeed we get them in the end,—which is not yet. . . . Mary is making her arrangements for the country, and a little previous visit to Eliza for a few days; was to have gone to-day to Fishkill, but one of her headaches has put a stop to it. She came over yesterday and drove us to the park.

It is perfectly beautiful there, and so filled with gay vehicles of every description, and happy faces, you would not dream of war and bloodshed in the land. So goes the world, and we a part of it. A telegram from Charley just arrived dated 8th—older than his notes; could not be sent I suppose. We are very fortunate in hearing from him so often in such a state of things; he is very attentive about writing to us under all circumstances. . . . The big box stands ready for your duds; if there is anything else you need, say so *at once*. "or forever after," etc., etc.

C. W. W. to Mother (Copy).

HEADQUARTERS, A. P.
FRIDAY, MAY 13, '64.

Dear Mother:

The enemy has been badly whipped and has fallen back again. We still have communication with Washington through Fredericksburg, but this is not intended to be our base, we only make a convenience of it for the wounded and for some supplies. Hancock and Wright and Burnside report the enemy as having withdrawn, maintaining though, a thin line in front of Burnside. Hancock's attack was by far the most brilliant thing so far, in this campaign. We have certainly 35 guns and a great many prisoners.

General Ned Johnson [The rebel general, taken prisoner with his entire force by bayonet charge under Hancock, in the fog, May 12.] was at our camp all this morning. It was he who nearly turned our right at Germania Ford.

General Stuart [Johnson's associate] refused to shake hands with General Hancock and was made to walk to the rear with his men.

We shall probably be cut off from any communication with Washington in a day or two, but I will scratch a few lines whenever I can.

It was an understood thing with the Sanitary Commission and myself (G.) that I was to be called on at any time for hospital service at the front; and immediately after these late battles (May 12th) the summons came—a courier arriving at the Fairfax Seminary Hospital to summon me. I left at once via boat down the Potomac for Fredericksburg.

A. H. W. to H. Gilman.

NEW YORK, MAY 16.

Mrs. Gibbons called here Saturday afternoon to let us know that she was going to the front. But we couldn't tell what to send by her to Georgy, and the trunk with G.'s boots, gloves and thin clothing had already started by express. Mother gave Mrs. G. some money to do army shopping with on her way up town—some *good tea* for G. and herself for one thing—and then we collected a quantity of old linen, towels, mosquito-bar, etc., whatever we had in the house, and took them up to Mrs. Gibbons.

Some of us went to General Rice's funeral at Dr. Adams' church yesterday afternoon. Mr. Prentiss was to assist Dr. Adams. The church was jammed to suffocation.

General Rice was a very devout as well as a gallant man. Just as the army marched, he had written to Dr. A. and enclosed him a manuscript tract of his, a little story of his own soldiers—the "Dying Sergeant," which will be published by the Tract Society.

The General's aide—Lieutenant Bush, a young fellow of 17—brought the body on, packed in ice, for he said they found many Virginia mansions with *ice-houses* well stocked, near the field, and everything was seized of course for the hospitals. There was an abundance of it. Dr. Adams asked Lieutenant B. how they all felt—in the fight. "Feel," he said, "why we are *worn out,* we couldn't feel—we couldn't eat—we did what we were told to do, mechanically."

A. H. W. to H. G.

We all had a very solemn week, last week; people felt that it was no time for shouting or flag waving, it was all too tremendous, too serious for that. They count up now our loss and our advance more than a thousand men to every mile probably, and feel that it is going to cost us very dear yet to conquer Lee or reach Richmond. Our personal anxieties were soon relieved by daily letters, or rather pencilled scraps, from Charley, which were always confident and hopeful about our movements, reflecting the tone of Army Headquarters. . . .

Charley, in his last note, says that Fredericksburg is not their real base—was only used as convenient for shipping the wounded, and that they will soon cut loose again from communication with Washington. Where they are going to swing to we do not know. . . .

You will have seen from the *Times* or *Tribune* that Georgy is at Belle Plain. She went off very suddenly last Thursday, through the "open door," she always sees,—the Sanitary Commission sending a courier out to the Hospital for her; and to-day we had a letter from her. On board the boat going down was "C. A. P.," Mr. Page, the *Tribune* reporter, a gentlemanly nice young fellow, the one who told the pretty little story of the wounded boy crawling about on the battlefield with his hands full of violets. So Georgy made friends with him, sent a note to Charley by him, and got him to promise he would sometimes say in his letters to the *Tribune* that the staff were all well.

He grants her request this morning, or some letter-writer does, by a publicity which neither she nor Charley will relish. . . .

Mother is well and weak by turns. She drives about the house faster than ever, to forget thought now. . . .

Mrs. Gibbons and Sally have gone from here, and Georgy will be with them when they reach Belle Plain; also with Mrs. John Barlow, who is active and first-rate, I believe. Her husband, General B., was carried about all summer at Brattleboro on a stretcher, after Gettysburg, but is now in the thick of the fight again. . . .

G. M. W. to J. S. W.

BELLE PLAIN ON THE POTOMAC, MAY 13, '64.

Dear Jane:

On the Sanitary Commission boat, pulling up to the shore the Government flat-boat of horses and cavalry recruits. There are no docks and the supplies are landed by pontoons—a constant stream of contrabands passing with bags of grain and barrels of pork on their shoulders. Drs. Agnew and Douglas and Cuyler are here. We have a feeding station on shore, and another two miles away, where ambulance-trains halt sometimes for hours. The mud is frightful and the rain coming on. We are to take the returning ambulance-train for Fredericksburg.

Just as I finished, the train of ambulances arrived *from* Fredericksburg. Nothing I have ever seen equals the condition of these men they have been two or three days in the train and no food. We have been at work with them from morning till night without ceasing, filling one boat, feeding the men, filling another and feeding them. There's no sort of use in trying to tell you the story. I can scarcely bear to think of it.

All the "Invalid Corps" from our Hospital, who marched off that day, are down here guarding prisoners, Generals Stuart and Bradley Johnson among them. The wounded arrive in ambulances, one train a day, but the trains are miles long, plunged in quagmires, jolted over corduroys, without food, fainting, filthy, frightfully wounded; arms gone to the shoulder, horrible wounds in face and head.

I would rather a thousand times have a friend killed on the field than suffer in this way; it is worse than White House, Harrison's, or Gettysburg. We found thirty-five dead in the ambulances yesterday, and five more died on the stretchers while being put on the boat. Mules, stretchers, army-wagons, prisoners, dead men and officials all tumbled and jumbled on the wretched dock, which falls in every little while and keeps the ambulances waiting for hours. We fed all the five boats that got off yesterday. There is no *Government* provision for this beyond bread: no coffee, soup, cups, pails or vessels of any kind for holding food. The men eat as if they were starving. We are ordered to Fredericksburg, where there is more misery than here. . . .

Mr. Andrew Cheesbro, of the Canandaigua "delegation," who was with Mother and G. at Gettysburg, and was now again at Belle Plain, working hard, writes:

WASHINGTON, MAY 20, 1864.

Dear Miss Woolsey:

Thinking you may have received my spasm of a note, written in a moment of desperation and an exaggerated condition of mules, mule drivers, nigs and other animals on that horrid pier on the Potomac—it should be spelt with a b—and that you may have answered the same, I take the liberty of saying that I am in Washington and not there, thank God! I didn't leave until the last minute (who ever did?), but I grew seasick and land sick till I would have thanked and absolved any rebel who would have shot me. Then I came away. The ladies didn't come. . . .

After you were gone on to Fredericksburg, imagination suggested that a face lying far off in the crowd was "Charley's;" I hurried to him through mule heels and the "innumerable caravan," but found, when I reached the utmost stretcher, the resemblance was gone—though the Captain's name *did* begin with a W. I treated him to punch for the suggestion

I hope that in no wounded man you will find a nearer resemblance than I did. I hear of you as cooking in the rear of some hospital. Let me serve you, if I can . . .

There's no news here. General Wadsworth's body went off yesterday A. M., under General Auger's escort to the cars, and five Congressmen to New York with it. . . .

Mr. Cheesbro's letter directed to Fredericksburg, was long in coming, but finally got round to G., endorsed in pencil in Charley's handwriting from the field: "Sent to the front by mistake, unless, indeed, Miss Woolsey has established a feeding station at Bowling Green, Virginia."

G. M. W. to Mother.

FREDERICKSBURG, SUNDAY, MAY 15.

Dear Mother:

Charley all safe by to-day's report as enclosed. Mrs. Barlow and I at Fredericksburg—town full of badly wounded, Commission feeding *all the houses*, for men are put in anywhere, the regular hospitals being full, and hundreds of poor fellows report to any one, or no one, as the case may be. The stores on both sides of the streets are full—filthy shops, old shoe stores, old blacksmiths' rooms, men lying on the floor without even straw under them, and with their heads on old bits of cast iron. I saw a boy sound asleep on a pile of old iron last night, as we made the rounds late after arriving. This A. M. we started a diet-kitchen, and have fed several hundred in the little rooms and houses about here. The Commission has a large corps of volunteer nurses, men, who go right in and work under the surgeons, and get all the supplies they want from the Commission. Lenox is here; I saw him in the street while we were at the purveyors this morning, wriggling a great camp stove out of the depot. You will have more good news before this reaches you, of our successes. The wounded men are as happy as possible over it, *some* of them. The road from Belle Plain over here is more abominable than anything you can imagine; corduroy, and filled with holes and bogs, and the wounded are sent in army wagons over them. We have our hands full here, and I am glad I came. The hospitals are delighted to have ladies come right in and feed the sick; we can go in any where. From the extreme difficulty in getting supplies, there has been very little food in town. To-day ten great wagons full of stores came for the Sanitary Commission, and really I don't know what the sick would do but for this society. Their nurses and supplies are every where. Ammunition was needed for the army two days ago, and was of course sent before all other things, which stopped all other transportation. I have sent a note to Charley to-night by the *Tribune* reporter, who comes and goes and brings us all the news. Good night.

G. to Mother.

FREDERICKSBURG, MONDAY, 16TH.

Dear Mother:

Charley's note was brought to me to-day by Charley Coit. How good it is to get a line the same day on which it is written! Mr. Clark and all the gentlemen were interested in reading it. I have almost daily communication with Charley, and have sent a note and two messages to-day.

Just as I was going to write, a message came from one of the hospitals to say that my little boy on the floor in the corner wanted me. Such a dear handsome young fellow—*going,* like all the rest. "Where is my lady?" he demanded, "Will she come soon?" And when I got to him he took hold of my hand tight, saying, "Is this my lady—that's all right then." No straw yet to put the men on. The transportation is dreadful; all the ammunition, food, and forage for the army, and all the food, clothing and medicines depending upon a line of army-wagons, over a frightful road, after reaching a distant and most inconvenient point on the Potomac. There has been no bread or hard-tack even, for twelve hours in town. We have beef only, and make soup all day long, and farina gruel. The supplies are *expected* to-night; also Sanitary Commission wagons, but none have come, and it is now II, and we shall have to turn our wits inside out for breakfast. Some hospitals have been provident and have drawn for several days in advance. I think, now that I *do* think of it, that some one said they saw hard-tack going up to the Sixth Corps hospital this evening, so that it may be here in time for to-morrow. The frightful wounds of these men need everything; everything is provided, and nothing, comparatively, *can be got here.* The Sanitary Commission have fifteen wagons going and coming daily, but that is a drop. The Post Quartermaster told me to-day that the supplies had been delayed by the absolute necessity for sending army stores to the front, and if the enemy could only succeed in cutting our wretched line, we should be lost, from starvation. I must go to bed. Please send this note to Jane, I shan't have time, perhaps, to write to-morrow to her. One from her just now, for which thanks. We are required to show reason for being here, or go to the guard house. I have a pass from the Surgeon-General as "volunteer nurse."

Lenox over at tent to-day; he has a Baptist Church for hospital, and the baptistry in the floor of the pulpit gives him a constant supply of fresh water.

Two stained and worn little leaves from Charley's war note-book give the following:

HEADQUARTERS ARMY OF THE POTOMAC, NEAR BOWLING GREEN, VA.
MAY 19, '64.

At 2.05 took dispatch to Tyler to attack enemy if advancing as reported on our left.

Hancock to move his command at 2 A. M. tomorrow to Bowling

Green.—About 5.30 P. M. enemy came round on our right, attacking Tyler with intent to capture our trains. I was sent to put Tyler's whole division in line of battle under fire. We drove them back, capturing 250."

[Charley adds: We used to say that the left boot heels of the whole army were worn down, there was such constant moving by "the left flank," fighting by day, marching past Richmond "by the left flank" at night.]

G.'s pencil notes from Fredericksburg were scratched off when a spare moment came, which was but seldom, and show by their disconnected sentences that they were written under great pressure.

G. M. W. to J. S. W.

FREDERICKSBURG, MAY 19.

All right. Hard work, dirt and death everywhere. Mrs. Gibbons arrived last night and she and her daughter are assigned to a fearful place and are working hard.

Men are brought in and stowed away in filthy places called distributing stations. I have good men as assistants, and can have more. We go about and feed them; I have a room of special cases, besides the station; three of these died last night. They had been several days on the field after being shot, in and out of the rebels' hands, taken and retaken. The townspeople refuse to sell or give, and we steal everything we can lay our hands on, for the patients; more straw-stealing, plank-stealing, corn-shuck-stealing; more grateful, suffering, patient men.

MAY 22.

No confusion was ever greater. Tent hospitals have been put up, and the surgeons ordered *not to fill them.* Orders came from Washington that the railroad should be repaired, then orders came withdrawing the guard from the road. Medical officers refuse to send wounded over an unguarded road. Telegram from Washington that wounded should go by boat. Telegram back that wounded were already over the pontoons, ready to go by rail if *protected.* Telegram again that they should go by boat. Trains came back to boat, river falling. One boat got painfully off; second boat off; ambulance trains at many hospital doors; got on train and fed some poor fellows with egg nogg; moved on with the slow moving procession; at every moment a jolt and a "God have mercy on me," through the darkness over the pontoons to the *railroad,* again! I cooked and served to-day 926 rations of farina, tea, coffee, and good rich soup, chicken, turkey, and beef, out of those blessed cans.

The government rations are drawn *this* way: The contract surgeon in charge of a little shop or room full of wounded, reports to the surgeon in charge of a *group* of such; this officer reports to the surgeon of division, the surgeon of division to the corps surgeon; the corps surgeon draws on the commissary for the number of rations he needs for the day. It has often been 10 o'clock at night before dinner was ready.

You may easily see how important the *irregular* supplies of the Sanitary Commission and other organizations have been.

We are lodged with a fine old lady, mild and good, in a garden full of roses. We board ourselves. We have crackers, sometimes soft bread, sometimes beef. Last night we had a slice of ham all round. The town will be deserted in a few days. We are sweeping and cleaning Mrs. ——'s rooms to leave the old lady as well off as we can, for all her slaves have packed their feather-beds and frying-pans, and declare they will go with us.

One bright spot there was in the midst of all this horror.

G. to Mother.

FREDERICKSBURG.

Augur's reinforcements have passed through; as the troops went forward they were all met by the ambulances from the front full of wounded men, who thrust out their poor hands and waved, and weakly cheered them.

Mrs.——'s house has a large old-time garden full of roses; indeed, the whole town is brimming with early flowers. We begged and received permission to take all we could gather, and filled the baskets and trays and skirts of our gowns with snowballs, lemon-blossoms, and roses, yellow, white and red. The 8th New York Heavy Artillery was in the advancing column. In the headstall of Colonel Porter's horse I fastened a knot of roses, and tossed roses and snowballs over the men. They were delighted "In *Fredericksburg!*" they said; "O! give me one," "Pray give me one," "I will carry it into the fight for you," and another cheerily, "and I will bring it back again."

Three days afterwards the ambulances came, and in them came some of the same men, shattered, dying, and dead. We went out, but this time it was with pails of soup and milk punch; one and another recognized us—all were cheery enough. "A different coming back, ma'am," "no roses to-day"; and one said, pointing over his shoulder, "The Lieutenant is there on the stretcher, and he's brought the flowers back, as he promised." I went to his side, hoping to help a wounded man. The Lieutenant lay dead, with a bunch of roses in the breast of his coat.

Our friend and fellow-worker at Beverly Hospital later, Miss Sever, sent me, a year after, this little allusion to Fredericksburg:

"Levi Thaxter (Celia Thaxter's husband) sat with me a long while the other day, and we talked of you, dear Miss Georgy. He says the most beautiful moment he has ever seen in life was at Fredericksburg, last summer, when you were giving roses to the regiment who were marching to almost certain death, and a soldier stepped from the ranks and seized your hands."

C. C. W. to G. M. W.

NEW YORK, MONDAY.

Dear G.:

If you were not frightened away by the teamsters' reports on Friday, I suppose you are still pursuing your "labors of love" in Fredericksburg. Your old tow-headed friend of the Peninsula is a co-worker; perhaps not equally efficient with yourself, but willing to be obnoxious in any way. . . .

Door-bell—Miss E. M. wants to know if I wrote those everlasting *Three Weeks at Gettysburg*. Having read them, she cannot stay at home, and would like a little information as to what was needed for a nurse. We have just finished breakfast, and she is the second anxious inquirer this morning. We think of opening a branch office of information and drawing a salary from the Sanitary Commission. This elderly spinster wants to know if she can have a bath daily, and if her night's rest will be interrupted, as her health depends upon those two things. I haven't heard of any bath-tubs, and I believe day and night are all one in Fredericksburg. What it is to be the sister of an authoress! especially one who "has a brother on General Williams' staff!" I wish we could send both of you something to eat and to wear. . . .

Yesterday (Sunday) we got into our new chapel for the first time—a long, narrow room, lighted from one end, aired in the same way.

Mr. Prentiss could scarcely conceal his delight at being there, and tried to convince us all that it was "built by God, stone on stone," though we saw evident signs of James Renwick, and thought the ventilation was not altogether providential.

Later, A. H. W. writes:

Miss P. has called to get Mother to go on a Literature Committee and collect matter for a book she wants to publish—advertising first the names and residences of the committee, and appealing to mothers and families to forward the dying speeches, messages, battlefield-incidents, etc., of their sons and brothers! Mother sent her down word that she had a son in the army herself, and that all such matters as "dying words" were too sacred for intrusion. She declined going upon any committee, or appealing to any mother for such a purpose. Whereupon Miss P. said she would scratch out those words and modify her purpose, which didn't modify Mother, however.

Now that we are receivers for the North Carolina refugees, every time the door-bell rings Carry says, "Cooking stoves!" or Hatty cries "Bed-ticks!" but nothing has come, except five dollars through the city post from some gentleman signing himself "Pity." . . .

Mother to Mary and Eliza.

BEFORE "TAPS,"
MONDAY P. M., MAY 23D.

I have made several attempts to write a line to you to-day, my dear girls, for I hope Mary is still at Fishkill, but this has been a day of unusual inter-ruptions, and I have now only a few minutes and half a sheet, but shall make the most of it. . . .

Home is our best place, "until these calamities be overpass," which are now keeping us in a state of anxiety and uncertainty as to what is best for us to do.

We have thought perhaps G. may like to run on for a little rest and refreshment after Fredericksburg. I wish it may be so that she and Jane will both come. I send you their letters received to-day. Jane writes "chirkly," and seems to require no sympathy or aid; in fact, she scorns them both. Amongst a host of others, Lizzie Thompson called to-day. Her husband is at Dalton as Christian Commission delegate, aiding the poor men there in every way; was in the front of the battle there and saw the whole thing; is very busy and deeply interested in his work. His letters are charming. Mrs. McKeever was here too, and asked for you all; asked me to "let her know some day when I go to see Mary, that she might join me."

We think of adding "Army Gen'l Directory" to our door-plate, so many people of all sorts come to us for information, and for aid in various enterprises. . . .

From C. W. W. at the Front.

MAY 24TH, 1864, 7 A. M.

Dear Mother:

All day yesterday we were marching South by many roads, to the North Anna; and towards night Warren, who had reached an excellent position, was attacked by the enemy, and for an hour before dark and half an hour after, there was a heavy artillery fire and some musketry, which resulted in his favor. It was a fair stand-up fight, neither side having any other defence than the lay of the land. Wright was in Warren's rear, on the same roads, and is up this A. M., and Hancock farther to the south and left. Burnside is on the right in her rear of marching column. The Ninth Corps marches badly and there has been difficulty about their trains each day. Headquarters saw nothing of the fight yesterday, but we are to go nearer the front to-day. We are over the North Anna, and shall probably come up with the enemy in force to-day or to-morrow. The fight yesterday was by advanced guards of either army—the enemy hoping to find us in column, before line of battle could be formed. We are more than half way to Richmond—last night camping just half way—30 miles, at the house of a proud old F. F. V., whose sheep and chickens, I regret to say, were paid for.

We have heard from Sheridan to-day: the staff officer who came through brought word that he was 35 miles from here, and he will join us to-night or to-morrow. His command is all right except for fatigue and hunger, and he will return from his raid in better condition than ever before after so long a march. The North Anna divides our army, but it is an easy stream to cross, and the rest of the troops can easily be thrown over, if that is the intention.

The wounded from Warren's fight last night will be sent to Port Royal, I suppose.

Getting Sheridan back will be a great gain to us; two days' rest and recuperation will fit them for duty and they will be invaluable on our flanks. They can easily avoid the rebel infantry,—the confederate cavalry, the prisoners ace knowledge, "is about gone up."

12 MAY.

We have our Headquarters in a roadside church, Mt. Carmel Church, and General Grant is in a pew near me, whittling and talking to General Meade. We are making up a mail! and I am just in from Burnside in time to put my letter in.

The weather is very pleasant and the country beautiful, so different from our winter camps.

I have found the negroes very friendly and useful as guides. Their masters and missuses have, as a general thing, "done gone clar out."
Aff'ly, C. W. W.

A. H. W. to E.

THURSDAY, MAY 26TH.

Dear Eliza:

It is raining so hard that there is little chance of sending to the Post Office, and you will lose the pleasure of getting Charley's letter, in *two days,* from beyond the North Anna. You see it was written at noon on Tuesday, and we had it at 8 this Thursday morning. Carry and Hatty came home late last night from Newark, N. J. A young officer was in the Fourth Avenue car with them who said that he was "just up from the Army of the Potomac by way of Port Royal. Grant was swinging round onto the Peninsula, and White House was again to be the base!"

We have nothing more from Georgy at Fredericksburg. Dr. Buck has got home; said he couldn't stand the work any longer, he *had* to come away. He was here night before last—it was he who brought G's letter that was left at our door. When he left Fredericksburg things were more comfortable; straw was beginning to arrive, or hay. He left from 7,000 to 8,000 wounded there, so I don't believe the *Times* despatch, that "all the wounded had been removed to Washington." If they have been, the Medical Department has murdered a good many in doing it.

By May the 28th, Charley found himself on the old ground again. Gaines Mill, where Joe was wounded two years before, was close by, and each army occupied the position its opponent held during the fight of those seven days in 1862;—Lee's men taking their turn in the Chickahominy Swamps now.

Mother to G.

MONDAY EVENING.

My dear Georgy:

You don't know how we grab at your letters and how eagerly we read them; nor do you know how much I long to be down *there* with you. I would give anything to start off to-morrow morning, and take the "new Tent Hospital Kitchen!" or even an "umbler" station. What scenes you are surrounded with, and what an experience you are having! . . . It is a great pleasure and comfort to me to have you and Charley so near as to keep up almost daily communication. Yours of day before yesterday! enclosing his little note of same date, reached us this afternoon—only think how quickly they came. I am glad, too, good old Dr. Buck has been with you; it seems to bring you nearer home. Oh! Georgy, what heart-sickening sufferings our men are subjected too. . . . It is, I suppose, miserable management somewhere.

It was a great day for the Church of the Covenant—the day we assembled in our new room. . . . Mr. Prentiss seemed inspired, and good old Dr. Skinner looked as if he could scarcely refrain from an outburst of applause while Mr. Prentiss was preaching. . . . When you all come home we will have our nice seats there all ready for you. Oh, the happy day when we shall *all* as a family assemble there together once more! . . .

Impress it upon Charley not to expose himself *unnecessarily* to the enemy. Of course he must do as he is ordered, but I know he is anxious to be in the very front. I wonder if he realizes what it would be to be maimed for life with the loss of a leg or an arm, perhaps both! I do not think young men think soberly enough about it. Surely, Charley has seen suffering that might put him on his guard. I tremble for him, and a dread comes over me when I take up a newspaper. We are all well, and shall not go out of town till the army is at rest. A loving kiss to you, my dear child. Take care of yourself for the sake of your loving

MOTHER.

Mother's longing for our meeting as a family once more, was never satisfied. Our dear, beautiful Mary died, May the 31st, in her Astoria home. Rose Terry, who had been with her there a year before, wrote: "I used to sit and look at your sister like a person in a dream. I did not think any mortal woman could be so exquisite, so like a *flower* with a soul in it. She was not less human, but more spiritual, than any other mortal I ever saw; and now she is immortal."

These are, we think, the last verses Mary wrote, "Taps,"—the army bugle-call to sleep, to put out the light. "The notes rising and falling, say as plainly as music can say anything:

"Put it out; put it out; put it out!"

"It is a clear, golden call, almost a human voice, falling softer and slower to the end, and, when well played, lingering a little at the last, like some one very cautiously hushing a baby to sleep":—

"TAPS."

Put it out! Put it out! Put it out!
The clear notes rising, climb
A ladder of sweet sound,
And from each golden round
The ascending angels, nearing heaven, do chime,
"God's watch begins, put your dim lanterns out!"

Put out each earthly light;
It is God's shadow falls

Along the darkening walls,
Closing us round, when men say "it is night,"
He draws so near it shuts the daylight out.

Put it out! Put it out! Put it out!
Forbear each scheme of ill;
Good angels walk the ward,
And heaven is all abroad
When twilight falls, and earth lies hushed and still;
Room for the angels! Put the dark deeds out.

Put out all thoughts of care:
Rest gently, aching head;
He stands beside the bed
Who brings in peace and healing, unaware
And sends soft-footed sleep to shut pain out.

Put it out! Put it out! Put it out!
Put out—quite out—the light.
Hark! as the notes grow faint,
Was that a new-voiced saint
Who climbed with them, and scaled the starry height?
Has from among us any soul gone out?

God's love falls as a screen.
Where lights burn dim and pale
No flickering flame shall fail,
For with His hand held steadfastly between,
No wind can blow to put these life-lamps out.

Through earth's long night He waits,
Till, to the soul's glad eyes
Filled with divine surprise,
Heaven opens wide her golden morning gates:
Then, day being come, He breathes the candle out.

We had hurried home, too late, from hospital work. Jane went back to her duties at Fairfax. Two of us were not needed there longer, and I (G.) felt that I had wounded in our own home to care for, a while. Charley was still at the front.

C. W. W. to E. J. W.

HEADQUARTERS A. OF P.
JULY 13TH, 1864.

This is but a line to acknowledge the receipt of the package and to say how much I should like to take a breath of Lenox air with you. Things don't look to me over-promising just *now*, but I shall not give way to any feeling of discouragement.

I wish I could be at home for a while with Mother, but this is impossible.

Always aff'ly yours.

Georgeanna Woolsey's commission as nurse at the Beverly, N. J. Hospital, signed by Dorothea Dix, Superintendent of Army Nurses.
National Library of Medicine

CHAPTER FOURTEEN

How Can We Go Home?

THE EFFORT to out-flank Lee and push on to Richmond by the old line was unsuccessful. Great battles with enormous losses had occurred—though, as Grant reported to the Secretary of War, with general results "in our favor"; adding, "I propose to fight it out on this line if it takes all summer." There was no retreating under Grant, but a concerted plan to close in on the enemy, which included a settling down before Petersburg, on the line of railroad by which the rebels received their principal supplies.

Here occurred the explosion of the mine and its utter failure through the blunder of some commanding officer, to which Charley's letter, copied and sent to a friend abroad, refers. Grant had established his headquarters at City Point on the James.

C. W. W. to Mother.

HEADQUARTERS ARMY OF THE POTOMAC.

July 27, 1864.

The movement of troops yesterday, which we have tried to keep very quiet, is part of a programme which, if successfully carried out, will change the look of things in our front. A very important move is to be made to-morrow. I try, on principle, to expect success, but the chances for it to-morrow seem small to me. Complete defeat is, I think, impossible, for no matter how severely we may be repulsed in the offensive, our line of *defence* is a very strong one. I shall feel more at liberty to write to-morrow.

JULY 31ST.

Got back to camp at 2 P. M. yesterday, but went off to sleep after much hard riding. We had been expecting the explosion of Burnside's mine for

361

weeks, and though *I* have not felt at liberty to speak of it, I dare say it has been kept so little secret, that you, and no doubt the enemy, have been expecting it too. Here, scarcely any one expected complete success, and it had been so delayed from day to day that we expected a counter-mine to blow *us* up. The movement of Foster and Hancock to the north of the James was a successful diversion. The secret service proved that the enemy detached large bodies of troops and maintained but a thin line in our front.

But for the invariable delay of the 9th Corps we might have had Petersburg at noon yesterday. The 18th Corps held the trenches on the right of our line and had orders to form, with the 9th, the assaulting column. The 5th Corps, holding our left, had orders to reduce its front line to a minimum and mass in the rear of its trenches to follow up the 9th. The cavalry had orders to demonstrate on the extreme left and threaten from the south. The mine was to explode at 3.30 A. M., when our artillery on either flank of the crater was to open, leaving the space of the breach through which the assaulting column was to pass. The mine did not explode until 4.45, but even then the attack would have succeeded if the troops had been promptly advanced. An hour passed, and no advance. Daylight came, the enemy recovered from their scare and concentrated what troops they had at the breach, and got an enfilading fire on our column as it was forming, a thing which couldn't have happened in the dark. The column was heavily shelled and somewhat broken, and the men were advanced down the covered way, artificial approach, two abreast (instead of regimental front, as might have been in the dark), and over the open. The wounded began to come back, blocking the way and halting the column. Our men were hit before they got out of the approach. Finally the column advanced to the crater, with its tail end still in the narrow approach, found that the enemy had had time to make the best dispositions, and received a tremendous fire, front and both flanks, lost very heavily, and were withdrawn.

Many lay the blame on a regiment of negroes that broke. This may be part cause of the failure, but I will not make them responsible for it because they are "niggers," as do many of the officers here. I think, if the assault had been made immediately after the explosion, that any troops, even the greenest and blackest, would have gone through. The Brigade that led our column was chosen by lot. It fell upon Bartlett, but he has a wooden leg, and they drew again. It fell upon a brigade of dismounted cavalry, some artillery-men, and a mixed-up lot not fit to lead a forlorn hope.

When it was found they wouldn't and couldn't advance, General Grant, who, with General Meade, was at Burnside's headquarters (General B. being at the front), said: "Well, we've made the attempt and it has failed; that's the amount of it. The troops had better be withdrawn." General Burnside's failure and a more personal matter will, I am afraid, bring him to grief. I am sorry. I'm afraid he'll go under. It is but a hundred yards between the lines, *called* fifty,—and the wounded are lying in the sun. The rebels have refused General Meade's flag of truce; why on earth I see no reason. We took one gun and left three in the ruins. The mines are occupied by the rebel sharpshooters, who fire incessantly at us over the wounded on the field. We shall have a quiet spell I suppose before trying again. It was a golden chance and a disgraceful failure.

AUGUST 2ND.

The failure of the assault has given us a bluish tinge here. General Grant and General Meade are a good deal cut up by it. Our loss is heavy. I went with the flag of truce *yesterday*. At the point of the explosion the rebels and our officers and men mingled freely. The rebels and the nationals, in their shirtsleeves, are not to be told apart, for very many of the rebels had on United States regulation blue trousers. The hot sun had done dreadful work. Nine-tenths of the men I saw were negroes. They had apparently been killed in running to the rear, but beyond the crater they (the blacks) had held their ground well, some of them to the last. The officers and men were friendly with us. To-day there is a court holding in our mess-tent. Burnside's telegraph men are accused of intercepting messages between Generals Meade and Grant. Their defence is that they did it under General B.'s orders. All this will "lead to complications." The explosion, I fear, has made a wider breach than the one in the enemy's lines. Some changes in command and movements of troops are taking place. I will tell you when the right time comes. Private letters from this army are opened by the secret service men. I congratulate H. J. on his 30-day bullet. No chance for me.

We have no more of Charley's army letters this summer, but Rev. H. Hopkins, who had at last accomplished his desire and was a chaplain *in the field*, tells of some of the experiences of the A. P.

Camp 120th N. Y. Vols., A. P.,
August 11th, 1864.

Dear Georgy:

Since our expedition to Deep Bottom, and short sojourn in the trenches at the time of the explosion of the mine and assault on the enemy's lines, we have been enjoying regular camp life. . . .

The industry of the men has provided deep wells abounding in cool, clear water; so that for all, the heat is endurable.

Here at Headquarters we luxuriate. We no longer creep on hands and knees into our sleeping places, but *live* in ample wall-tents. . . .

All the routine of the camp, even to the school in tactics, has been re-established and the calls from reveille to tattoo are regularly sounded. Our regimental band, an unusually fine one, plays for us after dress parade, while we take our tea, and all goes pleasantly on.

In a Bomb-proof,
August 20th,'64.

My experience since the above was written is a good commentary on the uncertainty of human affairs, and a good illustration of a soldier's life.

I was going on to tell you of the rural chapel we had built, and the services we were daily holding, etc., when I was interrupted. I went over and dined with your brother and returned to finish my letter, when lo! my home, the camp, my flock, my property, had vanished like the baseless fabric of a dream. The whole Corps had gone towards City Point. It was a week of excitement and danger. Several lay dead by the roadside before we reached City Point, though the troops were marched more reasonably than usual . . . .

A profound mystery shrouded the whole movement and was a delightful feature of it. Division generals were as much in the dark as any of us; and as the fleet dropped down the river, every place from Mobile to Atlanta was looked forward to as our destination, by the sagacious prophets on board. It was generally supposed that we were going to Washington.

It was a beautiful sight at sunset on the James, that night, as our thirty-two transports turned their heads up stream and cast anchor just above *Harrison's bar....*

The army was back again at the same spot from which it and the Sanitary Commission—ourselves part of it—had retreated two years before; but the Chaplain's regiment, far from falling back on Washington, as we did, was to engage later in heavy fighting for the capture of Petersburg.

G. to Mother at Fishkill.

NEW YORK, AUGUST 6, '64.

I have been in to see Mrs. Gibbons, who has written to know whether Carry and I would go with her to Beverly, fifteen miles from Philadelphia, and help put in running order Dr. Wagner's new hospital, to open on Tuesday, for 2,000 men. He implores Mrs. Gibbons to come and help him. She is to appoint all his nurses, and do as she pleases. *She* is to go at once, so as to be there for the first arrival of sick, which will be early in the week, and is to let us know all about the place—diet-kitchens, accommodations, etc., etc.—after she gets there, and then we are to decide and join her if we like the look of it. If she won't go, Dr. Wagner says he will not have any women nurses, and that is such a loss to a hospital, that she feels obliged on that account, if on no other, to help him....

Scrap in Mother's handwriting:

About Mrs. G.'s plan you must let me know. It seems much more desirable *to me* than going to the front, but you must judge for yourselves, of course. Pennsylvania is a more healthy region by far, than the South at present. My love to you all....

A. H. W. to H. Gilman.

AUGUST, '64.

The girls' new summons to hospital work came a few days ago, and yesterday Georgy and Carry started for Beverly, N. J., where Mrs. Gibbons and others have been hard at work for a month organizing a new military hospital to accommodate 3500. She says they are very short of help, and there is a village full of malignant people who are ready to make trouble if they are not allowed to sail through the wards with *their* help. It will be new life for Carry, but she is quick-witted and "handy," and was very anxious to go, and we couldn't refuse when there were hundreds of badly wounded, and few nurses to be had. . . . I don't believe you will be long without finding what you wanted—"something to do"—in Norwich. Trust you for not being "lazy" long! or blue either.

Abby herself was still hard at work cutting out shirts, and packing boxes, wherever she happened to be.

A. H. W. to H. G.

CORNWALL, N. Y., SEPTEMBER 23, 1864.

The bale of "California flannel" came, and no doubt the Ladies' Army Sewing Circle will need it all, and justify my purchase. A few of them who had heard of it have sent me money enough already to pay for one-third the expense, so we shall begin swimmingly. We came to this place last Saturday, and at first felt forlorn enough, but we secured an extra little room which Mother has taken pleasure in fitting up as our so-called private parlor. . . .

I cannot help wishing that we could have maintained a longer seclusion, just among our own family. This coming among outsiders seems to bury our sorrow deep from sight, to put it far back in the past. . . .

We can see Eliza's house plainly across the bay, and with a spyglass make out some signal, which, hung from an attic window, means, "We shall drive over this morning to see you," or, a story lower down, "Expect us this afternoon." It takes three days for a letter to come or go, all mail communication between this township and the universe being by stage to Newburgh, so we drive over when we want to say anything to Eliza! . . .

We have nothing very recently from Georgy and Carry. Their experience has been new and very trying—more wearing, Georgy says, than anything she has gone through before, because of the mental anxiety to provide for so many wounded men without means to do it with, and without authority to *compel* the means from the hands of dishonest stewards and indifferent doctors. She and Carry have been buying *all* the food that *all* their worst patients needed—forty in number, at the Beverly grocery.

The cooks and stewards make a clean steal of at least one meal a day from these two surgical wards—and the meals, when they *are* served from the hospital, are just the usual pork fat, and greasy slops. The men cry like babies, and *Carry* cries with them, and then laughs with them, and then does better than that, by taking the eggs she has sent to the grocer's for, and scrambling them on a spirit-lamp—to feed and keep life in some dying man. They are common ward nurses—Mrs. Gibbons having the position at the head of the women. . . .

The girls say they ask each other, every day, *"How* can we stay? and yet how *can* we go home?"* They will wait and see this set of men on the road to recovery, if possible.

John Packard goes up from Philadelphia every day as a sort of Inspector—to show the contract men what to do—with the wounds, etc.! Of course the girls' own accommodations are miserable, but that is nothing Georgy says she has really "at last an opportunity of exercising some of that self-sacrifice which her misguided friends have sometimes given her credit for." They say, however, we must not think it is all gloom and forlornness. They have rare fun between themselves about what goes on, and the airs and ignorance of the young doctors, etc., etc.

As a sample of this G. writes from Beverly to Mother:

SEPTEMBER, '64.

This set of regulations was promulgated this morning regarding "female nurses:"

"All deliberations, discussions and remarks having the object of expressing comparative praise, or censure, of the medical officers of this hospital, or their individual course or conduct, are positively prohibited!" The provision against our *"praise"* is truly judicious. C. and I have 100 men in our wards, all in bed. It is grimly amusing to hear the ward-surgeon say day after day, "Milk and eggs for 38." For two days there have been no eggs at all, and the milk rations are always short. The ladies are not allowed in the kitchen, or to have anything to do with the food for the patients. No steak or potatoes or milk punch come into this ward. We have opened a private account for bread, and milk, and butter and eggs, enough for this ward, with the village store. Our ward-surgeon has gone to a horse race, which seems a pretty long one! The surgeon-in-charge is kind in manner, and draws rations strictly according to army regulations; and seems to think that the stewards are the best persons to manage the food business. The object of the minor officers seems to be to subsist the men on nothing, and avoid making a row. We cannot keep our men alive; eleven of them have died in three days.

Rocking-chairs were still our craze. The Government furnished absolutely nothing for a sick man to sit on. These were for our Beverly ward:

H. L. H. to G.

PHILADELPHIA, SEPTEMBER, '64.

Dear Georgy:

I hope that Pomegranate rind has already reached you in packages as desired. As you suggested, I have ordered 10 Boston Rockers. . . . I have on hand twenty-six dollars and forty-five cents; . . . subject to your order. Do let me know whenever I can be of service in any way. . . . I am glad to hear that Dr. Packard is on duty at Beverly, as he may be of service to you and your patients, if you will only give him a hint.

We had a good-natured laugh over a visit from Miss Dix, who, poor old lady, kept up the fiction of appointing all the army nurses. She descended upon Beverly for this purpose, when, finding us already established without consultation with her, she served this printed assignment to duty—not on me only, but on Carry, whom she had never spoken to and knew nothing about!

OFFICE OF SUPERINTENDENT OF WOMEN NURSES,
WASHINGTON, D. C., AUGUST 30, 1864.

Miss Woolsey having furnished satisfactory evidence of her qualifications for the position of a "Nurse" in the employment of the Medical Department U. S. A., is approved.

D. L. Dix, Superintendent.

Assigned to duty at U. S. General Hospital, Beverly, New Jersey, 1864, upon application of Surgeon in charge.

A. H. W. to H. G.

Carry writes us about the visit of a Christian commission delegate to their hospital and the gloomy sermons on death he preaches to the convalescents, till her hair stands on end. He also haunts the wards early and late when no one is on the lookout for visitors, loaded with pocket-handkerchiefs and *pickled quinces*, demanding all round who has the diarrhea, and quite pleased to find that *no one* has and all glad to get the sour fruit, though in truth eleven of the men had died in three days of that chronic complaint.

Carry writes: "If *I* owned a hospital no philanthropist should ever enter. I could have pounded two benevolent old ladies yesterday on a tour of "inspection" through my ward. One of my poor little boys, feverish and restless, tired of lying in bed for days and days, had crawled to the stove and been tucked up in one of our rocking-chairs in his blanket. I had given him a hot drink and he had fallen into a doze, when these elderly philanthropists arrived, shook him by the arm, yelling, "Poor fellow, what's the matter, fever? O! my! you're too near the stove; get right back to bed. There now, that's it, you're too weak to sit up;" and so having saved one life as they thought, they passed on to the next."

You see Carry has *her* trials like all hospital nurses.

Jane writes at this date from her hospital:

I should think Beverly must be one of the worst conducted places in the service except Willett's Point Government Hospital, Long Island, where in August I saw them handing about pieces of fat pork on newspapers, to wounded men, for their dinners.

The Beverly Hospital was perhaps the worst one claiming to be a Regular Army establishment that I (G.) ever went into, and the conditions exasperating, because it was in the midst of a land of plenty. But it was dominated by the same Regular Army spirit which we had encountered all along, from the very first day of our army experience.

As in our late Spanish war, the system adapted to the case of a frontier regiment in time of peace was expected to cover all the emergencies of a large army in time of war. At Beverly the surgeon in charge was kind, but strangled in red tape. Mrs. Gibbons made the effort to keep us comfortable, and her daughter herself prepared in one corner of the kitchen articles for our table, to mitigate the army ration. Our own discomforts on the top floor of the board shanty are not worth speaking of, but one incident will illustrate the general conduct of affairs. I was pursued up-stairs one day by the man detailed to wait on the nurses' table, (a huge private in shirt-sleeves and *bare feet),* and violently berated for taking a piece of dry bread from the table to eat in peace in my own room, "contrary to regulations," I supposed.

Cousin Margaret Hodge and home friends helped us constantly to feed our poor men, and Robert sent weekly boxes of fruit and flowers. At last a tent hospital took the place of this wretched old tooth-brush factory building (where, through the wide cracks in the single plank floor of my ward, we looked down into the dead-house), and, matters having improved, we came away.

The poor fellows' Christmas day was happy. Miss Sever, our co-laborer, who remained, in acknowledging Christmas boxes from us, writes: "The dinner was a great success, and Mrs. Grant, the General's wife, spent the day going about among the men, which delighted them."

In the course of this summer of 1864, Admiral Farragut's splendid taking of Mobile came as a comfort, after the failure of the mine explosion before Petersburg; and Sherman and Sheridan were working out, through victories elsewhere, their part of Grant's plan for closing in round the rebel Lee.

McClellan, the "lost leader," while his old command still faced the enemy in the field, was occupied in offering himself as a rival to Mr. Lincoln's second presidency, and as the regular nominee of the Democratic party with its "peace at any price" morals. Chaplain Hopkins' letter fills a gap in the record.

Chaplain Hopkins to E. W. H.

IN THE FIELD.

CAMP OF 120TH NEW YORK, SEPTEMBER 29TH, 1864.

My dear Mrs. Howland:

I have just returned to camp from City Point, whence I have just dispatched over eighteen thousand dollars out of their pay to the homes of our men. I find tents down, baggage sent to the rear, and everything ready for a move at a moment's notice. . . . Thank you for your kind, good letter. . . . It is pleasant to know that one has the hearty approval of his friends in a step like that which I took in leaving the hospital. To be congratulated therefore by you, through whom I was first introduced to hospital life, on my escape from it, is peculiarly gratifying. . . . It was three years ago last Saturday, I think, that I waited in the parlor of the Ebbitt House, filled with misgivings at the thought of my temerity, to see the two elderly ladies to whom Prof. Smith had bidden me to report! I trembled lest, like a gentleman in New York whose son I offered to teach, they should look at me through their spectacles and think me too young for such a work. . . .

While I write Fort Morton, a hundred yards from me, is thundering with its heavy guns and mortars, to try the enemy, but they scarcely deign to reply. . . .

These soldiers, so apparently remorseless at times, were yesterday stealing out between the lines to talk and trade together, exchanging papers, and comparing news or politics. They wrote each other notes as "My dear Johnny Reb," "My dear Yank." They had a little dog for a mail carrier, and enclosed the orders of opposing generals, inviting desertions. The Johnnies were coming over to us a dozen or more a day. This afternoon in the hottest firing a rebel jumped up, swung a towel and called out, "Stop firing, and we will!" and in a moment it was as quiet as a New England Sunday. Their officers did not agree to this, and ordered firing to begin; so they shouted, "Get down, Yanks, we are going to open." I long for victory not less that the enemy may be defeated, than that the peace party of the North may be utterly confounded. Not an officer in our regiment will support McClellan. . . .

To-day I hear that Col. —— and Lieut.-Col. ——, both New York city democrats of the baser sort, who were never known to swerve from any nomination of the party, have declared themselves against little Mac. They can't, they say, as soldiers vote for him. Poor man! the loyal thousands of the army used to greet the mention of his name with a perfect enthusiasm. Now he is cheered for by traitors and their friends, and builds his fortunes on the disgrace of his government.

Your letter, which said in every line from beginning to end, "Let the war go on!" came to me just as I had come in from gazing on the noble, manly face of one of our Lieutenants, who half an hour before had been killed by a rebel bullet. There was not a more promising young officer in the regiment. We all expected much of him, and at home he was the idol of his mother and sisters. I was pondering on how best to tell them the heart-rending news when your letter came; and I confess, that even then, with those pale features before my eyes and that desolate home in my thoughts, I could say too, "Let the war go on!"

A. H. W. to H. G.

CORNWALL, OCTOBER 13TH.

Charley writes us with great pleasure of the gradual change that seems to be coming in the opinions of army officers. Those who have always had *personal* friendship for McClellan begin to see that they cannot vote for anybody on the Chicago platform, and are coming over to the right side. Colonel McMahon of Dix's staff had been down to Headquarters on a visit, and carried them the assurance that "McClellan was sure to be the next President; bets in New York ran four to one in his favor." He *came away* from camp rather cast down at the growing confidence of the army in the administration. [It is satisfactory to record even at this late date McClellan's overwhelming defeat, he received 21 votes of the Electoral College, in a total of 212.]

Charley has not been at home since March, and is not likely to come until the election is over; when, if Lincoln is successful, there may be a "let up" in military movements. That is *my* idea you know, at least. . . .

This afternoon we shall take an early start after dinner and drive up to Newburg and over the river to Eliza's at Fishkill, where Robert Howland and our four dear little girls are staying on a little visit. This is to fill up the time for them, till we go back to New York, when they are all coming to live with us for the winter, a long, long visit. Mother is going to give them the third story, and we shall find them the life of the house; I think, though, it will bring some responsibility. *That* we should feel, however, wherever they lived. May tells us, she "saw that there was a bill on their house in 23rd street, and asked papa what it meant, and where she and little sisters were going to live;" and then he told her Moremamma's and his secret.

The wretched men who had lived through the brutalities attending their imprisonment in Southern pens, were now being exchanged for the hearty, healthy rebels we had so frequently seen during our service, Government established a large receiving hospital at Annapolis; good women were put in charge, and steamers brought their appalling loads to that port. Our old commanding officer, Dr. Smith, was called to superintend the transportation, and sent Jane, just then at home from the Hospital on leave, an account of this service.

J. S. W. to a friend abroad.

NEW YORK, NOVEMBER, 29TH, 1864.

We are painfully interested just now in the coming home of our long-captive soldiers from the South. Our friend, Surgeon Smith, went down with the truce fleet. Perhaps you will let me quote a sentence or two from his letter dated at Savannah, November 20th. "I have just received 560 poor, wretched, miserable sufferers. All their being, all mind, seems to be absorbed in the one idea of living. They are too low, too utterly wrecked to have hope. They can't even conceive the idea that they are going home. Hope and remembrance are lost. They are sunk almost to the level of beasts. God help and pity them and take home the wretches that will die to-night. These living skeletons and puling idiots are worse to see than any sight on battlefields. In helping them on board it is frightful. You see a head, then a double handful of something in a bit of blanket or heap of rags! It weighs what the bones would weigh. Whiskey and hot strong broth are being served out rapidly."

Same day, later: "The whiskey and broth, sweet soft bread and onions are working wonders. One poor skeleton said to me just now, 'Why, Major, I could but just crawl on board, and now I'm bully.' 'How is that?' said I. 'Oh, it's the grub; I was starving to death.' Another skeleton head near by, speaks; 'This is Heaven; I have often envied my father's pigs their food and shelter.' O my God! it is dreadful to see these things." This surgeon is no weakling. He is called a hard man. He tells me later that our men are ill only with hunger and abuse, and the *incident diseases*. He says they have been subjected to every cruelty, every infamy of cruelty, we can conceive of. I have seen the prison camp and hospitals at Point Lookout, have lived in them for a month, and I *know* what the contrast is. How can I help bitter indignation when I read the over-seas talk of how the war is degenerating on the part of the North into a system of violence and cruelty, etc., etc.!

From the Army of the Potomac we get no important news. The "Turkey fleet" for Thanksgiving day arrived on time, and there was great merry-making in the camps. It looks like winter quarters, and then again it doesn't look like winter quarters, and they are holding their breaths for Sherman, and wondering when General Butler is going to give another "on to Richmond." That is the substance of our advices. Headquarters A. P. have a standing feud with Headquarters A. J. Butler is a thorn in the flesh of Meade.

Charley is copying and *punctuating* Meade's report of the unsuccesses of the A. P. since May 1st, with the reasons therefor; he feels the responsibility of his semi-colons, and thinks that if the American people would only mind their stops, all might yet be well. He sighs for promotion (there is no promotion in the General Staff) and wants to be a Captain in a colored regiment; but when I think of the dreadful anxiety it would cause Mother, I hope, unless it is a very clear case of duty, he will not join the black brigade. He was a prisoner for an hour or two in the late advance of the left, but after some hard and unequal fighting got away with his orderly and his dispatches, safe to our lines again. It would have been a terrible thing for us to have known him a prisoner in Richmond or Andersonville.

Colonel and Mrs. Howland are well. Georgy is with them, recruiting after her rather hard campaign at Beverly. . . .

We are all lighter-hearted since the election although we never allowed ourselves to doubt seriously of the result. As far as I know there are no McClellan men left anywhere. They are gone, no one knows where, and the "era of good feeling" appears to have set in. . . .

The newest sensation is the incendiary fires and the registration of secessionists. It is astonishing how many of these people are here "eating of our bread and lifting the heel against us." I hear stories every day of the impertinence of Southern women who are in sanctuary, so to speak, here, while their husbands are fighting against us. But we can afford magnanimity, even though our magnanimity be called weakness by the over-seas people, whom we cannot please.

All that could be done for the saving of the wretched exchanged prisoners was at last done. Supplies were sent from the Sanitary Commission and many homes from Eliza's and ours among them, to the lady in charge, an old friend of ours since the first days of the war, who writes:

ANNAPOLIS, DECEMBER 15TH, '64.

Dear Mrs. Howland:—

The boxes of lemons, wine and brandy came in perfect order, and in good season. Many thanks for the kind and generous response to my suggestions for the benefit of our boys. The condition of them is very sad. I am afraid to say how many have died in the hospital. . . .

A most touching letter was written a little while ago, dictated by a man to his wife. If I can get a copy of it I will send it to you—expressing simply the feeling of contentment to die, since he had once more come under the "starry folds of the dear old flag"; and, commending her and their one child to God, he bade her good-bye in the full consciousness of the nearness of death.

The flannel shirts will be most acceptable to us. The Sanitary Commission have so far furnished us large quantities of them, but as fast as the boys get their furloughs they go off, wearing in many instances the shirts that we have given them. The Government shirts are so rough and harsh that, if they can get others, the boys do not feel willing to wear them, and for my own part I have hardly the mind to put the poor skeletons into nutmeg graters, to lose what little flesh they have clinging to their bones.

Another boat is being unloaded.

From the Same.

ANNAPOLIS, DECEMBER 27TH, 1864.

Dear Mrs. Howland:—

The barrel containing the shirts from your Ladies' society was delivered promptly at my store-room on Saturday. . . .

I was very negligent not to tell you particularly of the condition of your pickles. They were in most excellent order. Nothing could have been more *àpropos* than that very barrel. In some of the wards I sent them every day, and actually believe that nothing else but pickles saved the life of one man who would eat nothing till he tasted them. After the first one, he could not live without a jar of them in his room, and said they seemed to "rouse up the vitals pretty sharp," and gave him an appetite that nothing else could do.

You may indeed consider the experiment a perfect success. [E. had them made by the barrel—sometimes by the hogshead—for this very purpose, as anti-scorbutics.]

Our Christmas passed off very well. I hesitate for a word to express *how* it went. "Happily" could hardly express the manner of it if I mention at the same time that *ten deaths* were reported to me the same day. But we had a very nice dinner of proper Christmas eatables, such as turkey, cranberry, celery, pies, plum pudding, with vegetables, for all full diets, and all sorts of goodies for the sick ones. Our decorations were not extensive, and confined mostly to the chapel, for all the ladies were too busy to trim the wards. The general condition of the patients is improving, I think, but the mortality has been fearful. Large numbers of the returned men were able to get off for home before Christmas and others are still going.

Very truly yours,

MARIA M. C. HALL.

Work for the Union Refugees was meantime going on all over the North. As an indication of the general interest in them, the "Highland Serenaders," a village band of Matteawan, N. Y., sent E. W. H. a check for $100, asking her to "accept this small sum, the profits of their first concert," and to use it for the benefit of the Union Refugees. They add, "We hold ourselves in readiness to do our part in anything for our Free Country."

Mrs. Joseph P. Thompson to E. W. H.

32 WEST 36TH ST., N. Y. DECEMBER.

My dear Eliza:—

Abby tells me that your Fishkill ladies are busily at work for the refugees, and she says you want to know what organization there is at the Southwest, for receiving and distributing the supplies. . . . The Union Commission are exploring through all those states, and reporting constantly. The most urgent calls at present are from Memphis, Nashville, from Helena, and from Cedar Keys, Florida, all reconquered from the rebels, where the destitution has been most appalling. Twenty barrels of clothing, potatoes, &c., have been shipped to Cedar Keys, to the care of Captain Pease, of the 2nd U. S. Infantry. There will be shipped for Memphis to-morrow seven barrels and boxes of the largest kind, of second-hand clothing, and there are probably at the rooms 40 barrels and boxes that will be forwarded as soon as possible.

A. H. W. to H. G.

NEW YORK, DECEMBER 21, '64.

Our household moves on with the usual ups and downs. We see and hear nothing from the outside world except what the newspapers bring, but that is stirring enough. Sherman's march proves, at last, our numerical superiority. We have *one* army free to move where it likes and have an "agreeable time" in the enemy's country. We may soon have *two* surplus armies, for Thomas' victory over Hood seems to have been a crushing one. Hood had forty thousand men engaged in that fight, but, a very large number of them Tennesseans, who are evidently "demoralized"—if that slang word has not lost all its force, and he has three swollen rivers to cross in his retreat . . .

I must see Lizzie Thompson soon, and hear how the refugees fare. Carry went round one morning to the office, but her zeal only held out for that one day over the rags and vermin which some people find it convenient to dump on benevolent societies. We have packed one barrel, and hope to get off another before the close of the year, while Fishkill seems all agog on the subject. Poor creatures, homeless and hungry; these winter days must go hard with them in those border towns where the tide of war has stranded them. Our Thanksgiving box to Charley, which you were witness to, was so long delayed that the game in it must have been *very gamy,* so it has had to be followed by a *Christmas* box, which we sent off yesterday, and as another must go to the little Jerome children, (the Chaplain's family), at Fairfax Hospital, and another to the soldiers at Beverly, etc., we have, in that particular line, a rather busy time. . . . Carry is filling the month with weekly visits at Bloomingdale Orphan Asylum. She always comes back full of experience and pleasure, and has much to tell of her pow-wows with Mrs. Anthon and Mrs. Satterlee and the other elderly and revered ladies of the board. . . . They have been engaging two teachers, for the boys and girls' departments, the two young people who have had charge so far having romantically fallen in love . . .

The girls' teacher, it seems, was herself raised in the asylum, and great interest has been felt in her approaching marriage. . . . A sad and romantic turn has been given to the affair, however, by the appearance on the scene of a first-love whom she had secretly jilted for the sake of the new teacher. This first-love, a gallant, noble young Captain in the army, obtained a short leave and came dashing into Mrs. Pell's room the other night, to know what it all meant; why his engagement ring had been returned? So then, it all had to come out. The young Captain was, himself, an asylum boy once, and a match with him would have been the wisest thing. . . Poor young soldier, he is heartbroken, and has gone into the *regular* army, now, as a career. . . .

Surgeon Smith has been ordered back to Fairfax Hospital, the transfer of prisoners from Savannah and Charleston being nearly at an end. . . . I don't wonder that the girls are enthusiastic in their praise of him; he looks so carefully and personally into the condition of his patients, instead of being satisfied with giving orders to subordinates and sitting at his ease, as the surgeon who took his place for a time did. He has sent the girls *his* first two general orders issued on his return, and they are an indication of what sort of a man he is and of how shamefully his predecessor has acted, shutting up the chapel and snubbing the Chaplain. By "No. 1, December 14, Surgeon David P. Smith hereby assumes command of this hospital." In No. 2, dated next day, he orders the chapel opened, divine service held on Christmas Day and every Sunday thereafter at 10.15 o'clock. Also afternoon and evening weekly services at such hours as the Chaplain may appoint; and officers and soldiers are referred to certain articles of war and advised to be reverent and diligent in their attendance upon divine things. . . . Charley has been brevetted Captain, for "gallantry on the field," and all the rest of the "clap-trap" (as *he* says) that his complimentary letter was filled with.

"The complimentary letter" unfortunately is destroyed, and as we were all at home and no family letters were exchanged, there is nothing further to add to the simple fact that for "gallantry on the field" Charley could always be relied on. He came home for a while apparently, as this extract from a note from our co-worker at Beverly shows.

Miss Annie Sever to "Dear little Miss Carry."

BEVERLY HOSPITAL.

I was very glad to have the little note from you to-night and to think of your enjoyment in having your brother at home with you. You must let me give you my congratulations on his promotion.

And so the fourth year of the war closed with a united family—save one.

Fairfax Seminary Hospital

CHAPTER FIFTEEN

Brotherhoods & Sisterhoods

JANUARY, 1865, found Sherman master of Savannah. The victory at Fort Fisher under General Terry followed. Columbia and Charleston within a month were occupied by Sherman, and he was marching north. Sheridan was making harassing raids, cutting off supplies, and breaking up railroads, and the rebels under Lee, held to their position at Petersburg by Grant, were gradually being surrounded and shut in on every side.

In the absence of Charley's letters Chaplain Hopkins again helps to make the story continuous:—

CAMP 120TH N. Y. VOLS., A. P.
BEFORE PETERSBURG, JANUARY 8TH, 1865.

Dear Georgy:

That prince of Christmas boxes! . . . Fresh from the perusal of one of Dr. Bushnell's masterly sermons, with the linen pockets hanging "from the ridge-pole," paper-cutter, etc. enriching the pigeon holes before me, new books adorning my table, and a fabulous array of goodies close at hand, while the match-box lies lovingly beside a little copy of the Psalms in a safe pocket, and a sugar-plum is rolled even now as a sweet morsel under my tongue—what wonder that my heart is too full for utterance. . . .

I had been hard at work for many days with the axe, helping the men build the log chapel another Chaplain and myself are building for three regiments. We had had such trials and disappointments. . . . I had found coldness where I had expected sympathy, and even selfishness and meanness where I thought to be met with generous co-operation. My heart was as sombre as the winter sky when I came to my tent. *There was the box!*

Since then all has gone well; the afternoon was a happy one. The next day, teams, tools and willing men came with a pleasant day for the chapel, and to-day I have found in the huts of the men some such bright good souls that I feel strengthened and blessed by seeing them. See how much a box of sugar-plums can do! I beg you to distribute my thanks where they belong, not forgetting Bertha and Una. . . .

I have thought that part of your Mother's money could not be expended more satisfactorily than in supplying this brigade regularly with a number of copies of the *Messenger* and *Sunday School Times*. It would be a pleasant thing for your Mother to know that she was putting a copy of each one of these good sound preachers into every hut in a whole brigade, regularly, through the winter months. We mean to make a reading-room of the chapel, and I have already made arrangements for the secular papers.

I should like to give every soldier in the regiment a copy of "The Rainy Day in Camp." I never knew of a copy of it being destroyed; it is usually sent home in the first letter. Four hundred and fifty would be enough. Has Jane gone back to Fairfax Hospital? . . .

Both of my brothers are near me, one, Archy, in 37th Mass., 6th Corps, and the other, Lawrence, in the 1st Mass. Cavalry. I expect them to spend Thursday evening. I am about moving into a new and elegant shanty, and shall have a house-warming. I am saving cake, figs, prunes, nuts, etc. from the box, to garnish the feast. . . .

CAMP 120TH N. Y. VOLS., NEAR HATCHER'S RUN,
FEBRUARY 12TH, 1865.

Dear Georgy:

For the first time in a week I have a tent and table. Outside, the winds howl and shake the canvas like mad, but my little fury of a stove makes it summer within. . . .

I am unable to understand what we have accomplished by this week of fighting and exposure, unless it be a diversion in favor of Sherman.

When we came away from our old camp, there was a manifest improvement going on in the brigade, in the health, discipline and morals of the men. Our two chapels were none too large, and the attendance was increasing from night to night. The Dinwiddie Literary Association, carried on by officers of the brigade, was a capital institution. . . . Then we had, every Thursday evening, a general singing exercise under a first-rate leader. Besides I had an interested and interesting Bible class. . . .

To-day the chapel and the camp are desolate, and not one man in ten of the brigade knows that it is the Sabbath. By the end of the week we hope to have a new chapel up, though by the end of the week we may have made *another* move "by the left flank."

J. S. W. had gone back to the Fairfax Seminary Hospital, which was filling up with sick men from the camps abandoned as the army had advanced. Her hands were full of work again.

J. S. W. to J. H.

FAIRFAX HOSPITAL, FEBRUARY 16, 1865.

Dear Colonel:

Many thanks for your neat and appropriate gift. The thin disguise of writing backwards—not to mention the postmark—shall not prevent me from claiming "thee as my valentine." . . . The last camelia G. sent me remained "quite fresh yet," till yesterday, when I turned it upside down, and it lasted some hours longer. . . .

See how it is: you sit at home at ease, waxing fat on petroleum stock and *purée aux quafre saisons*, while we, whose bosoms are the bulwark (you may have heard something like this before) between you and your country's foes, are obliged to turn our camelias wrong side out to economise them. But you also have been in "Arcadia."

Here there is nothing but shop to tell, and nothing of shop, but that we are continually expecting to be reinforced with every species of the genus Bummer from the breaking up of Alexandria hospitals. *Some* among the men will be bad cases; they shall have the shirts of "the benevolent."

The individual who has ten small children to feed on four months' arrears of pay—*il y en a*—he shall have a shirt too; while "Mr." B., an inmate of ours, who boasts of having "jumped" a thousand dollars or two, has been six months in the service, in hospitals, and has just procured his discharge on the ground of epileptic fits of fifteen years standing, will be requested to clothe himself out of his last bounty. The doctor sends me up now, the names of all discharged men with a mark against those he considers "unworthy of my charity"; so I have only to refer to my list, on the application.

Ask Eliza how she gets the wine out of the "kag." Do you take off the hoops? or gimlet-hole it in the side? I was rather afraid of a *jet de vin* if I meddled with the little square piece of tin on the side of it.

My love to the orchid-house and incidentally to the members of the family.

A. H. W. to H. G.

We plod along here, one day very much like the rest, and a large proportion of them rainy ones, when we stay indoors, and sort over closets, or get a good pile of mending, and some lively story for one to read aloud.

Jane writes rarely, and always hurriedly; so many hospitals have been broken up in Alexandria that she has had a large accession of "lame backs" and despondent "chronics." It seems to be felt that the Department of Washington will not be the depot for the wounded from our next battle; but that they will either be kept in North Carolina or sent up North, here. We hear nothing from Headquarters, now that Charley has left temporarily, but are looking with interest for a letter from him from *Charleston,* where he was going with all speed when he last wrote. General Williams and himself went to Hilton Head a month ago on "inspecting" duty, and Charley has written us about his Savannah and Florida trips, which were all novel and charming to him. General Gilmore had given them the use of a little steamboat, the Delaware, and on that they live, and shoot in and out along the coast. He tells us of the excellent order, appearance, and "snap" of the colored troops—the Third United States particularly—and mentions one company of artillery garrisoning a battery, where the Sergeant was a field hand five months ago, but now "keeps the company books, and in excellent order"—no small mark of intelligence, in an officer of *any* standing, I am told. . . .

We have gone into a new business, Georgy and I, collecting fancy articles for a *colored fair* in Alexandria. We have made a few gay silk neckties, some fancy aprons for colored babies, highly-colored pincushions, &c. It seems that articles for a fair will fill a place that mere money won't. Mrs. Jacobs (perhaps you have heard of her), a mulatto, formerly a slave, long living in Nat Willis' family, and a "big, noble, Christian lady" as described to me, has gone back to Alexandria to help educate her race. She found so much coldness and reserve among the well to do—those who were free before the war, and live comfortably—so much fear on their part that this great influx of degraded contrabands would drag them all down to the same level in social estimation, that she has done her best to bring out their sympathies and break up this selfish, aristocratic notion. A fancy fair last spring, where the young colored "ladies" held tables, was most success-ful in more than mere money, and now Mrs. Jacobs wants to repeat it. The proceeds are to supply delicacies, &c., for the colored soldiers in the great dreary hospital at Alexandria appropriated to them.

Charley and General Williams completed their inspection of the troops at Southern stations, and were back again at Headquarters of the Army of the Potomac in time for the final act of the campaign.

On April 2d, Grant's whole line advanced against the rebel works at Petersburg, cutting Lee's army in two. The rebel General telegraphed to Jeff Davis that, his line being broken, he was compelled to abandon his position.

He evacuated Richmond and Petersburg, closely pursued by Grant, while loyal forces occupied both cities; Weitzel's black troops being first to march into Richmond. The rebel president fled before them towards North Carolina.

C. C. W. to E. W. H.

NEW YORK, MONDAY NIGHT, APRIL 3D, 1865.

Dear Eliza:

Isn't it Glorious? New York has stood on its head, and the bulls and bears of Wall street for once left their wrangling, and sang Old Hundred. "Bless the Lord, oh, my soul," and don't you hope Lee will not escape? We have felt very sorry you were not here to see it all; can't you come down? . . . Suppose you and Joe go to Charleston and take Hatty and me to see the flag-raising at Sumter? Com. Draper can give passes to *any one;* and the opportunity will never occur again. Go! do go! It is hard to sit still with the excitement and commotion which you know can never be repeated, and you not there. "Plenty of good times, only I ain't in 'em."

The lion has not yet lain down with the lamb, but one evidence of peace we just had. G. was sitting by the little table with her cup of tea on it, when, rooking up suddenly, we saw a small mouse quietly drinking the tea, his nose in the cup and his tail in the air! Glory, Hallelujah! Good-bye.

The following was the glorious sight that Carry longed to see:

GENERAL ORDERS, No. 50.
WAR DEPARTMENT,
ADJUTANT-GENERAL'S OFFICE,
WASHINGTON, MARCH 27, 1865.
ORDERED—

First. That at the hour of noon, on the 14th day of April, 1865, Brevet Major General Anderson will raise and plant upon the ruins of Fort Sumter, in Charleston harbor, the same United States flag which floated over the battlements of that Fort during the rebel assault, and which was lowered and saluted by him and the small force of his command when the works were evacuated on the 14th day of April, 1861.

Second. That the flag, when raised, be saluted by one hundred guns from Fort Sumter, and by a National salute from every fort and rebel battery that fired upon Fort Sumter. . . .

BY ORDER OF THE PRESIDENT OF THE UNITED STATES:
EDWIN M. STANTON,
SECRETARY OF WAR.

On April the 8th, held in a vise, cut off from all supplies, utterly and hopelessly beaten,—Lee surrendered. His starving troops were eating the buds from the trees to keep life in themselves, that pleasant spring day.

Grant's first act after the formal surrender, was to issue rations to the famished rebels. "If thine enemy hunger, feed him." Riding to his camp after a three hours' interview with Lee at Appomattox Court House, Grant heard the firing of salutes, and sent at once to stop them, saying: "The war is over, the rebels are again our countrymen; the best sign of rejoicing after this victory will be to abstain from all demonstration in the field."

Charley's letters at this time, it is remembered, gave us striking accounts of these last days. He wrote out one of the five copies of the terms of surrender from Grant's notes, which for a time he had in his hands; and he saw what has not been mentioned in any account of the closing scene.

The very small room in which Grant and Lee met was crowded with officers, and it was an easy thing to miss seeing an action which passed in an instant. At a certain moment, Charley is positive that he saw Lee make a motion as if to offer his side arms, and saw Grant also silently, and immediately, with a gesture, refuse to accept the humiliation.

And so the great Rebellion came to an end. The armies immediately under Grant had captured in Virginia 75,000 men and 689 cannon; and the forces under his general command had, in addition, taken 147,000 prisoners and 997 cannon in the final campaign of April and May. So that it was not altogether the giving in of a remnant of dissipirited men to superior numbers, but the out-generaling by Grant of the traitor Lee, false to the Government which had educated him, and to the flag which, as an officer of that Government, he had solemnly sworn to protect.

It was just and comforting that what was virtually the final surrender of the rebel cause, should have been made to the General in personal command of the Army of the Potomac,—that courageous, long-suffering army, whose fortunes we have followed, and with which it seemed to the members of this special family they themselves had been marching, for four weary years.

On the day that the news of the surrender of Lee's Army came to New York, it was impossible for this family to accept it as a matter of course. The silence and lack of enthusiasm up town, and the sight of the women going in and out of the dry goods shops as usual, was unbearable. Mother and I (G.) said to each other, "Come, let us see what Wall Street is doing." We took a Fulton Street omnibus, which was entirely empty but for ourselves, and drove down to the neighborhood of the Custom House. As we came near, the streets were more and more blocked, thousands and thousands of men standing, crowding upon each other, not a woman's face among them,—all the narrow streets which converge to that point black with men, thousands more, solidly packed. As the omnibus came to a stand, not able to move a step further, they were singing as if their hearts would burst:

> Praise God from whom all blessings flow,
> Praise Him all creatures here below;
> Praise Him above ye heavenly host,
> Praise Father, Son and Holy Ghost.

A young man, half fainting with fatigue, threw himself into the omnibus, saying, "They have been at it for hours."

At Joe's and Eliza's home at Fishkill peace was celebrated by the building, in the spring and summer of 1865, of the Tioronda School House. Two little framed photographs—one of the tattered battle-flags of the 16th N. Y. as *War,* and the other of the School House as *Peace,*—always hung side by side in J. H.'s dressing room, and travelled with him whenever he and E. went abroad.

Mother to E.

NEW YORK, APRIL 13TH.

My dear Eliza:—

Your very jolly, hallelujah letter came yesterday, while Mrs. Joseph Thompson was sitting with us, and I could not keep it to myself, but read it aloud, and we all enjoyed it together. Your patriotism is grand, and I have no doubt you have done your part in firing the hearts of the Fishkill people, and working them up to their unusual and commendable ardor in the cause, especially the women and "their sewing-machines." I really think your neighborhood has accomplished wonders, and the people of Fishkill deserve great praise for their energy and industry. I want you to come down for the grand illumination on the 20th to celebrate the surrender, which will be next Thursday, that you may see the city in its glory of thanksgiving display.

We have Abby's pretty silk flag in one of our windows pinned across the curtains, and Willy G.'s little one in the other, with our larger one over the front door outside, which has hung through the rains and sun, day and night, since Richmond was taken, and begins to lose its bright color.

You can bring your little silk one with you. The girls have been getting some colored lanterns to decorate the balcony and street door; and this, with the gas all lighted and the windows open, will be the extent of our illumination, but we can drive round and see the city. I hope you will come certainly.

Calvin Goddard and his wife made us a long call last night, and this evening Calvin came in again. . . .

I enclose our last from Charley; he is undoubtedly in Richmond before this—probably one of Lee's escort into the city, as the papers mention General Grant and his staff accompanying him. Isn't it grand to have all these victories coming so fast, and the rebels giving up, in a forlorn hope, their boasted Confederacy.

Robert told me last night he meant to spend August at Sharon Springs—taking the children with him, to be with Mary G. Poor little darlings, they are very precious to me. My love to Joe and your dear self. Mother.

P. S.—Charley is in Washington with General Williams. . . . Drafting stopped!!—all over the country!!!

From a letter of E. W. H.'s

April, '65.

Charley is still in Washington He had just had an interview with an old friend, Captain Carpenter, who is now a miserable cripple, all doubled up with wounds from the *blood-hounds* which chased and seized him when he tried to escape from the rebel prison at Columbia.

The great President's second term of office began with such lofty words as these:

"The judgments of the Lord are true and righteous altogether. With malice towards none; with charity for all; with firmness in the right, as God gives us to see the right, let us strive to finish the work we are in; to bind up the Nation's wounds; to do all which may achieve and cherish a just and lasting peace."

Mr. Lincoln was personally with the army for the last few days of the campaign, entering Richmond immediately after its surrender, riding

through the city in a common U. S. ambulance, greeted with the bene-
dictions of the negroes whom he had set free.

On April 14th the civilized world was startled with the news of his
assassination. He was shot in his box at Ford's Theatre in Washington
by a rebel bullet, and died in a small house on the opposite side of the
street, without regaining consciousness, at about 7 A. M. on April 15.
The joy over the return of peace was eclipsed by the grief of the whole
nation.

All that I can remember about the first moments of that awful morning at home, is that I rushed to Hatty's and Carry's bedroom door,
pounding it, and crying, "Let me in, let me in! Mr. Lincoln is murdered."

C. C. W. to E. W. H.

SATURDAY MORNING, APRIL 15TH, 1865.

Dear Eliza:

What can one do? We are all dumb with grief. The extra has just been
cried giving the awful moment of his death. What a moment for America! When you think of his unvarying kindness toward those very men
who now rejoice,—how his whole career has been one of goodness and
mercy, and now at the very first beginning of reward, it is too hard to
bear. The papers were brought up while we were in bed this morning. You
have hardly heard it now. I suppose you will not come down to-day, but
you must on Monday. Charley is in Washington, in rooms with General
Williams, on 15th Street. New York seems dead, the streets are quiet and
the flags all covered with black crape—even the 'extra' boys subdue their
voices. Work is suspended, and Wall Street is thronged with silent men.

Do come down; we ought to be together in these awful times.

Men, women and children went about the streets of New York,
crying, and hardly a single poor tenement in the most impoverished
quarters of the city was without its little black streamer. Clocks were
stopped at the hour of his death; and on the anniversary of it, for years,
on some of the principal buildings of New York.

GENERAL ORDERS, No. 66.

WAR DEPARTMENT,
ADJUTANT GENERAL'S OFFICE.
WASHINGTON, APRIL 16, 1865.

The following order of the Secretary of War announces to the Armies of the United States the untimely and lamentable death of the illustrious ABRAHAM LINCOLN, late President of the United States:

WAR DEPARTMENT,
WASHINGTON CITY, APRIL 16, 1865.

The distressing duty has devolved upon the Secretary of War to announce to the Armies of the United States, that at twenty-two minutes after seven o'clock, on the morning of Saturday, the fifteenth day of April, 1865, ABRAHAM LINCOLN, President of the United States, died of a mortal wound inflicted upon him by an assassin.

The Armies of the United States will share with their fellow-citizens the feelings of grief and horror inspired by this most atrocious murder of their great and beloved President and Commander-in-Chief, and with profound sorrow will mourn his death as a national calamity.

The Headquarters of every Department, Post, Station, Fort, and Arsenal will be draped in mourning for thirty days, and appropriate funeral honors will be paid by every Army, and in every Department, and at every Military Post, and at the Military Academy at West Point, to the memory of the late illustrious Chief Magistrate of the Nation, and Commander-in-Chief of its Armies.

Lieutenant General Grant will give the necessary instructions for carrying this order into effect.

EDWIN M. STANTON,
Secretary of War.

On the day after the receipt of this order at the Headquarters of each Military Division, Department, Army, Post, Station, Fort, and Arsenal, and at the Military Academy at West Point, the troops and cadets will be paraded at 10 o'clock A. M., and the order read to them; after which all labors and operations for the day will cease and be suspended, as far as practicable in a state of war.

The national flag will be displayed at half-staff.

At dawn of day thirteen guns will be fired, and afterwards, at intervals of thirty minutes, between the rising and setting sun, a single gun, and at the close of the day a national salute of thirty-six guns.

The officers of the Armies of the United States will wear the badge of mourning on the left arm and on their swords, and the colors of their commands and regiments will be put in mourning for the period of six months.

By command of
LIEUTENANT GENERAL GRANT.
W. A. NICHOLS
ASSISTANT ADJUTANT GENERAL.

Mother to E. W. H.

NEW YORK, APRIL 25, '65.

My dear Eliza:

I was very glad to get your letter this morning, which was handed in with the enclosed from Charley. . . .

I am sorry you postpone your visit, as you would have seen something of the funeral pageant. It will be weeks before the country recovers from the first great shock of this terrible event, and as long, before the people of New York are quieted down again to their every-day occupations. We all feel unsettled, and can really do little else than read the newspapers. Robert left home on Thursday P. M. for Washington.

Georgy means to deluge Lee with Northern newspapers. Commenced this morning by sending him the *Post* of last evening, with an editorial marked very strikingly, headed "General Lee."

It must have been about this time that Charley was brevetted Major, and then Lieutenant Colonel; we have no date, the record is destroyed.

The following letter contains the first intimation that earth was pleasant to Abby, since the war began nearly five years before:

A. H. W. to H. Gilman.

FISHKILL, MAY, '65.

When I came up here last Tuesday, I did not think that I should let a week of this easy, idle life pass without writing a letter or two that were due. But it is *so* easy to do nothing but read the newspapers and stroll in the garden, if you only tried! . .

This is the fifth season that I have failed to watch the gradual development of nature, as it used to be such an occupation and pleasure to do, even in city back yards and corner grass plats. For five years there has been something else, so overwhelming, so pre-occupying that Spring has burst upon us unknown, or rather, come quietly, unnoticed, till some day when we have looked up into the trees or out of the window, and found that it was Summer!

And *peace* has come, like the Spring this year, unheralded, unobserved, like the changes of the season. And, strangely enough, there is a dash of sadness in the thought of peace,—the scattering of the troops and the breaking up of brotherhoods and sisterhoods of patriotic efforts and hopes.

Jane thinks her duties will hold out, however, for awhile, and says she "shall stand by Mr. Micawber"—Fairfax Hospital. They have the great armies camped all about them now, the glimmer of the white tents by day and the fires by night being pretty to see, and the sick, who have borne up bravely through the march, or have been wearily dragged hither or thither after their regiments, are all brought into Fairfax,—it is so handy, and dumped, as if it were a matter of course. So *she* has plenty to do.

The following list found among Abby's papers gives an inadequate idea of the labors she needed to rest from. She cut out and had made a very large number of the garments mentioned, knitted an untold number of the socks, and saw that all the articles in this list, and many more not mentioned, were safely forwarded to us at the front.

PARTIAL LIST OF SUPPLIES SENT FROM NO. 8 BREVOORT PLACE TO THE
ARMY HOSPITALS; MOST OF THEM THROUGH G. AND E. AND JANE:

667 flannel and cotton shirts.

134 pairs of drawers.

165 men's wrappers.

628 pairs of socks.

107 pairs of slippers.

104 woolen mufflers.

1144 pocket handkerchiefs.

1036 towels and napkins.

203 pillow-cases.

121 pillow-sacks and twenty-five pounds of curled hair towards filling
them.

26 sheets and several pieces of unmade sheeting and ticking.

36 woolen caps and 24 pairs wristlets.

58 pieces of mosquito netting.

Several dozen rocking chairs.

Blankets, air-pillows, india-rubber cloth, no end of lint, bandages, old
linen, oil-silk, &c.

18 or 20 cases of brandy, wine, &c., of which ten cases were old port
wine from Uncle Edward.

Cologne by the dozen boxes at a time.

Tobacco in large quantity.

Tobacco boxes; jack knives.

300 boxes of games, checkers, dominoes, &c., &c.

Lead pencils by the gross.

Tooth brushes, pocket-combs and pocket mirrors by the hundred.

Quantities of prepared beef and chicken.

Beef-tea, cocoa.

Canned tomatoes, &c.

Arrow-root, barley, farina.

Condensed milk.

Lemons, tea, crackers.

Pickles, oatmeal.

Currant jelly, &c., &c., &c.

Large quantities of clothing and other supplies were also sent South for the Freedmen and the poor white refugees.

A. H. W. to H. G.

FISHKILL, MAY, 1865.

Charley, frightened partly into resignation by the hint of the War Department that "resignations would be accepted until the 15th," and considering himself wholly superfluous now that General Williams is camped in E street, Washington, is out of the service.

Jane Eliza Newton Woolsey
Woolsey Papers, Ferriday Archives

CHAPTER SIXTEEN

The Mad, Sad, Noble War Was Over

WHEN PEACE HAD FINALLY COME we were all eager that Mother, who had seen so much of the dark side of the War and had known its anxieties so keenly, should see something also of the victorious army and of Washington with the smile of Peace upon it.

A. H. W. to H. G.

FISHKILL, MAY, 1865.

Charley has expressed a hope that Mother would go on to Washington before he leaves and let him show her about a little and take a peep at Jane, etc., etc. So quite suddenly at the last, after a good deal of that good-natured, kindly-intentioned goading with which people often press their attentions upon unwilling relatives, Mother was got off to Baltimore, with Georgy, Hatty and Carry. There Charley met them,—Robert Howland was also of the party—and to-day we hear for the first time of their further progress down the Bay and up the James to Richmond! the goal of so many of *Georgy's* desires. They reached there on Thursday night, and to our great pleasure were still in time for the passage of a portion of Sherman's army through Richmond next day. . . . I don't enjoy traveling at any time, least of all rebelward, and so came up here to be with Eliza and our little children, who are making their usual spring visit and revelling in the wealth of "daisy-lions" and blue violets on the lawn and in the ravine. There is soldier work here for Eliza to do too,—a returned prisoner, who is getting well on her good tea and brandy and fresh eggs, in a cottage up at Glenham, and another elsewhere who must die, and the family of a third who did die after two months of sickness, five miles from here, in a "copperhead" neighborhood, where folks said "rebel prisons served him just right, he oughtn't to have been such a fool as to go to the war." . . .

397

Mother to A. H. W.

BALTIMORE, TUESDAY EVENING, MAY 10, 1865.

My dear Abby:

So far "on to Richmond" safe and well, without let or hindrance; no mishap except the opening, in some miraculous way, of my inkstand in my handbag and spoiling a few articles—my paper, as you see, for one. We were scarcely in this city's precincts when Charley appeared in the car, taking us by surprise; said he had walked out to meet us, and it was the third train he had met, not knowing by which we would come. He is looking very well, and seems greatly pleased to be a citizen again; and as Carry says is "extremely civil." He had rooms all ready for us; nice ones on the first floor; we have had a hearty supper, waited upon by Gettysburg John, who was our cook there, and is head waiter here. We had a shaking of hands all round, and he got us up a very nice supper. . . . We are agitating the question of boats, whether to try the new line, which makes it first trip to-morrow from here, or to go to Washington, where, as Charley says, Mr. Dana, the Assistant Secretary of War, will be happy to give us passes in the Government boat. We think it will be pleasant to go on from here and return by the other way, and Charley says he can write to Mr. Dana to reserve our passes till then. . . . Robert is well and glad to meet Charley. I hope you are safely housed with Eliza. Kiss the dear children for me and remember me to Ann.

Public conveyances had their discomforts just after the war! as Hatty's letter shows:—

H. R. W. to A. H. W.

RICHMOND, MAY 14, 1865.

Dear Abby:

Robert, I believe, gave you an account of our night on the boat with its accompaniment of drunken women and "b flats". . . But in spite of it all we are *in Richmond!* and glad we are,—(knock at the door, and two bouquets with the "compliments of Major Scott, Fourth Massachusetts Cavalry," handed in, for Mrs. Woolsey and Mrs. Woolsey's daughter Carry, with whom he rode on horseback yesterday). We arrived too late for the grand display, but on Wednesday, all day long, Sherman's troops were passing through the city as quietly as possible; no display of any kind, no review by Halleck; grim, fierce-looking men some of them, marching along splendidly, but giving no sign. . . . (G. M. W. takes up the letter) Sherman and Halleck are deadly enemies, since the latter's order to disregard any orders received from Sherman, and a hot interchange of letters, before the troops came up, ended in an announcement by note to Halleck from Sherman that "he had better not show himself in the streets, as Sherman could not answer for the reception he might receive from the soldiers." So they marched sullenly through, leaving the Fourteenth and Seventeenth Corps to follow next day. We were all ready to review them, when, to our horror, at 9.30, as we were finishing breakfast, the announcement came that all the troops had gone through. No one was told of it; General Curtis,—our wounded Captain of the old Sixteenth, now Brigadier-General of Volunteers, who is here—knew nothing of it, and they began at 5.30 A. M., and went as quietly as possible. Saturday there was still left one corps to pass, and we went up to the State House and watched them, but they broke up, passed through different streets, and took no more notice of our handkerchiefs and the flag, than if we were posts—sullen fellows, espousing Sherman's cause, and determined not to show the slightest interest in the place where Halleck was. So this personal fight deprived us and the army of what might have been a splendid sight. General Curtis is doing everything for us. We have our order for as many ambulances as we want as long as we stay; we never drive with less than four horses and eight outriders; have been all over the city and to Cold Harbor, going there yesterday with four officers and General Curtis and wife, and seeing the field and line of works. To my great pleasure we broke down on this side, and were not obliged to eat our dinner on any battle field, though we did stop where the rebel army must have camped, and somewhere in the neighborhood of *Gaines Mill*, where Joe was wounded. . . .

We came back safely to receive Generals Ord, Turner and someone else, and Captains and Lieutenants thrown in—Mrs. Ord with them. This morning Mother and I have been at home, the girls at a colored church, where, to their great delight, the announcement was made of *Jeff. Davis' capture*. The whole church was overcome with delight, blessing the Lord, crying and kissing Hatty's and Carry's hands. They were charmed to see the northern ladies, and gave them chief places among them, and a bunch of roses each. Numbers of notices were read; people asking information about lost relations, and where to find their own families.

To-morrow (Monday), we have been induced by three Major-Generals to go with them to Fort Harrison, and they promise to see that we get off to Petersburg on Tuesday A. M., by General Ord's private boat or special train. What *can* we do against the Union Army? We *have* to stay of course, and shall not get to Washington before Thursday, probably. General Curtis wants me to urge Joe and Eliza to come on soon; he may be sent off from here, and wants them while he is here. They must be sure to, it is all full of interest. Carry is in her glory; goes on horseback with the officers when we are in ambulances, and is delighted with all; Hatty, too. Mother keeps up her interest in all she sees. I shall leave the scraps at Lee's house to-day; we marched by it with General Curtis the other day.

G. had collected for some time past all the striking editorials from the *Tribune* and *Post,* on the abuses of the Belle Isle and Libby prisons by the keepers of those shameful pens, which were in daily sight of Lee's own house, and which he could by one condemnatory order have closed. She left the package so collected at his door in Richmond, first ascertaining that he was in the house, and knowing that in the dearth of southern news they would certainly be read.

Jane was at Fairfax Seminary Hospital all this time, and in forwarding the following letter of Mother's she writes to E. at Fishkill, "You will be glad to get this nice letter from Mother. I am so glad she went. All well here. Six hundred and twenty-five men received since this night week, fever, diarrhoea &c., and many broken down by the 'quick march home' that sounds so pretty in the papers. Come to the 'Great Review'."

Mother to J. S. W.

RICHMOND! SUNDAY, MAY 14TH, 1865.

My dear Jane:

I do not realize the heading of my letter, in spite of the filthy rebel room we are in at the "Spottiswood," and the strange sights and sounds all about us,—and despair of giving you any clear idea of the fact that we are actually in this Rebel capital. . .

On Wednesday, at 4 P. M., we took the "Adelaide," from which I would warn all who come after us! Of all filthy, disgusting conveyances *that* is the most so. Crowded with men, women, children and b.b's. The lowest set of females, too, that could possibly be congregated together. We had smooth, pleasant weather, however, which in some measure compensated, and after our night of discomfort had a glorious sun-rising, and at Fortress Monroe we took a joyful leave of the nasty Adelaide for a nice new boat, and had a charming sail (or steam) on to Richmond,—stopping awhile at City Point, which, with the whole of the James River from that on, was very interesting, with the fortifications, broken bridges, soldiers at different points guarding the shores still, and Dutch Gap, etc. Our own troops now garrison all the rebel works on the approach to the city. We glided along to it most peacefully, arriving about 7 P. M., an immense crowd waiting the boat's arrival—civil and military, black and white, Union and rebel, men, women and children, all mixed in, and forming a dense mass. It was a sight to behold! We got through with difficulty, a military guard taking down all our names as we passed out of the boat, and we were packed into the Spottiswood stage and soon found ourselves in this hotbed of rebels, which name may still belong with truth to it. We are disgusted to find as many rebels as Union people here, and although officers have been forbidden to appear here in uniform, they swarm in their gray coats, with their families and friends. We had the pleasure of dining with a party of them opposite us at dinner to-day. I have been expecting to be assailed at every turn by some of my old Southern friends, but no one I know has yet crossed my path. . . .

We found rooms kept for us; Robert being along, he took Charley's, but C. has a cock-loft by himself now. As we drove up the evening we arrived, we saw General Curtis to our great pleasure, who stopped his ambulance in front till we came up alongside, and told us he would come immediately to call on us, which he did, and has been doing ever since. We saw Chaplain Gray too, Charley's friend, and he with all the staff of the Massachusetts 4th Cavalry have been at our service all the while. . . .

We have seen the rebel house of Representatives and the Senate; in one of these we waited for some time, seeing and hearing a number of rebels taking the oath of allegiance, a poor, forlorn, weather-beaten, hollow-checked-looking set, with sad, dispirited countenances, that made one feel very sorry for them. We have been to the cemetery, from which we had a very good view of Belle Isle,—a wretched, barren point of land, the very worst spot in the whole country they could have selected for our poor prisoners. In the cemetery we saw J. E. B. Stuart's grave, which has only a headstone, no monument, but is kept constantly covered with fresh flowers; so were many rebel graves. We had an ambulance with four horses and four orderlies put at our service, and wherever we go it is in this style! We drove to the cavalry camp of the 4th Mass., by invitation of Mr. Gray, Major Scott and Dr. Garvin, who have been our escort all the while, and their splendid band was called out on Friday afternoon and gave us charming music. We make quite a sensation, I assure you, when we move anywhere with our four grays and outriders. Yesterday we started off in this same style, with the addition to our party of General Curtis and wife, and spent the day on the battlefields of Gaines' Mill, thrice fought over, you remember.

It was a most interesting day, the weather was superb, the trees all in full leaf, and flowers, seemed in contrast to the lines of graves, with their wooden stakes marking the spots, and whole lines, as far as you could see, of earthworks and rifle pits, with fragments of garments hanging about them, and still, in many places, miserable human fragments unburied. A burial detachment is sent out every few days to do its sad work. We took a grand lunch of meats, ice-cream, strawberries and cake, all of which we collected from confectioneries and markets, and borrowed a supply of saucers, spoons, etc. When we had selected a rural spot, not on the battlefield, and spread our cloth, which was the india rubber blanket of one of our aides, we found the officers had also brought from camp a lunch of their own getting up, which, all together, made a large and attractive display of viands. We were sixteen in company and did ample justice to the feast. General Curtis and wife were our guests, Major Scott, Chaplain Gray, Major Garvin, Robert, Charley and ourselves, with our orderlies. Carry rode on horseback with her military escort, feeling grand as possible, and had a real jolly time. Her dress and cap were very handsome, and she rode Major Scott's fine war horse. Altogether the day was a success, and was crowned in the evening by a *line* of distinguished callers, Major General Ord and his wife heading the column, (which we consider a great attention.) General Turner, Captain Gibbs, Captain Baker, Chaplain Trumbull,

Captain Franklin, brother of the old General, General Curtis and wife, Major Scott and Chaplain Gray were all our guests here that evening.

I am so glad Hatty and Carry are having such a grand time. We have had every attention these officers could show us, and they are all very busy and pushed hard for time, too. They think it a great treat for themselves to have Northern Union ladies to call on—so they say. Baker is an English officer of the regular army, and has been in some of our late battles, joining himself with good will to the Union army.

Monday noon.—I wrote this far yesterday and laid it aside to visit the Libby prison and walk round the burnt district, while Robert, H. and C. were at church. I was too tired to finish it last evening, and to-day we have been off on another excursion since 9 o'clock this morning. General Turner sent his own carriage, a very nice low barouche, for my use, in which Georgy, Robert and I went, and in the Headquarters ambulance—which is a very handsome one, cushioned, and seats running across to accommodate eight persons, and which we have had the use of all the time—General Curtis and wife, General Turner and Captain Gibbs accompanied Hatty and Carry. We were very sorry to leave Charley behind with a slight indisposition. We left him a bowl of arrowroot, with a small phial of brandy, and made him promise to keep quiet, which he did, and we found him fast asleep on our return, feeling better, but still out of sorts. This determines us to wait here till to-morrow morning, instead of leaving this afternoon for Petersburg. We drove this morning to Fort Harrison, and all over the battlefields there, getting out and walking all over the forts, and poking our heads into bomb-proofs and rifle pits, and walking into the log tents so recently deserted, first by the rebels, and then by our own soldiers, where their cooking utensils are all left, and their blankets still hanging over poles, and canteens strung on the doors, and old clothing of all sorts strewn about, and everything having the appearance of being left but yesterday.

It is a city of log tents, inside of Fort Harrison, a very extensive one, where the Army of the James were encamped, excellently built and wide avenues between the rows of huts,—their tables, benches, stoves, tin cups and plates all there. We were saying it would be a capital plan to send the poor of Richmond there, either white or black; they could live quite comfortably. To-day has been a more interesting one than Saturday. We saw at the Libby yesterday the quarters of our men and the pit where our officers were buried, without air or light. I wonder any one of them ever lived to tell the story of their sufferings. There are a few rebels there in the upper room still, and we saw them from the street, sitting on the window sills with their legs hanging through the bars outside. Their rebel friends are down there constantly, talking with them, and, until very lately, have been allowed to send them up baskets of provisions, which they managed to draw up by strings furnished them in some way or other. The windows are near enough to the street for their friends to throw up a ball of string, oranges, apples, letters, etc.

This is very different from the rebel treatment of our poor prisoners, who were shot if they showed themselves at a window. We saw the place where the notorious jailer Turner escaped since we have been here, and also the subterranean passage made by Colonel Streight and others, and had some idea of the horrid work it must have been; also, the mine that was prepared by Lee's order in the prison, to blow it up with its inmates in case the city was taken! This same Lee is living here now peacefully in his own residence, and being fed by our military authorities on all the luxuries of the season. We have passed his house repeatedly, but have not yet seen his Satanship. Georgy has plied him well with reading matter from our papers, making any little darky who happens to pass at the moment ring the door-bell and hand them in, having directed them beforehand to Robert Lee, Franklin Street. She sent him a lot of Sunday reading yesterday. I would like much to know the effect it has. Some say he is very much subdued of late, never goes out except early in the morning or late at night, avoids every one, and is *intending* to take the oath of allegiance! I hope he will not be allowed to do so, as it will only be to get to Europe, where his friends will join him. Only think of Jeff. in his wife's clothes! It is good to secure him in any garb, though I am sorry to have womanly garments so desecrated. I have no doubt he will manage to slip through the fingers of his captors, and get off yet out of reach of our Government. It is to be hoped not, and that they will make quick work with him.

Judge Campbell is here in this hotel—in the parlor, sitting near us every evening. General Curtis pointed him out to us, with the remark, "There is a man under arrest and who will probably be hung." The house is full of rebel women, who are here from all parts looking up their brothers and husbands and sons. It is annoying to have them swarm into the dining room at meals, and then to the parlors, occupying all the sofas and chairs. We sometimes cannot tell whether the new arrivals are rebels or Union, till we see their gray-coated males coming in to greet them.

Carry went with Robert yesterday to see Miss VanLew, the celebrated Union lady here, and took her a handsome flag, and some new books brought from New York for her. She was very much delighted, and you shall see a letter which came from her to-day. She sent Carry an elegant bunch of flowers this morning, and wanted her to promise that by and by, when things are more settled here, she would come and make her a visit. She invited Carry and Robert, and any of us who would accompany them, to tea with her this evening. We are not going to tea, but some of us mean to drive and see her. She lives in a fine old "mansion," with beautiful grounds. We mean also to call on Mrs. Ord and Mrs. Curtis to pay our farewell compliments; and tomorrow morning at 10.40 we take our leave of Richmond, feeling that our visit here has been a brilliant success.

This evening the girls are expecting a bevy of new officers to call on them, and are going in the meantime to General Turner's Headquarters, across the river,—Captain Gibbs coming for them in the General's private carriage. . . .

I don't know how we shall get along at home again without two or more orderlies in full trappings behind us. Wherever we go here on excursions, officers and orderlies are armed, there are so many stragglers and marauders about.

The air is filled with the burning brick and mortar smell through the whole city. The entire block through to the next street in front of us is in ruins, and all the way down the long street not a house is standing; banks, churches, private dwellings and stores without number, all lie in ruins. By moonlight the sight is beautiful. They are putting up slightly-built shanties here and there for the sale of different articles, mostly "beer and cakes," which spoil the picturesqueness.

The city is a beautiful one, with its fine old trees and large gardens, now filled with every variety of roses. We average about four large bouquets a day in our room, from military friends, and our mantelpiece is filled all in a row with roses, syringes, honeysuckles and magnolias. I wish every day

you had come with us. I am sure you would enjoy it. Do join Eliza and Joe
when they come on . . . .

We shall be in Washington by Wednesday or Thursday sometime. Do
not give yourself any trouble about meeting us; we will go and see you as
soon as we can, and G. can stay as long as pleases her and you. . . .

Best love to you.

Yours,

MOTHER.

Your Grandmother's next letter is given because its anxiety over a
slight illness of G's, shows how unusual such a thing was. This was the
first "sick leave" in four years. G's campaign had made a hardened veteran of her, though at last the Sanitary Commission came even to *her*
rescue.

Mother to A. H. W.

PETERSBURG, VA., MAY 18TH.

My dear Abby:

The only drawback to our enjoyment of the trip has been Georgy's illness, but I am very happy to speak of this now as past away. We left Richmond Tuesday morning. She was not very well, I could see plainly, though
she would not allow it, and on reaching this place, she was in a high fever,
and obliged to give up to the care of a physician. We called in Dr. Prince,
the medical director and surgeon of the post, who was highly spoken of
as a good man and excellent doctor. The fever raged for a day and night,
so that we were extremely anxious lest it might run into typhoid, or some
other rapid and fearful disease, but God was pleased to order otherwise,
and she is now so much relieved that we think of pursuing the journey
to-morrow, as it is desirable to get on by "easy stages" to Washington.
We could not have been better off in every way. . . . An attentive, skilful
and gentlemanly physician, and the *Sanitary Commission* close at hand to
supply us the wine which we could not get anywhere else; also excellent
black tea. . . . G's bed is literally covered with roses, we have them in such
profusion; our little silk flag (your make) is hung by her bedside for effect;
and on a table near her every variety of flower the country produces, and
this is a great one, with superb roses of every kind. Ice, lemonade, ice-

cream when wanted, and very good, too, with whatever else she needs or fancies—looking like an interesting princess. . . .

The 1st Division of the 6th Corps passed through from Danville to-day. It was splendid; the band was drawn up in front of the hotel, playing while they passed, and a crowd of Union people in the piazzas and windows of the house looking on. The girls and Charley displayed our flag, and there was a large collection of officers in front below us to see them pass along. Dreadfully burnt and weather-beaten they looked, too, poor fellows, under their weight of knapsacks, etc.—they seemed too wearied for even the thought of going home to cheer them. There was no cheering or waving at all as they passed. I do not understand why this is the case. The feelings of the rebels present everywhere seem to be too much regarded, I think, in this; I hope in northern cities it will be different. These brave fellows should be met with the applause they deserve, and be made to feel their welcome from all hearts. . . . We will not stay long in Washington, just to rest and see Jane, unless there is something very attractive and interesting going on. I must say I would wait there a week to see Jeff. in his wife's petticoats! This is talked of with great glee amongst the blacks here; one or two have asked me, grinning from ear to ear, if "dey was gwine to bring Jeff. dis way." Wasn't it a joke? it finishes up his reputation amongst his own people. . . .

I add a P. S. to ask if you will write a line to Mrs. Turner at Cornwall, or perhaps you and E. will drive over and see her about a room for Charley—he seems to want a quiet rest somewhere for a while—an airy, nice room, as he will sit in it a good deal. . . . We hope to meet Dr. Bacon at City Point, who will be on hand if needed.

G. M. W. to A. H. W.

EBBITT HOUSE, WASHINGTON,
SATURDAY, MAY 21, '65.

We have just arrived; the boat from City Point touching at Alexandria long enough to let Mother and Robert off. They were to take a carriage and drive out two-and-a-half miles to see Jane, and bring her in to spend Sunday (if she will come). We came on with Charley to this House and find it packed. We are all four put in one room until to-morrow night, when possibly we may have something better. The city is full, to see the Review. I hope Joe has telegraphed for rooms. . . .

I am delighted that they are coming, and very much disappointed that you are not. We really thought that you might be induced just to look at the brave fellows on Tuesday and Wednesday before everything marched off into the past, forever and ever. . . . I am seeing doctors and taking doses without number in a perfectly docile way, and you have nothing to say about *me*. . . . We had Vance of North Carolina a prisoner on board the boat up, (under guard of officers and four privates) strutting about,—great fat, chewing fellow. He called for potatoes at breakfast, and Mother, sitting next, said, "Here is a very small, and cold one." "Thank you," he said, quite fiercely, "I wish a large and a hot one." "Small potatoes" might answer his purposes under the circumstances. . . .

Mother to A. at Fishkill.

WASHINGTON, MAY 21, 1865.

My dear Abby:

Robert will probably have seen you before this reaches you and told you all about us. . . . He had telegraphed Joe and Eliza that he would be at home on Monday, so that they could come on to the Review. . . Georgy is much better, gains every day, but will gain faster going north, out of this oppressive air, which seems to have no vitality whatever in it. Dr. Smith says it is all malaria everywhere in this region. As Robert will tell you, he and I left the boat on the journey up and drove from Alexandria to the Fairfax Seminary Hospital. We found Jane well, and very glad to see us. It was a very busy time with her, just making out her orders for special diet, and giving out the stores. We only staid an hour, and did not go into the wards, or to see Mrs. Jerome, only into Jane's department. I looked into her poorly furnished little bedroom, which seemed to me very bare, and very unsuited to Jane's ideas and tastes, but which she seems perfectly contented and happy with.

It is a fine building, airy and beautifully situated, very clean, and everything about in perfect order, and Jane the supreme directress. It was strange indeed to see her there, all alone, and hundreds of men waiting their portion at her hands. Things are so arranged that she can sit quietly in her office, (which is a pleasant room, with its seven wardrobes, sure enough, all in a row!) and move the whole machinery of the kitchen and wards, with apparently little labor. This had just been scoured, and a large wood fire was burning, to dry the board floor. The wardrobes! are fitted up with shelves, and form a row of very nice closets, filling one side of the room; there is one very large window with a beautiful view, and on the sill a flower box with growing plants; in the middle of the floor is her business table covered with papers relating to the work of the hospital, her writing implements and piles of diet-lists, etc. Between this table and the huge fire-place is spread her rug, the only piece of floor covering she has anywhere; across the window, with space from it to admit a chair, stands another table, filled with books and flowers—two vases of beautiful roses,—and I added a splendid magnolia, which I brought her from Petersburg, and managed to keep perfectly fresh in water on the boat.

Jane seemed very well, though she *looks* no stronger than when at home. . . . We left her with the promise from her that she and Dr. Smith would drive up in the afternoon to see G. They did so in spite of the rain, made us a short call, and took Hatty back with them to stay till tomorrow, when Charley is to drive down for her. Jane promises to come up and see the Review on Tuesday, so that we will all *but you*, dear Abby, be here together. . . . Dr. Bacon is staying here in the house, so that we can have his medical advice if needed. . . . General Williams came in last night in his little, modest, quiet way to call, and offered his services in any way to aid us in our getting about; invited us to a seat in his pew. Will Winthrop was here too, last night. Mrs. John Rockwell, her two sons, and Miss Foote are in the house, and a great crowd of queer-looking people coming to see their husbands and brothers the "Jyggydeers" of the army. Miss Prime and some of her family are here, too; we have had several little talks with her; she is very pleasant, as usual. Robert will tell you all about our trip on the horrid boat, only a very little better than the Adelaide, and our seeing the vessel with Jeff. Davis and his party on board.

C. C. W. to A. H. W.

WASHINGTON, MAY 23, 1865,

Dear Abby:

Joe and Eliza arrived safely last night at 12 o'clock, and E. was taken into our room, we having fortunately an extra bed, an extraordinary thing in these times. The city is crammed, and no accommodations to be had at any price; hundreds of people have left, finding no sleeping place, and great numbers stay at Baltimore and come up for the day; among the latter is Charles Rockwell, who with the Tracys came in the train yesterday with Eliza. Charley gave up his third of a room to Joe and took his old quarters with General Williams. The old General has been daily to see us and secured us a window in the avenue for to-day; but as nothing was to be seen from it, we wisely accepted six tickets on a platform which our usual luck threw in our way, in fact forced upon us. Miss Prime's uncle procured in some way twenty seats on the Connecticut State platform, opposite the President's, and insisted on our taking six, which we gladly did. General Sherman's box or covered platform was immediately next, and Admiral Wilkes, who was in it, made several of us come in there. Georgy would not lose the Review and came slowly up, escorted by Joe and Charley, and followed by the family, chiefly Mother, who brought a feather pillow and an air cushion for her to sit on and put at her back, a box for her feet, and a bag of sandwiches, and port wine. She stood it remarkably well, and with three glasses of wine, etc., declared it did her great good to go. She takes frequent sherry-cobblers and strong drinks generally, and the "bar" must think the "sick lady eats and drinks awful."

The Review was sublime! As each general officer rode up to the President's stage, which was gorgeously dressed with flags and hot-house plants, he dismounted and took his seat in the great circle of great men, till we had directly opposite us and under our inspection, President Johnson, Secretary Welles, Mr. Stanton, Generals Grant, Meade, Hancock, Sherman, Butterfield, Merritt, etc., etc. Whenever a pause occurred the mass rushed to the front of the staging to get a nearer view of the great men. Three superb bands relieved each other and kept up a constant clang of splendid music just alongside of us. There were no drawbacks, no accidents. Little General Custer came near being run away with; his horse took fright and got beyond his control, tore down the lines, his hat blew off, and there was a good deal of excitement, but he finally stopped him without any damage. One splendid Colonel there would not have fared as well—a fine looking fellow, sitting like an arrow on his horse, his sword drawn and a beautiful bouquet in his hand; we noticed he made a fine salute, as they all did, to the President, but with his *left* hand; then we saw his right arm was gone to the shoulder! What could he have done if his horse had started, with his sword, his flowers, and the reins all in one hand? Have we not been just in the nick of time everywhere! To-morrow we have our same seats for Sherman's Army; we could not have had a better time for Richmond, and our first night here was Sheridan's last. He spent some time in the parlor, so we had a good look at him; short and stubby, but jolly. That night his troops gave him the most superb serenade you can imagine, right under our windows; there must have been three or four bands united, and all the people of the city must have turned out, from the cheering. Early next morning his troops passed, to give a farewell cheer, and at noon he left for Texas, the men to follow, I believe.

We have had a number of callers as usual, the Wilkes, the Knapps, Mr. Huntington Wolcott, Dr. Smith, Mr. "Conversation Clark," Harry Hopkins, etc., and Dr. Bacon in the house. We are glad to have him near in case of need, though G. really is better. I think the last four years is the matter with her. It would not be human that she could endure, without some ill effects, the constant exposure and trials of that time. We have only seen Jane for a few moments; she is very busy and did not care to come to the procession.

E. and G. were at the Ebbitt House again for the first time since they sailed away with the Sanitary Commission in '62. E. writes:

E. W. H. to A. H. W.

EBBITT HOUSE, WASHINGTON, MAY 24, '65.

Dear Abby:

I wish you could have been here at least for this second day, and have seen Sherman's splendid army. Far from flagging, the interest greatly increased, and there was much more enthusiasm and life to-day than yesterday, both among the men themselves and the lookers on. Nothing ever was more false than the report that Sherman's braves were all "bummers," and beyond his control, or if so, it would be well for all armies to have "'alf their complaint." They beat the A. P. all to pieces in their marching, which is an easy swinging gait but in perfect time and uniformity; and in physique they seemed half a head taller and broad and straight in proportion,—great big, brave, brawny men with faces brown as Indians and a pleased smile on every one. The Army of the Tennessee came first with Logan at its head, though Sherman, of course, preceded him, and both were greeted with roars of delight, as indeed was the case with every general officer, every particularly torn flag, and all the men! Flowers—many more than yesterday—were showered among them, great wreaths of laurel hung around many of the horses' necks or over the flagstaffs,, and one of the prettiest parts of all was to watch Mrs. Sherman, who, with her little boy, sat next the general all day, cheer and wave and toss flowers to one after another of the color-bearers. When she couldn't toss far enough herself the general himself would throw them, and they were always caught with great cheers and tossing of caps by the men. Indeed Sherman won back our hearts to-day by his perfect delight in watching the ovation to his soldiers and his zeal in helping it on. Most of the day he and *Stanton* sat at the two extremes of the platform, by design we supposed but it could not have been so, for when it was all over the last thing we noticed before the grandees separated were the two standing with their arms around each other! Perhaps a grand review in Richmond would have had an equally happy effect in Halleck's case.

After Logan's army came old Slocum, for whom we all rose and gave a special cheer—and who was cheered by everyone,—and the splendid army of Georgia. The 20th Corps more than any other impressed us with its immense size. Each division seemed an army in itself, and after each came the drollest mule-train loaded with blankets and camp-kettles and *poultry!* and darkies of all sizes, just as they came through Georgia and South Carolina,—"Slocum's baggage," the people shouted, as they laughed and cheered. By this time the crowd of spectators had increased and encroached on the street so much, that the infantry guards were unable to keep them back, and a file of cavalry were detailed to ride in advance of each division or brigade to clear the way, and Joe means to laugh at Slocum for his dodge in making a little force appear like a great one, for the company filed around behind the White House, as in a theater, and reappeared on the scene every few minutes like new troops.

I can't begin to tell you all about it—the newspapers will do that better than I could, but it was a sublime spectacle and one I am very, very sorry you have missed. . . .

I am writing in the parlor with talking all about me and therefore incoherently. Capt. Joe Rockwell is just telling the girls about his ten months in Libby Prison. . . . Here come General Williams and Mr. Knapp, so I must say good night.

We are very glad you stayed at our home, always *yours*, too, dear, instead of going down to town. Best love to you and the little darlings.

Mother to A. H. W.

WASHINGTON, MAY 27TH, SATURDAY.

My dear Abby:

Here we are yet, detained by a cheerless, hopeless, steady pour of rain. . . .Georgy is at the Fairfax Seminary with Jane, and cannot get back to us until the weather changes decidedly for the better; but such roads! as this rain made. Their condition reminds me of our McClellan winter here, though the deep yellow mud is now tramped through by the "homeward bound," those who have escaped and survived the hardships and horrors of the "cruel war" now over. . . .

On Thursday we made up a little party to visit Jane, as she could not come to us—a good-bye call. Miss Prime and Eliza, with Charley and Joe, went on horseback, Miss P. riding Charley's new horse, which is a beauty. Mrs. Clarkson, with Georgy, Carry and me, in an open carriage, with Harry Hopkins on the box, all started together from the door. On reaching the Long Bridge, we found to our dismay an interminable line of troops coming this way, the Fourteenth Army Corps, with all their wagons, etc., and no chance whatever of getting on in that direction,—no vehicles are allowed to pass these trains on the bridge. The equestrians found they could do so, and rode on. We had the choice of driving to the boat, with the chance of finding that too crowded for our carriage, or driving out over the Aqueduct Bridge, and passing through Arlington grounds and Freedman's Village, finally reaching the Seminary road. All this was very attractive, and we made the drive, losing very little time and seeing a great deal that was extremely interesting. On arriving at the Seminary we met the rest of our party just emerging from one of the wards with Jane and Dr. Smith, who had been showing Miss Prime through them, to her great delight. You know she doats on soldiers and hospitals. Jane seemed quite well, and did the honors with a grace that delighted her stranger guests. I was introduced to the chaplain and wife, Mr. and Mrs. Jerome, in their own room, and we all then assembled in Jane's office, where she gave us some claret and crackers, of her private stores.

We lost our way in coming back; our driver, a darkey, unacquainted with the country; our horseback party far ahead of us, and cross roads innumerable everywhere. We drove about over hill and dale for two hours, and eventually found ourselves on the Leesburg turnpike! Where we should have spent the night I know not, but for an old house on the roadside which at length showed itself, whose occupant informed us where we were; and on further inquiry we found we were much nearer to the *Seminary!* than to the Long Bridge which had been the object of our search. Of course we had only to drive back there and beg a guide. You can imagine the surprise and regret of Dr. S. and Harry Hopkins when we drove up at that late hour, and told them our experience. . . .We did not let Jane and G. know anything about it, and Dr. Smith and Harry both ordered horses and saw us safely back. We reached the hotel at a little before 10. . . . Charley is well, but tired out with hanging about here, and I shall be glad to leave. . . . Kisses to the dear children. I dare not look back to this time last year! or speak of those days of sorrow, but my heart is heavy within me, these *anniversary days*, with unspoken sorrow.

Mother to J. S. W.

WASHINGTON MAY 28, 1865.
SUNDAY EVENING.

My dear Jane:

As we propose leaving Washington to-morrow morning on the 10.30 train, I write you a line of "good bye" tonight, and shall leave it at the desk in case the orderly should call here—and with it some lovely roses which Charley brought in to us this afternoon. I wish you had them now. It is very hard for me to go off and leave you all alone behind us, though you *do seem* happier where you are than at home. I hope, however, when all military hospitals and every vestige of war are done away with, you will be contented to make us happy at home by sharing home with us, and being happy there yourself. . . . Joe and Eliza went off to Richmond on Friday in spite of the rain. . . .

The city has been very quiet the last two or three days—no serenades, no excitements of any sort. To-day Charley and I went to Dr. Gurley's church, while H. and C., attended by General Williams, went to Dr. Hall's. . . . It is very tiresome here now, and disagreeable; the house is wretchedly kept. If it were not for our colored waiter, young "George Washington Jerome Buonaparte me lord," we should have no attention at all; he remembered us at Gettysburg, and has devoted himself to us. . . . We shall go through to-morrow, reaching home on Tuesday. . . .

A loving good night to you, my dear child.

MOTHER.

The splendid sweep of the great army passing away for ever, seemed to carry with it out of sight all the stormy four years of our family life. The mad, sad, noble war was over. Those dear to us, who had been in peril, were safe at home once more. All we had longed for, and fought for, was ours. Slavery was dead, and one flag covered the land *"Across a Kindling Continent."*

> We with uncovered head
> Salute the sacred dead,
> * * * * * *
> Through whose desert a rescued Nation sets
> Her heel on treason.

The home circle of which your Grandmother was the center and the charm, was broken and scattered long ago, but it has not been forgotten by those who knew it in the days of war:—Chaplain Hopkins,—writing of it after all these years, says:—

"I stopped once on my way to the army at the New York home, and it seemed to me that I got for a little time into a climate and country entirely different from this poor cold world. The house was all aglow with light and warmth; there was an atmosphere of earnest faith, courage, and good cheer, that filled me with a new sense of the sacredness of the cause of our country. Some of the faces in the groups there are dim in my memory, but not your Mother's. She seemed to me very noble and very beautiful the first time I saw her, and later she was good to me after such a fashion, that

I put an aureole about her head, and counted her among the saints long before she went to be where the saints are."

A paragraph in a letter from this dear Mother, written six years after the war, expresses her constant love for us, and allows us to close these chapters of our family story with her benediction.

This 9th day of November, 1871, completes my "three score years and ten!" and how has God blessed me all the way along, and in nothing so richly as in my beloved children! What aid, and comfort, and strength, and life have they given me always! and how my heart yearns over each one as my dearest treasure on earth! They have been my staff and support in God's hands, when He was leading me through deep waters, and have kept my head up so that I did not sink. I bless God to-day for *my children*. May He continue to be their God!

Georgeanna Woolsey Bacon and Eliza Woolsey Howland
Woolsey Papers, Ferriday Archives

Their Useful Hands

Who can quit young lives after being long in company with them, and
not desire to know what befell them in their after-years?
                                        —George Eliot, Middlemarch

WITH THE PEACE, Jane Eliza Woolsey returned to her life as the New York matron, gathering her family around her. In the next four years, she watched as Georgeanna, Carry, Charles, and Hatty married. At times, the old faces reappeared. Abby described one such scene, writing, "One man was almost convulsed at seeing Mother, and, with tears, would hardly let her hand go. 'I knew you, ma'am, the minute you came in. You were at Gettysburg, and were the first one that dressed my arm.'" She died on Christmas Eve, 1874.[1]

For three sisters, the war years dramatically changed their lives. As Georgeanna commented on the effect of the war:

> Many of these women, who after four or five years had been forced to recognize the value of their own work, and had developed genuine ability for organization, were not willing to fold their useful hands when the war was over, and let the old order of things reestablish itself.[2]

Abby, Jane, and Georgeanna are important transitional figures as the "system of women-nurses" progressed from a temporary wartime measure to an entrenched profession within the medical establishment.

Abby Woolsey remained active in New York charitable work, primarily through the Church of the Covenant. In 1872, her friend and wartime associate, Louisa Schuyler, asked her to assist with the newly formed New York State Charities Aid Association. This organization sent visiting teams to evaluate charitable work in hospitals, poor houses, and other public institutions—mirroring the Sanitary Commission inspection teams. Abby sat on the Board of Managers for twelve years and on the Committee on Hospitals for twenty-one years.

She served on the Board of Managers of Bellevue Training School of Nursing, drafting its plan of organization. This school, one of the first in the country, provided a model that dominated nursing education for the next fifty years. Drawing on the medical experiences of her family, she brought a moral passion to a central argument of the day, that is, whether nurses should be a glorified maid or a trained professional. She wrote, "In spite of sentimental notions, women are no more born nurses than men are born chemists and engineers. Nursing is serious business. The thrusting of persons, without previous education for the duties, into such responsible positions is trifling with human life and suffering." In 1876, Abby traveled throughout Europe, studying nursing schools and hospital administration. Her observations resulted in *Handbook for Hospital Visitors* (1877), *Handbook for Hospitals* (1883), *Hospital Laundries* (1880), which became standard works in hospital administration. She also wrote *Lunacy Legislation in England* (1884). Abby Howland Woolsey died in 1893.[3]

Jane Stuart Woolsey managed the close of the Fairfax Seminary Hospital in August 1865. After a brief rest at home, she returned to Virginia to work at the Lincoln Industrial School for Freedman in Richmond. In 1868, she came back to New York and wrote her memoir, *Hospital Days*. The book, printed for the family, included a thoughtful analysis of the "system of women-nurses." With the book completed, she accepted a post at the Hampton Normal and Agricultural Institute with Georgeanna's sister-in-law, Rebecca Bacon. At the Institute, Woolsey supervised the "girl's industries," teaching sewing and housework classes.[4]

Jane took the position of resident directress at New York Presbyterian Hospital in 1872. Working with her sister, Abby, she implemented the lessons learned at Fairfax Seminary Hospital. The job gave her considerable authority, causing tensions with a cadre of physicians who resented a woman with such wide responsibilities. The issue came to a head when Woolsey charged that one doctor had admitted an infectious case against hospital rules. The hospital's board resolved the conflict with the removal of the recalcitrant doctors.[5]

Jane suffered from ill health following a bout with rheumatic fever in the early 1870s and resigned her hospital position in 1876. She remained in poor health for the rest of her life, cared for by Abby. She died on 9 July 1891.

Georgeanna Woolsey married her long-time beau, Dr. Francis Bacon, in 1866. Bacon had already embarked on a distinguished career as professor of surgery at the Yale Medical School. In New Haven, Georgeanna found a rich field for her leadership skills. She worked with the organizing committee for the Connecticut Training School for Nurses, serving as a board member, secretary, and advisor. Lacking a sound textbook for nurses' training, Georgeanna wrote the widely distributed manual, *A Handbook of Nursing for Family and General Use*, in 1879. This book remained a standard text for several decades, and Georgeanna completed revisions for a new edition just before her death.[6]

Her philanthropy extended across several fields. When the Connecticut State Board of Charities organized in 1883, the governor appointed Georgeanna to the Board of Managers. As part of that work, she testified before the Connecticut State Legislature on behalf of reform school methods in 1889. Moved by her inspection visits to children's institutions, she threw her energies into the Connecticut Children's Aid Society and the Newington Hospital for Crippled Children. With her husband, she built a retreat home for children, called Playridge, in Woodmont, Connecticut. She died 27 January 1906. Although Francis Bacon lived until 1912, a family member noted, "After Georgy's death, he lost interest in life and grew much older."[7]

The rest of the family returned to a quiet life.

The Howlands lived at their Fishkill home, Tioronda. Joseph Howland, widely respected for his war service, made a brief foray into politics and became New York State Treasurer in 1865. Politics was not his passion, however, and he spent his days as a gentleman farmer, community philanthropist, and world traveler. He died in France in 1886. In her later years, Eliza took on the role of family historian, organizing the Civil War letters and writing the *Woolsey Family Records 1620–1840*. She died in July 1917.[8]

Harriet married her cousin, Dr. Hugh Lenox Hodge, in 1869. Hodge was a surgeon and taught at the University of Pennsylvania Medical School. Hatty had two children, Hugh Lenox and Jane Eliza Woolsey. The infant girl, however, died at birth. Hatty died in 1878.

Caroline Woolsey married Edward Mitchell—a highly respected lawyer—in 1867. They had one child, Eliza. Caroline died in 1914. That daughter's summer home in Bethlehem, Connecticut was given to the Antiquarian & Landmarks Society in 1990 and is open to the public. The family papers passed down to Caroline Woolsey's granddaughter, Caroline Ferriday, and are now part of the collections of the Bellamy-Ferriday House and Gardens.

Charles William Woolsey married Arixene Southgate Smith (Zenie) in 1868. As his obituary noted, "As a man of leisure, he was able to devote much time to travel and the careful study of art." He pursued this cultured life in Ossining, New York until health concerns led him to move to Asheville, North Carolina. Of his three children, only Alice Bradford lived to adulthood. Charles remained active in Asheville community affairs until his death in 1907.

Endnotes

1. *My Heart Toward Home*, 322.

2. Georgeanna Woolsey Bacon, "Connecticut Training School," *Trained Nurse*, October, 1895: 187-193.

3. Abby Howland Woolsey, *Handbook for Hospitals* (NY: New York State Charities Aid Association, 1883, 1895); *Handbook for Hospital Visitors* (NY: New York State Charities Aid Association, 1877, 1883); *Hospital Laundries* (NY: New York State Charities Aid Association, 1880); *Lunacy Legislation in England* (NY: New York State Charities Aid Association, 1884). For a discussion of the Woolsey sisters within the context of nursing history, see Philip and Beatrice Kalisch, *The Advance of American Nursing* (Philadelphia: J. B. Lippincott, 1995), 47-50, 53-54.

4. Jane Stuart Woolsey, *Hospital Days: Reminiscence of a Civil War Nurse* (Roseville: Edinborough Press, 1996); Robert Francis Engs, *Educating the Disenfranchised and Disinherited: Samuel Chapman Armstrong and Hampton Institute, 1839–1893* (Knoxville: University of Tennessee Press, 1999), 87.

5. Austin, 123-129; Dr. Albert Lamb, *The Presbyterian Hospital and the Columbia Medical Center, 1868-1943* (New York: Columbia University Press, 1955), 19; Abby Howland Woolsey, *A Century of Nursing*, 122.

6. Georgeanna Woolsey Bacon, "Connecticut Training School," *Trained Nurse*, October, 1895: 187-193; Georgeanna Woolsey Bacon, *A Handbook of Nursing for Family and General Use* (Philadelphia: J. B. Lippincott, 1879).

7. "Reform School Methods," *Hartford Evening Post*, 30 March 1889; Obituary, *Hartford Evening Post*, 27 January 1906; Obituary, *HEP*, 26 April 1912.

8. "Joseph Howland," *Fishkill Standard*, 3 April 1886; Eliza Howland, editor, *Family Records 1620-1840* (New York: Tuttle, Morehouse & Taylor, 1900).

Index